SUICIDE RESEARCH: SELECTED READINGS

Volume 13

A. Sheils, J. Ashmore, K. Kõlves, D. De Leo

Australian Institute for Suicide Research and Prevention

Griffith
UNIVERSITY

WHO Collaborating Centre for
Research and Training in Suicide Prevention

National Centre of Excellence in Suicide Prevention

First published in 2015
Australian Academic Press
18 Victor Russell Drive,
Samford QLD 4520
Australia
www.australianacademicpress.com.au

ISBN: 978 1 9221 1748 9

Typesetting and cover design by Maria Biaggini — The Letter Tree.

Contents

Foreword vii

Acknowledgments viii

Introduction
    Context..1
    Methodology 2

Key articles

Barker et al, 2014. Suicide around anniversary times............................9

Bernert et al, 2014. Association of poor subjective sleep quality with
risk for death by suicide during a 10-year period: A longitudinal,
population-based study of late life 11

Boyd et al, 2015. Gender differences in mental disorders and
suicidality in Europe: Results from a large cross-sectional
population-based study...14

Brent et al, 2015. Familial pathways to early-onset suicide attempt:
A 5.6-year prospective study...17

Campbell et al, 2015. The prevalence and correlates of chronic pain
and suicidality in a nationally representative sample 20

Carroll et al, 2014. Hospital management of self-harm patients and
risk of repetition: Systematic review and meta-analysis 22

Coupland et al, 2015. Antidepressant use and risk of suicide and
attempted suicide or self harm in people aged 20 to 64: Cohort study
using a primary care database 25

De Beurs et al, 2015. The effect of an e-learning supported
train-the-trainer programme on implementation of suicide guidelines
in mental health care..29

Delforterie et al, 2015. The relationship between cannabis involvement
and suicidal thoughts and behaviors...32

Erlangsen et al, 2015. Short-term and long-term effects of psychosocial
therapy for people after deliberate self-harm: A register-based,
nationwide multicentre study using propensity score matching..........35

Gibbs et al, 2015. Religious conflict, sexual identity, and suicidal behaviors among LGBT young adults 38

Gould et al, 2014. Newspaper coverage of suicide and initiation of suicide clusters in teenagers in the USA, 1988-96: A retrospective, population-based, case-control study. 40

Hunt et al, 2014. Safety of patients under the care of crisis resolution home treatment services in England: A retrospective analysis of suicide trends from 2003 to 2011...43

Kramer et al, 2015. The mental health of visitors of web-based support forums for bereaved by suicide...46

Kim et al, 2015. Suicide risk among perinatal women who report thoughts of self-harm on depression screens 49

Law et al, 2015. Health and psychosocial service use among suicides without psychiatric illness 52

Mehlum et al, 2014. Dialectical behavior therapy for adolescents with repeated suicidal and self-harming behavior: A randomized trial 55

Mitchell et al, 2014. Exposure to websites that encourage self-harm and suicide: Prevalence rates and association with actual thoughts of self-harm and thoughts of suicide in the United States 58

Nordt et al, 2015. Modelling suicide and unemployment: A longitudinal analysis covering 63 countries, 2000-11 61

Oude et al, 2015. Suicide in patients suffering from late-life anxiety disorders; a comparison with younger patients 64

Pritchard et al, 2014. Examining undetermined and accidental deaths as source of 'under-reported-suicide' by age and sex in twenty Western countries 67

Rees et al, 2014. Perceptions of paramedic and emergency care workers of those who self harm: A systematic review of the quantitative literature 70

Rimkeviciene et al, 2015. Impulsive suicide attempts: A systematic literature review of definitions, characteristics and risk factors...........................73

Sinyor et al, 2014. Suicide in the oldest old: An observational study and cluster analysis 76

Skerrett et al, 2015. Are LGBT populations at a higher risk for suicidal behaviors in Australia? Research findings and implications 79

Soole et al, 2014. Suicides in Aboriginal and Torres Strait Islander children: Analysis of Queensland Suicide Register 81

Ueda et al, 2015. The effectiveness of installing physical barriers for preventing railway suicides and accidents: Evidence from Japan. 83

Vyssoki et al, 2014. Suicide among 915,303 Austrian cancer patients:
Who is at risk? 86

Wasserman et al, 2014. School-based suicide prevention programmes:
The SEYLE cluster-randomised, controlled trial 89

Recommended readings 93

Citation list
Fatal suicidal behaviour:
    Epidemiology 147
    Risk and protective factors 153
    Prevention 159
    Postvention and bereavement 160
Non-fatal suicidal behaviour:
    Epidemiology 162
    Risk and protective factors 165
    Prevention 202
    Care and support 204
Case reports 210
Miscellaneous 217

Foreword

This volume contains quotations from internationally peer-reviewed suicide research published during the semester November 2014 – April 2015; it is the thirteenth of a series produced biannually by our Institute with the aim of assisting the Commonwealth Department of Health in being constantly updated on new evidences from the scientific community.

As usual, the initial section of the volume collects a number of publications that could have particular relevance for the Australian people in terms of potential applicability. These publications are accompanied by a short comment from us, and an explanation of the motives that justify why we have considered of interest the implementation of studies' findings in the Australian context. An introductory part provides the rationale and the methodology followed in the identification of papers.

The central part of the volume represents a selection of research articles of particular significance; their abstracts are reported *in extenso*, underlining our invitation at reading those papers in full text: they represent a remarkable advancement of suicide research knowledge.

The last section reports all items retrievable from major electronic databases. We have catalogued them on the basis of their prevailing reference to fatal and non-fatal suicidal behaviours, with various sub-headings (e.g. epidemiology, risk factors, etc). The deriving list guarantees a level of completeness superior to any individual system; it can constitute a useful tool for all those interested in a quick update of what is most recently published on the topic.

Our intent was to make suicide research more approachable to non-specialists, and in the meantime provide an opportunity for a *vademecum* of quotations credible also at the professional level. A compilation such as the one that we provide here is not easily obtainable from usual sources and can save a considerable amount of time to readers. We believe that our effort in this direction may be an appropriate interpretation of one of the technical support roles to the Government that the status of National Centre of Excellence in Suicide Prevention — which has deeply honoured our commitment — entails for us.

The significant growth of our centre, the Australian Institute for Suicide Research and Prevention, and its influential function, both nationally and internationally, in the fight against suicide, could not happen without the constant support of Queensland Health and Griffith University. We hope that our passionate dedication to the cause of suicide prevention may compensate their continuing trust in our work.

Diego De Leo AO, DSc

Director, Australian Institute for Suicide Research and Prevention

Acknowledgments

This report has been produced by the Australian Institute for Suicide Research and Prevention, WHO Collaborating Centre for Research and Training in Suicide Prevention and National Centre of Excellence in Suicide Prevention. The assistance of the Commonwealth Department of Health in the funding of this report is gratefully acknowledged.

Introduction

Context

Suicide places a substantial burden on individuals, communities and society in terms of emotional, economic and health care costs. In Australia, about 2000 people die from suicide every year, a death rate well in excess of transport-related mortality. At the time of preparing this volume, the latest available statistics released by the Australian Bureau of Statistics[1] indicated that, in 2013, 2,522 deaths by suicide were registered in Australia, representing an age-standardised rate of 10.7 per 100,000.

Despite the estimated mortality, the prevalence of suicide and self-harming behaviour in particular remains difficult to gauge due to the often secretive nature of these acts. Without a clear understanding of the scope of suicidal behaviours and the range of interventions available, the opportunity to implement effective initiatives is reduced. Further, it is important that suicide prevention policies are developed on the foundation of evidence-based empirical research, especially as the quality and validly of the available information may be misleading or inaccurate. Additionally, the social and economic impact of suicide underlines the importance of appropriate research-based prevention strategies, addressing not only significant direct costs on health system and lost productivity, but also the emotional suffering for families and communities.

The Australian Institute for Suicide Research and Prevention (AISRAP) has, through the years, gained an international reputation as one of the leading research institutions in the field of suicide prevention. The most important recognition came via the designation as a World Health Organization (WHO) Collaborating Centre in 2005. In 2008, the Commonwealth Department of Health (DoH) appointed AISRAP as the National Centre of Excellence in Suicide Prevention. This latter recognition awards not only many years of high quality research, but also of fruitful cooperation between the Institute and several different governmental agencies.

As part of this mandate, AISRAP is committed to the creation of a databank of the recent scientific literature documenting the nature and extent of suicidal and self-harming behaviour and recommended practices in preventing and responding to these behaviours. The key output for the project is a critical bi-annual review of the national and international literature outlining recent advances and promising developments in research in suicide prevention, particularly where this can help to inform national activities. This task is not aimed at providing a critique of new researches, but rather at drawing attention to investigations that may have particular relevance to the Australian context. In doing so, we are committed to a user-friendly language, in order to render research outcomes and their interpretation accessible also to a non-expert audience.

In summary, these reviews serve three primary purposes:

1. To inform future State and Commonwealth suicide prevention policies;
2. To assist in the improvement of existing initiatives, and the development of new and innovative Australian projects for the prevention of suicidal and self-harming behaviours within the context of the Living is for Everyone (LIFE) Framework (2008);
3. To provide directions for Australian research priorities in suicidology.

The review is presented in three sections. The first contains a selection of the best articles published in the last six months internationally. For each article identified by us (see the method of chosing articles described below), the original abstract is accompanied by a brief comment explaining why we thought the study was providing an important contribution to research and why we considered its possible applicability to Australia. The second section presents the abstracts of the most relevant literature — following our criteria — collected between November 2014 and April 2015; while the final section presents a list of citations of all literature published over this time-period.

Methodology

The literature search was conducted in four phases.

Phase 1

Phase one consisted of weekly searches of the academic literature performed from November 2014 to April 2015. To ensure thorough coverage of the available published research, the literature was sourced using several scientific electronic databases including: PubMed, ProQuest, Scopus, Safetylit and Web of Science, using the following key words: *suicide OR suicidal OR self-harm OR self-injury OR parasuicide.*

Results from the weekly searches were downloaded and combined into one database (deleting duplicates).

Specific inclusion criteria for Phase 1 included:

- Timeliness: the article was published (either electronically or in hard-copy) between November 2014 to April 2015;
- Relevance: the article explicitly referred to fatal and/or non-fatal suicidal behaviour and related issues and/or interventions directly targeted at preventing/treating these behaviours.
- The article was written in English.

Articles about euthanasia, assisted suicide, suicide terrorist attacks, and/or book reviews, abstracts and conference presentations were excluded.

Also, articles that have been published in electronic versions (ahead of print) and therefore included in the previous volume (Volumes 1 to 12 of *Suicide Research: Selected Readings*) were excluded to avoid duplication.

Phase 2

Following an initial reading of the abstracts (retrieved in Phase 1), the list of articles was refined down to the most relevant literature. In Phase 2 articles were only included if they were published in an international, peer-reviewed journal.

In Phase 2, articles were excluded when they:

- were not particularly instructive or original
- were of a descriptive nature (e.g. a case-report)
- consisted of historical/philosophical content
- were a description of surgical reconstruction/treatment of self-inflicted injuries
- concerned biological and/or genetic interpretations of suicidal behaviour, the results of which could not be easily adoptable in the context of the LIFE Framework.

In order to minimise the potential for biased evaluations, two researchers working independently read through the full text of all articles selected to create a list of most relevant papers. This process was then duplicated by a third researcher for any articles on which consensus could not be reached.

The strength and quality of the research evidence was evaluated, based on the *Critical Appraisal Skills Programme (CASP) Appraisal Tools* published by the Public Health Resource Unit, England (2006). These tools, publically available online, consist of checklists for critically appraising systematic reviews, randomized controlled trials (RCT), qualitative research, economic evaluation studies, cohort studies, diagnostic test studies and case control studies.

Phase 3

One of the aims of this review was to identify research that is both evidence-based and of potential relevance to the Australian context. Thus, the final stage of applied methodology focused on research conducted in countries with populations or health systems sufficiently comparable to Australia. Only articles in which the full-text was available were considered. It is important to note that failure of an article to be selected for inclusion in Phase 3 does not entail any negative judgment on its 'objective' quality.

Specific inclusion criteria for Phase 3 included:

- applicability to Australia
- the paper met all criteria for scientificity (i.e., the methodology was considered sound)
- the paper represented a particularly compelling addition to the literature, which would be likely to stimulate suicide prevention initiatives and research
- inevitably, an important aspect was the importance of the journal in which the paper was published (because of the high standards that have to be met in order

to obtain publication in that specific journal); priority was given to papers published in high impact factor journals

- particular attention has been paid to widen the literature horizon to include sociological and anthropological research that may have particular relevance to the Australian context.

After a thorough reading of these articles ('Key articles' for the considered time frame), a written comment was produced for each article detailing:

- methodological strengths and weaknesses (e.g., sample size, validity of measurement instruments, appropriateness of analysis performed)
- practical implications of the research results to the Australian context
- suggestions for integrating research findings within the domains of the LIFE framework suicide prevention activities.

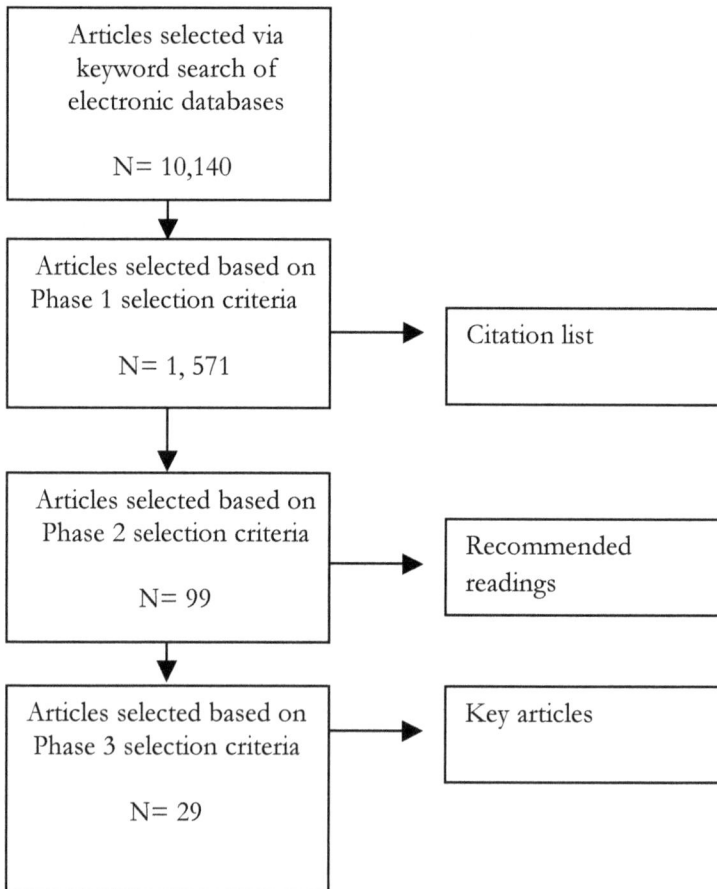

Figure 1 — Flowchart of process.

Phase 4

In the final phase of the search procedure all articles were divided into the following classifications:

- *Fatal suicidal behaviour* (epidemiology, risk and protective factors, prevention, postvention and bereavement)
- *Non-fatal suicidal/self-harming behaviours* (epidemiology, risk and protective factors, prevention, care and support)
- *Case reports* include reports of fatal and non-fatal suicidal behaviours
- *Miscellaneous* includes all research articles that could not be classified into any other category.

Allocation to these categories was not always straightforward, and where papers spanned more than one area, consensus of the research team determined which domain the article would be placed in. Within each section of the report (i.e., Key articles, Recommended readings, Citation list) articles are presented in alphabetical order by author.

References

1   Australian Bureau of Statistics (2015). *Causes of death, Australia, 2013. Suicides.* Cat. no. 3303.0. Canberra: ABS.

Key Articles

Suicide around anniversary times

Barker E, O'Gorman J, De Leo D (Australia)
Omega 69, 305-310, 2014

The anniversary of the loss of a loved one is known to induce negative emotions, which for some can be significant. The present study examined the incidence of suicide around the time of such anniversaries using data from the Queensland Suicide Register for the years 1998 to 2008. There were statistically significant increases in suicide events immediately after the loss of a loved one and around the anniversary of the loss. Limitations of the study are noted.

Comment

Main Findings: Limited research has been conducted on the incidence of suicides on or around the anniversary of a loved one's death. As bereavement of a loved one can be enduring, eliciting psychiatric and physiological reactions surrounding the anniversary[1], this study aimed to evaluate the anniversary of a loved one's death as a potential risk factor for suicide. Cases from the Queensland Suicide Register (QSR) during 1998 until 2008 were examined to identify suicides that occurred around the anniversary of a loved one's death. A total of 137 cases had bereavement listed as a possible trigger for suicide, and the exact date of death of their respective loved one was recorded in the available documents. The number of days between the anniversary of a loved one's death and suicide was calculated and subsequently analysed. Of 137 cases, 94 suicides (68.6%) occurred before the first anniversary of a loved one's death, with the average number of days from death to suicide equating to 220.5 days, 97 (70.8%) were males and 40.8 years was the average age at time of death. Twenty-four suicides (17.5%) of the 137 cases were bereaved by the loss of a spouse whereas 56.2% were bereaved by a family member. For 34.3% of cases, the loved one died by suicide whilst in 51.8% of cases, the loved one died by other causes. Seventy-nine (57.7%) occurred within the first six months of the death of a loved one and of these, 25.3% occurred within the first five days and 49.4% occurred within the first 30 days. Of the remaining 58 (42.3%) suicides that occurred more than six months after the death, 22.4% occurred within five days of an anniversary of the death and 29.3% occurred within 30 days. Of those suicides occurring within 30 days of an anniversary, 88.2% involved the death of a family member whilst no deaths involved the anniversary of the death of a spouse.

Implications: Although the authors attempted to ensure recording was comprehensive and systematic, there is no guarantee that all cases, in which bereavement was a potential trigger, were included. Furthermore, whilst 137 cases were selected for analysis based on provision of exact dates of the loved one's death, this sample represents a sub-sample of a larger collection of people who suffered loss and subsequently died by suicide. Despite such limitations, this study highlights the significant life event of losing a loved one as being a possible etiological factor for suicide. A remarkable number of suicides in the days following loss, and a lower but still relevant incidence of suicides within 30 days of the anniversary, were identified in the study. The anniversary of the death is likely to engender memories of a loved one and associated emotions, as suggested by other studies of anniversary reactions[1]. In light of these findings, there is a need for increased vigilance by those people in the bereaved person's social environment. Particular organisations in Australia, such as Lifeline, aim to provide useful information for helping someone who is grieving and offer services such as face-to-face interviews for those dealing with grief and loss[2].

Endnotes

1. Renvoize EB, Jain J (1986). Anniversary reactions. *The British Journal of Psychiatry* 148, 322-324.
2. Website of Lifeline (2015). Retrieved from https://www.lifeline.org.au/

Association of poor subjective sleep quality with risk for death by suicide during a 10-year period:
A longitudinal, population-based study of late life

Bernert RA, Turvey CL, Conwell Y, Joiner TE, Jr. (USA)
JAMA Psychiatry 71, 1129-1137, 2014

Importance: Older adults have high rates of sleep disturbance, die by suicide at disproportionately higher rates compared with other age groups, and tend to visit their physician in the weeks preceding suicide death. To our knowledge, to date, no study has examined disturbed sleep as an independent risk factor for late-life suicide.

Objective: To examine the relative independent risk for suicide associated with poor subjective sleep quality in a population-based study of older adults during a 10-year observation period.

Design, Setting, and Participants: A longitudinal case-control cohort study of late-life suicide among a multisite, population-based community sample of older adults participating in the Established Populations for Epidemiologic Studies of the Elderly. Of 14 456 community older adults sampled, 400 control subjects were matched (on age, sex, and study site) to 20 suicide decedents.

Main Outcomes and Measures: Primary measures included the Sleep Quality Index, the Center for Epidemiologic Studies-Depression Scale, and vital statistics.

Results: Hierarchical logistic regressions revealed that poor sleep quality at baseline was significantly associated with increased risk for suicide (odds ratio [OR], 1.39; 95%CI, 1.14-1.69; P < .001) by 10 follow-up years. In addition, 2 sleep items were individually associated with elevated risk for suicide at 10-year follow-up: difficulty falling asleep (OR, 2.24; 95%CI, 1.27-3.93; P < .01) and nonrestorative sleep (OR, 2.17; 95%CI, 1.28-3.67; P < .01). Controlling for depressive symptoms, baseline self-reported sleep quality was associated with increased risk for death by suicide (OR, 1.30; 95% CI, 1.04-1.63; P < .05).

Conclusions and Relevance: Our results indicate that poor subjective sleep quality is associated with increased risk for death by suicide 10 years later, even after adjustment for depressive symptoms. Disturbed sleep appears to confer considerable risk, independent of depressed mood, for the most severe suicidal behaviors and may warrant inclusion in suicide risk assessment frameworks to enhance detection of risk and intervention opportunity in late life.

Comment

Main Findings: Research has indicated a link between sleep disturbances such as nightmares, insomnia and poor sleep quality with an increased risk for suicidal ideation, suicide attempts and death by suicide[1]. Considering that depression is one of the important predictors of suicide[2], much past research has failed to account for depression's confounding presence and thus has been unsuccessful in determining whether sleep disturbance is an independent risk factor for suicide. This cohort study explored whether subjective sleep disturbance conferred independent risk for suicide compared with control subjects in older adults across a 10-year time span. It was hypothesised that disturbed sleep would predict increased suicide risk and this effect would hold true after adjusting for concomitant mood symptoms. An exploratory evaluation of individual sleep items was conducted in regard to their prediction of suicide risk. Participants were recruited between 1981 and 1991. Data was collected from 14,456 older adults aged 65 years and older, as sleep difficulties are especially common in late life[3]. Complete data files were available for 20 out of the 21 suicide decedents, and they were subsequently matched with controls by age, sex and location. As a result, the final sample consisted of 400 controls and 20 suicide decedents.

Participants ranged from 66 to 90 years of age. Suicide decedents' deaths occurred, on average, within two years from baseline. Ninety-five percent of suicide decedents were males. The most common method of suicide was firearms (62%) followed by hanging (9.5%), cutting (9.5%), poisoning, drowning, lethal jump and suffocation (all 4.8%). Poor subjective sleep quality at baseline was associated with increased suicide risk at 10 year follow-up (p<.001), with those reporting poorer sleep quality showing a 1.4 times increased risk of suicide. This effect remained statistically significant (p<.05), after controlling the effect of depressed mood, showing those with poor sleep quality at baseline at a 1.2 times increased risk of suicide death during the 10 year period. When individual items measuring sleep quality were analysed, two were significantly associated with increased risk of suicide at 10 year follow-up: non-restorative sleep (p<.01) and difficulty falling asleep (p<.01). However, after adjusting for the influence of depressed mood, this effect was only significant for non-restorative sleep (p<.05).

Implications: Several limitations were present in this study. Firstly, the subjective nature of measuring sleep quality using a self-report questionnaire may have impacted on the results, as participants potentially presented with underlying sleep disorders (i.e. chronic insomnia). Moreover, other important covariates (i.e. medical conditions) that may have impacted sleep quality were not included in this study. Despite limitations, findings prove valuable, demonstrating the importance of assessing sleep quality in the presence of other well renowned risk factors for suicide. This study also identifies sleep as a potential intervention tool and a novel therapeutic target for evidence-based suicide risk assessment frameworks, suicide prevention strategies and clinical practice guidelines for those in late life. Overall findings give rise to potential future research that may identify possible explanatory mechanisms for the relationship between poor sleep quality and suicide risk. As the sample for this study consisted of mostly white older males from the United States, additional research should be conducted with a more generalisable sample. The majority of the research regarding the link between sleep quality and risk of suicide has come from the United States and there is no known research on this topic in Australia. Australian research is therefore encouraged. Furthermore, as suicides occurred within approximately two years of the study commencing, further efforts into whether there is indication that disturbed sleep may confer risk within a relatively acute timeframe is viable.

Endnotes

1. Bernert RA, Joiner TE Jr, Cukrowicz KC, Schmidt NB, Krakow B (1986). Suicidality and sleep disturbances. *Sleep* 28, 1135-1141.
2. Nierenberg AA, Gray SM, Grandin LD (2001). Mood disorders and suicide. *Journal of Clinical Psychiatry* 62 (Suppl 25), 27-30.
3. McCall WV (2004). Sleep in the elderly: Burden, diagnosis, and treatment. *The Primary Care Companion to the Journal of Clinical Psychiatry* 6, 9-20.

Gender differences in mental disorders and suicidality in Europe: Results from a large cross-sectional population-based study

Boyd A, Van de Velde S, Vilagut G, de Graaf R, O'Neill S, Florescu S, Alonso J, Kovess-Masfety V (France, Belgium, Spain, The Netherlands, Northern Ireland, Romania)

Journal of Affective Disorders 173, 245-254, 2015

Introduction: When evaluating gender differences in mental disorders and suicidality, specifically between European countries, studies are sparse and frequently hindered by methodological issues, such as the limited items evaluated and inconsistent sampling designs.

Methods: In ten European countries participating in the World Mental Health Survey Initiative, lifetime internalizing and externalizing disorders and suicidality were assessed among 37,289 respondents. Disorders were classified using DMS-IV criteria. Odds ratios (OR) for gender differences were calculated using logistic regression, while trends across age-groups were tested via gender × age interaction.

Results: Within countries, prevalence of any lifetime internalizing disorder ranged from 10.8% to 44.5% among women and 5.9% to 26.5% among men, with women having consistently higher odds than men (OR range: 1.52-2.73). Prevalence of any lifetime externalizing disorders ranged from 0.2% to 6.6% among women and 2.2% to 22.4% among men, with women having consistently lower odds than men (OR range: 0.05-0.35). Any lifetime suicide attempt was found in 0.8-5.4% of women and 0.3-2.4% of men, showing inconsistent relative gender-differences across countries (OR range: 0.77-4.72). Significant effects in gender OR across age-groups were not observed for any internalizing disorder or suicide attempt, yet were present for any externalizing disorder in France ($p=0.01$), the Netherlands ($p=0.05$), and Spain ($p=0.02$).

Limitations: Mental disorders were assessed with the CIDI 3.0 and not psychiatric evaluations. Suicidality does not fully represent more important clinical events, such as suicide mortality.

Conclusions: Consistent across European countries, internalizing disorders are more common among women and externalizing disorders among men, whereas gender differences in suicidality varied.

Comment

Main Findings: Research has proposed a notable difference between women and men in how mental disorders manifest[1], indicating women are twice as likely to have mood and anxiety disorders whereas men are four times more likely to have impulsive and substance-use disorders[2]. The main aim of this study was to compare the prevalence of mental disorders and suicidality between genders in a variety of European counties (Belgium, France, Germany, Italy, the Netherlands, Spain, Bulgaria, Romania, Northern Ireland and Portugal). Trends across different age groups were also analysed. Data was obtained via the World Mental Health Survey Initiative during the period of 2001 to 2009 from a total of 37,289 respondents across the ten different countries. Questions were administered by interviewers using a computer-assisted face-to-face interview. Mental disorders were categorised into two groups, internalising disorders (mood and anxiety disorders) and externalising disorders (including attention-deficit, conduct, alcohol and drug-use disorder). In addition, specific questions were asked regarding suicidal thoughts, suicide plans and suicide attempts.

Results showed disparity in the prevalence of internalising disorders between women and men, with women having a significantly higher prevalence than men across all ten European countries. Romania presented with the lowest prevalence for both men and women (5.9% and 10.8% respectively) whereas France presented with the highest prevalence of internalising disorders (26.5% and 44.5% respectively). Conversely, a variation was also found regarding the prevalence of externalising disorders between women and men, with men having significantly higher incidences than women in all ten counties. Italy presented with the lowest prevalence of externalising disorders for both women and men (0.2% and 2.2% respectively) whereas Northern Ireland presented with the highest (6.6% and 22.4% respectively). All countries in this study showed a trend in lower prevalence of internalising and externalising disorders with increasing age-categories for both men and women. Suicide attempts varied between women (0.8% in Bulgaria to 5.4% in France) and men (0.3% in Bulgaria to 2.4% in Northern Ireland) with women exceeding or equalling those of men across all ten countries, with statistically significantly higher prevalence in six countries (Belgium, France, Germany, Bulgaria, Italy and Portugal). Severity of suicide attempt was measured when participants were asked to describe their attempt as either high, moderate or low, ranging from "I made a serious attempt to kill myself and it was only luck that I did not succeed" to "My attempt was a cry for help, I did not intend to die". No significant differences were found between genders across all countries except for men in Bulgaria who were less likely to report severe attempts than women (53% vs 63.6% out of all suicide attempts respectively). In general, most countries showed lower prevalence of suicidal thoughts (except Germany, Bulgaria and Romania), plans (except Bulgaria, Romania and Portugal), and attempts (except Romania) in older age-groups. Women had a lower median age of onset for suicidal attempts than men, with a statistically significant difference only in France (21 years vs 29 years) for women and men respectively (p=0.02).

Implications: Several limitations were addressed by the authors. Firstly, the way in which mental disorders and suicidality were measured was from self-reported responses, making the subjective nature of the data vulnerable to recall bias. In addition, lower response rates for certain countries may have impacted on their overall representativeness with France having the lowest response rate of 45.9% and Spain having the highest of 78.6%. The between-gender odds ratios for certain countries may have been inflated due to the low occurrence of externalising disorders and suicide attempts. Previous research has shown that women are more likely to meet the criteria for depressive disorder as they tend to report more traditional symptoms of depression than males[3], possibly contributing to the higher prevalence of internalising disorders in this study. This study found that both genders have similar prevalence of mental health problems; however the way in which these mental health problems are expressed differs considerably between men and women. Nevertheless, women were two times more likely to have internalising disorders than men and the inverse occurred for externalising disorders. However, an association between higher rates of suicidal behaviour in women, and their increased risk of developing an internalising disorder, has been also shown in an Australian mental health survey[4]. In addition, higher suicide fatalities have been associated with life-threatening behaviours, including alcohol abuse, which are more prevalent in males[5]. In conclusion, gender-distinct prevalence of mental disorders is clinically vital in guiding mental health professionals to understand the need to asses certain disorders, especially for men as they are less likely to seek help for their suicidality and mental health problems[6]. Differences between genders, regarding onset of both mental disorders and suicide attempts, need to be considered to help initiate better gender-specific interventions.

Endnotes

1. Alonso J, Angermeyer MC, Bernert S, Bruffaerts R, Brugha TS, Bryson H, de Girolamo G, Graaf R, Demyttenaere K, Gasquet I, et al. (2004). Prevalence of mental disorders in Europe: Results from the European Study of the Epidemiology of Mental Disorders (ESEMeD) project. *Acta Psychiatrica Scandinavica*, 109, 21-27

2. Seedat S, Scott KM, Angermeyer MC, Berglund P, Bromet EJ, Brugha TS, Demyttenaere K, de Girolamo G, Haro JM, Jin R, et al. (2009). Cross-national associations between gender and mental disorders in the World Health Organization World Mental Health Surveys. *Archives of General Psychiatry* 66, 785-795.

3. Piccinelli M, Wilkinson G (2000). Gender differences in depression. Critical review. *British Journal of Psychiatry* 177, 486-492.

4. Slade T, Johnston A, Teesson M, Whiteford H, Burgess P, Pirkis J, Saw S (2009). *The mental health of Australians 2. Report on the 2007 National Survey of Mental Health and Wellbeing.* Department of Health and Ageing, Canberra.

5. Pompili M, Serafini G, Innamorati M, Dominici G, Ferracuti S, Kotzalidis GD, Serra G, Girardi P, Janiri L, Tatarelli R, et al (2010). Suicidal Behavior and Alcohol Abuse. *International Journal of Environmental Research and Public Health* 7, 1392-1431.

6. Milner A, De Leo D (2010). Who seeks treatment where? Suicidal behaviors and health care: Evidence from a community survey. *Journal of Nervous and Mental Disease* 198, 412-419.

Familial pathways to early-onset suicide attempt: A 5.6-year prospective study

Brent DA, Melhem NM, Oquendo M, Burke A, Birmaher B, Stanley B, Biernesser C, Keilp J, Kolko D, Ellis S, Porta G, Zelazny J, Iyengar S, Mann JJ (USA)

JAMA Psychiatry 72, 160-168, 2015

Importance: Suicide attempts are strong predictors of suicide, a leading cause of adolescent mortality. Suicide attempts are highly familial, although the mechanisms of familial transmission are not understood. Better delineation of these mechanisms could help frame potential targets for prevention.

Objective: To examine the mechanisms and pathways by which suicidal behavior is transmitted from parent to child.

Design, Setting, and Participants: In this prospective study conducted from July 15, 1997, through June 21, 2012, a total of 701 offspring aged 10 to 50 years (mean age, 17.7 years) of 334 clinically referred probands with mood disorders, 191 (57.2%) of whom had also made a suicide attempt, were followed up for a mean of 5.6 years.

Main Outcomes and Measures: The primary outcome was a suicide attempt. Variables were examined at baseline, intermediate time points, and the time point proximal to the attempt. Participants were assessed by structured psychiatric assessments and self-report and by interview measures of domains hypothesized to be related to familial transmission (eg, mood disorder and impulsive aggression).

Results: Among the 701 offspring, 44 (6.3%) had made a suicide attempt before participating in the study, and 29 (4.1%) made an attempt during study follow-up. Multivariate logistic regression revealed that proband suicide attempt was a predictor of offspring suicide attempt (odds ratio [OR], 4.79; 95% CI, 1.75-13.07), even controlling for other salient offspring variables: baseline history of mood disorder (OR, 4.20; 95% CI, 1.37-12.86), baseline history of suicide attempt (OR, 5.69; 95% CI, 1.94-16.74), and mood disorder at the time point before the attempt (OR, 11.32; 95% CI, 2.29-56.00). Path analyses were consistent with these findings, revealing a direct effect of proband attempt on offspring suicide attempt, a strong effect of offspring mood disorder at each time point, and impulsive aggression as a precursor of mood disorder.

Conclusions and Relevance: Parental history of a suicide attempt conveys a nearly 5-fold increased odds of suicide attempt in offspring at risk for mood disorder, even after adjusting for the familial transmission of mood disorder. Interventions that target mood disorder and impulsive aggression in high-risk offspring may attenuate the familial transmission of suicidal behavior.

Comment

Main findings: Several studies have suggested the familial transmission of suicidal behaviours; however, few have examined the pathways by which this phenomenon occurs[1,2]. Previous research has indicated that children of suicide attempters have a four to six times greater risk of a suicide attempt and that familial transmission of mood disorders, impulsive aggression and childhood maltreatment may mediate this relationship[2,3]. This study followed up the offspring of parents with mood disorders, with half of parents having had a previous suicide attempt. The authors hypothesised that parental attempted suicides would predict children's suicide attempts and this effect would stand true after controlling for the familial transmission of mood disorders. Furthermore, the familial transmission of suicidal behaviour was expected to be mediated by familial transmission of mood disorders, physical or sexual abuse and childhood and impulsive-aggressive traits. Data were collected from 701 offspring of 334 parents with mood disorders, with 57.2% having made a suicide attempt during the period spanning from July 1997 through to June 2012. Offspring were followed up from baseline for a mean of 5.6 years. Per proband, there was an average of 2.1 offspring siblings. Data were collected at three time points: 1) baseline; 2) intermediate time points, which were all time points between baseline and proximal time point; and, 3) a proximal time point, which was the point immediately before the onset of an attempt (or, for non-attempters, a maximum time point).

Offspring whose parent had a suicide attempt displayed a five times greater risk of suicide attempts, with a mean age of 20.1 years. At baseline, proband suicide attempts were significantly related to risk of offspring suicide attempt (p=.005). This effect also held constant after controlling for the significant direct effects of other significant variables: history of mood disorders in offspring at baseline (p<.001), mood disorders at the proximal time point (p<.001) and, finally, history of offspring suicide attempts at baseline (p<.001). Furthermore, the relationship also remained significant after accounting for familial transmission of mood disorders. No support was found for the prediction that familial transmission of mood disorders, physical or sexual abuse in childhood and impulsive aggressive traits would mediate the pathway between proband suicide attempts and offspring attempts. An important variable that contributed to an increased risk of offspring suicide attempt was impulsive aggression, which increased the likelihood of the development of a mood disorder, and then increased the risk of a suicide attempt. This was evident as the pathway between offspring suicide attempt at baseline and attempt at the proximal time point was mediated by offspring impulsive aggression (p=.03) and mood disorder (p=.05).

Implications: Overall, this study indicated that parental suicide attempts conveyed an almost five-fold increase in the likelihood of suicide attempts in their offspring, which was also evident when the effect of familial transmission of mood disorder was accounted for. Despite the fact that familial transmission of suicide attempts occurred independently from the transmission of a mood disorder, the variable (transmission of a mood disorder) was a significant pathway to early onset of suicidal behavior. Clinical implications include the need for assessment and early intervention in families with parents who have a mood disorder or a history of suicide attempts. Prevention and treatment strategies would prove useful by targeting mood disorders in youth in order to reduce incidence of suicide attempts. Impulsive aggression was an important precursor of mood disorders and could be targeted in interventions designed to prevent those youth at high familial risk of making a suicide attempt. Such interventions need to focus on assisting young individuals with impulsive aggression to maintain better emotion regulation, which subsequently may reduce likelihood of suicide by reducing the risk of acting on suicidal impulses and developing a mood disorder. Further research should be conducted by examining bio-behavioural phenotypes to explain mechanisms by which suicidal behavior is transmitted from parent to child.

Endnotes

1. Brent DA, Melhem N (2008). Familial transmission of suicidal behavior. *Psychiatric Clinics of North America* 31, 157-177.

2. Mann JJ, Bortinger J, Oquendo MA, Currier D, Li S, Brent DA (2005). Family history of suicidal behavior and mood disorders in probands with mood disorders. *American Journal of Psychiatry* 162, 1672-1679.

3. Brodsky BS, Mann JJ, Stanley B, et al (2008). Familial transmission of suicidal behavior: Factors mediating the relationship between childhood abuse and offspring suicide attempts. *Journal of Clinical Psychiatry*, 69, 584-596.

The prevalence and correlates of chronic pain and suicidality in a nationally representative sample

Campbell G, Darke S, Bruno R, Degenhardt L (Australia)

Australian and New Zealand Journal of Psychiatry. Published online: 19 February 2015. doi: 0.1177/0004867415569795

Background: Research suggests that people suffering from chronic pain have elevated rates of suicidality. With an ageing population, more research is essential to gain a better understanding of this association.

Aims: To document the prevalence and correlates of chronic pain and suicide, and estimate the contribution of chronic pain to suicidality.

Method: Data from the 2007 Australian National Survey of Mental Health and Wellbeing, a nationally representative household survey on 8841 people, aged 16-85 years, was analysed.

Results: The odds of lifetime and past 12-month suicidality were two to three times greater in people with chronic pain. Sixty-five percent of people who attempted suicide in the past 12 months had a history of chronic pain. Chronic pain was independently associated with lifetime suicidality after controlling for demographic, mental health and substance use disorders.

Conclusions: Health care professionals need to be aware of the risk of suicidality in patients with chronic pain, even in the absence of mental health problems.

Comment

Main findings: While suicidality amongst people with chronic pain is still under-investigated, emerging research suggests that people with chronic pain have almost double the risk of death by suicide[1]. This study used data from 8,841 participants in the 2007 Australian National Survey of Mental Health and Wellbeing, based on the World Mental Health Survey Initiative version of the Composite International Diagnostic Interview[2]. To ensure data were representative of the Australian population, person and replicate weights generated by the Australian Bureau of Statistics were applied. Results indicated that more than 6 million people (more than one-fourth of the Australian population) were likely to suffer from chronic pain conditions. Logistic regression analyses revealed that compared to people without chronic pain, people with chronic pain had: 2.3 times greater odds of lifetime suicidal thoughts, 2.5 times greater odds of having made a suicide plan at some point, and 2.7 times the odds of a lifetime suicide attempt. Just over 50% of those with lifetime suicidal thoughts had a history of chronic pain, and two-thirds of those had attempted suicide in the previous 12 months, equating to 42,000 people out of the estimated 64,000 who had attempted suicide nationally. After adjustment for socio-demographic characteristics, all specific pain conditions (arthritis, migraines, and back/neck problems) and an 'any pain' condition (any one chronic pain condition) were significantly associated with life-time suicidality. After adjusting for socio-demographic factors and mental health disorders (including substance disorders), most chronic pain conditions were independently associated with lifetime suicidality (suicide ideation, plans and attempts), other than associations between suicide plans for migraine pain, and suicide attempts for arthritis and migraine pain. The study found substantial variation in the levels of the different types of suicidal behaviours across different pain conditions. These conditions are usually highly comorbid, and more focussed research may be neccessary to help clarify the effect that specific pain conditions have on suicidality.

Implications: There appears to have been little formal recognition in Australia of people with chronic pain as a high risk group for suicidal behaviour[3]. Past studies investigating the association between suicidality and chronic pain have generally been based on small samples; it is unknown if a similar pattern exists in the general population of those with chronic pain. This study is believed to be among the first to estimate the contribution of chronic pain to suicidality in the general population, and to specifically examine its impact on an Australian population. The prevalence of chronic pain in Australia found by this study was higher than found previously[4], although an ageing population may explain some of the difference. The study supports recent epidemiological research findings that chronic pain is independently associated with suicidality, after controlling for demographic and mental health factors[5]. While the link between depression and chronic pain is generally well known[6], these findings suggest that clinicians should be aware of this increased risk amongst clients presenting with chronic pain, regardless of their mental health status.

Endnotes

1. Tang NK, Crane C (2006). Suicidality in chronic pain: A review of the prevalence, risk factors and psychological links. *Psychological Medicine* 36, 578-586.
2. Kessler RC, Ustun TB (2004). The World Mental Health (WMH) Survey Initiative Version of the World Health Organization (WHO) Composite International Diagnostic Interview (CIDI). *International Journal of Methods in Psychiatric Research* 13, 93-121.
3. Senate Community Affairs References Committee (2010). *The hidden toll: Suicide in Australia.* Canberra: Commonwealth of Australia.
4. Blyth FM, March LM, Brnabic AJM, Jorm LR, Williamson M, Cousins MJ (2001). Chronic pain in Australia: A prevalence study. *Pain* 89, 127-134.
5. Ilgen MA, Kleinberg F, Ignacio RV, Valenstein M (2013). Pain and suicidal thoughts, plans and attempts in the United States. *General Hospital Psychiatry* 30, 521-527.
6. Holmes A, Christells N, Arnold C (2012). Depression and chronic pain. *MJA Open* 1, 17-20.

Hospital management of self-harm patients and risk of repetition: Systematic review and meta-analysis

Carroll R, Metcalfe C, Gunnell D (UK)

Journal of Affective Disorders 168, 476-483, 2014

Background: Self-harm is a common reason for hospital presentation; however, evidence to guide clinical management of these patients to reduce their risk of repeat self-harm and suicide is lacking.

Methods: We undertook a systematic review to investigate whether between study differences in reported clinical management of self-harm patients were associated with the risk of repeat self-harm and suicide.

Results: Altogether 64 prospective studies were identified that described the clinical care of self-harm patients and the incidence of repeat self-harm and suicide. The proportion of a cohort psychosocially assessed was not associated with the recorded incidence of repeat self-harm or suicide; the incidence of repeat self-harm was 16.7% (95% CI 13.8-20.1) in studies in the lowest tertile of assessment levels and 19.0% (95% CI 15.7-23.0) in the highest tertile. There was no association of repeat self-harm with differing levels of hospital admission (n=47 studies) or receiving specialist follow-up (n=12 studies). In studies reporting on levels of hospital admission and suicide (n=5), cohorts where a higher proportion of patients were admitted to a hospital bed reported a lower incidence of subsequent suicide (0.6%, 95% CI 0.5-0.8) compared to cohorts with lower levels of admission (1.9%, 95% CI 1.1-3.2).

Limitations: In some analyses power was limited due to the small number of studies reporting the exposures of interest. Case mix and aspects of care are likely to vary between studies.

Discussion: There is little clear evidence to suggest routine aspects of self-harm patient care, including psychosocial assessment, reduce the risk of subsequent suicide and repeat self-harm.

Comment

Main Findings: There is sparse and conflicting research regarding the association between routine aspects of managing patients with self-harm and the risk of subsequent fatal and non-fatal self-harm[1,2]. For instance, whilst some evidence suggests that patients receiving a psychosocial assessment are at a reduced risk of subsequent self-harm, the evidence is feeble and lacks consistency[3]. Furthermore, there is a great amount of variation in the use of management protocols across health care settings[2,4]. This systematic review examined aspects of self-harm patient care that impact on risk of subsequent fatal and non-fatal self-harm. Specifically, the authors investigated whether the estimations of risk of subsequent self-harm are associated with psychosocial assessment, admission to hospital beds, and outpatient follow-up in different studies. Of the 64 articles that were included in the analysis, the majority were from Europe (82.8%), followed by Asia (7.8%),

Australia and New Zealand (6.3%), and lastly, North America (3.1%). Forty-two studies had recorded one-year repetition rates alongside psychosocial assessment, and found no association between psychosocial assessment and reduced risk of subsequent non-fatal self-harm (p>.05). Of these 42 studies, 20 measured suicide after one year and found no association between psychosocial assessment and suicide (p>.05). In addition, results showed no association between the proportion of patients admitted to hospital (46 studies) with a reduced risk of subsequent self-harm (p>.05) and no evidence to suggest that there was a relationship between admission to hospital and suicide in the year after presenting with self-harm (p>.05). However, a small sub-group of studies (n=5) provided an indication of the latter, as a 10% increase in the proportion of patients admitted was associated with a decline in the mean odds of repetition by 27.4% (p=.03). Lastly, of the 11 studies that reported the proportion of patients who received outpatient follow-up and six studies that recorded the proportion of patients who were discharged home without any specific after-care, there was no evidence to suggest a link between patient management (either receiving after-care or not) and subsequent non-fatal self-harm or suicide one year after presentation.

Implications: The findings from this systematic review and meta-analysis provided limited indication of the association between psychosocial assessment, outpatient follow-up for patients who self-harm and subsequent fatal and non-fatal self-harm. There was some evidence to suggest that admission to hospital was associated with a reduced risk in subsequent suicide a year after presenting with self-harm, which requires further investigation. The difficulty in finding consistent results is likely a reflection of the heterogeneity in self-harm populations, the interventions they receive and difficulties in evaluating the effects of treatment in observational data[2,5]. Future research aiming to identify the most effective interventions for this high risk population should focus on randomised controlled trials and causal analysis. A report on Australian and New Zealand clinical practice guidelines for the management of adult deliberate self-harm concluded that, in Australia, recommended psychological treatments are not widely available to patients who self-harm and those interventions that are available are not known to reduce repetition of self-harm[1]. Furthermore, the effect of follow-up in Australian psychiatric hospitals is poorly understood[1,5] and the need to develop and evaluate interventions that aim to reduce subsequent non-fatal self-harm and suicide should be a priority.

Endnotes

1. Royal Australian and New Zealand College of Psychiatrists Clinical Practice Guidelines Team for Deliberate Self-harm (2004). Australian and New Zealand clinical practice guidelines for the management of adult deliberate self-harm. *Australian & New Zealand Journal of Psychiatry* 38, 868-884.
2. Bennewith O, Gunnell D, Peters T, Hawton K, House A (2004). Variations in the hospital management of self harm in adults in England: Observational study. *British Medical Journal* 328, 1108–1109.

3. Kapur N, Steeg S, Webb R, Haigh M, Bergen H, Hawton K, Ness J, Waters K, Cooper J (2013). Does clinical management improve outcomes following self-harm? Results from the multi-centre study of self-harm in England. *PLoS One* 8, e70434.

4. Cooper J, Steeg S, Bennewith O, Lowe M, Gunnell D, House A, Hawton K, Kapur N (2013). Are hospital services for self-harm getting better? An observational study examining management, service provision and temporal trends in England *BMJ Open* 3, e003444.

5. Carter G, Whyte I, Ball K, Carter N, Dawson A, Carr V, Fryer J (1999). Repetition of deliberate self-poisoning in an Australian hospital-treated population. *Medical Journal of Australia* 170, 307-311.

Antidepressant use and risk of suicide and attempted suicide or self harm in people aged 20 to 64: Cohort study using a primary care database

Coupland C, Hill T, Morriss R, Arthur A, Moore M, Hippisley-Cox J (UK)

BMJ. Published online: 18 February 2015. doi: http://dx.doi.org/10.1136/bmj.h517

Objective: To assess the associations between different antidepressant treatments and the rates of suicide and attempted suicide or self harm in people with depression.

Design: Cohort study.

Setting: Patients registered with UK general practices contributing data to the QResearch database.

Participants: 238 963 patients aged 20 to 64 years with a first diagnosis of depression between 1 January 2000 and 31 July 2011, followed up until 1 August 2012.

Exposures: Antidepressant class (tricyclic and related antidepressants, selective serotonin reuptake inhibitors, other antidepressants), dose, and duration of use, and commonly prescribed individual antidepressant drugs. Cox proportional hazards models were used to calculate hazard ratios adjusting for potential confounding variables.

Main outcome measures: Suicide and attempted suicide or self harm during follow-up.

Results: During follow-up, 87.7% (n=209 476) of the cohort received one or more prescriptions for antidepressants. The median duration of treatment was 221 days (interquartile range 79-590 days). During the first five years of follow-up 198 cases of suicide and 5243 cases of attempted suicide or self harm occurred. The difference in suicide rates during periods of treatment with tricyclic and related antidepressants compared with selective serotonin reuptake inhibitors was not significant (adjusted hazard ratio 0.84, 95% confidence interval 0.47 to 1.50), but the suicide rate was significantly increased during periods of treatment with other antidepressants (2.64, 1.74 to 3.99). The hazard ratio for suicide was significantly increased for mirtazapine compared with citalopram (3.70, 2.00 to 6.84). Absolute risks of suicide over one year ranged from 0.02% for amitriptyline to 0.19% for mirtazapine. There was no significant difference in the rate of attempted suicide or self harm with tricyclic antidepressants (0.96, 0.87 to 1.08) compared with selective serotonin reuptake inhibitors, but the rate of attempted suicide or self harm was significantly higher for other antidepressants (1.80, 1.61 to 2.00). The adjusted hazard ratios for attempted suicide or self harm were significantly increased for three of the most commonly prescribed drugs compared with citalopram: venlafaxine (1.85, 1.61 to 2.13), trazodone (1.73, 1.26 to 2.37), and mirtazapine (1.70, 1.44 to 2.02), and significantly reduced for amitriptyline (0.71, 0.59 to 0.85). The absolute risks of attempted suicide or self harm over one year ranged from 1.02% for amitriptyline to 2.96% for venlafaxine. Rates were highest in the first 28 days after starting treatment and remained increased in the first 28 days after stopping treatment.

Conclusion: Rates of suicide and attempted suicide or self harm were similar during periods of treatment with selective serotonin reuptake inhibitors and tricyclic and related antidepressants. Mirtazapine, venlafaxine, and trazodone were associated with the highest rates of suicide and attempted suicide or self harm, but the number of suicide events was small leading to imprecise estimates. As this is an observational study the findings may reflect indication biases and residual confounding from severity of depression and differing characteristics of patients prescribed these drugs. The increased rates in the first 28 days of starting and stopping antidepressants emphasise the need for careful monitoring of patients during these periods.

Comment

Main findings: Rates of suicide and self-harm have been found to be greatly increased in people with depression. While antidepressants have been found to be effective in reducing depressive symptoms, concerns have been expressed that they may contribute to risk of suicide and self-harm. Various studies to date have suggested that particular antidepressants may result in higher levels of risk than others, but findings have been inconsistent. This large-scale cohort study from the UK sought to quantify associations between antidepressant types and suicide, attempted suicide and self-harm during five years of general practice follow-up with people diagnosed with depression. The most commonly prescribed antidepressant, citalopram, was used as a reference category for comparison. Findings provided support for previous studies indicating that venlafaxine may be associated with greater risks of suicide and self-harm at a population level[1]; fewer studies have reported increased risks for mirtazapine or trazodone. No significant differences were found in suicide risks associated with individual SSRIs, or between SSRIs and tricyclic antidepressants (TCAs). However compared to SSRIs, adjusted hazard ratios for suicide, attempted suicide and self-harm increased significantly in treatment with "other" antidepressants – these were mainly venlafaxine and mirtazapine, usually classed as a serotonin–norepinephrine reuptake inhibitor (SNRI) and a noradrenergic and specific serotonergic antidepressant (NaSSA) respectively. Amongst individual antidepressants, when compared to citalopram, the adjusted hazard ratio for suicide was significantly increased for mirtazapine (p<0.001, 3.7, 95% CI: 2.0-6.84), and for venlafaxine (p<0.02, 2.23, 95% CI: 1.14-4.39). In the case of attempted suicide or self-harm, hazard ratios were significantly higher for venlafaxine, mirtazapine, and the TCAs trazodone and amitriptyline. The study also found an association of increased risk of attempted suicide or self-harm with combinations of antidepressants (eg simultaneous use of an SSRI and a TCA), compared to SSRIs alone (p<0.001, 2.00, 95% CI: 1.54-2.59). Increased hazard ratios for suicide, attempted suicide and self-harm were reported not only within the first 28 days after stopping treatment, but also within the first 28 days of beginning treatment.

As selection of an antidepressant may depend on patient characteristics, the researchers adjusted for a range of potential confounding factors which could influence the choice of antidepressant, including severity of depression. As patients were prescribed drugs for a condition in itself associated with a risk of suicidality, only patients with a recorded diagnosis of depression were included to ensure all patients had the same rationale for treatment. The authors noted that higher hazard ratios for death from suicide associated with venlafaxine and mirtazapine, compared with attempted suicide and self-harm, could be due to higher lethality in overdose than with SSRIs; however, this would not explain the higher hazard ratios reported for SSRIs when compared to TCAs, which also have higher toxicity.

Implications: Past Australian studies have associated reductions in suicide rates with increasing rates of antidepressant use[2]. Australian dispensing of antidepressant medication by dosage has been reported to have increased by 95% between 2000 and 2011, particularly due to an increase in dispensing of SSRIs; there has also been a marked increase in dispensing of SNRIs and NaSSAs, and a decline in dispensing of TCAs and MAOIs[3]. Dispensing of venlafaxine increased threefold over this period, making up 13.9% of total antidepressant doses reported[3]. Considerable focus has been placed on possible associations between antidepressants and suicidality in young people, particularly SSRIs[4]. Confirmation of the current study may prompt review of Australian recommendations for prescribing of antidepressants across patient groups, such as consideration of venlafaxine in cases of severe and complicated depression resistant to initial treatment[5]. Current Australian guidelines for medical practitioners recommend avoidance of antidepressants which can be toxic in overdose when prescribing for patients who are already suicidal, including TCAs, venlafaxine and combinations of antidepressants; mirtazapine has been noted to be relatively safe in overdose[6]. Although simultaneous combination of antidepressants has been controversial in Australia, a survey of doctors working in psychiatry found that 79% of participants had prescribed combinations of antidepressants; SSRIs combined with TCAs were most common, followed by combinations of mirtazapine with venlafaxine and other antidepressants[7]. Although Australian guidelines stress risks during discontinuation of medication, there is less focus on risks during the initial period of beginning an antidepressant treatment. Further research is necessary to confirm the results of the current study, and to identify the mechanism behind associations between specific antidepressants and increased suicidal behaviour, and why individual patients may respond differently[1]. Antidepressants continue to be a valuable resource in treating depressed patients, but great care should be taken in selecting appropriate medication for each person, with careful monitoring of medication use, and disclosure of known risks to patients.

Endnotes

1. Sinyor M, Cheung AH (2015). Antidepressants and risk of suicide. *BMJ*. Published online: 19 February 2015. doi: 10.1136/bmj.h783. Hall WD, Mant A, Mitchell PB, Rendle VA, Hickie IB, McManus P (2003). Association between antidepressant prescribing and suicide in Australia, 1991-2000: Trend analysis. *BMJ* 326, 1008.

2. Stephenson CP, Karanges E, McGregor IS (2012). Trends in the utilisation of psychotropic medications in Australia from 2000 to 2011. *Australian & New Zealand Journal of Psychiatry* 47, 74-87.

3. Royal Australian and New Zealand College of Psychiatrists, Royal Australian College of General Practitioners, Royal Australasian College of Physicians. *Clinical guidance on the use of antidepressant medications in children and adolescents.* http://www.racgp.org.au/folder.asp?id=1180

4. Royal Australian and New Zealand College of Psychiatrists Clinical Practice Guidelines Team for Depression (2004). *Australian and New Zealand clinical practice guidelines for the treatment of depression.* https://www.ranzcp.org/Publications/Statements-Guidelines.aspx

5. National Prescribing Service (2004). Choosing an antidepressant for special patient groups. *NPS News* 35. http://www.nps.org.au/__data/assets/pdf_file/0020/15824/news35_depression_in_children_0804.pdf

6. Horgan D, Dodd S, Berk M (2007). A survey of combination antidepressant use in Australia. *Australasian Psychiatry* 15, 26-29.

The effect of an e-learning supported train-the-trainer programme on implementation of suicide guidelines in mental health care

De Beurs DP, De Groot MH, De Keijser J, Mokkenstorm J, Van Duijn E, De Winter RFP, Kerkhof AJFM (the Netherlands)

Journal of Affective Disorders 175, 446-453, 2015

Background: Randomized studies examining the effect of training of mental health professionals in suicide prevention guidelines are scarce. We assessed whether professionals benefited from an e-learning supported Train-the-Trainer programme aimed at the application of the Dutch multidisciplinary suicide prevention guideline.

Methods: 45 psychiatric departments from all over the Netherlands were clustered in pairs and randomized. In the experimental condition, all of the staff of psychiatric departments was trained by peers with an e-learning supported Train-the-Trainer programme. Guideline adherence of individual professionals was measured by means of the response to on-line video fragments. Multilevel analyses were used to establish whether variation between conditions was due to differences between individual professionals or departments.

Results: Multilevel analysis showed that the intervention resulted in an improvement of individual professionals. At the 3 month follow-up, professionals who received the intervention showed greater guideline adherence, improved self-perceived knowledge and improved confidence as providers of care than professionals who were only exposed to traditional guideline dissemination. Subgroup analyses showed that improved guideline adherence was found among nurses but not among psychiatrists and psychologists. No significant effect of the intervention on team performance was found.

Limitations: The ICT environment in departments was often technically inadequate when displaying the video clips clip of the survey. This may have caused considerable drop-out and possibly introduced selection bias, as professionals who were strongly affiliated to the theme of the study might have been more likely to finish the study.

Conclusions: Our results support the idea that an e-learning supported Train-the-Trainer programme is an effective strategy for implementing clinical guidelines and improving care for suicidal patients.

Comment

Main Findings: There have been concerns regarding mental health workers' adherence to evidence-based guidelines[1]. This is particularly alarming as they exist to inform professionals of diagnosis and treatment practices of patients with suicidality and mental health problems[2]. Based on international guidelines, the Netherlands issued practice guidelines in May 2012 for the assessment and treatment of suicidal behaviour (PDSB). The PDSB describes suicidal behaviour as an outcome of in interaction between biological, psychological, environmental and situational factors[3]. A Chronological Assessment of Suicidal Events interview is conducted measuring protective and risk factors of suicide, concluding in a diagnosis, treatment strategy, as well as a safety plan to maintain consistent care and involvement of significant others in the treatment process. In order to implement these guidelines in the mental health care system, staff of psychiatric departments participated in a program entailing a face-to-face training session by peers and subsequent e-learning modules (TtT-e). PDSB guidelines were also disseminated via other means such as professional institution websites, which was considered as the implementation as usual (IAU). This study examined the effectiveness of the TtT-e program by comparing professionals who received TtT-e with professionals who only received IAU. Participants completed an online survey (T0) and conducted a follow-up assessment three months after baseline assessment (T1). The primary outcome measure of this study was guidance adherence, which was measured via five video clips that displayed psychiatrists, psychologists and nurses interacting with a suicidal patient. Twenty-five different responses that could be given to the patient were provided. Participants were required to rate from one to 100 their likelihood of using each response (i.e. 'ask whether the patient thinks about suicide'). The authors also measured professionals' self-evaluation regarding their knowledge about suicidal behaviour and their confidence in their ability to assess and treat suicidal patients.

A total of 199 from the TtT-e group (intervention) and 104 participants from the IAU (control) condition were analysed from 18 and 16 different health care departments respectively. The TtT-e group comprised of masters (experts in the field of suicide prevention), trainers (selected as role models in the team and acquired exceptional training skills) and trainees (mental health professions that made up the team). Trainers were taught by masters who then subsequently trained their team of trainees. Of the initial 567 participants who started at T0, 53% completed assessment at T1 for both groups. There were significantly higher scores regarding adherence of guidelines (p=.02), self-evaluation of knowledge (p<.001) and greater confidence (p<.001) in the intervention condition than the control groups. Of those in the intervention condition, 61% viewed the e-learning module. E-learning did not display a significant effect on adherence to guidelines beyond that of face-to-face training (p>.05). A multidisciplinary comparison showed that at follow-up nurses in the intervention group showed greater adherence to guidelines than controls (p<.001) but this was not evident in psychiatrists/psychologists (p>.05). However, both groups showed significantly improved self-evaluation of knowledge and confidence in the intervention condition compared with the control group (nurses, p<.001 and p=.009, respectively; psychiatrists/psychologists, p=.005 and p=.007, respectively).

Implications: The findings from this study have many implications for the implementation of suicide prevention guidelines in the mental health care system. Firstly, the authors showed that the TtT-e program provides high quality training to health care professionals which has a more hands-on, systematic approach in addressing suicidality and can be directly applied to clinical practice. Such guidelines are important as they reflect everyday practice of professionals. When guidelines were disseminated via implementation as usual (IAU), mental health care professionals displayed limited adherence, reflecting the importance of implementing appropriate training programs such as TtT-e. Furthermore, nurses are more likely to benefit from the TtT-e training in relation to guideline adherence. This reflects the possibility that psychiatrists/psychologists are more often involved in assessment and treatment of suicidal patients, which suggests that nurses should be more involved in the assessment and treatment process also. In summary, this study suggested that TtT-e program was effective over at least a three month period. Additional research regarding the prolonged effect of this type of training would be useful in determining whether booster sessions are required. In order to determine the effectiveness of different elements of TtT-e programs, further research should involve randomised trials to make causal inferences regarding each element of TtT-e, so that targeted programs can be developed.

Endnotes

1. Weinmann S, Koesters M, Becker T (2007). Effects of implementation of psychiatric guidelines on provider performance and patient outcome: systematic review. *Acta Psychiatrica Scandinavica* 115, 420–433.
2. Wobrock T, Weinmann S, Falkai P, Gaebel W (2009). Quality assurance in psychiatry: quality indicators and guideline implementation. *European Archives of Psychiatry and Clinical Neuroscience* 259, 219-226.
3. Wasserman D, Rihmer Z, Rujescu D, Sarchiapone M, Sokolowski M, Titelman D, Zalsman G, Zemishlany Z, Carli V (2012). The European Psychiatric Association (EPA) guidance on suicide treatment and prevention. *European Psychiatry* 27, 129–142.
4. Palmieri G, Forghieri M, Ferrari S, Pingani L, Coppola P, Colombini N, Rigatelli M, Neimeyer RA (2008). Suicide intervention skills in health professionals: A multidisciplinary comparison. *Archives of Suicide Research* 12, 232–237.

The relationship between cannabis involvement and suicidal thoughts and behaviors

Delforterie MJ, Lynskey MT, Huizink AC, Creemers HE, Grant JD, Few LR, Glowinski AL, Statham DJ, Trull TJ, Bucholz KK, Madden PAF, Martin NG, Heath AC, Agrawal A (Australia)

Drug and Alcohol Dependence 150, 98-104, 2015

Background: In the present study, we examined the relationship between cannabis involvement and suicidal ideation (SI), plan and attempt, differentiating the latter into planned and unplanned attempt, taking into account other substance involvement and psychopathology.

Methods: We used two community-based twin samples from the Australian Twin Registry, including 9583 individuals (58.5% female, aged between 27 and 40). The Semi-Structured Assessment of the Genetics of Alcoholism (SSAGA) was used to assess cannabis involvement which was categorized into: (0) no cannabis use (reference category); (1) cannabis use only; (2) 1-2 cannabis use disorder symptoms; (3) 3 or more symptoms. Separate multinomial logistic regression analyses were conducted for SI and suicide attempt with or without a plan. Twin analyses examined the genetic overlap between cannabis involvement and SI.

Results: All levels of cannabis involvement were related to SI, regardless of duration (odds ratios [ORs]=1.28-2.00, p<0.01). Cannabis use and endorsing $\geq$3 symptoms were associated with unplanned (SANP; ORs=1.95 and 2.51 respectively, p<0.05), but not planned suicide attempts (p>0.10). Associations persisted even after controlling for other psychiatric disorders and substance involvement. Overlapping genetic (rG=0.45) and environmental (rE=0.21) factors were responsible for the covariance between cannabis involvement and SI.

Conclusions: Cannabis involvement is associated, albeit modestly, with SI and unplanned suicide attempts. Such attempts are difficult to prevent and their association with cannabis use and cannabis use disorder symptoms requires further study, including in different samples and with additional attention to confounders.

Comment

Main Findings: Research has found a strong relation between substance use behaviours, including cannabis use and suicidal ideation (SI), suicide planning and attempts[1]. Some studies have suggested that the relationship between cannabis use and suicidal thoughts and behaviours (STB) may in fact be explained by shared risk influences, such as substance use[2]. Both SI and cannabis use have been shown to be influenced to a similar degree by genetic factors with evidence for non-additive genetic influences on SI[3]. However, little is known regarding the magnitude of which shared genetic factors contribute to their comorbidity. Interestingly, a study from the USA found an association only between substance use and suicide attempts without planning (SANP), and not those that were planned prior to the event (SAP)[4]. This Australian study aimed to expand upon prior knowledge by examining different levels of cannabis involvement (including use and use disorders). SI and suicide attempts were examined separately and the magnitude of genetic overlap between cannabis involvement and STB was estimated. The authors predicted that cannabis involvement would be associated with SI and suicide attempts in a dose-response fashion; however, associations with suicide attempts would only be restricted to those reporting SANP. It was also hypothesised that there would be moderate genetic and individual-specific environmental correlations to contribute to the association between cannabis involvement and SI. The study used data from the Australian Twin Registry. The first sample comprised of 6,257 participants who were interviewed between 1996 and 2000. The second sample included 3,326 twins who were interviewed during 2005 and 2009. Cannabis involvement was categorised as no cannabis use, cannabis use only, one to two cannabis use disorder (CUD) symptoms and lastly, three or more symptoms. Data was collected through interviews on participants' demographics, other substance use and use disorders, psychopathology and early adversity.

Exploratory analyses found that after cannabis use 16.7% (1602) of participants had reported SI which lasted less than a day and 9.5% (n=907) reported SI which had lasted more than a day. Of those with SI, 17% (n=427) reported having a suicide plan without actually attempting. From the total sample 4.3% (n=408) reported suicide attempts, 2.6% (n=246) which were SAP and 1.7% (n=162) reporting never making a plan (SANP). Rates of substance use, psychopathology and a history of sexual abuse as a child were significantly higher in participants who reported STB (p<.05). The lifetime prevalence of cannabis use was 62.8% (n=6,017) and of these, 32.1% (n=1,933) reported at least one CUD symptom. Covariates between cannabis involvement and STBs were explored which showed that all levels of cannabis involvement remained significantly associated with SI after accounting for covariates, both less than a day (p<.05) and more than a day (p<.01). A dose-response relationship was observed as those who presented with three or more CUD symptoms were most likely to report having had SI for less or more than one day (p<.01 for both). After adjusting for the effects of other substance use involvement and psychopathology, cannabis use and presenting with three or more symptoms of CUD remained significantly related to SANP (p<.05 for both variables). By contrast, no significant association was found between any level of cannabis involvement and SAP. Through twin analyses, the authors established that the link between cannabis involvement and SI was strongly influenced by overlapping genetic and environmental factors.

Implications: The results from this Australian twin study provide evidence for the association between cannabis use and STB after adjusting for potential confounding variables. The evidence that linked cannabis use with SANP only could possibly be explained by either the self-medication hypothesis or the impaired functioning hypothesis. The former suggests that substances are used to cope with overwhelming aggression and negative affective states[5]. The latter suggests that physical/psychological/emotional functioning is impaired by repeated use of cannabis and early onset, subsequently leading to a higher risk of suicidal behaviours[6]. Further research should examine the etiological mechanisms that underlie the finding that cannabis use and endorsement of CUD exacerbates the likelihood of STBs. Due to SI being reported by 26.2% of the participants and the nature of SANPs being particularly difficult to prevent[7], uncovering factors that are associated with the link between cannabis use and SANPs as well as replicating such research across different samples is important for suicide preventative strategies by accurately identifying at risk populations.

Endnotes

1. Byrne P, Jones S, Williams R (2004). The association between cannabis and alcohol use and the development of mental disorder *Current Opinion in Psychiatry* 17, 255-261.
2. Price C, Hemmingsson T, Lewis G, Zammit S, Allebeck P (2009). Cannabis and suicide: longitudinal study. *British Journal of Psychiatry* 195, 492-497.
3. Maciejewski DF, Creemers HE, Lynskey MT, Madden PAF, Heath AC, Statham DJ, Martin NG, Verweij KJH (2014). Overlapping genetic and environmental influences on nonsuicidal self-injury and suicidal ideation: Different outcomes, same etiology? *JAMA* 71, 699-705.
4. Borges G, Walters EE, Kessler RC (2000). Associations of substance use, abuse, and dependence with subsequent suicidal behaviour. *American Journal of Epidemiology* 151, 781-789.
5. Khantzian EJ (1997). The self-medication hypothesis of substance use disorders: A reconsideration and recent applications. *Harvard Review of Psychiatry* 4, 231-244.
6. Van Ours JC, Williams J, Fergusson D, Horwood LJ (2013). Cannabis use and suicidal ideation. *Journal of Health Economics* 32, 524-537.
7. Conner KR (2004). A call for research on planned vs. unplanned suicidal behaviour. *Suicide and Life-Threatening Behaviour* 34, 89-98.

Short-term and long-term effects of psychosocial therapy for people after deliberate self-harm: A register-based, nationwide multicentre study using propensity score matching

Erlangsen A, Lind BD, Stuart EA, Qin P, Stenager E, Larsen KJ, Wang AG, Hvid M, Nielsen AC, Pedersen CM, Winsløv JH, Langhoff C, Mühlmann C, Nordentoft M (Denmark)
The Lancet Psychiatry 2, 49-58, 2015

Background: Although deliberate self-harm is a strong predictor of suicide, evidence for effective interventions is missing. The aim of this study was to examine whether psychosocial therapy after self-harm was linked to lower risks of repeated self-harm, suicide, and general mortality.

Methods: In this matched cohort study all people who, after deliberate self-harm, received a psychosocial therapy intervention at suicide prevention clinics in Denmark during 1992-2010 were compared with people who did not receive the psychosocial therapy intervention after deliberate self-harm. We applied propensity score matching with a 1:3 ratio and 31 matching factors, and calculated odds ratios for 1, 5, 10, and 20 years of follow-up. The primary endpoints were repeated self-harm, death by suicide, and death by any cause.

Findings: 5678 recipients of psychosocial therapy (followed up for 42.828 person-years) were matched with 17 034 individuals with no psychosocial therapy in a 1:8 ratio. During 20 year follow-up, 937 (16.5%) recipients of psychosocial therapy repeated the act of self-harm, and 391 (6.9%) died, 93 (16%) by suicide. The psychosocial therapy intervention was linked to lower risks of self-harm than was no psychosocial therapy (odds ratio [OR] 0.73, 95% CI 0.65-0.82) and death by any cause (0.62, 0.47-0.82) within a year. Long-term effects were identified for repeated self-harm (0.84, 0.77-0.91; absolute risk reduction [ARR] 2.6%, 1.5-3.7; numbers needed to treat [NNT] 39, 95% CI 27-69), deaths by suicide (OR 0.75, 0.60-0.94; ARR 0.5%, 0.1-0.9; NNT 188, 108-725), and death by any cause (OR 0.69, 0.62-0.78; ARR 2.7%, 2.0-3.5; NNT 37, 29-52), implying that 145 self-harm episodes and 153 deaths, including 30 deaths by suicide, were prevented.

Interpretation: Our findings show a lower risk of repeated deliberate self-harm and general mortality in recipients of psychosocial therapy after short-term and long-term follow-up, and a protective effect for suicide after long-term follow-up, which favour the use of psychosocial therapy interventions after deliberate self-harm.

Comment

Main Findings: Deliberate self-harm (DSH) has been established as a significant predictor of suicidal behaviour[1]. The World Health Organization (WHO) has emphasised the need for health-care providers to use operative treatment as a means of suicide prevention strategies; however, evidence for effective interventions is limited due to suicide being a relatively rare event as an outcome measure[2]. This study examined DSH as a risk factor of suicide and whether patients receiving a psychosocial therapy intervention after a self-harming event had lower risk of suicidal behaviour than those not receiving such treatments. The psychosocial therapy (PT) group included those who received psychosocial therapy intervention at one of the eight suicide prevention clinics in Denmark after their first episode of DSH during 1992 to 2010. This was compared with the no psychosocial therapy (NPT) group which included those who presented with an episode of DSH at a psychiatric hospital in Denmark but did not receive an intervention. A total of 5,678 patients who received PT were included in the study. Out of the 58,282 patients in the NPT group, 17,034 individuals from the NPT group were matched with the PT group (ratio 1:3) on 31 variables (i.e. gender, age, marital status, socio-economic status, psychiatric diagnosis, parental history of suicidal behaviour/psychiatric disorder, etc.).

In the PT group, 56.9% were referred to the clinic from hospitals or emergency departments (EDs), 10.1% by GPs, 10.9% were self-referrals and of the remaining, 7.4% were referred from an unspecified location and 14.8% had missing data. During the first year, those in the PT group significantly less often repeated DSH (6.7%) compared with 9% of those in the NPT group (p<.0001). However, suicide rates did not significantly differ between the two groups after the first year. Comparisons made at 10 years showed that 15.5% of those in the PT group had readmitted with a self-harm episode versus 18.4% of those in the NPT group. Unlike at one year follow-up, suicide rates were significantly lower for the PT group (p=.009). Based on odds ratios, repeated DSH and suicide risk were assessed. After one-year follow-up, there was a lower risk of repeated DSH in the PT group with an absolute risk reduction of 2.3% for those receiving therapy. At 20 year follow-up, risk of repeated DSH and suicide was lower for those in the PT group. Authors also estimated events avoided — a total 145 repeated episodes of DSH and 30 suicides were avoided in association with provision of the PT.

Implications: A main limitation in this study was the inability to randomise patients which potentially lent itself to self-selection bias in that patients who attended treatment at the clinic were more willing and motivated to make a difference despite the authors intending to adjust for this through matching. Notwithstanding this limitation, psychosocial interventions that were offered to individuals after their first episode of DSH was associated with a reduced risk of repeated DSH and general mortality, short- and long-term. Risk of suicide was lower for those in the PT group during the long-term follow-up. In summary, patients who present with DSH constitute a high-risk population for suicidal behaviour for which preventative efforts are important. A study conducted in Queensland evaluated the effectiveness of intensive case management in suicide attempters after discharge from inpatient psychiatric care[3]. Patient needs were addressed using a holistic approach by meeting with case managers face-to-face on a weekly basis for 12 months and received outreach telephone calls from experienced telephone counsellors. Compared with those who received usual treatment in accordance with existing hospital standards, the authors concluded that intensive case management of high-risk patients was associated with improvements in their mental health as well as increased use of health care services, reduced suicidal ideation and increased satisfaction with community-based mental health services[3].

Despite such promising findings, little research in Australia has examined the effectiveness of treatment services for patients who present with DSH explicitly. According to a report published in 2014 evaluating suicide prevention activities funded under Australia's National Suicide Prevention Strategy, those targeting people who have self-harmed accounted for 7.7% of all prevention activities[4]. However, there is a lack of prevention activities that offer follow-up services for patients who present to hospitals with DSH[5]. The findings from this study provide a foundation for policymakers state- and nation-wide. Implementing PT interventions for those people who present to hospital with DSH should be considered. Research regarding the different types of psychosocial treatments would be valuable to examine their effectiveness in reducing DSH and suicide.

Endnotes

1. Hawton K, van Heeringen K (2009). Suicide. *Lancet* 373, 1372-1381.
2. WHO (2014). *Preventing suicide: A global imperative.* Geneva: World Health Organization.
3. De Leo D, Heller T (2007). Intensive case management in suicide attempters following discharge from inpatient psychiatric care. *Australian Journal of Primary Health* 13, 49-58.
4. Australian Healthcare Associates (2014). *Evaluation of Suicide Prevention Activities.* Accessed online: 27 May 2015. http://www.health.gov.au/internet/main/publishing.nsf/Content/4FD5C304 C536BDE3CA257 CAF0017ADE9/$File/evalsuic.pdf
5. Arnautovska U, Kõlves K, Ide N, De Leo D (2013). Review of suicide prevention programs in Queensland: State and community level activities. *Australian Health Review* 37, 660-665.

Religious conflict, sexual identity, and suicidal behaviors among LGBT young adults

Gibbs JJ, Goldbach J (USA)

Archives of Suicide Research. Published online: 12 March 2015. doi: 10.1080/13811118.2015.1004476

Objectives: This is the first known study to explore how religious identity conflict impacts suicidal behaviors among lesbian, gay, bisexual, and transgender (LGBT) young adults and to test internalized homophobia as a mediator.

Methods: A secondary analysis of 2,949 youth was conducted using a national dataset collected by OutProud in 2000. Three indicators of identity conflict and an internalized-homophobia scale (mediator), were included in logistic regressions with three different suicide variable outcomes.

Results: Internalized homophobia fully mediates one conflict indicator and partially mediates the other two indicators' relationship with suicidal thoughts. Internalized homophobia also fully mediates the relationship between one conflict indicator and chronic suicidal thoughts. Two indicators were associated with twice the odds of a suicide attempt.

Conclusion: LGBT young adults who mature in religious contexts are at higher odds for suicidal thoughts, and more specifically chronic suicidal thoughts, as well as suicide attempt compared to other LGBT young adults. Internalized homophobia only accounts for portions of this conflict.

Comment

Main findings: Involvement in religion has generally been considered a protective factor against negative mental health outcomes. However, studies investigating the relative impact of religious affiliation and religiosity on mental health outcomes in lesbian, gay, bisexual and transgender (LGBT) adults have generally been inconclusive. This study used data from 2,949 18- to 24-year olds collected in a large, internet-based survey by OutProud in 2000. The majority identified themselves as gay or lesbian (61%), with 21% identifying as bisexual, 10% as 'questioning', 2% as 'other' and less than 1% as heterosexual. About 45% identified with a Christian denomination, about 16% reported a diversity of religious affiliations, and others were not religious or not sure of their current affiliation. Forty-three percent with a religious upbringing experienced conflict between religious beliefs and sexuality; 40% reported religious upbringing without conflict, and 17% were raised in a non-religious environment. Thirty-three percent reported suicidal thoughts in the last month, with 15% of these being chronically occurring thoughts; 3% reported suicide attempts in the last year. The study used three indicators of religious and sexual orientation identity conflict: having left a religion due to its views on sexuality, parents with anti-homosexual religious beliefs, and self-reported conflict in relation to religious upbringing. Logistic regression found that all three indicators were associated with (general) suicidal thoughts in the last month. Parental anti-homosexual religious beliefs were associated with chronic suicidal thoughts, and two indicators (leaving one's religion and parental religious beliefs about homosexuality) were associated with suicide attempt in the last year. The two indicators were associated with more than two times the odds of having attempted suicide in the last year. Internalised homophobia has an established relationship with suicide, so it was included as a mediator to determine if religious conflict independently explained variance in suicidality beyond that of internalised homophobia. Internalised homophobia only partially mediated the relationship between religious conflict and suicidal thoughts. After consideration of internalised homophobia, the relationship between leaving one's religion and suicidal thoughts was significant. A dual relationship was found whereby leaving one's religion was related to lower internalised homophobia, leading to lower odds of suicidal thought, but increasing risk of suicidal thoughts directly.

Implications: The results of this study suggest that LGBT young adults who experience religious identity conflict are at increased risk for suicide. This may not seem surprising given that a strong association exists between level of religiosity and negative attitudes towards non-heterosexuality[1]. An Australian study found that young same-sex attracted people who mentioned religion in a survey were also more likely to have had thoughts of self-harm, to have self-harmed, and to have had thoughts of suicide[2]. The study highlights the ongoing influence of parental religious beliefs in adulthood. Although internalised homophobia fully mediated the direct impact of religious conflict, through parental beliefs, on suicidal thoughts, it had a lower impact on the relationships between two indicators (combination of parental beliefs and leaving one's religion due to conflict) on suicidal thoughts. Leaving one's religion of origin due to conflict with sexual identity may seem a functional way of dealing with the conflict. However, it was also associated with a higher risk of suicidal thoughts. This may be due to other associated losses experienced such as loss of family relationships, community and supportive resources. Mental health professionals assessing and treating LGBT clients from religious backgrounds must consider such complexities in assessing risk; interventions with parents and families may be considered where feasible. Further research should particularly seek to define aspects of religious identity conflict, and apply them to the Australian context. Australia is generally a far more secular country than the United States[3], and the secular community and national environment may have an impact. The particular influences of diverse religions should also be considered.

Endnotes

1. Rowatt W C, LaBouff J, Johnson M, Froese P, Tsang J (2009). Associations among religiousness, social attitudes, and prejudice in a national sample of American adults. *Psychology of Religion and Spirituality* 1, 14–24.

2. Hillier L, Turner A, Mitchell A (2005). *Writing themselves in again: 6 years on. The 2nd national report on the sexual health & wellbeing of same sex attracted young people in Australia.* Melbourne, Australia: Australian Research Centre in Sex, Health & Society (ARCSHS).

3. Australian Bureau of Statistics (2013). *4102.0 - Australian Social Trends, Nov 2013. Losing my religion?* http://www.abs.gov.au/ausstats/abs@.nsf/Lookup/4102.0Main+Features30Nov+2013

Newspaper coverage of suicide and initiation of suicide clusters in teenagers in the USA, 1988-96: A retrospective, population-based, case-control study

Gould MS, Kleinman MH, Lake AM, Forman J, Midle JB (USA)

Lancet Psychiatry 1, 34-43, 2014

Background: Public health and clinical efforts to prevent suicide clusters are seriously hampered by the unanswered question of why such outbreaks occur. We aimed to establish whether an environmental factor — newspaper reports of suicide — has a role in the emergence of suicide clusters.

Methods: In this retrospective, population-based, case-control study, we identified suicide clusters in young people aged 13-20 years in the USA from 1988 to 1996 (preceding the advent of social media) using the time-space Scan statistic. For each cluster community, we selected two matched non-cluster control communities in which suicides of similarly aged youth occurred, from non-contiguous counties within the same state as the cluster. We examined newspapers within each cluster community for stories about suicide published in the days between the first and second suicides in the cluster. In non-cluster communities, we examined a matched length of time after the matched control suicide. We used a content-analysis procedure to code the characteristics of each story and compared newspaper stories about suicide published in case and control communities with mixed-effect regression analyses.

Findings: We identified 53 suicide clusters, of which 48 were included in the media review. For one cluster we could identify only one appropriate control; therefore, 95 matched control communities were included. The mean number of news stories about suicidal individuals published after an index cluster suicide (7.42 [SD 10.02]) was significantly greater than the mean number of suicide stories published after a non-cluster suicide (5.14 [6.00]; p<0.0001). Several story characteristics, including front-page placement, headlines containing the word suicide or a description of the method used, and detailed descriptions of the suicidal individual and act, appeared more often in stories published after the index cluster suicides than after non-cluster suicides.

Interpretation: Our identification of an association between newspaper reports about suicide (including specific story characteristics) and the initiation of teenage suicide clusters should provide an empirical basis to support efforts by mental health professionals, community officials, and the media to work together to identify and prevent the onset of suicide clusters.

Funding: US National Institute of Mental Health and American Foundation for Suicide Prevention.

Comment

Main findings: Past research has indicated that suicides may increase after increased media reporting about suicide, with young people being particularly susceptible[1]. Adolescents and young adults are also vulnerable to inclusion in suicide clusters, the occurrence of an exceptionally greater number of deaths than would be expected in a location over a particular time. The aim of the present study was to identify the possible role of newspaper suicide stories in the initiation of suicide clusters by examining the largest known group of youth suicide clusters studied to date, systematically identified through US national mortality data, and compared with matched non-cluster suicides. The study analysed 48 suicide clusters, occurring close in time and location, of young people aged 13 to 20 years living in populations of less than 500,000 between 1988 and 1996. Matched (non-cluster) suicides in 95 communities comprised young people who died within one year of the clusters, from the same states but not bordering counties. Newspaper articles from within each cluster community, printed between the first and second suicides in that cluster, were analysed for content about suicide; non-cluster community newspapers were examined for identical periods following non-cluster suicides.

Regression analyses revealed that the mean number of stories about the index suicide cases in the cluster communities (7.42; SD 10.02) was significantly greater than the mean number of stories about the non-cluster suicide cases in the control communities (5.14; SD 6.00; $p<0.0001$). At least one news story about the first adolescent suicide was published in 12 (25%) cluster communities compared with 13 (14%) control communities. Cluster communities were more likely than control communities to have two or more stories about the local teenage suicide; the mean number of stories about other suicidal individuals was also significantly greater following the initial cluster suicide than after the non-cluster suicide. Articles about suicidal individuals, rather than other articles about suicide, were found to be associated with subsequent suicides. Mixed effect regression analyses for characteristics of newspaper articles found that only two types of characteristics were significantly independently associated with cluster suicides: an accompanying sad picture, and celebrity status of the person who died by suicide. Potential confounding variables such as location or method of death were not found to have had a significant effect on results.

Implications: Although causality cannot be assumed, the findings of this study are consistent with considerable past research indicating that news media dissemination of a suicide can increase the risk of subsequent suicides[1]. The study's findings support theories that media effect can operate through identification with models[2], such as articles about other young people or celebrities. Young people seem to be more vulnerable to suicide contagion, largely because they identify more strongly with the actions of their peers, and because adolescence is a period of increased vulnerability to mental health problems that increases the risk of suicide[3]. Reporting of suicides has also been linked to negative effects, such as imitation, through glamourising and sensationalising suicide, detailed and repeated reports, prominent placement, and use of images and headlines[4]. However, the potential for a positive effect exists; responsible reporting following celebrity suicide has been linked to increased help-seeking[4]. In Australia, Mindframe, the National Media Initiative, has developed recommendations on responsible suicide reporting[5], and the Australian Press Council Standards of Practice include updated standards on coverage of suicide[6]. This study was based on suicides that took place before the widespread use of online social media technologies; while further research is needed, studies have indicated that online ability to rapidly spread information and rumour has an impact on suicide contagion amongst young people[7]. Avoiding discussion of suicide with young people does not manage risk of suicide contagion, especially if a suicide has already occurred amongst friends or peers. Providing a safe place to talk about their feelings, and referral to appropriate support or treatment where relevant, will help to reduce distress and reduce the likelihood that suicide will be romanticised[3].

Endnotes

1. Gould M, Jamieson P, Romer D (2003). Media contagion and suicide among the young. *American Behavioral Scientist* 46, 1269-1284.

2. Blood RW, Pirkis J. (2001). Suicide and the media: Part III. Theoretical issues. *Crisis* 2001, 163–69.

3. Headspace (2014). *Suicide contagion.* Retrieved 23 May 2015. http://www.headspace.org.au/media/9992/Suicide_Contagion.pdf

4. Kõlves K (2012). *The facts about safe reporting of suicide.* Webpage of The Conversation. Retrieved 23 May 2015. http://theconversation.com/the-facts-about-safe-reporting-of-suicide-9501

5. Mindframe National Media Initiative (2014). *Reporting and portrayal of suicide.* Retrieved 23 May 2015 from http://www.mindframe-media.info/for-media/reporting-suicide

6. Australian Press Council (2014). *Specific Standards on Coverage of Suicide.* Retrieved 23 May 2015 from http://www.presscouncil.org.au/uploads/52321/ufiles/SPECIFIC_STANDARDS_SUICIDE_-_July_2014.pdf

7. Robertson L, Skegg K, Poore M, Williams S, Taylor B (2012). An adolescent suicide cluster and the possible role of electronic communication technology. *Crisis* 33, 239-245.

Safety of patients under the care of crisis resolution home treatment services in England: A retrospective analysis of suicide trends from 2003 to 2011

Hunt IM, Rahman MS, While D, Windfuhr K, Shaw J, Appleby L, Kapur N (UK)

The Lancet Psychiatry 1, 135-141, 2014

Background: Community care provided by crisis resolution home treatment teams is used increasingly as an alternative to admission to psychiatric wards. No systematic analysis has been done of the safety of these teams in terms of rates of suicide. We aimed to compare the rate and number of suicides among patients under the care of crisis resolution home treatment teams with those of psychiatric inpatients. We also assessed the clinical features of individuals who died by suicide in both home and hospital settings.

Methods: We did a retrospective longitudinal analysis between 2003 and 2011 of all adults (aged 18 years or older) treated by the National Health Service in England who died by suicide while under the care of crisis resolution home treatment services or as a psychiatric inpatient. We obtained data from the National Confidential Inquiry into Suicide and Homicide by People with Mental Illness and from the Mental Health Minimum Dataset.

Findings: 1256 deaths by suicide (12% of all patient suicides) were recorded among patients cared for under crisis resolution home treatment teams, an average of 140 deaths per year. Different denominators meant that direct comparison between groups was difficult, but the average rate of suicide under crisis resolution home treatment services (14.6 per 10 000 episodes under crisis care) seemed higher than the average rate of suicide among psychiatric inpatients (8.8 per 10 000 admissions). The number of suicides in patients under the care of crisis resolution home treatment teams increased from an average of 80 per year (in 2003 and 2004) to 163 per year (in 2010 and 2011) and were twice as frequent as inpatient suicides in the last few years of the study. However, because of the growing number of patients under the care of crisis resolution home treatment teams, the average rate of suicide fell by 18% between the first and last 2 years of the study. 548 (44%) patients who died by suicide under the care of crisis resolution home treatment teams lived alone and 594 (49%) had had a recent adverse life event. In a third of patients (n=428) under the care of crisis resolution home treatment teams, suicide happened within 3 months of discharge from psychiatric inpatient care.

Interpretation: Although the number of suicides under the care of crisis resolution home treatment teams has risen since 2003, the rate has fallen. However, suicide rates remain high compared with the inpatient setting, and safety of individuals cared for by crisis resolution home treatment teams should be a priority for mental health services. For some vulnerable people who live alone or have adverse life circumstances, crisis resolution home treatment might not be the most appropriate care setting. Use of crisis resolution home treatment teams to facilitate early discharge could present a risk to some patients, which should be investigated further.

Comment

Main Findings: Crisis resolution home treatment services (CRHTS) provide treatment for those psychiatric patients with acute episodes of mental illness, who might otherwise be admitted in hospital, and have been initiated in Europe, the USA and Australia[1,2]. Not only do they provide a hospital-at-home service but are also responsible for gate-keeping functions for admission into other psychiatric services. There have been recent concerns regarding the safety of this service, indicating that suicides amongst people in the care of these teams may have been increasing, with some suggestion that there were more suicides in CRHTS than among those admitted to inpatient care[3]. However, it is unknown whether this is due to increasing caseloads of these services or a real increase. As a result, this study aimed to measure the incident of suicides in patients under the care of CHRTS in England since it was implemented in 2003 and examined particular trends. Furthermore, clinical characteristics of victims of suicide whilst under the care of CRHTS were assessed and compared with inpatients who were also victims of suicide.

A total of 39, 361 suicides were recorded, from the beginning of 2003 to the end of 2011, of people aged over 18 years with 27% (n=10,744) of these having had contact with mental health services during the year prior to death. Of those, questionnaires were sent to the consulting psychiatrist regarding the treatment each individual received prior to suicide. The response rate was high (98%), with 10,497 completed questionnaires. Of these, 10% (1,057) were inpatients at time of death and 12% (1,256) were receiving care under CRHTS. The average number of suicide deaths per year for people under care of CRHTS versus inpatients was 140 and 117 respectively. The overall suicide rate from 2003 to 2011 was 14.6 per 10,000 episodes for those under care of CRHTS as against 8.8 suicides per 10,000 admissions. However, due to episodes and admissions reflecting different events, a straight comparison is difficult. There were 7.8 suicides in the community per 10,000 people in contact with mental health services. Trend analysis showed a significant increase in annual number of suicides for patients under care of CRHTS from 80 to 163 (p<.0001). On the other hand, there was a significant decline for inpatient suicides from 163 to 76 across the study period (p<.0001). Despite this escalation in CRHTS, suicide rates significantly reduced by 18% from 15.3/10,000 episodes at the beginning of the study period in 2003 to 12.5/10,000 in the final year in 2011 (p=.004). Similarly, suicide rates significantly reduced amongst inpatients also from 9.9/10,000 admissions to 6.3/10,000 (p<.0001). This was also true for suicides in the community (from 9.4/10,000 of those in contact with mental health services to 7/10,000, p<.0001). The following characteristics describe CRHTS patient suicide cases: median age was 48 years; hanging/strangulation and self-poisoning were the most common methods (45% and 21% respectively); 44% lived alone; 30% had been ill for less than a year; nearly half reported an adverse life event in three months prior to death (28% reported multiple events), with most common events being relationship break-up (22%), workplace problems

(19%) and financial difficulties (11%); one-third of cases occurred within three months of discharge form inpatient care and 40% of these were within two weeks. In addition, risk of suicide was assessed by clinicians as moderate-to-high in 27% for short-term and 50% for long-term. Comparisons between CRHTS patients and inpatients showed that CRHTS suicide cases had less frequent history of self-harm (p<.0001) and drug misuse (p<.0001) but more often had been dealing with a physical illness (p<.0001), experienced an adverse event in three months prior to death (p<.0001), and more often showed symptoms of mental illness at last contact with a health service, particularly emotional distress (p<.0001) and depression (p<.0001). Lastly, CRHTS patients were more often assessed by a clinician as moderate-to-high short term risk of suicide (p<.0001).

Implications: This study was the first of its kind to examine the incidence and suicide rates of patients under the care of CRHTS. Despite the decline in suicide rates of those CRHTS patients, the average number of deaths in this service was 20% higher than those inpatients at the beginning of the study period and increased to twice as many in the last five years. These results, plus the finding that suicide rates were consistently higher in CRHTS care than inpatient care settings across the time span, indicate the need for improved attention to safety in CRHTS environments. However, it is also important to note that patients under the care of CRHTS were assessed more often as being at high-to-moderate short-term risk of suicide by a clinician at their last contact, which suggests that it was more likely that these patients included individuals with acute mental illness at high risk of suicide. In conclusion, safety of those patients under the care of CRHTS should be a priority for mental health services.

Endnotes

1. Johnson S, Nolan F, Pilling S, Hoult J, McKenzie N, White IR, Thompson M, Bebbington P (2005). Randomised controlled trial of acute mental health care by a crisis resolution team: The north Islington crisis study. *BMJ* 331-599.
2. Carroll A, Pickworth J, Protheroe D (2001). Service innovations: An Australian approach to community care — the Northern Crisis Assessment and Treatment Team. *Psychiatric Bulletin* 25, 439–41.
3. Appleby L, Kapur N, Shaw J, Hunt I, Flynn S, While D, Windfuhr K (2013). *The national confidential inquiry into suicide and homicide by people with mental illness: Annual report - England, Northern Ireland, Scotland and Wales.* University of Manchester, Manchester.

The mental health of visitors of web-based support forums for bereaved by suicide

Kramer J, Boon B, Schotanus-Dijkstra M, van Ballegooijen W, Kerkhof A, van der Poel A
(Netherlands)

Crisis 36, 38-45, 2015

Background: Persons bereaved by suicide are reluctant to ask for social support when they experience feelings of guilt and blame. A web-based peer forum may provide a safe and anonymous place for mutual support.

Aims: This study examined the mental health changes of visitors of two online support forums for persons bereaved by suicide and their experiences with the forum over 1 year.

Method: Visitors of two forums completed self-report measures at baseline and at 6 and 12 months' follow-up. Repeated measures analyses were used to study changes in well-being, depressive symptoms, and complicated grief. Additionally, participants were interviewed about their experiences with the forum.

Results: The 270 participants were mostly female, low in well-being, with high levels of depressive symptoms and complicated grief. Suicidal risk was high for 5.9%. At 12 months, there were small to medium-sized significant improvements in well-being and depressive symptoms (p <.001) and nearly as much for grief (p =.08). About two thirds reported benefit from visiting the forum. Because of the pre-post design we cannot determine whether a causal relationship exists between the form and changes in mental health.

Conclusion: After 1 year some positive changes but a large group was still struggling with their mental health. Interviews indicate that the forum was valued for finding recognition.

Comment

Main findings: Past research has suggested that mutal support amongst those bereaved by suicide can be beneficial, but may also increase risk of complicated grief[1]. Research specifically examining how use of online support forums affects the mental health of people bereaved by suicide has returned inconsistent results to date. Participants in this study were 270 adults bereaved by suicide who accessed either of two government-funded online support forums for those bereaved by suicide; 87% of participants were female. The online forums were both linked to open-access websites based in The Netherlands and Belgium. The Belgian website specifically focussed on the bereaved by suicide and the Dutch website was primarily designed for people who were suicidal, with some resources for the bereaved. Both forums were moderated by volunteers who monitored the messages, and ensured rules were followed. About two-thirds of participants reported low levels of well-being and clinical depression at the commencement of the study, and one-third reported complicated grief. Suicide risk was medium to high for nearly one-quarter of participants. Assessments were made at baseline, and at six and 12 months after commencement. Repeated measures analysis showed significant increases in well-being and decreases in depressive symptoms over the period of the study (p<.001). Effect sizes were small to medium for well-being (6 months: d=0.24; 12 months: d=0.36) and small for depressive symptoms (6 months: d=0.18, 12 months: d=0.28). However, it could not be concluded that these changes were brought about by use of the forum. Changes in symptoms of grief and in suicide risk did not reach significance; at 12 months, 17.2% of participants had a medium to high risk for suicide. Follow up telephone interviews were conducted with 29 participants including those who did and did not indicate benefit from the forum. Nearly all of those interviewed mentioned positive aspects of the forum; these included indication that they were greatly helped by finding recognition (65%), support (13.8%), and having a place to go when in need (24.1%). Participants had a high level of social support other than the online forum; 72% indicated that they had support from their social network and from professionals. The researchers suggested that the forum may not have been used as an alternative to general social support, but in addition.

Implications: Although people bereaved by suicide share many reactions with others who have lost loved ones, there are some unique features of grief such as a heightened sense of shame, responsibility, rejection and guilt. These may be linked to stigma about suicide, which can contribute to development of complicated grief[2]; risk of suicide is also believed to be greater amongst bereaved relatives of people who have died by suicide[1]. There has been some indication that the bereaved by suicide experience personal conflict about seeking help from social support networks[3], and it has been estimated that only about 25% of people bereaved by suicide have found their way to support groups or therapy where this is available[4]. Online forums may may provide an anonymous means for those bereaved by suicide to gain support and share grief with others who have had similar experiences. Given that the increasing use of online communication has prompted shifts in the way that people grieve[5], further empirical and longitudinal research is needed to better understand the potential benefits and dangers this may present. A variety of online resources are available to provide information and access to support to people bereaved by suicide; Australian resources include online information offered by Lifeline and Standby Response Service[6,7]. Clinicians should seek to understand how clients bereaved by suicide are using online communities and information, and be prepared to recommend the most appropriate options[5].

Endnote

1. de Groot M, Kollen BJ (2013). Course of bereavement over 8-10 years in first degree relatives and spouses of people who committed suicide: Longitudinal community based cohort study. *British Medical Journal* 347, f5519.
2. Kõlves K, De Leo D (2014). Is suicide grief different? In D. De Leo, A. Cimitan, K. Dyregov, O. Grad & K. Andriesson (Eds), *Bereavement after traumatic death: Helping the survivors.* Boston: Hogrefe.

3. Sveen CA & Walby FA (2008). Suicide survivors' mental health and grief reactions: A systematic review of controlled studies. *Suicide and Life-Threatening Behavior* 38, 13-29.

4. Dyregrov K (2002). Assistance from local authorities versus survivors' needs for support after suicide. *Death Studies* 26, 647-668.

5. Falconer K, Sachsenweger M, Gibson K, Norman H (2011). Grieving in the internet age. *New Zealand Journal of Psychology* 40, 79-88.

6. Lifeline (2010). *Suicide Bereavement.* Retrieved 14 May 2015 from https://www.lifeline.org.au/Get-Help/Facts — -Information/Suicide-Bereavement/Suicide-Bereavement

7. United Synergies (2015). *Standby Response Service.* Retrieved 14 May 2015 from http://www.unitedsynergies.com.au/program/standby-response-service/

Suicide risk among perinatal women who report thoughts of self-harm on depression screens

Kim JJ, La Porte LM, Saleh MP, Allweiss S, Adams MG, Zhou Y, Silver RK (USA)
Obstetrics and Gynecology 125, 885-893, 2015

Objectives: To estimate the incidence and clinical significance of suicidal ideation revealed during perinatal depression screening and estimate the associated suicide risk.

Methods: Retrospective cohort study of women completing the Edinburgh Postnatal Depression Scale at 24-28 weeks of gestation and 6 weeks postpartum through a suburban integrated health system with approximately 5,000 annual deliveries on two hospital campuses. Suicidal ideation on the Edinburgh Postnatal Depression Scale and prediction of suicide risk were examined through multivariable modeling and qualitative analysis of clinical assessments.

Results: Among 22,118 Edinburgh Postnatal Depression Scale questionnaires studied, suicidal ideation was reported on 842 (3.8%, 95% confidence interval [CI] 3.5-4.1%) and was positively associated with younger maternal age (antepartum mean age 30.9 compared with 31.9 years, P=.001), unpartnered relationship status (antepartum 29.5% compared with 16.5%, P<.001 and postpartum 25.0% compared with 17.5%, P<.01), non-Caucasian race (antepartum 62.1% compared with 43.8%, P<.001 and postpartum 62.4% compared with 45.2%, P<.001), non-English language (antepartum 11.0% compared with 6.6%, P<.001 and postpartum 12.4% compared with 7.7%, P<.01), public insurance (antepartum 19.9% compared with 12.5%, P<.001 and postpartum 18.2% compared with 14.2%, P<.001), and preexisting psychiatric diagnosis (antepartum 8.4% compared with 4.2%, P<.001 and postpartum 12.0% compared with 5.8%, P<.001). Multivariable antepartum and postpartum models retained relationship status, language, relationship status by language interaction, and race; the postpartum model also found planned caesarean delivery negatively associated with suicidal ideation risk (odds ratio [OR] 0.56, 95% CI 0.36–0.87) and severe vaginal laceration positively associated with suicidal ideation risk (OR 2.1, 95% CI 1.00–4.40). A qualitative study of 574 women reporting suicidal ideation indicated that 330 (57.5%, 95% CI 53.5–61.5%) experienced some degree of suicidal thought. Six patients (1.1%, 95% CI 0.2–1.9%) demonstrated active suicidal ideation with plan, intent, and access to means. Within this highest risk group, three patients reported a suicide attempt within the perinatal period.

Conclusion: Among perinatal women screened for depression, 3.8% reported suicidal ideation, but only 1.1% of this subgroup was at high risk for suicide. These findings support the need for systematic evaluation of those who report suicidal ideation to identify the small subset requiring urgent evaluation and care.

Comment

Main findings: Although pregnancy is regarded as a protective factor against suicide[1], subgroups of women may be at an increased risk before or after a birth. This study sought to estimate the overall incidence of suicidal ideation in a perinatal population, and to examine clinical correlates, characteristics of patients who reported suicidal thoughts and their explanations in order to estimate the magnitude of suicide risk. The study accessed data from a large suburban health system in the United States, where expectant mothers were routinely screened using the Edinburgh Postnatal Depression Scale (EPDS) during pregnancy and after delivery. First available antepartum and postpartum EPDS results were included, even if the screens were from different pregnancies, resulting in 22,118 unique screens. Suicidal ideation was indicated on 842 questionnaires (3.8%), with report rates similar across antepartum (4.1%) and postpartum (3.4%) questionnaires. The study identified subgroups of women more likely to report suicidal ideation in the perinatal period, including women without a partner, non-Caucasian women, and patients with a prior mental health diagnosis. Obstetric outcomes of birth modified postpartum suicide risk; greater risk was found in women with severe lacerations, but risk was reduced in caesarean delivery. The one perinatal suicide which occurred during the study period involved a patient whose obstetrician had chosen not to screen her because of her "positive affect" during a postpartum visit. Women who screened positively for suicidal ideation were interviewed by telephone within 48 hours of screening. Qualitative analysis of 574 of these interviews revealed that 330 women were experiencing some degree of suicidal thought at the time of the interview, both low and high risk. Six (1.1%) of the women interviewed (representing 0.7% of all screens in the study) reported high-risk active suicidal ideation, with a plan, intent and access to means. Three women reported a suicide attempt within the current perinatal period. A low rate of current mental health engagement was noted among the women reporting suicidal ideation. The majority (521 - 90.8%, 95% CI 88.4-93.13%) were not engaged in any form of mental health treatment.

Implications: Recent research has indicated that suicide in the perinatal period is a leading contributor to maternal death[2]. Australian and international studies have consistently found significant rates of mental health disorders in the perinatal period[3]. In the past, Australian maternal mortality associated with psychiatric illness in the perinatal period has been under-reported due to limitations in data collection and methods of detection[4]. An Australian review of perinatal maternal mortality (defined here as occurring from pregnancy to the end of the first year post-partum)[4] indicated significant rates of suicide in both pregnancy and the postnatal period. Between 1994 and 2002, 26 maternal deaths were found to be associated with mental health issues, comprising 17 suicides by violent means (65%), and nine deaths by overdose from prescription or illegal drugs (35%). At least three of the women (12%) were Indigenous, despite Indigenous women representing only 3.5% of the total number of women giving birth during the period studied. The creation of the National Perinatal Depression Initiative in 2008 led to the development of national clinical practice guidelines for managing various perinatal mental health issues, including suicide risk[3,5]. In addition to assessment in the primary care setting, the guidelines recommend universal screening using the EPDS, with specific principles for managing suicide risk[3]. The current study adds to the evidence regarding the value of routine mental health screening of women during the perinatal period, with follow-up where suicide risk is identified. Ongoing research in this field is much needed to ensure that the most effective methods of detection and management of suicidality are in place. Continued focus on this issue by policymakers, clinicians and researchers is imperative in order to ensure the wellbeing of this vulnerable population.

Endnotes

1. Oates M (2003). Suicide: The leading cause of maternal death. *British Journal of Psychiatry* 183, 279-281.
2. Palladino, Singh V, Campbell J, Flynn H, Gold KJ (2011). Homicide and suicide during the perinatal period: Findings from the national violent death reporting system. *Obstetrics & Gynecology* 118, 1056-1063.
3. Austin M-P, Highet N, Guidelines Expert Advisory Committee (2011). *Clinical practice guidelines for depression and related disorders – anxiety, bipolar disorder and puerperal psychosis – in the perinatal period. A guideline for primary care health professionals.* Melbourne: beyondblue: the national depression initiative.
4. Austin M-P, Kildea S, Sullivan E (2007). Maternal mortality and psychiatric morbidity in the perinatal period: Challenges and opportunities for prevention in the Australian setting. *MJA* 186, 364-367.
5. Austin M-P, Middleton PF, Highet NJ (2011). Australian mental health reform for perinatal care. *MJA* 195, 112-113.

Health and psychosocial service use among suicides without psychiatric illness

Law YW, Wong PWC, Yip PSF (Hong Kong)
Social Work 60, 65-74, 2015

Although mental illness is a major suicide risk factor, some cases of suicide list no symptoms of mental disorder at the time of death. Studying suicides without psychiatric illness has important implications for social work because this group's service needs seem to have been overlooked. The authors of this article conducted a psychological autopsy study of 150 people who committed suicide and 150 age- and gender-matched living controls. Suicides without psychiatric illness showed similar detectable psychopathology as the suicide and living control groups with nonpsychotic psychiatric disorders. Though suicides without psychiatric disorders showed fewer warning signs that could be noticed by their informants, they experienced more negative life events than living controls. The suicide cases without psychiatric illness also seemed to be less protected by enabling factors (such as social support and employment) than living controls with and without psychiatric disorders. Furthermore, they had lower use of services than the control and deceased-with-diagnosis groups. With fewer at-risk signs and poorer enabling resources, they were undetected or unengaged by the existing physical, psychiatric, and psychosocial services. This group should be of concern to social workers, who may develop community-based health education programs and preventive services to meet this vulnerable population's psychosocial needs.

Comment

Main findings: Mental health treatment is an important strategy in suicide prevention; however, interventions focusing on mental health problems only may not reach vulnerable people who do not possess a diagnosable mental disorder. This study examined whether suicides without psychiatric illness had different characteristics. The study accessed 150 cases from a psychological autopsy study in Hong Kong, where it is estimated that about 20% of suicide cases do not have a diagnosable psychiatric illness[1]. Suicide cases were matched by age and gender with living controls; background information and history were collected from informants and relatives. Retrospective psychiatric diagnosis was assessed by trained interviewers using the Structured Clinical Interview for DSM-IV Axis I Disorders (SCID-I)[2]. Cases not given a diagnosis included those with no apparent symptoms, or symptoms not at a level to warrant a diagnosis. As diagnoses assigned to living controls did not include psychotic disorders, only suicides with non-psychotic disorders were analysed. Data analysis was conducted on a sample of 265 cases including suicides with (n=86) and without (n=29) psychiatric diagnosis, and living controls with (n=15) and without (n=135) diagnosis. Chi-square and t tests were used to test differences between the suicide without diagnosis group and the three other groups on relevant variables. The study found that suicides without diagnosis were significantly younger (M=34.1, SD=11.64) than suicides with diagnosis (M=39.9, SD=11.06, p=.016) and living controls with diagnosis (M=43.7, SD=10.16, p=.01). They were also significantly better educated (p=.047) and less impulsive (p=.001) than the suicide group with diagnosis. Of the four groups, suicides without diagnosis had the highest proportion of indebtedness (approximately 43%). Suicides without diagnosis showed lower depression levels than suicides with diagnosis (p<.001), but these were higher than the living control group with no diagnosis (p<.001). Suicides without diagnosis were less likely to seek consultation for mental health problems (p=.007) and physical problems (p=.007) than the suicide with diagnosis group. In general, both suicide groups received less social support than living controls, had greater financial constraints and unemployment, and were more impacted by negative life events than living controls without diagnoses, but not those with a diagnosis. Although less likely to use health services, those without psychiatric diagnoses did show detectable psychopathology and other characteristics which should be further investigated as a means of identifying those at risk.

Implications: There has been minimal research into suicide in the absence of mental illness in high-income western countries such as Australia[3]. While there are methodological issues in obtaining retrospective information from proxies[3], psychological autopsy studies provide a means of attempting to understand the experience of those at risk prior to death. Past psychological autopsy studies have generally reported that most people who have died by suicide have an identifiable psychiatric condition, whether or not it had been diagnosed before death[4]. However, it should be noted that recent Australian research has found prevalence of psychiatric problems to be significantly lower among older suicides (61.6% in those 60+ years of age) than in middle age suicides (80.1%); the prevalence of psychiatric disorders in older suicides was also lower than reported in earlier studies (71.4 to 96.5%)[5]. The current study reflects findings of previous research from outside Europe and the United States, where higher proportions of suicide without diagnosable mental illness have been reported; major stressors in such cases included life events, and economic and social stress[3]. The current study has also suggested that those at risk, without a clear mental illness, may not be high users of health services for either physical or mental health problems. Research has consistently shown that while identifiable mental illness is a major risk factor for suicide, it is not the only one. Other important risk factors, which may or may not be accompanied by symptomology of mental illness include job or financial loss, hopelessness, chronic pain or other physical illness, genetic or biological factors, family history of suicide, and influence of alcohol[6]. It is clear that it is not adequate to confine suicide prevention strategies to alleviation of mental illness, or only intervene through health services[7]. Further Australian research would assist to identify those risk factors other than mental illness more specific to the Australian population, which would in turn allow the design of better informed prevention strategies and determination of intervention points in the community.

Endnotes

1. Chen EY, Chan WS, Wong PW, Chan SS, Chan CL, Law YW, Beh PSL, Chan KK, Cheng JW, Liu KY, Yip PS (2006). Suicide in Hong Kong: A case-control psychological autopsy study. *Psychological Medicine* 36, 815-825.

2. American Psychiatric Association (1997). *Structured Clinical Interview for DSM-IV Axis I Disorders (SCID-I): Clinician Version, Administration Booklet.* Washington, DC: American Psychiatric Publishing.

3. Milner A, Sveticic J, De Leo D 92013). Suicide in the absence of mental disorder? A review of psychological autopsy studies across countries. *International Journal of Social Psychiatry* 59, 545-554.

4. Bertolote JM, Fleischmann A, De Leo D, Wasserman D (2004). Psychiatric diagnoses and suicide: Revisiting the evidence. *Crisis 25*, 147-155.

5. De Leo D, Draper BM, Snowdon J, Kõlves K (2013). Suicides in older adults: A case-control psychological autopsy study in Australia. *Journal of Psychiatric Research 47*, 980-988.

6. World Health Organization (2014). *Preventing suicide: A global imperative.* Geneva: World Health Organization.

7. Fleischmann A, De Leo D (2014). The World Health Organization's report on suicide: A fundamental step in worldwide suicide prevention. *Crisis 35*, 289-291.

Dialectical behavior therapy for adolescents with repeated suicidal and self-harming behavior: A randomized trial

Mehlum L, Tormoen AJ, Ramberg M, Haga E, Diep LM, Laberg S, Larsson BS, Stanley BH, Miller AL, Sund AM, Groholt B (Norway)

Journal of the American Academy of Child and Adolescent Psychiatry 53, 1082-109, 2014

Objective: We examined whether a shortened form of dialectical behavior therapy, dialectical behavior therapy for adolescents (DBT-A) is more effective than enhanced usual care (EUC) to reduce self-harm in adolescents.

Method: This was a randomized study of 77 adolescents with recent and repetitive self-harm treated at community child and adolescent psychiatric outpatient clinics who were randomly allocated to either DBT-A or EUC. Assessments of self-harm, suicidal ideation, depression, hopelessness, and symptoms of borderline personality disorder were made at baseline and after 9, 15, and 19 weeks (end of trial period), and frequency of hospitalizations and emergency department visits over the trial period were recorded.

Results: Treatment retention was generally good in both treatment conditions, and the use of emergency services was low. DBT-A was superior to EUC in reducing self-harm, suicidal ideation, and depressive symptoms. Effect sizes were large for treatment outcomes in patients who received DBT-A, whereas effect sizes were small for outcomes in patients receiving EUC. Total number of treatment contacts was found to be a partial mediator of the association between treatment and changes in the severity of suicidal ideation, whereas no mediation effects were found on the other outcomes or for total treatment time.

Conclusion: DBT-A may be an effective intervention to reduce self-harm, suicidal ideation, and depression in adolescents with repetitive self-harming behavior.

Comment

Main findings: High rates of adolescent self-harm, with or without suicidal intent, have been reported across many countries; population studies indicate that approximately 10% of adolescents report past year self-harm[1]. Among the most vulnerable young people are those with features of borderline personality disorder (BPD), such as emotion dysregulation and high sensitivity to stress[2]. There has been little evidence that intervention treatments specifically targeting adolescent self-harm are more effective than "usual care", i.e. standard available treatments. The current study was the first published randomised controlled trial (RCT) of the efficacy of DBT-A, a short version of dialectial behavior therapy (DBT) adapted for self-harming adolescents with features of BPD[2]. Participants received 19 weeks of treatment and were randomly allocated to either "enhanced usual care" (EUC) (psychodynamically oriented therapy or CBT) or to DBT-A, consisting of individual therapy, skills training involving parents or caregivers, and other contact as needed. Symptomology was measured throughout the trial by independent interviewers blind to treatment allocation. No suicides were observed during treatment and there were few overall hospital admissions or emergency department visits. Self-harm frequency of EUC participants showed a mean of 4.7 (SD=5.5) episodes in the first nine weeks and 3.3 (SD=6.8) in the subsequent six weeks. For DBT-A participants, the mean self-harm frequency was 4.1 (SD=5.8) and 1.2 (SD=2.0) episodes respectively. Analysis using a logarithmic scale showed a highly significant average drop in self-harm frequency in the DBT-A group (slope=-1.28, 95%CI=-1.77 to -0.80, p<.001), whereas the drop in the EUC group was not statistically significant (slope=-0.36, 95%, CI=-0.99 to 0.26, p=.254). Both treatment groups had a mean baseline severity of suicidal ideation of 36.91, well above clinical cut-off of 31; this reduced at a similar rate in both groups over the first 15 weeks of treatment, and continued to drop amongst DBT-A participants. At the end of the trial, the mean rate of suicidal ideation of the DBT group was 18.30 (SD=11.11), and for the EUC group, was 32.56 (SD=23.99). Effect sizes for treatment outcomes were 0.89 for the DBT condition and 0.16 for EUC. There were no significant differences between groups for participant drop-out, reported as 25.6% for DBT-A and 28.9% for EUC; other studies involving suicidal teens with BPD have reported drop-out rates exceeding 60%[3]. Although adequately powered, the sample size was small; given that participants were mostly female, sample size was inadequate to study gender differences.

Implications: Athough some mental health practioners may have been traditionally reluctant to diagnose personality disorders in adolescents, current Australian clinical practice guidelines confirm that diagnostic criteria for BPD are as reliable and valid for people under 18 years as they are in adults[4]. Although the condition often goes unrecognised in young people, adolescents with BPD are believed to be commonly seen in outpatient mental health services; given the propensity for self-harm and suicidal behaviours, and the high levels of distress experienced, early intervention is advisable to reduce potential for negative outcomes[5]. However, there has been no consensus on Australian best practice interventions for this age group, considered difficult to treat because of reduced patient compliance, a tendency to drop out of treatment, and an apparent lack of understanding about the nature of BPD amongst practitioners[5]. The findings of the current study lend support to previous uncontrolled studies suggesting the efficacy of DBT-A, including a 2013 Australian study assessing a pilot program in a community mental health service which treated self-harming and suicidal adolescent females with BPD features[6]. Benefits of this treatment include its flexibility for application across clinical settings, encouragement of family validation and support, and shorter treatment length increasing cost-effectiveness and financial accessibility, while reducing the risk of drop-out[2]. Ideally, further controlled studies looking to confirm these results would be conducted in Australian settings, involve larger sample sizes and provide longer-term follow-up evaluations.

Endnotes

1. Madge N, Hewitt A, Hawton K, de Wilde EJ, Corcoran P, Fekete S, van Heeringen K, De Leo D, Ystgaard M (2008). Deliberate self-harm within an international community sample of young

people: Comparative findings from the Child and Adolescent Self-harm in Europe (CASE) study. *Journal of Child Psychology and Psychiatry* 49, 667-677.

2. Miller AL, Rathus JH, Linehan MM (2007). *Dialectical behavior therapy with suicidal adolescents.* New York: Guilford Press.

3. Miller AL, Glinksi J (2000). Youth suicidal behavior: Assessment and intervention. *Journal of Clinical Psychology* 56, 1131-1152.

4. National Health and Medical Research Council (2013). *Clinical practice guideline for the management of borderline personality disorder.* Canberra: Commonwealth of Australia.

5. Headspace (2009). *Evidence summary: Treating borderline personality disorder (BPD) in adolescence: What are the issues and what is the evidence?* Retrieved from http://www.headspace .org.au/media/101064/coe3461_es_bpdtreatment_v2.pdf

6. Geddes K, Dziurawiec S, Lee CW (2013). Dialectical behavior therapy for the treatment of emotion dysregulation and trauma symptoms in self-injurious and suicidal adolescent females: A pilot programme within a community-based child and adolescent mental health service. *Psychiatry Journal* 145219, doi: 10.1155/2013/145219

Exposure to websites that encourage self-harm and suicide: Prevalence rates and association with actual thoughts of self-harm and thoughts of suicide in the United States

Mitchell KJ, Wells M, Priebe G, Ybarra ML (USA)

Journal of Adolescence 37, 1335-1344, 2014

This article provides 12-month prevalence rates of youth exposure to websites which encourage self-harm or suicide and examines whether such exposure is related to thoughts of self-harm and thoughts of suicide in the past 30 days. Data were collected via telephone from a nationally representative survey of 1560 Internet-using youth, ages 10-17 residing in the United States. One percent (95% CI: 0.5%, 1.5%) of youth reported visiting a website that encouraged self-harm or suicide. Youth who visited such websites were seven times more likely to say they had thought about killing themselves; and 11 times more likely to think about hurting themselves, even after adjusting for several known risk factors for thoughts of self-harm and thoughts of suicide. Given that youth thinking about self-harm and suicide are more likely to visit these sites, they may represent an opportunity for identification of youth in need of crisis intervention.

Comment

Main findings: In recent years, considerable concern has been expressed about the ease of access vulnerable young people may have to online content which actively encourages self-injury and suicide, including information about techniques and graphic visual images[1]. Some research has suggested an association between suicide-related online searches and the incidence of suicide amongst young people[2], but much is still unknown about the level of exposure to such content, and the characteristics of those who access it. This study was based on data gathered through the third Youth Internet Safety Survey (YISS-3) in the United States; participants aged 10 to 17 years had used the internet at least once a month for the past six months. Measures included rates of self-harm and suicidal thoughts during the past month, and past year exposure to websites which encouraged suicide and self-harm. There has been little published research reporting self-harm prevalence within national samples of adolescents in the United States; this study found that 5% reported thoughts of self-harm in the past 30 days. The 12-month rate for visiting websites encouraging self-harm or suicide was low (1%, 95% CI: 0.51%, 1.49%); however, those who did access such sites presented with similar characteristics to those who reported thoughts of self-harm and suicide: for example, elevated depressive symptoms, being a victim of abuse or harassment, problem behaviours, conflict with parents, and low income households. Even after taking into account several known risk factors, stepwise logistic regression analysis showed that exposure to self-harm and suicide sites that may encourage these behaviours was associated with a seven-fold increase in likelihood of concurrent thoughts of suicide, and an eleven-fold increase in likelihood of thoughts of self-harm. It was conjectured that these young people may have used the internet to find information, or connect with others, in order to reinforce intentions; however, due to cross-sectional study design, it was not clear whether higher rates of risk-factors for suicide and self-injury caused them to be influenced by the sites, or whether probability of carrying out these behaviours was increased by exposure to the websites.

Implications: Suicide is the leading cause of death among young Australians aged 15 to 24[3]. Australian research suggests that 6-7% of young people aged 15-24 years engage in self-harm in any 12-month period[4], and that lifetime prevalence rates of self-harm are as high as 24% of females and 18% of males aged 20-24 years, and 17% of females and 12% of males aged 15-19[5] years. Australia became the first country to criminalise pro-suicide websites in 2006, and in recent years, various technology companies and social networking sites have increased monitoring and restriction of potentially harmful content[1]. Research has noted that general searches for information about self-harm do not usually produce results for those websites encouraging self-harm or suicide, but rather show those that provide preventative information and support; more sophisticated searches may be necessary to access pro-self-injury sites[6]. Given the constant evolution of online technologies, and the increasing technological skills of younger people[1], it is not thought to be possible to completely prevent access to potentially harmful online content[6]. In Australia during 2012–13, 15 to 17 year olds had the highest proportion of internet use (97%) compared to other age groups[7]; it has been recognised that the tendency of young people to turn to online content to help solve problems presents powerful opportunities to provide preventative and protective resources to those experiencing thoughts of suicide or self-harm[1]. Findings of the current study provide further information about the characteristics of young people accessing potentially harmful content, which may be useful in designing online interventions targeting these risk factors. While further research into the processes of how young people at risk access and use online information would be beneficial, health providers should also review how young clients experiencing self-harm or suicidal ideation may be using online technologies.

Endnotes

1. Robert A, Suelves JM, Armayones M, Ashley A (2015). Brief communications. Internet use and suicidal behaviors: Internet as a threat or opportunity? *Telemedicine and e-Health* 21, 306-311.
2. Hagihara A, Miyazaki S, Abe T (2012). Internet searches and the incidence of suicide in young people in Japan. *European Archives of Psychiatry and Clinical Neuroscience* 262, 39-46.
3. Australian Bureau of Statistics (2015). *3303.0 ABS Causes of Death, Australia, 2013. Underlying causes of death (Australia) Table 1.3.* http://www.abs.gov.au/AUSSTATS/ abs@.nsf/DetailsPage/3303.02013?OpenDocument
4. De Leo D, Heller TS (2004). Who are the kids who self-harm? An Australian self-report school survey. *Medical Journal of Australia* 181, 140-144.

5. Martin G, Swannell SC, Hazell PL, Harrison JE, Taylor AW (2010). Self-injury in Australia: A community survey. *Medical Journal of Australia* 193, 506-510.

6. Swannell S, Martin G, Krysinka K, Kay T, Olsson K, Win A (2010). Cutting on-line: Self-injury and the internet. *Advances in Mental Health* 9, 177-189.

7. Australian Bureau of Statistics (2014). *Household use of information technology, Australia, 2012-13 (No. 8146.0).* http://www.abs.gov.au/ausstats/abs@.nsf/Latestproducts /DE28AB7779067 AACCA257C89000E3F98?opendocument

Modelling suicide and unemployment: A longitudinal analysis covering 63 countries, 2000-11

Nordt C, Warnke I, Seifritz E, Kawohl W (Switzerland)

The Lancet Psychiatry 2, 239-245, 2015

Background: As with previous economic downturns, there has been debate about an association between the 2008 economic crisis, rising unemployment, and suicide. Unemployment directly affects individuals' health and, unsurprisingly, studies have proposed an association between unemployment and suicide. However, a statistical model examining the relationship between unemployment and suicide by considering specific time trends among age-sex-country subgroups over wider world regions is still lacking. We aimed to enhance knowledge of the specific effect of unemployment on suicide by analysing global public data classified according to world regions.

Methods: We retrospectively analysed public data for suicide, population, and economy from the WHO mortality database and the International Monetary Fund's world economic outlook database from 2000 to 2011. We selected 63 countries based on sample size and completeness of the respective data and extracted the information about four age groups and sex. To check stability of findings, we conducted an overall random coefficient model including all study countries and four additional models, each covering a different world region.

Findings: Despite differences in the four world regions, the overall model, adjusted for the unemployment rate, showed that the annual relative risk of suicide decreased by 1.1% (95% CI 0.8-1.4) per year between 2000 and 2011. The best and most stable final model indicated that a higher suicide rate preceded a rise in unemployment (lagged by 6 months) and that the effect was non-linear with higher effects for lower baseline unemployment rates. In all world regions, the relative risk of suicide associated with unemployment was elevated by about 20-30% during the study period. Overall, 41-148 (95% CI 39-552-42-744) suicides were associated with unemployment in 2007 and 46-131 (44-292-47-970) in 2009, indicating 4983 excess suicides since the economic crisis in 2008.

Interpretation: Suicides associated with unemployment totalled a nine-fold higher number of deaths than excess suicides attributed to the most recent economic crisis. Prevention strategies focused on the unemployed and on employment and its conditions are necessary not only in difficult times but also in times of stable economy.

Comment

Main Findings: The most recent data from the USA, Europe and Asia suggests there is an association between the Financial Crisis in 2008, increased unemployment rates and increased suicide rates, however, the significance of this effect has not been clearly revealed[1,2]. As a result, the authors of this study aimed to improve understanding of the effect of unemployment on suicide rates by analysing global data from the WHO mortality database and the International Monetary Fund's world economic outlook database from 2000 to 2011. Other economic factors that may have impacted on suicide rates were also considered. The 63 countries analysed were categorised into four world geographic regions which were Americas (i.e. the USA, Brazil, Argentina, Mexico, etc.), northern and western Europe (i.e. Denmark, Austria, Estonia, Ireland, the UK, etc.), southern and eastern Europe (i.e. Greece, Italy, Spain, etc.) and non-Americas and non-Europe (i.e. Australia, Japan, Singapore, South Korea, etc.). Suicide rates were analysed by age groups, separated by gender; 15-24 years, 25-44 years, 45-64 years and 65 + years. Economic data was collected on four indicators; unemployment rates, Gross Domestic Product (GDP), growth rate and inflation.

The authors examined the best model fit and the estimated effects of each economic variable across the four world regions. Only unemployment rates were associated with suicide rates with similar effects across each world regions of the economic variables tested. The best fit model was the non-linear, six month time-lagged unemployment rate displaying similar estimates for each world region. In other words, rates of suicide tended to increase six months prior to unemployment rates rising and this affected both genders equally as well as different age groups. Using the best final model, the authors suggested that across all world regions between 2000 and 2011, the rate of suicide associated with unemployment had increased by 20-30%, estimating that of the average 233,000 suicides that occurred per year during this period, unemployment accounted for roughly 45,000 suicides. In 2007 and 2009, unemployment rates were associated with 41,148 and 46,131 suicides respectively, suggesting that the recession was responsible for an additional 4,983 suicides. As a result, this proposes unemployment was responsible for a nine-fold higher number of suicides than those attributed to the economic crisis. The impact of unemployment rate on suicide rate was more robust in those countries that had a lower pre-crisis unemployment rate.

Implications: In general, the findings of this study support prior research that has indicated a link between unemployment and suicide rates[1,3] corroborating this effect as time-lagged and non-linear. The authors suggest that for those countries that do not commonly have unemployment prior to economic downturn, the unexpected increase in such rates may in fact elicit more severe insecurity and fears for this population than those countries with higher unemployment rates pre-crisis. This six month time lag may be in in part due to restricting the labour market and corporate downsizing during economic contraction; impacts on employee job security, work-load, and work-related stress may result in poorer mental health[4]. Training of human resource departments is necessary to identify those at increased risk of suicide, for those both in and out of work. Suicide interventions need to focus more on those negative health effects that are consequences of unemployment during times of both economic crisis and economic stability. In addition, investing in programs that promote health work climates and integrate people into the job market is essential for those countries that have low unemployment rates as the impacts of economic downturn appear to be greater on countries where unemployment is uncommon.

Endnotes

1. Stuckler D, Basu S, Suhrcke M, Coutts A, McKee M (2009). The public health effect of economic crises and alternative policy responses in Europe: An empirical analysis. *Lancet* 374, 315-323.

2. Chang S, Stuckler D, Yip P, Gunnell D (2013). Impact of 2008 global economic crisis on suicide: Time trend study in 54 countries. *BMJ* 347, f5239

3. Berk M, Dodd S, Henry M (2006). The effect of macroeconomic variables on suicide. *Psychological Medicine* 36, 181-189.

4. Melchior M, Caspi A, Milne BJ, Danese A, Poulton R, Moffitt TE (2007). Work stress precipitates depression and anxiety in young, working women and men. *Psychological Medicine* 38, 1119–1129.

Suicide in patients suffering from late-life anxiety disorders; a comparison with younger patients

Oude Voshaar RC, van der Veen DC, Kapur N, Hunt I, Williams A, Pachana NA (UK)

International Psychogeriatrics. Published online: 11 February 2015. doi: 10.1017/S1041610215000125

Background: Anxiety disorders are assumed to increase suicide risk, although confounding by comorbid psychiatric disorders may be one explanation. This study describes the characteristics of older patients with an anxiety disorder who died by suicide in comparison to younger patients.

Method: A 15-year national clinical survey of all suicides in the UK (n=25,128). Among the 4,481 older patients who died by suicide ($\geq$ 60 years), 209 (4.7%) suffered from a primary anxiety disorder, and 533 (11.9%) from a comorbid anxiety disorder. Characteristics of older (n=209) and younger (n=773) patients with a primary anxiety disorder were compared by logistic regression adjusted for sex and living arrangement.

Results: Compared to younger patients, older patients with a primary anxiety disorder were more often males and more often lived alone. Although 60% of older patients had a history of psychiatric admissions and 50% of deliberate self-harm, a history of self-harm, violence, and substance misuse was significantly less frequent compared to younger patients, whereas physical health problems and comorbid depressive illness were more common. Older patients were prescribed significantly more psychotropic drugs and received less psychotherapy compared to younger patients.

Conclusion: Anxiety disorders are involved in one of every six older patients who died by suicide. Characteristics among patients who died by suicide show severe psychopathology, with a more prominent role for physical decline and social isolation compared to their younger counterparts. Moreover, treatment was less optimal in the elderly, suggesting ageism. These results shed light on the phenomenon of suicide in late-life anxiety disorder and suggest areas where prevention efforts might be focused.

Comment

Main Findings: Despite the on-going debate that the association between anxiety disorders and suicide is confounded by comorbid psychiatric disorders, recent research has identified an independent contribution of anxiety to the onset of suicide attempts[1]. No research thus far has examined the clinical, behavioural and care characteristics of suicide amongst those older people who suffer from anxiety disorders. This study took the opportunity to explore the characteristics of suicide in late-life anxiety disorders with particular focus on comorbidity rates compared with younger people who died by suicide. The main population of interest were suicide victims with a lifetime primary diagnosis of anxiety disorders. In addition, data was extracted on patients with a comorbid diagnosis of an anxiety disorder in order to examine their primary diagnosis. Data were collected over a 15 year period

(1997-2012) on all suicides that occurred in the UK (n=94,922). A total of 25,128 suicide victims were in contact with mental health services in the year prior to their death. Questionnaires were sent to the consulting psychiatrist of each individual case and of those, 24,928 completed questionnaires were received which was the final sample used.

Suicide victims aged 60 years and older amounted to 4,481 with 16% having suffered from an anxiety disorder at the time of their death. Of these, 209 (4.7%) had a primary diagnosis of an anxiety disorder and 533 (11.9%) had an anxiety disorder comorbid with another primary diagnosis. These proportions were significantly higher in the older age group (p<.001). Comorbidity with depression was more common in the older age group with both a comorbid anxiety disorder and primary anxiety disorders (p<.001 and p=.001 respectively), whereas, younger patients suffered significantly more often from comorbid personality disorders and substance abuse disorders (p=.008 and p<.001 respectively). Analyses were then restricted to those with primary anxiety disorders to examine the clinical and behavioural characteristics of this population. Younger victims of suicide, when compared with older ones, were significantly more often male and less often lived alone (p=.002 and p=.001 respectively). Method of suicide differed between the two age groups (p<.001) with the older age group more often dying by suffocation and drowning and less often carbon monoxide poisoning or jumping. Substance taken for self-poisoning purposes did not differ between age groups with both young and old populations using opiates (n=70) either alone (n=43) or combined with paracetamol (n=27) the most often, followed by antidepressants (n=68). Frequency of previous hospitalisations did not differ between age groups, however older age groups had significantly less often a history of violence, self-harm, alcohol and drug misuse (p=.004, p<.001, p<.001 respectively), but suffered more often from chronic physical illnesses (p<.001). Interpersonal problems were more frequent in the younger age group (p<.001) and health-related events were more frequent in the older age group (p<.001). During the last contact with the older age group, deterioration in physical health was more frequently noted (p<.001) with less reported suicidal ideation (p=.03). Finally, the proportion of older suicide victims with an anxiety disorder who received psychological treatment was low (21%) and significantly lower compared to younger age group (p=.04).

Implications: This study from UK indicated that the proportion of those who died by suicide with anxiety disorders increased with age, as anxiety disorders were involved in roughly one of six suicides in older adults (16.6%) compared to 12.1% in younger age groups. In addition, there were other underlying mental health issues, in particular, the prominent role of late-life depression. When clinical characteristics were analysed using data from those who died by suicide with a primary anxiety disorder diagnosis, older groups with late-life anxiety presented with deteriorating health and concerns regarding this, as well as social isolation and significantly less suicidal thoughts and behaviours than the younger group. Furthermore, older populations less often missed their last appointment to see a doctor with reasons for visiting being urgent. This study highlights the difficulty in identifying older people at high risk of suicide in daily care. More caution should be exercised in assessing suicide risk amongst patients with late-life anxiety that may or may not present with suicidal thoughts or actions and make pharmacological and psychological treatments more accessible from a preventative perspective.

Endnotes

1. Nock MK, Hwang I, Sampson N, Kessler RC, Angermeyer M, Beautrais A, Borges G, Bromet E, Bruffaerts R, de Girolamo G, de Graaf R, Florescu S, Gureje O, Haro JM, Hu C, Huang Y, Karam E, Kawakami N, Kovess V, Levinson D, Posada-Villa J, Sagar R, Tomov T, Viana MC, Williams DR (2009). Cross-national analysis of the associations among mental disorders and suicidal behaviour: Findings from the WHO World Mental Health Surveys. *PLoS Medicine* 6, e1000123.

Examining undetermined and accidental deaths as source of 'under-reported-suicide' by age and sex in twenty Western countries

Pritchard C, Hansen L (UK)

Community Mental Health Journal 51, 365-374, 2014

Objectives: 'Undetermined' (UnD) and accidental deaths (AccD) are explored as possible sources of 'under-reported-suicides' (URS) in 20 Western countries.

Methods: WHO mortality rates per million of AccD, UnD and suicides analysed. UnD:suicides ratios of <1:5 calculated as likely URS versus ratios >1:10 unlikely URS and all correlated by sex and age.

Results: Male URS likely in 7 countries and in 11 for females. URS in AccD likely in 5 countries for both sexes only UnD and suicide rates the elderly (75+) significantly correlated.

Conclusion: Strong indication of URS in the UK, Portugal, Switzerland, Sweden, Denmark and Germany with likely URS in AccD in Greece, Portugal, Switzerland and USA. These findings have important implications, indicating that, with the exception of France and Japan, official reported suicide rates contain a degree of under-reporting, and especially for women yet it is essential to have accurate suicide data to ensure adequate service provision.

Comment

Main findings: The accuracy of suicide data has been an ongoing issue due to potential under-reporting of suicides (URS) which lessens the recognition of the extent of the problem[1]. This issue is highly reliant on the standardised diagnostic criteria of suicide that must be proved to be 'beyond reasonable doubt'[2]. Such decision-making can be influenced by numerous ethno-cultural factors regarding how suicide is viewed in each country[3]. Many researchers have suggested that the most likely cause of URS is through undetermined deaths (UnD) due to cause of death being very similar between the two[4]. Furthermore, this may also arise from coroners providing accidental or open verdicts in belief that it avoids adding to the family's distress[2]. This poses the detrimental issue of possibly distorting the true incidence of suicide. URS has also been proposed to comprise of accidental deaths which are particularly evident in the elderly population (i.e. car accidents)[5]. As a result, this study aimed to determine whether there are significant differences in patterns of suicide, UnD and accidental deaths by examination of possible URS amongst those UnD and accidental deaths (excluding transport related accidents). Data for this study were drawn from the WHO Annual Mortality Statistics and 20 Western countries were examined. Data was presented in age bands per million by gender. UnD:suicide ratios were calculated for each country for both males and females. Countries with a ratio less than 1:5 were classified as having a high likelihood of containing some URS, whereas countries with ratios that were more than 1:10 were less likely to contain URS.

Overall, there was a high chance that UnD contained URS in the following countries; Denmark, Germany, Switzerland, Ireland and particularly Portugal and the
UK as UnD: suicide ratios were less than 1:3 in every age bracket. USR appeared
smaller in Australia, New Zealand, Austria, Finland, France, Japan, Greece,
Netherlands, Norway and Spain, producing UnD:suicide ratios of >1:10. Results
indicated that URS was partly age and gender related as there appeared to be a
smaller UnD:suicide ratio for women than men suggesting that URS may be more
common amongst women. Only four countries reported high levels of URS for
males with a UnD:suicide ratio of <1:5 (the UK, Switzerland, Portugal and
Sweden). Whereas for females, 10 countries produced a similar ratio including the
UK, Switzerland, Portugal and Sweden, Germany, Denmark, USA, Canada, Italy
and Ireland. Data were not strong enough to suggest differences in mortality patterns between age brackets and gender in each country; however a few particular
trends were evident. In nine of the 20 countries, low ratios were noticeable in
elderly age groups for women and men displaying a possible source of URS.
Greece was found to have low suicide rates and no UnD for both genders which
suggests that accidental deaths may be a possible source of URS. This is also
apparent in the USA for both genders and Spain for males.

Implications: The findings of this study indicate a substantial degree of URS in
particular countries, such as Portugal, the UK, Sweden, Switzerland, Germany and
Denmark across the majority of age groups. The authors suggested possible socio-
religious-cultural factors such as age, sex, stigma and each individual mental
health delivery system that were not explored in this study may explain such differences, highlighting the need for further research to be conducted on this
matter. The main limitation that affects the results of this study is the decision of
the researchers to conclude that UnD: suicide ratios of <1:5 are more likely to
contain URS and those of >1:10 are unlikely to do so. Such ratios used in this
study are only indictors of possible URS; however, they do strongly indicate where
URS are likely to be due to internal consistency between and within countries
regarding gender and age. Overall, the findings from this study have implication
for policy and practice, as the extent of the problem is not adequately recognized,
hindering the ability to confront the issue of suicide and thus, services will be
under-resourced.

The accuracy of suicide reporting in Australia declined significantly since 2002[7].
This was due to a number of possible factors which include the lack of a central
authority for providing mortality data, coroners' inconsistencies in determining
intent (which is a consequence of inadequate information and suicide stigma),
and collecting and coding which entails the objective difficulty in interpreting the
cause of death (i.e. suicide-related single-vehicle road crashes)[6]. In addition, the
introduction of the National Coronial Information System (NCIS) in 2000/2001
also contributed to the escalation in underreporting as it increased the workload
of coroners and NCIS clerks in uploading electronic file, therefore an increasing
number of open cases[7,8]. In 2009, the problems with mortality statistics were

recognised and Australian Bureau of Statistics (ABS) introduced significant changes. Re-examining and revision of all coroner certified deaths at 12 and 24 months after initial processing and improved coding instructions for ABS coders were implemented[7,8].

Endnotes

1. Brieding M, Wiesema B (2006). Variability of undetermined manner of death classification in the US. *Injury Prevention* 12, 49–54.
2. Gunnell D, Hawton K, Kapur N (2011). Coroner's verdicts and suicide statistics in UK. *British Medical Journal* 343, 343–345
3. De Leo D, Conforti D, Carollo G (1997). A century of suicide in Italy: A comparison between old and young. *Suicide and Life-Threatening Behavior* 6, 122–126.
4. Pritchard C, Hansen L (2005). Adolescent and youth suicide in UK: An international comparison 1974–2000. *International Journal of Adolescent Medicine & Health* 17, 239–253.
5. Rockett IRH (2010). Counting suicides and making suicides count as a public health problem. *Crisis* 31, 227–230.
6. De Leo D, Dudley M, Aebersold C, Mendoza J, Barnes M, Harrison J, Ranson D (2010). Achieving standardised reporting of suicide in Australia: Rationale and program for change. *Medical Journal of Australia* 192, 452-456.
7. De Leo D (2010). Australia revises its mortality data on suicide. *Crisis* 31, 169-173.
8. De Leo D, Sveticic J, Kumpula E-K (2013). *Suicide in Queensland, 2008-2010. Mortality Rates and Related Data.* Brisbane: Australian Institute for Suicide Research and Prevention.

Perceptions of paramedic and emergency care workers of those who self harm: A systematic review of the quantitative literature

Rees N, Rapport F, Thomas G, John A, Snooks H (UK)

Journal of Psychosomatic Research 77, 449-456, 2014

Objective: The U.K. has one of the highest rates of self harm in Europe at 400 per 100,000 of population. Paramedics and emergency staff may be the first professionals encountered, therefore understanding their views and approaches to care is crucial. The aim of this study was to systematically review published quantitative literature relating to paramedic and emergency workers' perceptions and experiences of caring for people who self harm.

Methods: CINAHL®, MEDLINE®, OVID® and Psych INFO® databases were searched, PRISMA guidelines were followed, two researchers independently screened titles, abstracts and full papers against a priori eligibility criteria. Data synthesis was achieved by extracting and descriptively analysing study characteristics and findings.

Results: 16 studies met inclusion criteria; one included ambulance staff, all used questionnaires. Training, policies and guidelines improved staff knowledge and confidence in caring for people who self harm. Limited access to training was reported, ranging from 75% to 90% of staff lacking any. Limited departmental guidelines were also reported. Staff in acute settings exhibited increased feelings of negativity, becoming less positive closer to front line care. Recent studies report positive attitudes amongst emergency staff.

Discussion: Despite guidelines indicating need for education and policies to guide staff in self harm care, there is limited evidence of this happening in practice. The lack of literature including paramedics suggests a gap in our understanding about care for self harm patients. This gap warrants greater attention in order to improve care for patients who self harm in their first point of contact.

Comment

Main findings: There have been allegations regarding the attitudes of health care staff and the unsatisfactory quality of care they provide to those who intentionally self-harm[1]. Many patients who self-harm find that health professionals ignore them not only because of their negative attitudes towards the patient but because they are perceived as being difficult to deal with and untreatable[2]. As emergency department staff and paramedics are usually a first point of contact for those who self-harm, this can have detrimental effects on the individual during a vulnerable period[1,3]. This paper systematically reviewed quantitative research to investigate the current knowledge about the perceptions of emergency workers and paramedics that work with those who self-harm. Electronic searches of the literature were conducted using four databases (CINAHL®, MEDLINE®, OVID® and Psych INFO®). Searches were conducted and articles were reviewed by two researchers independently. Of the 864 studies that were screened for relevance, data was abstracted from 16 studies that were conducted in Australia (4), the UK (5), Ireland (4), Finland (2) and Taiwan (1).

Studies reported that staff believed they lacked the skills to care for people who presented with self-harm and would have more confidence if given the adequate training in communication and understanding of self-harm. Participation in training significantly improved their confidence, knowledge and attitudes towards self-harm. One particular study conducted with staff from EDs in Ireland found positive relationships between knowledge and effectiveness (p<.05) and also between confidence and effectiveness (p<.01). Older and more experienced nursing staff reported more supportive and positive attitudes and greater empathy for patients with self-harm (p<.05). Interestingly, another study from Northern Ireland indicated that 92% of more experienced nurses and 71% of less experienced nurses stated that most people who tried to kill themselves did not in fact really want to die (p<001)[4]. An Australian study found a relationship between staff members who had not been trained in self-harm and high levels of anger towards self-harming patients[5]. Some nurses reported feelings of frustration towards patients who repeatedly presented and were often ignored. Staff perceived those patients with self-harm as deserving a lower priority of care than those 'purely medical' patients with 76% of emergency staff stating that patients who attempt suicide are wasting staff time. Staff situated in large units and acute settings were more likely to report negativity toward self-harming individuals than those in non-acute settings. Two studies assessing gender differences in their attitudes towards self-harming patients found that males more likely expressed unfavourable attitudes (p<.01), less sympathy (p<.02) and greater irritation (p<.04) and frustration (p<.01) and alarmingly, a lack of willingness to help (p<.005) than women. Lastly, policies for dealing with people who self-harm and guidelines were lacking or underused in hospitals, either having no formal or informal procedures (46%), or nurses commonly had no knowledge of policy existence, with others reporting there were no guidelines to assess self-harm (82%).

Implications: This systematic review highlights a number of key issues that are faced by those who self-harm when they encounter paramedics and emergency staff. Quality of care was found to be influenced by a number of factors including education of staff, level of experience in caring for those who self-harm, age, gender, situational factors, availability of policies and guidelines for dealing with self-harm, confidence, assessment, and work load. As paramedics and emergency staff are often the first health professionals that patients with self-harm encounter, it is vital that they have an adequate level of knowledge and understanding regarding self-harm in order to provide quality care. As was seen from the review of the literature, this quality of care is compromised by staff in acute settings often exhibiting negativity towards self-harm patients, less positive attitudes, feelings of irritation and anger which often resulted in giving those patients lower priority and reduced entitlement to care. For the majority of staff their attitudes towards people who self-harm became more positive with increased knowledge, confidence in their ability and perceived personal effectiveness which goes hand in hand with training and education. Addressing the need for educational training and availability of formal and informal guidelines and policies is paramount in its potential to ensure equitable practice is provided by paramedics and emergency department staff and to have a positive impact on the quality of care for self-harming individuals. More specifically, an Australian study in this review that analysed nurses' actions and procedures for self-harm patients in Queensland emergency departments concluded that nearly all participants believed that they lacked specialised self-harm education and training[6]. It was recommended that health services in Australia must budget for continuing education and training of all emergency department staff, for experimental research funding that evaluates the effectiveness of clinical initiatives and implementing comprehensive and consistent guidelines of standard practice in assessing and treating patients who present with self-harm[6].

Endnotes

1. Chapman R, Martin C (2014). Perceptions of Australian emergency staff towards patients presenting with deliberate self-poisoning: A qualitative perspective. *International Emergency Nursing* 22, 140–145.
2. Vivekananda K (2000). Integrating models for understanding self-injury. *Psychotherapy in Australia* 7, 18-25.
3. Broadhurst M, Gill P (2007). Repeated self-injury from a liaison psychiatry perspective. *Advances in Psychiatric Treatment* 13, 228-235.
4. McLaughlin C (1994) Casualty nurses' attitudes to attempted suicide. *Journal of Advanced Nursing* 20, 1111-1118.
5. McAllister M, Creedy D, Moyle W, Farrugia C (2002). Nurses' attitudes towards clients who self-harm. *Journal of Advanced Nursing* 40, 578-586.
6. McAllister M, Creedy D, Moyle W, Farrugia C (2002). Study of Queensland emergency department nurses' actions and formal and informal procedures for clients who self-harm. *International Journal of Nursing Practice* 8, 184-90.

Impulsive suicide attempts: A systematic literature review of definitions, characteristics and risk factors

Rimkeviciene J, O'Gorman J, De Leo D (Australia)

Journal of Affective Disorders 171, 93-104, 2015

Background: Extensive research on impulsive suicide attempts, but lack of agreement on the use of this term indicates the need for a systematic literature review of the area. The aim of this review was to examine definitions and likely correlates of impulsive attempts.

Methods: A search of Medline, Psychinfo, Scopus, Proquest and Web of Knowledge databases was conducted. Additional articles were identified using the cross-referencing function of Google Scholar.

Results: 179 relevant papers were identified. Four different groups of research criteria used to assess suicide attempt impulsivity emerged: (a) time-related criteria, (b) absence of proximal planning/preparations, (c) presence of suicide plan in lifetime/previous year, and (d) other. Subsequent analysis used these criteria to compare results from different studies on 20 most researched hypotheses. Conclusions regarding the characteristics of impulsive attempts are more consistent than those on the risk factors specific to such attempts. No risk factors were identified that uniformly related to suicide attempt impulsivity across all criteria groups, but relationships emerged between separate criteria and specific characteristics of suicide attempters.

Limitations: Only published articles were included. Large inconsistencies in methods of the studies included in this review prevented comparison of effect sizes.

Conclusions: The vast disparities in findings on risk factors for impulsive suicide attempts among different criteria groups suggest the need to address the methodological issues in defining suicide attempt impulsivity before further research into correlates of such attempts can effectively progress. Specific recommendations are offered for necessary research.

Comment

Main findings: Despite description of impulsive suicide attempts in the literature as early as the 1890s[1], this is the first systematic review of the literature on the concept. The review examined how impulsive suicide attempts have been defined in research, and sought to establish characteristics of such attempts. A total of 179 papers were identified, comprising 161 quantitative studies and 18 case studies, case descriptions or qualitative studies; most of the research was conducted in Western countries. A substantial lack of agreement on the definition of impulsive suicide attempts hampered integration of research findings. Studies used a wide variety of criteria to identify an attempt as impulsive, particularly differing in whether they used proximal or distal identifiers of attempt impulsivity. The distal criteria assessed whether the attempter had ever made a suicide plan in their lifetime or the previous year, and proximal criteria assessed suicide ideation, planning and preparation just prior to the event. Results indicated that most attempts perceived as impulsive did not show signs of extensive preparation and planning proximally to the attempt, nor were attempts usually preceded by a long period of proximal suicide ideation. Even though the proportion of attempts that occurred without the person ever having made a suicide plan in their lifetime was smaller than those in which there had been a plan, it still comprised from 15% to 64% of all attempts. Given the problem with definitions, conclusions could only be drawn with a reasonable degree of support for approximately half of the 20 hypotheses advanced in the literature. These were that: impulsive suicide attempts are more likely to involve low intent to die, a low degree of expected lethality and readily available means, and were likely to be associated with deficits in executive function. Commonly held beliefs regarding associations with impulsive suicide attempts such as being male, a young age, substance use and alcohol intoxication[2], were not supported by present research. Previously associated factors such as lethality of the attempt, depression, hopelessness, aggression or trait impulsivity were complex and depended on the criteria used and population studied.

Implications: Past research has supported the development of suicidality along a continuum ranging from less severe forms, such as thoughts of death or suicide ideation, to more serious expressions of intent to die, including suicide attempts[2]. The claim that risk of suicide, and suicide attempts, can develop quickly with little prior premeditation has been countered by others who believe that most people who suicide, and attempt suicide, have experienced thoughts of suicide at some stage, whether recently or in their past[3]. The literature review revealed many inconsistencies in methodology which prevent better understanding of this concept, particularly in determining whether assessments of suicide attempt impulsivity are valid. International standardisation of suicide terminology would be a starting point to progress this area, and would greatly benefit communication between researchers and clinicians[4]. Future research is particularly needed to explore how proximal suicide ideation and planning relate to more distal elements of suicidality in the past of the attempters. Given that the research may not support commonly held assumptions of the characteristics of impulsive suicide attempts, it is possible that health workers may inappropriately minimise risk factors and intentions, or assume that there has been no prior risk of suicidality. Absence of warning signs should not be treated as absence of acute suicide risk. Exploring how this construct is used in clinical practice could assist to formulate more robust, relevant criteria to assess impulsivity. However, the presence of warning signs should not be trivialised; past suicidal thoughts or acts are highly statistically associated with subsequent suicide, and warrant careful professional attention[3].

Endnotes

1. Durkheim E (2005). *Suicide: A study in sociology* (2nd ed). Hoboken: Taylor and Francis (original work published 1897).
2. Conner KR (2004). A call for research on planned vs. unplanned suicidal behavior. *Suicide and Life-Threatening Behavior* 34, 89-98.
3. Sveticic J, De Leo D (2012). The hypothesis of a continuum in suicidality: A discussion on its validity and practical implications. *Mental Illness* 4, 73-78.
4. De Leo D (2011). DSM-V and the future of suicidology. *Crisis* 32, 233-239.

Suicide in the oldest old: An observational study and cluster analysis

Sinyor M, Tan LP, Schaffer A, Gallagher D, Shulman K (Canada)

International Journal of Geriatric Psychiatry. Published online: 24 March 2015. doi: 10.1002/gps.4286

Objectives: The older population are at a high risk for suicide. This study sought to learn more about the characteristics of suicide in the oldest-old and to use a cluster analysis to determine if oldest-old suicide victims assort into clinically meaningful subgroups.

Methods: Data were collected from a coroner's chart review of suicide victims in Toronto from 1998 to 2011. We compared two age groups (65-79 year olds, n=335, and 80+ year olds, n=191) and then conducted a hierarchical agglomerative cluster analysis using Ward's method to identify distinct clusters in the 80+ group.

Results: The younger and older age groups differed according to marital status, living circumstances and pattern of stressors. The cluster analysis identified three distinct clusters in the 80+ group. Cluster 1 was the largest (n=124) and included people who were either married or widowed who had significantly more depression and somewhat more medical health stressors. In contrast, cluster 2 (n=50) comprised people who were almost all single and living alone with significantly less identified depression and slightly fewer medical health stressors. All members of cluster 3 (n=17) lived in a retirement residence or nursing home, and this group had the highest rates of depression, dementia, other mental illness and past suicide attempts.

Conclusions: This is the first study to use the cluster analysis technique to identify meaningful subgroups among suicide victims in the oldest-old. The results reveal different patterns of suicide in the older population that may be relevant for clinical care.

Comment

Main Findings: Suicide in older populations, particularly the oldest old (80+ years) is an important public health issue due to having the highest suicide rates[1]. Suicide risk factors in the elderly that have been identified include: male sex, widowed or divorced, psychiatric illness, stressful life events (i.e. financial difficulties, bereavement, social isolation and relationship problems) and physical illness[2,3]. Compared to younger subjects, older individuals who die by suicide are less likely to report suicidal ideation to family members or physicians placing them at even higher risk of suicide due to a lack of help-seeking behaviours[3]. This study aimed to explore the issue of high suicide rates in the oldest-old (80+ years) when compared to young-old populations (65-79 years). Demographics, clinical and suicide-specific differences between the two groups were identified. A cluster analysis was conducted in order to examine whether suicide victims aged 80 years and over separate into meaningful subgroups in accordance with established risk factors (sex, living circumstances, marital status, mental illness, previous suicide attempts, recent stressors, recent emergency department/psychiatric care)[3]. Furthermore, a more specific sample of suicide victims (90+ years) was examined to identify any features that distinguish them from suicide victims of older adults aged less than 90 years. Data were collected from the coroner's office in Toronto, Canada, regarding all suicides that occurred between 1998 and 2011 in people aged between 65 and 79 years (n=335) and 80+ years (n=191), which included 25 aged 90+ years.

Comparisons between 65-79 year olds and 80+ year olds showed significant differences in marital status (p<.001) as the older group was more often widowed compared with younger group who were more often single. Living circumstances also significantly differed between the two groups (p<.001) in that the older group more often lived in a nursing home or retirement residence compared to young-old persons (8.9% vs 2.4% respectively) whereas the younger group more often lived alone compared with oldest-old persons (46.9% vs 38.2% respectively). Those aged 80+ years more likely had a physical health problem (p=.007) or dementia (p=.004). The younger group had more often recent stressors which were interpersonal (p=.04) or to do with finances/employment (p=.002). The two groups did not differ on depression, past attempts or suicide method. A cluster analysis of those 80 years and over of age showed three distinct constellations. The largest cluster comprised of those who were either widowed or married, had slightly higher rates of physical health issues and depressed moods. The second included almost all those who were single, majority living alone and had lowest rates of mental illness. Lastly, the third cluster was mostly single, lived in a nursing home or retirement residence and had the highest rates of depression, other mental illness, dementia and past attempts. Exploration of characteristics of those 90 years and older suicide victims (n=25) displayed the following findings: 15 were male, 14 depressed, 12 had a recent medical health issue in the previous year and of those 12, nine stated they were bothered by their deteriorating health/loss of independence, six were married and 10 widowed and none had come into contact with mental health professionals in the week prior to death.

Implications: This study was the first of its kind to explore clusters of those aged 80 years and above who died by suicide and examine characteristics associated with victims of suicide aged 90 years and above. Recent contact with mental health professionals was very low across all three clusters, which aligns with research from Australia[4]. The first cluster highlights the importance of mental health professionals screening adults with medical comorbidities for depression and possible suicide ideation, particularly those who are widowed but also those who are married. The second cluster that identified the majority of those who lived alone could be an indication of social isolation, which has been previously identified as a significant risk factor of suicide[5]. It is important to identify suicide risk in the population of older adults regardless of whether they have been diagnosed with a psychiatric illness, as low rates were found which may reflect under-reporting or under-detection. A study conducted in Northern Italy reduced social isolation in the elderly by using a telephone and emergency support intervention and concluded that service use was associated with fewer suicides when compared to the general population[6]. The final cluster demonstrated high risk in older populations that live in a nursing home or retirement residence with high rates of mental illness.

Further effort needs to be made to heighten vigilance of screening for suicidality and intervening when necessary in those older age groups with a history of mental illness or dementia, residing in retirement or nursing homes. In addition, this study also highlights deteriorating health as a significant stressor in those aged 90 years and above. With a lack of contact with mental health professionals, it is important for physicians who are treating such individuals for physical health conditions express caution in assuming that people of this age do not have suicidal ideation even if there is no evident psychiatric history. A recent review on suicide prevention programs in Queensland indicates that there is a lack of suicide prevention activities targeting older adults, uncovering six times more programs for younger populations (up to 24 years) when compared with the number of programs available for older people (65 years and above)[7]. Specific suicide prevention strategies to target elderly in Australia have been recommended which include: restricting access to means (i.e. using Webster packs to reduce stockpiling of medications), upskilling GPs and mental health staff and telephone counsellors in detecting and treating elderly people with suicidal ideations and behaviours and improving social support and reducing social isolation through community programs and telephone services[8].

Endnotes

1. Cattell H (2000). Suicide in the elderly. *Advances in Psychiatric Treatment* 6, 102-108.
2. De Leo D, Draper BM, Snowdon J, Kõlves K (2013). Suicides in older adults: A case–control psychological autopsy study in Australia. *Journal of Psychiatric Research* 47, 980–988.
3. Conwell Y, Duberstein PR, Caine ED (2002). Risk factors for suicide in later life. *Biological Psychiatry* 52, 193-204.
4. De Leo D, Draper BM, Snowdon J, Kõlves K (2013). Contacts with health professionals before suicide: Missed opportunities for prevention? *Comprehensive Psychiatry* 54, 1117–1123.
5. Kõlves K, Milner A, McKay K, De Leo D (2012). *Suicide in rural and remote areas of Australia*. Brisbane, Australia: Australian Institute for Suicide Research and Prevention.
6. De Leo D, Dello Buono M, Dwyer J (2002). Suicide among the elderly: The long-term impact of a telephone support and assessment intervention in northern Italy. *The British Journal of Psychiatry* 181, 226-229.
7. Arnautovska U, Kõlves K, Ide N, De Leo D (2013). Review of suicide prevention programs in Queensland: State and community level activities. *Australian Health Review* 37, 660-665.
8. Kõlves K, O'Dwyer S, De Leo D (2014). *Suicide in older adults in Australia*. Australian Institute for Suicide Research and Prevention, Brisbane.

Are LGBT populations at a higher risk for suicidal behaviors in Australia? Research findings and implications

Skerrett DM, Kolves K, De Leo D (Australia)

Journal of Homosexuality. Published online: 8 January 2015. doi:10.1080/00918369.2014.1003009

The aim of this article is to review the Australian literature about suicidality in minority sexual identity and/or behavior groups in order to determine the evidence base for their reported higher vulnerability to suicidal behaviors than heterosexual and non-transgendered individuals in the Australian context, as well as to identify the factors which are predictive of suicidal behaviors in these groups in Australia. A literature search for all available years (until the end of 2012) was conducted using the databases Scopus, Medline, and Proquest for articles published in English in peer-reviewed academic journals. All peer-reviewed publications that provided empirical evidence for prevalence and predictive factors of suicidal behaviors among LGBTI individuals (or a subset thereof) in Australia were included. Reference lists were also scrutinized to identify "gray" literature for inclusion. The results revealed that there is only limited research from Australia. Nevertheless, although no population-based studies have been carried out, research indicates that sexual minorities are indeed at a higher risk for suicidal behaviors. In order to further the understanding of suicidal behaviors and potential prevention among LGBT groups in the Australia, further research is needed, particularly on fatal suicidal behaviors.

Comment

Main findings: Despite Australian Government recognition of lesbian, gay, bisexual, transgender, and intersex (LGBTI) people as belonging to high risk groups for suicide[1], limited research has been conducted to examine suicidality within minority sexual identity and/or behaviour groups in Australia. This literature review, the first of its kind, aimed to determine the Australian evidence base for a heightened risk of suicidal behaviour. In total, 12 documents based on 11 empirical studies were identified for inclusion; the earliest study was published in 1988. Identified limitations in Australian studies to date included a lack of research based on suicide deaths, and reliance on cross-sectional studies and convenience sampling, often with self-selected participants. While no population-based studies had been published in Australia, the research indicated a higher risk of suicidal behaviours for populations studied. A 2002 study based on a sample of 4,824 people from the electoral roll found gay men at a higher risk for 'suicidality' than heterosexual men, and bisexual men at a higher risk than gay men[2]. A 2006 study found highly statistically significant differences in 'feeling suicidal' between both gay and bisexual men, and heterosexual men[3]. While LGBT populations and non-LGBT populations shared common risk factors for suicide attempt, such as substance abuse and psychiatric disorders, unique risk factors existed, including developmental stressors such as self-identifying ('coming out') in adolescence and adulthood. Homophobic abuse was associated with self-harming behaviours, as was rejection by a family member. Possible protective factors identified by the research included acceptance of one's sexuality, having a supportive family, positive fictional media portrayal of openly gay characters, and perceived school-based policy protection.

Implications: Sexual orientation is seldom recorded at death in Australia, increasing the likelihood that suicide deaths from LGBTI groups are under-reported[4]. The relatively recent recognition of the high risk inherent within LGBTI populations in Australia has sparked initiatives such as the world's first national suicide prevention project specifically targeting LGBTI indiviudals[5]. This literature review has provided support for predictive factors for suicidal behaviours specific to minority sexual identity and/or behaviour groups, in line with recent research identifying LGBT suicide deaths in Queensland as belonging to a distinct sub-group[4]. However, further methodologically sound research is needed; larger scale case-controlled studies would provide greater clarity as to the specific predictive factors within these populations, and help to close knowledge gaps such as those relating to lack of information about risk factors for transgender populations. Outcomes of such studies would be invaluable in informing targeted intervention strategies such as inclusive telephone counselling services staffed by counsellors specifically trained to help suicidal callers from LGBTI populations.

Endnotes

1. Commonwealth of Australia (2010). *Commonwealth response to The hidden toll: Suicide in Australia Report of the Senate Community Affairs Reference Committee.* Canberra: Commonwealth of Australia.

2. Jorm AF, Korten AE, Rodgers B, Jacomb PA, Christensen H (2002). Sexual orientation and mental health: Results from a community survey of young and middle-aged adults. *The British Journal of Psychiatry* 180, 423-427.

3. Abelson J, Lambevski S, Crawford J, Bartos M, Kippax S (2006). Factors associated with 'feeling suicidal': The role of sexual identity. *Journal of Homosexuality* 51, 59-80.

4. Skerrett DM, Kõlves K, De Leo D (2014). Suicides among lesbian, gay, bisexual and transgender populations in Australia: An analysis of the Queensland Suicide Register. *Asia-Pacific Psychiatry* 6, 440-446.

5. MindOUT! (2015). *Mindout: The National LGBTI Mental Health and Suicide Prevention Project.* Retrieved 27 February 2015 from http://www.lgbtihealth.org.au/mindout

Suicides in Aboriginal and Torres Strait Islander children: analysis of Queensland Suicide Register

Soole R, Kõlves K, De Leo D (Australia)

Australian and New Zealand Journal of Public Health 38, 574-578, 2014

Objective: Suicide rates among Indigenous Australian children are higher than for other Australian children. The current study aimed to identify factors associated with Indigenous child suicide when compared to other Australian children.

Methods: Using the Queensland Suicide Register, suicides in Indigenous children (10–14 years) and other Australian children in the same age band were compared.

Results: Between 2000 and 2010, 45 child suicides were recorded: 21 of Indigenous children and 24 of other Australian children. This corresponded to a suicide rate of 10.15 suicides per 100,000 for Indigenous children – 12.63 times higher than the suicide rate for other Australian children (0.80 per 100,000). Hanging was the predominant method used by all children. Indigenous children were significantly more likely to suicide outside the home, to be living outside the parental home at time of death, and be living in remote or very remote areas. Indigenous children were found to consume alcohol more frequently before suicide, compared to other Australian children. Current and past treatments of psychiatric disorders were significantly less common among Indigenous children compared to other Australian children.

Conclusions: Western conceptualisation of mental illness may not adequately embody Indigenous people's holistic perspective regarding mental health. Further development of culturally appropriate suicide prevention activities for Aboriginal and Torres Strait Islander children is required.

Comment

Main Findings: Research thus far has indicated that Aboriginal and Torres Strait Islander children were at a 10 times greater risk of suicide when compared to other Australian children living in Queensland; however, reasons for their over-representation in suicide statistics is unknown[1]. Potential explanations for this have been suggested which include intergenerational trauma due to colonisation and forceful removal, enduring racism and disintegrated cultural identity[2]. This study aimed to compare suicides rates of Aboriginal and Torres Strait Islander children with other Australian children and identify factors associated with Aboriginal and Torres Strait Islander child suicide when compared to other Australian children in Queensland. Data was collated from the Queensland Suicide Register (QSR). A total of 45 deaths by suicide were recorded for children 14 years and younger between 2000 and 2010 with Aboriginal and Torres Strait Islander children comprising 46.7% (n=21) of those 45. Aboriginal and Torres Strait Islander children had a suicide rate of 10.15 suicides per 100,000 whereas other Australian children's suicide rate was 0.8 suicides per 100,000, being 12.63 times higher for Aboriginal and Torres Strait Islander children. Suicide rates for Aboriginal and Torres Strait Islander children were highest for those living in remote areas where as other Australian children had their highest rate of suicide in metropolitan areas.

Despite usual residency being the most frequent for both groups, Aboriginal and Torres Strait Islander children were more likely than other Australian children to die by suicide in places other than their usual residence and less likely to leave a suicide note. For both groups, hanging was the most common suicide method (95.2% for Aboriginal and Torres Strait Islander children and 95.8% for other Australian children). Diagnosed psychiatric disorders were significantly less common in Aboriginal and Torres Strait Islander children (4.8%) than other Australian children (29.2%) who died by suicide. Furthermore, current or past treatment for a psychiatric condition was significantly higher in other Australian children (29.2%) than Aboriginal and Torres Strait Islander children (4.8%). Analysing toxicology reports revealed a significant trend of Aboriginal and Torres Strait Islander children consuming alcohol prior to suicide (33.3%) more frequently when compared to other Australian children (4.2%). In addition, analysis of life events uncovered that the most common life event for both groups was familial conflict.

Implications: Thus far, there is a lack of understanding regarding cultural specificities of Aboriginal and Torres Strait Islander Australians' mental health[3]. This is particularly alarming in the context of such high suicide rates amongst Aboriginal and Torres Strait Islander children. Much less than other Australian children, 5% of Aboriginal and Torres Strait Islander children who died by suicide had been diagnosed with a psychiatric disorder. This lower prevalence of psychiatric disorders in Aboriginal and Torres Strait Islander children may be a manifestation of the unsuitable application of the Western concept of psychiatric disorder, not accurately representing Aboriginal and Torres Strait Islander holistic perspectives regarding mental health[4]. One reason for this disparity might be the limited access to mental health professionals with skills required to recognise and subsequently treat mental health problems[5]. This is particularly important as more than half of Aboriginal and Torres Strait Islander children who died by suicide lived in remote or very remote areas. This study highlights the importance of developing targeted suicide prevention strategies that are culturally sensitive, incorporating the Aboriginal and Torres Strait Islander holistic conceptualisation of mental health for this population as well as providing accessible mental health services.

Endnotes

1. De Leo D, Sveticic J, Milner, A (2011). Suicide in Indigenous people in Queensland, Australia: Trends and methods, 1994–2007. *Australian & New Zealand Journal of Psychiatry* 45, 532-538.

2. Tatz C (2005). *Aboriginal Suicide is Different: A Portrait of Life and Self-destruction.* Canberra (AUST): Aboriginal Studies Press.

3. Chenhall R, Senior K (2009). "Those young people all crankybella": Indigenous youth mental health and globalization. *International Journal of Mental Health* 38, 28-43.

4. Vicary D, Westerman T (2004). 'That's just the way he is': Some implications of Aboriginal mental health beliefs. *Australian E-journal for the Advancement of Mental Health* 3, 1-10.

5. Hunter E (2007). Disadvantage and discontent: A review of issues relevant to the mental health of rural and remote Indigenous Australians. *Australian Journal of Rural Health* 15, 88-93.

The effectiveness of installing physical barriers for preventing railway suicides and accidents: Evidence from Japan

Ueda M, Sawada Y, Matsubayashi T (Japan)
Journal of Affective Disorders 178, 1-4, 2105

Background: Installing physical barriers, such as platform screen doors (PSDs), on train platforms is considered to be one of the most effective measures to prevent railway suicide. However, there is little evidence on the effectiveness of such barriers. In particular, the effectiveness of half-height, as opposed to full-height, PSDs has never been assessed.

Methods: Using suicide and accident data between 2004 and 2014 provided by a major railway company in the Tokyo metropolitan area, this study examines whether the installation of half-height PSDs has contributed to the reduction of the incidents of fatal and non-fatal railway suicide. In addition, the study tests whether the installation of PSDs has resulted in the reduction of unintentional falls onto railway tracks.

Results: Our estimation using a Poisson regression model showed that the introduction of PSDs resulted in a decrease in the number of suicides by 76% (CI: 33-93%). Yet, the installation of PSDs has not completely prevented suicide, as there were cases in which passengers climbed them over. As for unintentional accidents, no fall accidents occurred at stations with PSDs.

Limitations: Our data come only from one train operator, and thus the generalizability of our results may be limited. We do not fully examine potential substitution effects.

Conclusion: Platform screen doors are effective in reducing the number of railway suicides. However, half-height PSDs are less effective than the full-height PSDs in preventing intentional entry to the train tracks. Installation of PSDs is an extremely effective method to prevent fall accidents.

Comment

Main findings: Railway suicides have a far-reaching impact beyond the individuals loss of life and their family and friends but also the train drivers and general public[1]. For instance, in the metropolitan area of Tokyo, one railway suicide can affect up to 83,000 other people. This ranges from passengers simply disrupted by the normal operation of the train line to traumatised train conductors that witnessed the occurrence[1,2]. Installation of physical barriers (i.e. platform screen doors — PSDs) on train platforms is considered to be one of the most effective measures to prevent railway suicide in an effort to limit access to the platform by individuals who enter train tracks for the purpose of ending their lives[3]. PSDs in Japan are unique as they are 'half-height' (chest height) whereby adult persons have the ability to climb over the barrier in comparison with those 'full-height' PSDs that extend from ceiling to floor. Therefore, the current study explored PSDs in Japan in an attempt to provide evidence on their effectiveness to prevent suicides, examining whether the installation of half-height PSDs are associated with a reduction of fatal and non-fatal railway suicidal behaviours.

Data on both fatal and non-fatal suicidal behaviours was obtained during April 2004 to March 2014 from a major railway company in the metropolitan area of Tokyo. As the study occurred during the installation of PSDs, it was feasible to compare the number of fatal and non-fatal railway suicidal behaviours between stations with and without PSDs. Despite PSDs not completely preventing railway suicidal behaviours, the number of incidents was much larger at those stations without PSDs than those with PSDs from 2004 to 2013 (137 and seven respectively). Overall, the installation of PSDs resulted in a significant decrease in the number of railway suicidal behaviours by 76% (p=.007). The few stations in Tokyo that had full-height barriers installed had no incidents that occurred during the study period. Of the seven people who attempted suicide at stations with half-height PSDs, only two cases were fatal. Attempts at stations with PSDs were less likely to be fatal than those without PSDs due to the nature of the suicide method as wandering onto the track (more common at stations with PSDs) was less fatal than jumping in front of an oncoming train (common at stations without PSDs).

Implications: This study demonstrated that the installation of half-height barriers is an effective method of suicide prevention as it contributed to a significant reduction of fatal and non-fatal railway suicidal behaviours. Of the seven incidents of fatal and non-fatal suicidal behaviours that occurred at stations with half-height PSDs, five had climbed the barrier and all were in their 20s or 30s thus having the physical capability to do so. By contrast, no incidents of fatal and non-fatal railway suicidal behaviours had occurred during the study period at those stations with full-height PSDs installed. Despite the greater effectiveness of full-height PSDs, half-height barriers are more appealing to train operators as they can be easily retrofitted to stations and are lightweight thus more cost effective. Future research should examine in more detail the cost of stalling different heights of PSDs with the associated benefits of their installation. One main limitation in this study were the inability to assess whether there were possible substitution effects in that suicides which may have occurred at locations with PSDs were potentially shifted to other stations without PSDs or substituted with other suicide methods. Further examination into substitution phenomenon is suggested for additional research.

In Australia, TrackSAFE is currently working on initiatives to reduce suicidal behaviours on railways[4]. Recommendations that have been put forward as effective suicide prevention methods include creating physical barriers as a way of preventing individual from having access to the tracks[5]. However, due to this approach being expensive and also logistically difficult, as most suicides on Australian railways occur on open track areas, an assessment of suicide risk factors at station hot spots with the result in erecting barriers at bridges or platform ends is recommended[5].

Endnotes

1. Weiss KJ, Farrell JM (2014). PTSD in railroad drivers under the Federal employers' liability act. *Journal of the American Academy of Psychiatry and the Law* 34, 191-199.
2. Mishara BL (2007). Railway and metro suicides: Understanding the problem and prevention potential. *Crisis* 28, 36-43.
3. Law CK, Yip PS (2011). An economic evaluation of setting up physical barriers in railway stations for preventing railway injury: evidence from Hong Kong. *Journal of Epidemiology & Community Health* 65, 915-920.
4. Website of TrackSAFE (2015). Retrieved from http://tracksafefoundation.com.au/ on 8th May 2015
5. Kõlves K, Barker E, De Leo D. (2012). *Suicide prevention strategies for the reduction of rail-related suicides and suicide attempts. Report to Lifeline Foundation.* Australian Institute for Suicide Research and Prevention, Brisbane.

Suicide among 915,303 Austrian cancer patients: Who is at risk?

Vyssoki B, Gleiss A, Rockett IRH, Hackl M, Leitner B, Sonneck G, Kapusta ND (Austria)
Journal of Affective Disorders 175C, 287-291, 2015

Objectives: The aim of this study was to determine whether time since first diagnosis, site, and stage of cancer impacted suicide risk within a nationwide cohort of Austrian cancer patients.

Methods: Data for this population-based study were derived from the Austrian National Cancer Registry and Austrian Statistics on Causes of Death. The study of population comprised 915,303 patients diagnosed with cancer between 1983 and 2000 and 14,532,682 person-years of follow-up. Standardized suicide mortality ratios (SMRs) were calculated by sex, time since first diagnosis, site, and stage of cancer.

Results: A total of 2877 suicides were registered among all cancer patients over the observation period. Indicating excess suicide risk relative to the general Austrian population, the SMR for the patient cohort was 1.23 (95% CI: 1.19-1.28), and was higher for men (1.41; 95% CI: 1.35-1.47) than women (1.24; 95% CI: 1.15-1.34). This excess risk varied with time since first cancer diagnosis. SMRs peaked in year one after diagnosis (3.17; 95% CI: 2.96-3.40). An excess suicide risk was observed for patients with late locally advanced (SMR=1.59; 95% CI: 1.47-1.71) or metastasized cancer (SMR=4.07; 95% CI: 3.58-4.61), and cancers of the lung (SMR 3.86; 95% CI: 3.36-4.42) and central nervous system (SMR 2.81; 95% CI: 1.92-3.97).

Limitations: No data were available on psychiatric comorbidities, genetic variables, family characteristics, social factors, and community characteristics.

Conclusions: Our study shows that cancer patients have an excess risk for suicide, relative to the general population, which varies with time since first diagnosis, disease severity, and anatomical site. The diagnostic process needs to be sensitive and responsive to their mental health needs. Psychological care should be an integral component of cancer treatment programs

Comment

Main Findings: Receiving a cancer diagnosis can be a major stressor and traumatic experience for many patients[1], often leading to hopelessness and depression and the desire for accelerated death is common in the terminally ill[2]. Cancer is an important risk factor for depression and detection can be difficult due to symptoms being misinterpreted as 'normal' sadness from receiving the diagnosis, and many physical symptoms such as fatigue, loss of appetite and disturbed sleep are shared between the two[2]. Such misinterpretation may lead to underestimation of depression and thus a lack of pharmaceutical treatment and psychological interventions. As mood disorders are a major risk factor for suicide, this may indicate a high suicide risk that goes undetected in this population[3]. This study examined suicide deaths in a population of Austrian cancer patients for the purpose of identifying high-risk groups that might benefit from psychotherapeutic interventions.

Data was obtained on 915,303 patients who were initially diagnosed during 1983 to 2010 regarding their age, sex, site of cancer, stage of cancer, and cause of death.

Overall, during the time period of 1983-2010, trend data revealed higher suicide rates in cancer patients than the general population, with rates reaching twice as high for cancer patients in 2010. Of the 915,303 cancer patients 2,877 died by suicide with suicide rates peaking in the first year after diagnosis (Standardised Mortality Rate (SMR)=1.23, 95% CI: 2.96-3.40). This rate appeared to diminish between the first and second years (SMR=3.17, 95% CI: 1.54-1.89), and further between the second and third years (SMR=1.32, 95% CI: 1.17-1.50) and so on for subsequent years. Interestingly, patients beyond 10 years from initial diagnosis had a reduced risk of suicide when compared with the general population (SMR=0.74 for 11 to 15 years after diagnosis, 95% CI: 0.90-1.05). Higher risk of suicide was found in patients with more advanced cancer, as well as those with late locally advanced and metastasized cancer. Highest risk of suicide was found in patients with cancer of the lung, central nervous system (CNS) and a combined category of oesophagus, liver or pancreas cancer. Skin cancer patients showed no elevated risk of suicide.

Implications: Excess risk of suicide peaked in the first year following diagnosis. Such findings indicate that these immensely stressful months following diagnosis may induce a great deal of emotional distress, depression and possible suicidal ideation. As a result, improving the psychiatric and psychotherapeutic care of cancer patients, particularly focusing on the first year after diagnosis is crucial in suicide prevention. Lower rates of suicide in cancer patients 10 years after diagnosis compared to the general population point toward a possible ongoing and prosperous adaptation. Additional studies should be conducted to identify protective factors and coping mechanisms used by these long-term cancer survivors. This study also identified higher risk of suicide by anatomical site of cancer with those diagnosed with lung cancer at the highest risk followed by CNS tumours and combined combination of oesophageal, pancreatic, and liver cancer. Evidence has suggested that these cancers had poor prognosis with survival rates below 30% over five years[4]. In addition, suicide risk was higher in patients in the two most severe cancer stages. As full remission declines with tumour progression this, along with diagnosis of cancers with poor prognosis, probably intensifies distress and hopelessness in such patients. Given the apparent positive association between suicide risk and cancer severity, optimised psychotherapeutic and psychiatric care of these patients is vital, particularly in detecting and treating mood disorders.

A number of literature reviews have identified cancer as a risk factor for suicidal behaviours[5,6]. A study from Western Australia[7] indicated that the highest level of suicide risk in cancer patients was found during the three months following diagnosis explained by painful emotional reactions from receiving a cancer diagnosis. Feelings of despair, distress and hopeless were key features associated with those diagnosed with cancer particularly after failed treatment which increases risk of suicidal behaviours[7]. Suicide risk was found higher for those with cancers that affect vital functioning (i.e. pancreas, lung, head and neck, etc.) which often relate to impaired physical and social behaviours[5]. A key implication stressed in a literature review was the need to screen for suicidality, potentially incorporating into the admission questionnaire, a 3-item version of the Beck Hopelessness Scale[6].

Endnotes

1. Spiegel D, Giese-Davis J (2003). Depression and cancer: Mechanisms and disease progression. *Biological Psychiatry* 54, 269-282.
2. Rosenfeld BB, Pessin H, Kaim M, Funesti-Esch J, Galietta M, Nelson CJ, Brescia R (2000). Depression, hopelessness, and desire for hastened death in terminally ill patients with cancer. *JAMA* 284, 2907–2911.
3. Hem E, Loge JH, Haldorsen T, Ekeberg O (2004).Suicide risk in cancer patients from 1960 to 1999 *Journal of Clinical Oncology* 22, 4209-4216.
4. De Angelis R, Sant M, MD, Coleman MP, Francisci S, Baili P, Pierannunzio D, Trama A, Visser O, Brenner H, Ardanaz E, Bielska-Lasota M, Engholm G, Nennecke A, Siesling S, Berrino F, Capocaccia R, the EUROCARE-5 Working Group. (2014). Cancer survival in Europe 1999–2007 by country and age: Results of EUROCARE-5 – a population-based study. *The Lancet Oncology* 15, 23-34.
5. Spoletini I, Gianni W, Caltagirone C, Madaio R, Repetto L, Spalletta G (2011). Suicide and cancer: Where do we go from here? *Critical Reviews in Oncology/Hematology* 78, 206-219.
6. Anguiano L, Deborah DK, Piven ML, Rosenstein D (2012). A literature review of suicide in cancer patients. *Cancer Nursing* 35, E14-26.
7. Dormer NR, McCaul NA, Kristjanson LJ (2008). Risk of suicide in cancer patients in Western Australia, 1981-2002. *Medical Journal of Australia* 188, 140-143.

School-based suicide prevention programmes: The SEYLE cluster-randomised, controlled trial

Wasserman D, Hoven CW, Wasserman C, Wall M, Eisenberg R, Hadlaczky G, Kelleher I, Sarchiapone M, Apter A, Balazs J, Bobes J, Brunner R, Corcoran P, Cosman D, Guillemin F, Haring C, Iosue M, Kaess M, Kahn J-P, Keeley H, Musa GJ, Nemes B, Postuvan V, Saiz P, Reiter-Theil S, Värnik A, Värnik P, Carli V (Austria, Estonia, France, Germany, Hungary, Ireland, Italy, Romania, Slovenia, Spain)

Lancet 385, 1536-1544, 2015

Background: Suicidal behaviours in adolescents are a major public health problem and evidence-based prevention programmes are greatly needed. We aimed to investigate the efficacy of school-based preventive interventions of suicidal behaviours.

Methods: The Saving and Empowering Young Lives in Europe (SEYLE) study is a multicentre, cluster-randomised controlled trial. The SEYLE sample consisted of 11 110 adolescent pupils, median age 15 years (IQR 14-15), recruited from 168 schools in ten European Union countries. We randomly assigned the schools to one of three interventions or a control group. The interventions were: (1) Question, Persuade, and Refer (QPR), a gatekeeper training module targeting teachers and other school personnel, (2) the Youth Aware of Mental Health Programme (YAM) targeting pupils, and (3) screening by professionals (ProfScreen) with referral of at-risk pupils. Each school was randomly assigned by random number generator to participate in one intervention (or control) group only and was unaware of the interventions undertaken in the other three trial groups. The primary outcome measure was the number of suicide attempt(s) made by 3 month and 12 month follow-up. Analysis included all pupils with data available at each timepoint, excluding those who had ever attempted suicide or who had shown severe suicidal ideation during the 2 weeks before baseline. This study is registered with the German Clinical Trials Registry, number DRKS00000214.

Findings: Between Nov 1, 2009, and Dec 14, 2010, 168 schools (11 110 pupils) were randomly assigned to interventions (40 schools [2692 pupils] to QPR, 45 [2721] YAM, 43 [2764] ProfScreen, and 40 [2933] control). No significant differences between intervention groups and the control group were recorded at the 3 month follow-up. At the 12 month follow-up, YAM was associated with a significant reduction of incident suicide attempts (odds ratios [OR] 0.45, 95% CI 0.24-0.85; p=0.014) and severe suicidal ideation (0.50, 0.27-0.92; p=0.025), compared with the control group. 14 pupils (0.70%) reported incident suicide attempts at the 12 month follow-up in the YAM versus 34 (1.51%) in the control group, and 15 pupils (0.75%) reported incident severe suicidal ideation in the YAM group versus 31 (1.37%) in the control group. No participants completed suicide during the study period.

Interpretation: YAM was effective in reducing the number of suicide attempts and severe suicidal ideation in school-based adolescents. These findings underline the benefit of this universal suicide preventive intervention in schools.

Comment

Main findings: Worldwide, suicide is the second leading cause of death amongst young people aged 15 to 19 years[1]. As most adolescents attend school, it is an appropriate setting to conduct suicide prevention activities, yet few randomised controlled trials (RCTs) of school-based intervention programs have been conducted. The Saving and Empowering Young Lives in Europe (SEYLE) study is the first European, multi-country, RCT of the prevention of suicidal behaviour in adolescents, with the largest number of adolescent participants in any school-based preventive study. A total of 11,110 students, mostly aged 15 years, were recruited from 168 schools in Austria, Estonia, France, Germany, Hungary, Ireland, Italy, Romania, Slovenia and Spain; students who reported suicide attempts or severe suicidal ideation in the two weeks before baseline assessment were not included in the final analysis. Using a cluster-randomised design, schools were assigned to a control group with minimal intervention or to one of three intervention groups: Youth Aware of Mental Health Programme (YAM), developed for SEYLE, a manualised intervention targeting all students to raise awareness about suicide risk and protective factors, and enhance life skills; Question, Persuade and Refer (QPR)[2], a manualised gatekeeper program which trains school personnel to recognise risk of suicidal behaviour and help students at risk to seek professional care; and screening by Professionals (ProfScreen), developed for the study, which identified students at risk of mental health problems through the baseline questionnaire, and invited these students to receive clinical assessment and referral if necessary.

No suicides were reported during the study. At three months, 3.4% of participants reported either a suicide attempt or severe suicide ideation, and 0.9% reported both; no significant differences were found between the intervention groups and the control group. At the 12-month follow-up, the only intervention associated with a significant reduction of suicidality compared to the control group was YAM: suicide attempts (odds ratio [OR] 0.45, 95% CI 0.24-0.85, $p=0.014$); severe suicidal ideation (0.50, CI 0.27-0.92, $p=0.025$). While the other two interventions were associated with reductions in suicidality at 12 months compared to the control group, these were not significant: QPR suicide attempts (OR 0.70, CI 0.39-1.25, $p=0.229$) and severe suicide ideation (OR 0.95, CI 0.55-1.63, $p=0.858$); ProfScreen suicide attempts (OR 0.65, CI 0.36-1.18, $p=0.158$) and severe suicide ideation (OR 0.71, CI 0.40-1.25, $p=0.234$). Reliance on self-report may have been a limitation of the study; however, the authors did not believe that the YAM training in mental health awareness would affect self-report of suicidality.

Implications: Identification of effective suicide prevention measures is imperative in Australia, given that suicide is the leading cause of death amongst young Australians aged 15 to 24[3]. Although a range of youth suicide prevention activities and programs have been implemented in the past across Australia, a paucity of empirical evidence exists to guide decisions about the most effective types of programs[4]. The evidence generated by the current study is useful as it directly compares the three types of youth suicide interventions for which support has been generated to date[5]. The authors believed that the gatekeeper program in the study may have been hampered by teachers' subjective psychological wellbeing and the tendency of suicidality to be internalised and hidden, and that screening for early detection may be limited by the stigma of mental health issues. Population-based programs in which interventions are delivered to whole populations regardless of individual risk level, such as SEYLE, appear to have the benefit of increasing the likelihood of help-seeking by young people, and reducing stigma about suicidality amongst peers[4]. However, concerns have been expressed that population-based programs which directly target suicidal behaviour may adversely affect young people who are already vulnerable, and may normalise suicidality by minimising the relationship between suicidal behaviour and mental illness[5]. Various Australian schools have incorporated suicide prevention into more general mental health promotion programs, such as MindMatters[6]. While further empirical research into the effectiveness of suicide prevention programs in the Australian context is needed, it should be noted that the most effective way to assess suicide risk is to ask young people sensitively, but directly, about suicidal thoughts and behaviours; research has shown that this approach is not harmful[5].

Endnotes

1. Patton GC, Coffey C, Sawyer SM, Viner RM, Haller DM, Bose K, Vos T, Ferguson J, Mathers CD (2009). Global patterns of mortality in young people: A systematic analysis of population health data. *The Lancet* 374, 881-892.
2. Tompkins TL, Witt J, Abraibesh N (2010). Does a gatekeeper suicide prevention program work in a school setting? Evaluating training outcome and moderators of effectiveness. *Suicide and Life-Threatening Behavior* 40, 506-515.
3. Australian Bureau of Statistics (2015). *3303.0 ABS Causes of Death, Australia, 2013. Underlying causes of death (Australia) Table 1.3.*
4. Robinson J, Cox G, Malone A, Williamson M, Baldwin G, Fletcher K, O'Brien M (2013). A systematic review of school-based interventions aimed at preventing, treating and responding to suicide related behavior in young people. *Crisis* 34, 164-182.
5. Headspace (2011). *Position paper – suicide prevention.* Accessed online: 21 May 2015. http://www.headspace.org.au/media/10063/Suicide%20Position%20Paper.pdf
6. MindMatters (2014). *Mental health and school success.* Accessed online: 21 May 2015. http://www.mindmatters.edu.au/about-mindmatters/what-is-mindmatters

Recommended Readings

Inhibitory control in people who self-injure: Evidence for impairment and enhancement

Allen KJD, Hooley JM (USA)

Psychiatry Research 225, 631-637, 2015

Self-injury is often motivated by the desire to reduce the intensity of negative affect. This suggests that people who self-injure may have difficulty suppressing negative emotions. We sought to determine whether self-injuring individuals exhibit impaired inhibitory control over behavioral expressions of negative emotions, when responding to images containing aversive emotional content. Self-injuring participants and healthy controls completed a Stop Signal Task in which they were asked to judge the valence (positive or negative) of images. Three types of images depicted emotional content (neutral/positive/negative). A fourth type depicted self-cutting. An unpredictable "stop signal" occurred on some trials, indicating that participants should inhibit their responses to images presented on those trials. Compared to controls, self-injuring participants showed poorer inhibition to images depicting negative emotional content. Additionally, they showed enhanced inhibition to self-injury images. In fact, self-injuring participants showed comparable response inhibition to cutting images and positive images, whereas controls showed worse inhibition to cutting images compared to all other types of images. Consistent with the emotion regulation hypothesis of self-injury, people who self-injure showed impaired negative emotional response inhibition. Self-injuring individuals also demonstrated superior control over responses to stimuli related to self-injury, which may have important clinical implications.

The modal suicide decedent did not consume alcohol just prior to the time of death: An analysis with implications for understanding suicidal behavior

Anestis MD, Joiner T, Hanson JE, Gutierrez PM (USA)

Journal of Abnormal Psychology 123, 835-840, 2014

We identified and analyzed a total of 92 studies, representing 167,894 suicide decedents, to determine if there is evidence to support what appears to be a widely held cultural, clinical, and scholarly view that many people who die by suicide had been drinking at the time of death. It was determined that, based on weighted averages, approximately 27% of suicide decedents had above-zero blood alcohol concentrations (BACs) at the time of death. We emphasize that it was not 27% who were intoxicated at the time of death; rather, 27% had above-zero BACs and 73% had BACs of 0.00%. Among studies of suicide decedents, BACs differed as a function of race (higher in non-White individuals). We conclude that the role of alcohol use at the time of death may be less than some assume, and this interpretation can inform clinical practice and theories of suicide. Important unanswered questions are posed which will help refine research in this area going forward.

A modelling tool for policy analysis to support the design of efficient and effective policy responses for complex public health problems

Atkinson J-A, Page A, Wells R, Milat A, Wilson A (Australia)

Implementation Science 10, 26, 2015

Background: In the design of public health policy, a broader understanding of risk factors for disease across the life course, and an increasing awareness of the social determinants of health, has led to the development of more comprehensive, cross-sectoral strategies to tackle complex problems. However, comprehensive strategies may not represent the most efficient or effective approach to reducing disease burden at the population level. Rather, they may act to spread finite resources less intensively over a greater number of programs and initiatives, diluting the potential impact of the investment. While analytic tools are available that use research evidence to help identify and prioritise disease risk factors for public health action, they are inadequate to support more targeted and effective policy responses for complex public health problems.

Discussion: This paper discusses the limitations of analytic tools that are commonly used to support evidence-informed policy decisions for complex problems. It proposes an alternative policy analysis tool which can integrate diverse evidence sources and provide a platform for virtual testing of policy alternatives in order to design solutions that are efficient, effective, and equitable. The case of suicide prevention in Australia is presented to demonstrate the limitations of current tools to adequately inform prevention policy and discusses the utility of the new policy analysis tool. In contrast to popular belief, a systems approach takes a step beyond comprehensive thinking and seeks to identify where best to target public health action and resources for optimal impact. It is concerned primarily with what can be reasonably left out of strategies for prevention and can be used to explore where disinvestment may occur without adversely affecting population health (or equity). Simulation modelling used for policy analysis offers promise in being able to better operationalise research evidence to support decision making for complex problems, improve targeting of public health policy, and offers a foundation for strengthening relationships between policy makers, stakeholders, and researchers.

Change in emergency department providers' beliefs and practices after use of new protocols for suicidal patients

Betz ME, Arias SA, Miller M, Barber C, Espinola JA, Sullivan AF, Manton AP, Miller I, Camargo CA, Boudreaux ED (USA)

Psychiatric Services 66, 625-631, 2015

Objective: The study examined changes in self-reported attitudes and practices related to suicide risk assessment among providers at emergency departments (EDs) during a three-phase quasi-experimental trial involving implementation of ED protocols for suicidal patients.

Methods: A total of 1,289 of 1,828 (71% response rate) eligible providers at eight EDs completed a voluntary, anonymous survey at baseline, after introduction of universal suicide screening, and after introduction of suicide prevention resources (nurses) and a secondary risk assessment tool (physicians).

Results: Among participants, the median age was 40 years old, 64% were female, and there were no demographic differences across study phases; 68% were nurses, and 32% were attending physicians. Between phase 1 and phase 3, increasing proportions of nurses reported screening for suicide (36% and 95%, respectively, p<.001) and increasing proportions of physicians reported further assessment of suicide risk (63% and 80%, respectively, p<.01). Although increasing proportions of providers said universal screening would result in more psychiatric consultations, decreasing proportions said it would slow down clinical care. Increasing proportions of nurses reported often or almost always asking suicidal patients about firearm access (18%-69%, depending on the case), although these numbers remained low relative to ideal practice. Between 35% and 87% of physicians asked about firearms, depending on the case, and these percentages did not change significantly over the study phases.

Conclusions: These findings support the feasibility of implementing universal screening for suicide in EDs, assuming adequate resources, but providers should be educated to ask suicidal patients about firearm access.

Inflammation and lithium: Clues to mechanisms contributing to suicide-linked traits

Beurel E, Jope RS (USA)
Translational Psychiatry 4, e488, 2014

Suicide is one of the leading causes of death in the United States, yet it remains difficult to understand the mechanistic provocations and to intervene therapeutically. Stress is recognized as a frequent precursor to suicide. Psychological stress is well established to cause activation of the inflammatory response, including causing neuroinflammation, an increase of inflammatory molecules in the central nervous system (CNS). Neuroinflammation is increasingly recognized as affecting many aspects of CNS functions and behaviors. In particular, much evidence demonstrates that inflammatory markers are elevated in traits that have been linked to suicidal behavior, including aggression, impulsivity and depression. Lithium is recognized as significantly reducing suicidal behavior, is anti-inflammatory and diminishes aggression, impulsivity and depression traits, each of which is associated with elevated inflammation. The anti-inflammatory effects of lithium result from its inhibition of glycogen synthase kinase-3 (GSK3). GSK3 has been demonstrated to strongly promote inflammation, aggressive behavior in rodents and depression-like behaviors in rodents, whereas regulation of impulsivity by GSK3 has not yet been investigated. Altogether, evidence is building supporting the hypothesis that stress activates GSK3, which in turn promotes inflammation, and that inflammation is linked to behaviors associated with suicide, including particularly aggression, impulsivity and depression. Further investigation of these links may provide a clearer understanding of the causes of suicidal behavior and provide leads for the development of effective preventative interventions, which may include inhibitors of GSK3.

A cross-sectional study of major repeaters: A distinct phenotype of suicidal behavior

Blasco-Fontecilla H, Jaussent I, Olié E, Béziat S, Guillaume S, Artieda-Urrutia P, Baca-Garcia E, De Leon J, Courtet P (France)

Primary Care Companion to CNS Disorders. Published online: 7 August 2014. doi: 10.4088/PCC.14m01633.

Objective: The characterization of major repeaters (individuals with ≥ 5 lifetime suicide attempts) is a neglected area of research. Our aim was to establish whether or not major repeaters are a distinctive suicidal phenotype, taking into account a wide range of potential competing risks including sociodemographic characteristics, personal and familial history, psychiatric diagnoses, and personality traits.

Method: This cross-sectional study included 372 suicide attempters admitted to a specialized unit for suicide attempters in Montpellier University Hospital, Montpellier, France, between October 12, 2000, and June 10, 2010. Logistic regression models controlling for potential confounders were used.

Results: When compared with subjects who attempted suicide < 5 times, major repeaters were more likely to be female (odds ratio [OR]=5.54; 95% CI, 1.41-21.81), to have a lower educational level (OR=5.1; 95% CI, 1.55-17.2), to have lifetime diagnoses of anorexia nervosa (OR=3.45; 95% CI, 1.10-10.84) and substance dependence (OR=5.00; 95% CI, 1.37-18.27), and to have lower levels of anger expressed outward (OR=0.17; 95% CI, 0.06-0.47) and higher levels of trait anger (OR=2.82; 95% CI, 1.18-6.75). Major repeaters had significantly higher suicide risk (lethality) scores (OR=2.14; 95% CI, 1.08-4.23).

Conclusion: Major repeaters are a distinctive suicidal phenotype characterized by a distinctive sociodemographic (ie, female gender, low education) and clinical profile (ie, trait anger, substance dependence, anorexia nervosa). If our results are replicated, specific preventive plans should be tailored to major repeaters.

Associations between the Department of Veterans Affairs' suicide prevention campaign and calls to related crisis lines

Bossarte RM, Karras E, Lu N, Tu X, Stephens B, Draper J, Kemp JE (USA)

Public Health Reports 129, 516-525, 2014

Objective: The Transit Authority Suicide Prevention (TASP) campaign was launched by the Department of Veterans Affairs (VA) in a limited number of U.S. cities to promote the use of crisis lines among veterans of military service.

Methods: We obtained the daily number of calls to the VCL and National Suicide Prevention Lifeline (NSPL) for six implementation cities (where the campaign was active) and four control cities (where there was no TASP campaign messaging) for a 14-month period. To identify changes in call volume associated with campaign implementation, VCL and NSPL daily call counts for three time periods of equal length (pre-campaign, during campaign, and postcampaign) were modeled using a Poisson log-linear regression with inference based on the generalized estimating equations.

Results: Statistically significant increases in calls to both the VCL and the NSPL were reported during the TASP campaign in implementation cities, but were not reported in control cities during or following the campaign. Secondary outcome measures were also reported for the VCL and included the percentage of callers who are veterans, and calls resulting in a rescue during the study period.

Conclusions: Results from this study reveal some promise for suicide prevention messaging to promote the use of telephone crisis services and contribute to an emerging area of research examining the effects of campaigns on help seeking.

Treating prolonged grief disorder: A randomized clinical trial

Bryant RA, Kenny L, Joscelyne A, Rawson N, Maccallum F, Cahill C, Hopwood S, Aderka I, Nickerson A (Australia)
JAMA Psychiatry 71, 1332-1339, 2014

Importance: Prolonged grief disorder (PGD) is a potentially disabling condition that affects approximately 10% of bereaved people. Grief-focused cognitive behavior therapy (CBT) has been shown to be effective in treating PGD. Although treatments for PGD have focused on exposure therapy, much debate remains about whether exposure therapy is optimal for PGD.

Objective: To determine the relative efficacies of CBT with exposure therapy (CBT/exposure) or CBT alone for PGD.

Design, Setting, and Participants: A randomized clinical trial of 80 patients with PGD attending the outpatient University of New South Wales Traumatic Stress Clinic from September 17, 2007, through June 7, 2010.

Interventions: All patients received 10 weekly 2-hour group therapy sessions that consisted of CBT techniques. Patients also received 4 individual sessions, in which they were randomized to receive exposure therapy for memories of the death or supportive counseling.

Main Outcomes and Measures: Measures of PGD by clinical interview and self-reported measures of depression, cognitive appraisals, and functioning at the 6-month follow-up.

Results: Intention-to-treat analyses at follow-up indicated a significant quadratic time x treatment condition interaction effect (B [SE], 0.49 [0.16]; t(120.16)=3.08 [95% CI, 0.18-0.81]; P=.003), indicating that CBT/exposure led to greater PGD reductions than CBT alone. At follow-up, CBT/exposure led to greater reductions in depression (B [SE], 0.35 [0.12]; t(112.65)=2.83 [95% CI, 0.11-0.60]; P=.005), negative appraisals (B [SE], 0.68 [0.25]; t(109.98)=2.66 [95% CI, 0.17-1.18]; P=.009), and functional impairment (B [SE], 0.24 [0.08]; t(111.40)=3.01 [95% CI, 0.08-0.40]; P=.003) than CBT alone. In terms of treatment completers, fewer patients in the CBT/exposure condition at follow-up (14.8%) met criteria for PGD than those in the CBT condition (37.9%) (odds ratio, 3.51; 95% CI, 0.96-12.89; chi(2)=3.81; P=.04).

Conclusions and Relevance: Including exposure therapy that promotes emotional processing of memories of the death is an important component to achieve optimal reductions in PGD severity. Facilitating emotional responses to the death may promote greater changes in appraisals about the loss, which are associated with symptom reduction. Promotion of emotional processing techniques in therapies to treat patients with PGD is needed.

Everyday functioning of male adolescents who later died by suicide: Results of a pilot case-control study using mixed-method analysis

Buhnick-Atzil O, Rubinstein K, Tuval-Mashiach R, Fischer S, Fruchter E, Large M, Weiser M (Israel)
Journal of Affective Disorders 172, 116-120, 2014

Objective: Previous research has shown a link between difficulties in everyday functioning and suicidality in adolescence. The majority of research in this field focuses on suicidal ideation and attempts, rather than on completed suicide. The main goal of this study is to better characterize everyday functioning among young men who later completed suicide. Based on previous literature, we hypothesized that the functioning of adolescents who died by suicide would be poor, compared to controls.

Methods: The current study is a record-driven study, which examined summaries of screening interviews performed by the Israeli Defense Forces (IDF) of 20 male adolescents who later completed suicide, compared with 20 matched living controls. The current study is a pilot stage of a larger project. The study used unique data, collected as part of the IDF pre-induction process, in the months or years before the tragic outcome. The data were extracted by two psychologists, blinded to the participants' suicide or non-suicide outcome, using mixed-method technique, combining qualitative and quantitative analysis.

Results: The main findings indicated that, in comparison with controls, male adolescents who later died by suicide were described as having more interpersonal difficulties, were more likely to be involved in violent behavior, had more difficulties in dealing with problems in everyday functioning and had an avoidant conflict resolution style.

Conclusions: Functional difficulties are apparent in a wide range of behavioral domains in adolescents who later complete suicide. These findings indicate a need for interventions that might assist young persons, and it is possible that such assistance might reduce the likelihood of suicide. However, because suicide is a rare outcome and these behavioral traits are common in adolescence, the presence of such traits might not be useful in identifying people at risk of suicide.

Meta-analysis of the association between suicidal ideation and later suicide among patients with either a schizophrenia spectrum psychosis or a mood disorder

Chapman CL, Mullin K, Ryan CJ, Kuffel A, Nielssen O, Large MM (Australia)
Acta Psychiatrica Scandinavica 131, 162-173, 2015

Objective: Recent studies of patients with a mix of psychiatric diagnoses have suggested a modest or weak association between suicidal ideation and later suicide. The aim of this study was to examine the extent to which the association between expressed suicidal ideation and later suicide varies according to psychiatric diagnosis. *Method:* A systematic meta-analysis of studies that report the association between suicidal ideation and later suicide in patients with 'mood disorders', defined to include major depression, dysthymia and bipolar disorder, or 'schizophrenia spectrum psychosis', defined to include schizophrenia, schizophreniform disorder and delusional disorder.

Results: Suicidal ideation was strongly associated with suicide among patients with schizophrenia spectrum psychosis [14 studies reporting on 567 suicides, OR=6.49, 95% confidence interval (CI) 3.82-11.02]. The association between suicidal ideation and suicide among patients with mood disorders (11 studies reporting on 860 suicides, OR=1.49, 95% CI 0.92-2.42) was not significant. Diagnostic group made a significant contribution to between-study heterogeneity (Q-value=16.2, df=1, P < 0.001) indicating a significant difference in the strength of the associations between suicidal ideation and suicide between the two diagnostic groups. Meta-regression and multiple meta-regression suggested that methodological issues in the primary research did not explain the findings. Suicidal ideation was weakly but significantly associated with suicide among studies of patients with mood disorders over periods of follow-up of <10 years.

Conclusion: Although our findings suggest that the association between suicidal ideation and later suicide is stronger in schizophrenia spectrum psychosis than in mood disorders this result should be interpreted cautiously due to the high degree of between-study heterogeneity and because studies that used stronger methods of reporting had a weaker association between suicidal ideation and suicide.

Late-life homicide-suicide: A national case series in New Zealand

Cheung G, Hatters Friedman S, Sundram F (New Zealand)
Psychogeriatrics. Published online: 3 March 2015. doi: 10.1111/psyg.12120

Homicide-suicide is a rare event, but it has a significant impact on the family and community of the perpetrator and victim(s). The phenomenon of late-life homicide-suicide has not been previously studied in New Zealand, and there is only limited data in the international literature. The aim of this study is to systematically review coroners' records of late-life homicide-suicides in New Zealand. After ethics approval was granted, the Coronial Services of New Zealand was approached to provide records of all closed cases with a suicide verdict (age 65+)

over a five-year period (July 2007-December 2012). Of the 225 suicides, 4 cases of homicide-suicide were identified (an estimated incidence of 0.12 per 100 000 per persons year). All four perpetrators were men; three had been farmers. Their ages ranged from 65 to 82. One case occurred in the context of an underlying psychiatric illness (psychotic depression in bipolar disorder). Firearms were used in three cases. Two cases were categorized as spousal/consortial subtype, one case as filicide-suicide, and one case as siblicide-suicide. The prospect of major social upheaval in the form of losing their homes was present in all four cases. The findings of this case series were consistent with the limited existing literature on homicide-suicide. Age-related biopsychosocial issues were highlighted in this case series of late-life homicide-suicide. Additionally, evaluating firearm licences in high-risk groups may represent a prevention strategy.

Why are suicidal thoughts less prevalent in older age groups? Age differences in the correlates of suicidal thoughts in the English adult psychiatric morbidity survey 2007

Cooper C, Rantell K, Blanchard M, McManus S, Dennis M, Brugha T, Jenkins R, Meltzer H, Bebbington P (UK)

Journal of Affective Disorders 177, 42-48, 2015

Background: Suicidal ideation is more strongly associated with suicidal intent in later life, so risk factors may also differ by age. We investigated whether the relationship between suicidal ideation and established correlates varied by age in a representative population.

Methods: We used data from the 2007 Adult Psychiatric Morbidity Survey of England to assess the relationship between age and suicidal thoughts across 20-year age bands, using logistic regression, adjusted for survey weights. We used mediation analyses to assess the extent to which other factors mediate the relationship between suicidal thoughts and age.

Results: Reports of previous-year suicidal thoughts decreased with age. This was partly explained by (1) lower rates of reported child abuse (in those aged 75+), of depression, and of anxiety symptoms (in those aged 55+), factors all strongly associated with suicidal thoughts, and (2) higher rates of protective factors in people aged 35+, specifically homeownership and cohabitation. Rates of phobias, irritability and compulsions also decreased with age, and the association of these symptoms with suicidal thoughts was particularly strong in the youngest (16-34) age group. People who reported experiencing childhood abuse in all age groups reported more suicidal thoughts, suggesting abuse has lifelong negative effects on suicidal ideation.

Limitations: The response rate was 57%. Older people may be less likely to recall childhood abuse.

Conclusions: Sexual and physical abuse in childhood are associated with suicidal ideas throughout the lifespan, so screening for suicidal ideas in younger and older people should be routine and vigorous, and cover experiences in early life: management may require appropriate psychological interventions.

Help-seeking behaviour following school-based screening for current suicidality among European adolescents

Cotter P, Kaess M, Corcoran P, Parzer P, Brunner R, Keeley H, Carli V, Wasserman C, Hoven C, Sarchiapone M, Apter A, Balazs J, Bobes J, Cosman D, Haring C, Kahn JP, Resch F, Postuvan V, Varnik A, Wasserman D (Ireland)

Social Psychiatry and Psychiatric Epidemiology 50, 973-982, 2015

Purpose: To screen and clinically interview European adolescents reporting current suicidality (suicidal ideation and suicide attempt) and investigate attendance at the clinical interview.

Methods: The Saving and Empowering Young Lives in Europe (SEYLE) Project was carried out in 11 European countries. A baseline questionnaire was completed in school by 12,395 adolescents (mean age 14.9; SD 0.9). Those who screened positive for suicidality (attempting suicide and/or serious suicidal ideation or plans) in the past 2 weeks were invited to a clinical interview with a mental health professional.

Results: Of the 12,395 adolescents, 4.2 % (n=516) screened positive for current suicidality. The prevalence ranged from 1.1 % in Hungary to 7.7 % in Israel (p < 0.001). 37.6 % (n=194) of those who screened positive subsequently attended the clinical interview. Female students were more likely to attend for interview (42.0 % versus 30.6 %, p=0.010). The attendance rate varied considerably across countries, from 5.7 % in Italy to 96.7 % in France (p < 0.001). Improved attendance was associated with using school as the only interview setting (Mean attendance rate, MAR=88 vs. 31 %, p=0.006) and arranging the interview within 1 week of contacting the student (MAR=64 vs. 23 %, p=0.013). The greater the travel time to interview, the lower the attendance rate (Pearson's r=-0.64, p=0.034). Independent of the variation by country, at the individual level, adolescents with more depressive symptoms and a recent suicide attempt more often attended for interview.

Conclusion: A high rate of current suicidality was found amongst European adolescents. However, the majority of these displayed limited help-seeking behaviour. Future studies should investigate ways of making screening programmes and other interventions more acceptable and accessible to young people, especially young males.

Using participatory action research to prevent suicide in Aboriginal and Torres Strait Islander communities

Cox A, Dudgeon P, Holland C, Kelly K, Scrine C, Walker R (Australia)

Australian Journal of Primary Health 20, 345-349, 2014

The National Empowerment Project is an innovative Aboriginal-led community empowerment project that has worked with eight Aboriginal and Torres Strait Islander communities across Australia over the period 2012–13. The aim of the Project was to develop, deliver and evaluate a program to: (1) promote positive social and emotional well-being to increase resilience and reduce the high reported rates of psychological distress and suicide among Aboriginal and Torres Strait Islander people; and (2) empower communities to take action to address the social determinants that contribute to psychological distress, suicide and self-harm. Using a participatory action research approach, the communities were supported to identify the risk factors challenging individuals, families and communities, as well as strategies to strengthen protective factors against these challenges. Data gathered during Stage 1 were used to develop a 12-month program to promote social and emotional well-being and build resilience within each community. A common framework, based on the social and emotional well-being concept, was used to support each community to target community-identified protective factors and strategies to strengthen individual, family and community social and emotional well-being. Strengthening the role of culture is critical to this approach and marks an important difference between Aboriginal and Torres Strait Islander and non-Indigenous mental health promotion and prevention activities, including suicide prevention. It has significant implications for policy makers and service providers and is showing positive impact through the translation of research into practice, for example through the development of a locally run empowerment program that aims to address the social determinants of health and their ongoing negative impact on individuals, families and communities. It also provides a framework in which to develop and strengthen culture, connectedness and foster self-determination, through better-informed policy based on community-level holistic responses and solutions as opposed to an exclusive focus on single-issue deficit approaches.

Psychological distress because of asking about suicidal thoughts: A randomized controlled trial among students

de Beurs DP, Ghoncheh R, Geraedts AS, Kerkhof AJFM (The Netherlands)

Archives of Suicide Research. Published online: 9 March 2015. doi: 10.1080/13811118.2015.1004475

To investigate the effect of the questions from the Beck Scale for Suicide Ideation on psychological well-being among healthy participants.

Methods: A randomized controlled study. 301 participants completed the same four questionnaires on psychopathology. The experimental group additionally answered 21 items of the Beck Scale for Suicide Ideation. The control group answered 19 items on Quality of Life.

Results: The experimental group showed a significant smaller decrease of negative affect compared to the control condition. When analyzing participants with an increase in distress, 80% were part of the experimental group.

Conclusions: For most participants, answering questions about suicide does not affect their mood. A small group of participants did react with some distress to the questions about suicide. As the questions about suicide were administered immediately before the questions about negative affect, the questions about suicide could have worked as a negative mood challenge. Future experimental research should further investigate the effect of questions about suicide among healthy participants, especially on the long term.

Suicidal ideation and suicide attempts among adults with psychotic experiences: Data from the collaborative psychiatric epidemiology surveys

DeVylder JE, Lukens EP, Link BG, Lieberman JA (USA)
JAMA Psychiatry 72, 219-225, 2015

Importance: Suicide is a leading cause of preventable death, especially among individuals with psychotic disorders, and may also be common among nonclinical populations of adults with subthreshold psychotic experiences. Understanding this association has the potential to critically bolster suicide prevention efforts.

Objectives: To examine the association between 12-month suicidality and 12-month psychotic experiences and to test the hypotheses that psychotic experiences are associated with increased prevalence of suicidal ideation and suicide attempts during the concurrent period and with greater severity of suicidal behavior.

Design, Setting and Participants: Cross-sectional survey data were drawn from a large general population-based sample of households in the United States identified through the Collaborative Psychiatric Epidemiology Surveys (2001-2003). Adult household residents (n = 11,716) were selected using a clustered multistage sampling design with oversampling of racial/ethnic minority groups. Logistic regression models were adjusted for potential demographic confounders and co-occurring DSM-IV mental health conditions.

Exposures: Twelve-month psychotic experiences assessed with the Composite International Diagnostic Interview, version 3.0 psychosis screen.

Main Outcomes and Measures: Twelve-month suicidal ideation and suicide attempts.

Results: Respondents reporting psychotic experiences were more likely to report concurrent suicidal ideation (odds ratio [OR], 5.24; 95% CI, 2.85-9.62) and suicide attempts (OR, 9.48; 95% CI, 3.98-22.62). Most respondents with psychotic experiences (mean [SE], 65.2% [4.2%]) met criteria for a DSM-IV depressive, anxiety, or substance use disorder. Among respondents with suicidal ideation, those with psychotic experiences were likely to make an attempt during the con-current 12-month period (OR, 3.49; 95% CI, 1.05-11.58) when adjusting for co-occurring psychiatric disorders. In contrast, depressive (OR, 1.67; 95% CI, 0.62-4.52), anxiety (OR, 1.57; 95% CI, 0.40-6.09), and substance use disorders (OR, 1.64; 95% CI, 0.24-11.17) did not reliably identify those at risk for attempts among respondents with suicidal ideation. The mean (SE) 12-month prevalence of suicide attempts among individuals reporting ideation and psychotic experi-ences and meeting criteria for any psychiatric disorder was 47.4% (10.9%) com-pared with 18.9% (4.8%) among those with just ideation and a disorder. Psychotic experiences were especially prevalent among individuals reporting severe attempts and may account for nearly one-third of attempts with intent to die (population attributable risk, 29.01%) in the United States annually.

Conclusions and Relevance: Assessment of psychotic experiences among individ-uals with suicidal ideation has potential clinical and public health utility in reduc-ing the prevalence of suicide attempts, particularly attempts with intent to die.

Suicide ideation and attempts in children with psychiatric disorders and typical development

Dickerson Mayes S, Calhoun SL, Baweja R, Mahr F (USA)

Crisis 36, 55-60, 2015

Background: Children and adolescents with psychiatric disorders are at increased risk for suicide behavior.

Aims: This is the first study to compare frequencies of suicide ideation and attempts in children and adolescents with specific psychiatric disorders and typical children while controlling for comorbidity and demographics.

Method: Mothers rated the frequency of suicide ideation and attempts in 1,706 children and adolescents with psychiatric disorders and typical development, 6-18 years of age.

Results: For the typical group, 0.5% had suicide behavior (ideation or attempts), versus 24% across the psychiatric groups (bulimia 48%, depression or anxiety dis-order 34%, oppositional defiant disorder 33%, ADHD-combined type 22%, anorexia 22%, autism 18%, intellectual disability 17%, and ADHD-inattentive type 8%). Most alarming, 29% of adolescents with bulimia often or very often had suicide attempts, compared with 0-4% of patients in the other psychiatric groups.

Conclusion: It is important for professionals to routinely screen all children and adolescents who have psychiatric disorders for suicide ideation and attempts and to treat the underlying psychiatric disorders that increase suicide risk.

The impact of patient suicide and sudden death on health care professionals

Draper B, Kõlves K, De Leo D, Snowdon J (Australia)
General Hospital Psychiatry 36, 721-725, 2014

Objective: To compare the professional and personal impact of patient suicide and sudden death on health care professionals (HCPs) and determine factors associated with these impacts.

Method: The sample was derived from a sudden death-controlled psychological autopsy study of suicide. HCPs were identified by deceased's next of kin, by other HCPs, from coroners' files and from medical records. The HCPs were interviewed about their last contact with the deceased and the impact of the death on their lives.

Results: Two hundred eleven HCPs were interviewed following suicide; 92 after sudden death. Suicide deaths were significantly more likely to impact upon the HCP's professional practice [suicide n=79 (37.4%); sudden death n=9 (9.9%); chi(2)=22.06, P<.001] and personal life [suicide deaths n=55 (26.1%); sudden death n=12 (13.0%); chi(2)=5.58, P=.018] than sudden deaths. Using multinomial logistic regression, being female and suicide within a week of the consultation predicted professional and personal impacts; having less than 5 years experience predicted professional impact and receipt of support/counseling predicted personal impact.

Conclusion: Suicide deaths have a greater impact than sudden deaths upon the life of HCPs. Clinical inexperience influences impacts on professional practice and availability of support impacts on personal life.

Impact of a suicide-specific intervention within inpatient psychiatric care: The collaborative assessment and management of suicidality

Ellis TE, Rufino KA, Allen JG, Fowler JC, Jobes DA (USA)
Suicide and Life-Threatening Behavior. Published online: 12 January 2015. doi: 10.1111/sltb.12151

A growing body of literature indicates that suicidal patients differ from other psychiatric patients with respect to specific psychological vulnerabilities and that suicide-specific interventions may offer benefits beyond conventional care. This naturalistic controlled-comparison trial (n=52) examined outcomes of intensive psychiatric hospital treatment (mean length of stay 58.8 days), comparing suicidal patients who received individual therapy from clinicians utilizing the Collaborative Assessment and Management of Suicidality (CAMS) to patients whose individual therapists did not utilize CAMS. Propensity score matching was used to control for potential confounds, including age, sex, treatment unit, and severity of depression and suicidality. Results showed that both groups improved significantly over the course of hospitalization; however, the group receiving CAMS showed significantly greater improvement on measures specific to suicidal ideation and suicidal cognition. Results are discussed in terms of the potential advantages of treating suicide risk with a suicide-specific intervention to make inpatient psychiatric treatment more effective in reducing risk for future suicidal crises.

Relationship of suicide rates to economic variables in Europe: 2000-2011

Fountoulakis KN, Kawohl W, Theodorakis PN, Kerkhof AJ, Navickas A, Hoschl C, Lecic-Tosevski D, Sorel E, Rancans E, Palova E, Juckel G, Isacsson G, Korosec Jagodic H, Botezat-Antonescu I, Warnke I, Rybakowski J, Azorin JM, Cookson J, Waddington J, Pregelj P, Demyttenaere K, Hranov LG, Injac Stevovic L, Pezawas L, Adida M, Figuera ML, Pompili M, Jakovljevi M, Vichi M, Perugi G, Andrasen O, Vukovic O, Mavrogiorgou P, Varnik P, Bech P, Dome P, Winkler P, Salokangas RK, From T, Danileviciute V, Gonda X, Rihmer Z, Forsman Benhalima J, Grady A, Kloster Leadholm AK, Soendergaard S, Nordt C, Lopez-Ibor J (Greece, Switzerland, The Netherlands, Lithuania, Czech Republic, Serbia, USA, Latvia, Slovakia, Germany, Sweden, Slovenia, Romania, Poland)

British Journal of Psychiatry 205, 486-496, 2014

Background: It is unclear whether there is a direct link between economic crises and changes in suicide rates.

Aims: The Lopez-Ibor Foundation launched an initiative to study the possible impact of the economic crisis on European suicide rates.

Method: Data was gathered and analysed from 29 European countries and included the number of deaths by suicide in men and women, the unemployment rate, the gross domestic product (GDP) per capita, the annual economic growth rate and inflation.

Results: There was a strong correlation between suicide rates and all economic indices except GPD per capita in men but only a correlation with unemployment in women. However, the increase in suicide rates occurred several months before the economic crisis emerged.

Conclusions: Overall, this study confirms a general relationship between the economic environment and suicide rates; however, it does not support there being a clear causal relationship between the current economic crisis and an increase in the suicide rate.

Disagreement between self-reported and clinician-ascertained suicidal ideation and its correlation with depression and anxiety severity in patients with major depressive disorder or bipolar disorder

Gao K, Wu R, Wang Z, Ren M, Kemp DE, Chan PK, Conroy CM, Serrano MB, Ganocy SJ, Calabrese JR (USA)

Journal of Psychiatric Research 60, 117-124, 2015

Objectives: To study the disagreement between self-reported suicidal ideation (SR-SI) and clinician-ascertained suicidal ideation (CA-SI) and its correlation with depression and anxiety severity in patients with major depressive disorder (MDD) or bipolar disorder (BPD).

Methods: Routine clinical outpatients were diagnosed with the MINI-STEP-BD version. SR-SI was extracted from the 16 Item Quick Inventory of Depression Symptomatology Self-Report (QIDS-SR-16) item 12. CA-SI was extracted from a modified Suicide Assessment module of the MINI. Depression and anxiety severity were measured with the QIDS-SR-16 and Zung Self-Rating Anxiety Scale. Chi-square, Fisher exact, and bivariate linear logistic regression were used for analyses.

Results: Of 103 patients with MDD, 5.8% endorsed any CA-SI and 22.4% endorsed any SR-SI. Of the 147 patients with BPD, 18.4% endorsed any CA-SI and 35.9% endorsed any SR-SI. The agreement between any SR-SI and any CA-SI was 83.5% for MDD and 83.1% for BPD, with weighted Kappa of 0.30 and 0.43, respectively. QIDS-SR-16 score, female gender, and ≥ 4 year college education were associated with increased risk for disagreement, 15.44 ± 4.52 versus 18.39 ± 3.49 points (p=0.0026), 67% versus 46% (p=0.0783), and 61% versus 29% (p=0.0096). The disagreement was positively correlated to depression severity in both MDD and BPD with a correlation coefficient $R2=0.40$ and 0.79, respectively, but was only positively correlated to anxiety severity in BPD with a $R2=0.46$.

Conclusion: Self-reported questionnaire was more likely to reveal higher frequency and severity of SI than clinician-ascertained, suggesting that a combination of self-reported and clinical-ascertained suicidal risk assessment with measuring depression and anxiety severity may be necessary for suicide prevention.

Acute alcohol use among suicide decedents in 14 US States: Impacts of off-premise and on-premise alcohol outlet density

Giesbrecht N, Huguet N, Ogden L, Kaplan MS, McFarland BH, Caetano R, Conner KR, Nolte KB (USA)
Addiction 110, 300-307, 2015

Aims: To estimate the association between per capita alcohol retail outlet density and blood alcohol concentration (BAC) from 51,547 suicide decedents and to analyse the relationship between alcohol outlet density and socio-demographic characteristics among alcohol positive suicide decedents in the United States by racial/ethnic groups and method of suicide.

Design: Analysis of U.S. data, 2003-11, National Violent Death Reporting System.

Setting: Suicide decedents from 14 U.S. States.

Cases: A total of 51,547 suicide decedents tested for blood alcohol content.

Measurements: Blood alcohol content and levels were derived from coroner/medical examiner reports. Densities of county level on-premises and off-premises alcohol retail outlets were calculated using the 2010 Census.

Findings: Multilevel logistic regression models suggested that higher off-premises alcohol outlet densities were associated with greater proportions of alcohol-related suicides among men — for suicides with alcohol present (BAC>;0; adjusted odds ratio [AOR]= 1.08, 95% confidence interval [CI]= 1.03-1.13). Interactions between outlet density and decedents' characteristics were also tested. There was an interaction between off-premises alcohol availability and American Indian/Alaska Native race (AOR=1.36; 95% CI=1.10-1,69) such that this sub-group had highest BAC positivity. On-premises density was also associated with BAC > 0 (AOR=1.05; 95% CI=1.03-1.11) and BAC ≥ 0.08 (PubMed AOR=1.05; 95% CI=1.02-1.09) among male decedents.

Conclusions: In the US, the density of both on- and off-premises alcohol outlets in a county is positively associated with the alcohol-related suicide rate, especially among American Indians/Alaska Natives.

Suicide attempts in a longitudinal sample of adolescents followed through adulthood: Evidence of escalation

Goldston DB, Daniel SS, Erkanli A, Heilbron N, Doyle O, Weller B, Sapyta J, Mayfield A, Faulkner M (USA)

Journal of Consulting and Clinical Psychology 83, 253-264, 2015

Objectives: This study was designed to examine escalation in repeat suicide attempts from adolescence through adulthood, as predicted by sensitization models (and reflected in increasing intent and lethality with repeat attempts, decreasing amount of time between attempts, and decreasing stress to trigger attempts).

Method: In a prospective study of 180 adolescents followed through adulthood after a psychiatric hospitalization, suicide attempts, and antecedent life events were repeatedly assessed (M=12.6 assessments, SD=5.1) over an average of 13 years 6 months (SD=4 years 5 months). Multivariate logistic, multiple linear, and negative binomial regression models were used to examine patterns over time.

Results: After age 17-18, the majority of suicide attempts were repeat attempts (i.e., made by individuals with prior suicidal behavior). Intent increased both with increasing age, and with number of prior attempts. Medical lethality increased as a function of age but not recurrent attempts. The time between successive suicide attempts decreased as a function of number of attempts. The amount of precipitating life stress was not related to attempts.

Conclusions: Adolescents and young adults show evidence of escalation of recurrent suicidal behavior, with increasing suicidal intent and decreasing time between successive attempts. However, evidence that sensitization processes account for this escalation was inconclusive. Effective prevention programs that reduce the likelihood of individuals attempting suicide for the first time (and entering this cycle of escalation), and relapse prevention interventions that interrupt the cycle of escalating suicidal behavior among individuals who already have made attempts are critically needed.

Paracetamol poisoning in adolescents in an Australian setting: Not quite adults

Graudins A (Australia)
Emergency Medicine Australasia 27, 139-144, 2015

Objective: To describe and compare the characteristics of paracetamol poisoning in adolescent and adult patients.

Method: Descriptive retrospective case series of adolescent (12-17 years) and adult (>18 years) patients presenting to a metropolitan hospital network ED, diagnosed with paracetamol poisoning from October 2009 to September 2013.

Results: There were 220 adolescent (median age 16 years, 47% treated with acetyl-cysteine [NAC]) and 647 adult presentations (median age 27 years, 42% treated with NAC) for paracetamol poisoning in the study period. Adolescent patients were more frequently women (89% vs 76%; odds ratio [OR] 2.4; 95% confidence interval [CI] 1.5-3.8) and ingested similar amounts of paracetamol (18 g) when requiring NAC treatment. Adolescents were more likely to ingest paracetamol as a single agent (53% vs 34%; OR 2.2; 95% CI 1.6-3.0) and less likely to ingest compound paracetamol products than adults (18% vs 29%; OR 0.54; 95% CI 0.36-0.79). Adolescents were less likely to report accidental supratherapeutic ingestion of paracetamol (0.02% vs 10%; OR 0.23; 95% CI 0.09-0.58), or co-ingestion of prescription medications (25% vs 43%; OR 0.4; 95% CI 0.31-0.62). Adolescents had more frequent histamine release reactions to NAC than adults (17% vs 8%; OR 2.3; 95% CI 1.2-4.5). No cases required liver transplantation or resulted in death.

Conclusion: Adolescents ingested comparable amounts of paracetamol to adults, when presenting with deliberate self-poisoning. However, there were significant differences in co-ingested medications and the reason for ingestion of paracetamol. Histamine reactions to NAC were more common in adolescents; however, most were mild. Overall, outcome was favourable in both cohorts.

Mental health treatment patterns among adults with recent suicide attempts in the United States

Han B, Compton WM, Gfroerer J, McKeon R (USA)
American Journal of Public Health 104, 2359-2368, 2014

Obejctives: We examined mental health treatment patterns among adults with suicide attempts in the past 12 months in the United States.

Methods: We examined data from 2000 persons, aged 18 years or older, who participated in the 2008 to 2012 National Survey on Drug Use and Health and who reported attempting suicide in the past 12 months. We applied descriptive analyses and multivariable logistic regression models.

Results: In adults who attempted suicide in the past year, 56.3% received mental health treatment, but half of those who received treatment perceived unmet treatment needs, and of the 43.0% who did not receive mental health treatment, one fourth perceived unmet treatment needs. From 2008 to 2012, the mental health treatment rate among suicide attempters remained unchanged. Factors associated with receipt of mental health treatment varied by perceived unmet treatment need and receipt of medical attention that resulted from a suicide attempt.

Conclusions: Suicide prevention strategies that focus on suicide attempters are needed to increase their access to mental health treatments that meet their needs. To be effective, these strategies need to account for language and cultural differences and barriers to financial and treatment delivery.

Self-reported contacts for mental health problems by rural residents: Predicted service needs, facilitators and barriers

Handley TE, Kay-Lambkin FJ, Inder KJ, Lewin TJ, Attia JR, Fuller J, Perkins D, Coleman C, Weaver N, Kelly BJ (Australia)

BMC Psychiatry 14, 249, 2014

Background: Rural and remote Australians face a range of barriers to mental health care, potentially limiting the extent to which current services and support networks may provide assistance. This paper examines self-reported mental health problems and contacts during the last 12 months, and explores cross-sectional associations between potential facilitators/barriers and professional and non-professional help-seeking, while taking into account expected associations with socio-demographic and health-related factors.

Methods: During the 3-year follow-up of the Australian Rural Mental Health Study (ARMHS) a self-report survey was completed by adult rural residents (N=1,231; 61% female; 77% married; 22% remote location; mean age=59 years), which examined socio-demographic characteristics, current health status factors, predicted service needs, self-reported professional and non-professional contacts for mental health problems in the last 12 months, other aspects of help-seeking, and perceived barriers.

Results: Professional contacts for mental health problems were reported by 18% of the sample (including 14% reporting General Practitioner contacts), while non-professional contacts were reported by 16% (including 14% reporting discussions with family/friends). Perceived barriers to health care fell under the domains of structural (e.g., costs, distance), attitudinal (e.g., stigma concerns, confidentiality), and time commitments. Participants with 12-month mental health problems who reported their needs as met had the highest levels of service use. Hierarchical logistic regressions revealed a dose-response relationship between the level of predicted need and the likelihood of reporting professional and non-professional contacts, together with associations with socio-demographic characteristics (e.g., gender, relationships, and financial circumstances), suicidal ideation, and attitudinal factors, but not geographical remoteness.

Conclusions: Rates of self-reported mental health problems were consistent with baseline findings, including higher rural contact rates with General Practitioners. Structural barriers displayed mixed associations with help-seeking, while attitudinal barriers were consistently associated with lower service contacts. Developing appropriate interventions that address perceptions of mental illness and attitudes towards help-seeking is likely to be vital in optimising treatment access and mental health outcomes in rural areas.

The access study: Zelen randomised controlled trial of a package of care for people presenting to hospital after self-harm

Hatcher S, Sharon C, House A, Collins N, Collings S, Pillai A (New Zealand)
Journal of Psychiatry 206, 229-236, 2015

Background: The problem of people presenting to hospitals with self-harm is important because such presentations are common, there is a clear link to suicide and a high premature mortality. However, the best treatment for this population is unclear.

Aims: To see whether a package of measures, that included regular postcards and problem-solving therapy, improved outcomes at 1 year compared with usual care in people who presented to hospital with self-harm

Method: The design of the study was a Zelen randomised controlled trial. The primary outcome was re-presentation to hospital with self-harm within 12 months of the index episode.

Results: There were no significant differences in the primary outcome and most of the secondary outcomes between the two groups. About half the people offered problem-solving therapy did not receive it, for various reasons.

Conclusions: The package as offered had little effect on the proportion of people re-presenting to hospital with self-harm. The dose of problem-solving therapy may have been too small to have an effect and there was a difficulty engaging participants in active treatment.

Suicide following self-harm: Findings from the multicentre study of self-harm in England, 2000-2012

Hawton K, Bergen H, Cooper J, Turnbull P, Waters K, Ness J, Kapur N (UK)
Journal of Affective Disorders 175C, 147-151, 2015

Background: Self-harm is a key risk factor for suicide and it is important to have contemporary information on the extent of risk.

Methods: Mortality follow-up to 2012 of 40,346 self-harm patients identified in the three centres of the Multicentre Study of Self-harm in England between 2000 and 2010.

Results: Nineteen per cent of deaths during the study period (N=2704) were by suicide, which occurred in 1.6% of patients (2.6% of males and 0.9% of females), during which time the risk was 49 times greater than the general population risk. Overall, 0.5% of individuals died by suicide in the first year, including 0.82% of males and 0.27% of females. While the absolute risk of suicide was greater in males, the risk relative to that in the general population was higher in females.

Risk of suicide increased with age. While self-poisoning had been the most frequent method of self-harm, hanging was the most common method of subsequent suicide, particularly in males. The number of suicides was probably a considerable underestimate as there were also a large number of deaths recorded as accidents, the majority of which were poisonings, these often involving psychotropic drugs.

Limitations: The study was focussed entirely on hospital-presenting self-harm.

Conclusions: The findings underline the importance of prevention initiatives focused on the self-harm population, especially during the initial months following an episode of self-harm. Estimates using suicide and open verdicts may underestimate the true risk of suicide following self-harm; inclusion of accidental poisonings may be warranted in future risk estimates.

General hospital-treated self-poisoning in England and Australia: Comparison of presentation rates, clinical characteristics and aftercare based on sentinel unit data

Hiles S, Bergen H, Hawton K, Lewin T, Whyte I, Carter G (UK, Australia)
Journal of Psychosomatic Research 78, 356-362, 2015

Objective: Hospital-treated deliberate self-poisoning (DSP) is common and the existing national monitoring systems are often deficient. Clinical Practice Guidelines (UK and Australia) recommend universal psychosocial assessment within the general hospital as standard care. We compared presentation rates, patient characteristics, psychosocial assessment and aftercare in UK and Australia.

Methods: We used a cross sectional design, for a ten year study of all DSP presentations identified through sentinel units in Oxford, UK (n=3042) and Newcastle, Australia (n=3492).

Results: Oxford had higher presentation rates for females (standardised rate ratio 2.4: CI 99% 1.9, 3.2) and males (SRR 2.5: CI 99% 1.7, 3.5). Female to male ratio was 1.6:1, 70% presented after-hours, 95% were admitted to a general hospital and co-ingestion of alcohol occurred in a substantial minority (Oxford 24%, Newcastle 32%). Paracetamol, minor tranquilisers and antidepressants were the commonest drug groups ingested, although the overall pattern differed. Psychosocial assessment rates were high (Oxford 80%, Newcastle 93%). Discharge referral for psychiatric inpatient admission (Oxford 8%, Newcastle 28%), discharge to home (Oxford 80%, Newcastle 70%) and absconding (Oxford 11%, Newcastle 2%) differed between the two units.

Conclusions: Oxford has higher age-standardised rates of DSP than Newcastle, although many other characteristics of patients are similar. Services can provide a high level of assessment as recommended in clinical guidelines. There is some variation in after-care. Sentinel service monitoring routine care of DSP patients can provide valuable comparisons between countries.

Geography of suicide in Hong Kong: Spatial patterning, and socioeconomic correlates and inequalities

Hsu C-Y, Chang S-S, Lee EST, Yip PSF (China)
Social Science & Medicine 130, 190-203, 2015

Past urban research on Western nations tends to show high suicide rates in inner city and socioeconomically deprived areas. However, little is known about geographic variations in suicide in non-Western cities. We used Bayesian hierarchical models to estimate smoothed standardised mortality ratios (2005-2010) for suicide in people aged 10 years or above in each geographic unit in Hong Kong at two levels, i.e. large street block (n=1639; median population=1860) and small tertiary planning unit group (n=204; median population=14,850). We further analysed their associations with a range of area socioeconomic characteristics and a deprivation index. The "city centre" of Hong Kong, a generally non-deprived area, showed mostly below average suicide rates. However, there were high rates concentrating in some socioeconomically deprived, densely populated areas, including some inner city areas, across the city. Males had greater geographic variations in rates than females, except the elderly group. The use of smaller geographic units revealed finer detailed suicide distribution than the use of larger units, and showed that suicide rates were associated with indicators of socioeconomic deprivation (population with non-professional jobs and low median household income), and social fragmentation (proportions of unmarried adults and divorced/separated adults), but not with Gini coefficient. Sex/age groups had different associations with suicide rates. Areas in the most deprived quintile had a suicide rate more than two times higher than the least deprived. The association between suicide and deprivation was stronger in males than females and more marked in the younger populations compared to the elderly. The spatial distribution of suicide in Hong Kong showed distinct patterning and a stronger association with income compared to findings from Western countries. Suicide prevention strategies should consider tackling the marked socioeconomic gradient in suicide and high risk in young and middle-aged males living in deprived areas.

Predicting suicide in older adults — a community-based cohort study in Taipei City, Taiwan

Hung GCL, Kwok CL, Yip PS, Gunnell D, Chen YY (Taiwan)

Journal of Affective Disorders 172, 165-170, 2015

Background: Older adults worldwide are at a greater risk of suicide than other age groups. There is a scarcity of prospective studies exploring risk factors for suicide in older people and their discriminative ability to identify future suicide.

Methods: We examined a prospective cohort of senior Taipei City residents between 2005 and 2009 (N=101,764). Cox proportional hazards regression analysis was used to determine significant risk factors and to construct a predictive score. The accuracy of the derived score in the prediction was tested by Receiver Operating Characteristic analysis.

Results: Male sex (Hazard Ratio [HR]=3.41, p<0.001), lower education (HR=3.31, p<0.001) and lower income (HR=2.52, p=0.01) were associated with an increased risk of suicide, as well as depressed mood (HR=1.44, p=0.02; per unit increase in a 4-point scale) and insomnia (HR=1.30, p=0.03; per unit increase in a 4-point scale). The derived prediction score yielded a sensitivity of 0.63 a specificity of 0.73 and an area under curve of 0.73. Removing depressed mood from the prediction model did not significantly alter suicide predictability (P=0.11).

Limitations: The dataset examined did not contain information regarding to important risk factors such as substance misuse and prescribed medications and the measures of mental health were relatively limited.

Conclusion: Prediction of suicide based on factors recorded in a routine health screen of elderly people was unsatisfactory; the strongest predictors were factors that cannot be easily altered. Further understanding of how the socioeconomic condition of seniors contributes to suicide may provide valuable insights for intervention targeting this growing population-at-risk.

Interventions to prevent repeat suicidal behavior in patients admitted to an emergency department for a suicide attempt: A meta-analysis

Inagaki M, Kawashima Y, Kawanishi C, Yonemoto N, Sugimoto T, Furuno T, Ikeshita K, Eto N, Tachikawa H, Shiraishi Y, Yamada M (Japan)

Journal of Affective Disorders 175, 66-78, 2015

Background: A huge number of patients with self-harm and suicide attempt visit emergency departments (EDs). We systematically reviewed studies and examined the effect of interventions to prevent repeat suicidal behavior in patients admitted to EDs for a suicidal attempt.

Method: We searched the databases of MEDLINE, PsychoINFO, CINAHL, and EMBASE through August 2013. Eligible studies were randomized controlled trials assessing the effects on repeat suicidal behavior of interventions initiated in suicidal patients admitted to EDs. Interventions in each trial were classified into groups by consensus. Meta-analyses were performed to determine pooled relative risks (RRs) and 95% confidence intervals (CIs) of repetition of suicide attempt for interventions in each group.

Results: Out of 5390 retrieved articles, 24 trials were included and classified into four groups (11 trials in the Active contact and follow-up, nine in the Psychotherapy, one in the Pharmacotherapy, and three in the Miscellaneous). Active contact and follow-up type interventions were effective in preventing a repeat suicide within 12 months (n=5319; pooled RR=0.83; 95% CI: 0.71 to 0.97). However, the effect at 24 months was not confirmed (n=925; pooled RR=0.98; 95% CI: 0.76-1.22). The effects of the other interventions on preventing a repetition of suicidal behavior remain unclear.

Limitation: Caution is needed regarding the heterogeneity of the effects.

Conclusion: Interventions of active contact and follow-up are recommended to reduce the risk of a repeat suicide attempt at 12 months in patients admitted to EDs with a suicide attempt. However, the long-term effect was not confirmed.

Suicide risk among 1.3 million veterans who were on active duty during the Iraq and Afghanistan wars

Kang HK, Bullman TA, Smolenski DJ, Skopp NA, Gahm GA, Reger MA (USA)
Annals of Epidemiology 25, 96-100, 2015

Purpose: We conducted a retrospective cohort mortality study to determine the post-service suicide risk of recent wartime veterans comparing them with the US general population as well as comparing deployed veterans to nondeployed veterans.

Methods: Veterans were identified from the Defense Manpower Data Center records, and deployment to Iraq or Afghanistan war zone was determined from the Contingency Tracking System. Vital status of 317,581 deployed and 964,493 nondeployed veterans was followed from the time of discharge to December 31, 2009. Underlying causes of death were obtained from the National Death Index Plus.

Results: Based on 9353 deaths (deployed, 1650; nondeployed, 7703), of which 1868 were suicide deaths (351; 1517), both veteran cohorts had 24% to 25% lower mortality risk from all causes combined but had 41% to 61% higher risk of suicide relative to the US general population. However, the suicide risk was not associated with a history of deployment to the war zone. After controlling for age, sex, race, marital status, branch of service, and rank, deployed veterans showed a lower risk of suicide compared with nondeployed veterans (hazard ratio, 0.84; 95% confidence interval, 0.75-0.95). Multiple deployments were not associated with the excess suicide risk among deployed veterans (hazard ratio, 1.00; 95% confidence interval, 0.79-1.28).

Conclusions: Veterans exhibit significantly higher suicide risk compared with the US general population. However, deployment to the Iraq or Afghanistan war, by itself, was not associated with the excess suicide risk.

Suicide after nonfatal self-harm

Karasouli E, Owens D, Latchford G, Kelley R (UK)

Crisis 36, 65-70, 2015

Background: Nonfatal self-harm is the strongest predictor of suicide, with some of the risk factors for subsequent suicide after nonfatal self-harm being similar to those for suicide in general. However, we do not have sufficient information regarding the medical care provided to nonfatal self-harm episodes preceding suicide.

Aims: Our study sought to explore hospital care and predictive characteristics of the risk of suicide after nonfatal self-harm.

Method: Individuals with history of nonfatal self-harm who died by suicide were compared with those who had a nonfatal self-harm episode but did not later die by suicide. Cases were identified by cross-linking data collected through a self-harm monitoring project, 2000-2007, and comprehensive local data on suicides for the same period.

Results: Dying by suicide after nonfatal self-harm was more common for male subjects than for female subjects (OR=3.3, 95% CI=1.7-6.6). Self-injury as the method of nonfatal self-harm was associated with higher risk of subsequent suicide than was self-poisoning (OR=2.0, 95% CI=1.04-3.9). More urgent care at the emergency department (OR=2.7, 95% CI=1.1-6.3) and admission to hospital (OR=2.0, 95% CI=1.0-4.0) at the index episode were related to a heightened risk of suicide.

Conclusion: The findings of our study could help services to form assessment and aftercare policies.

Farmers' contact with health care services prior to suicide: Evidence for the role of general practitioners as an intervention point

Kavalidou K, McPhedran S, De Leo D (Australia)

Australian Journal of Primary Health 21, 102-105, 2015

Suicide in Australian rural communities has received significant attention from researchers, health practitioners and policymakers. Farmers and agricultural workers have been a focus of particular interest, especially in relation to levels of help seeking for mental health concerns. A less explored area, however, is the level of contact that Australian farming and agriculture workers who die by suicide have had with health providers for physical, rather than mental, health conditions. It is often assumed that farmers and agricultural workers have lower levels of contact with health care services than other rural residents, although this assumption has not been well tested. Using data from the Queensland Suicide Register, this paper describes levels of contact with health care providers in the 3 months before death by suicide among men in farming and agriculture occupations and other occupations in rural Queensland. No significant differences were found in farming and agricultural workers' levels of contact with a general practitioner when compared with other rural men in Queensland. The current findings lend weight to the view that rural general practitioners represent an important intervention point for farming and agriculture workers at risk of suicide (whether or not those individuals exhibit accompanying psychiatric illness).

Predicting suicides after psychiatric hospitalization in US army soldiers: The Army Study to Assess Risk and Resilience in Servicemembers (Army STARRS)

Kessler RC, Warner CH, Ivany C, Petukhova MV, Rose S, Bromet EJ, Brown M, III, Cai T, Colpe LJ, Cox KL, Fullerton CS, Gilman SE, Gruber MJ, Heeringa SG, Lewandowski-Romps L, Li J, Millikan-Bell A, Naifeh JA, Nock MK, Rosellini AJ, Sampson NA, Schoenbaum M, Stein MB, Wessely S, Zaslavsky AM, Ursano RJ, Army SC (USA)
JAMA Psychiatry 72, 49-57, 2015

Importance: The US Army experienced a sharp increase in soldier suicides beginning in 2004. Administrative data reveal that among those at highest risk are soldiers in the 12 months after inpatient treatment of a psychiatric disorder.

Objective: To develop an actuarial risk algorithm predicting suicide in the 12 months after US Army soldier inpatient treatment of a psychiatric disorder to target expanded posthospitalization care.

Design, Setting and Participants: There were 53 769 hospitalizations of active duty soldiers from January 1, 2004, through December 31, 2009, with International Classification of Diseases, Ninth Revision, Clinical Modification psychiatric admission diagnoses. Administrative data available before hospital discharge abstracted from a wide range of data systems (sociodemographic, US Army career, criminal justice, and medical or pharmacy) were used to predict suicides in the subsequent 12 months using machine learning methods (regression trees and penalized regressions) designed to evaluate cross-validated linear, nonlinear, and interactive predictive associations.

Main Outcomes and Measures: Suicides of soldiers hospitalized with psychiatric disorders in the 12 months after hospital discharge.

Results: Sixty-eight soldiers died by suicide within 12 months of hospital discharge (12.0% of all US Army suicides), equivalent to 263.9 suicides per 100 000 person-years compared with 18.5 suicides per 100 000 person-years in the total US Army. The strongest predictors included sociodemographics (male sex [odds ratio (OR), 7.9; 95% CI, 1.9-32.6] and late age of enlistment [OR, 1.9; 95% CI, 1.0-3.5]), criminal offenses (verbal violence [OR, 2.2; 95% CI, 1.2-4.0] and weapons possession [OR, 5.6; 95% CI, 1.7-18.3]), prior suicidality [OR, 2.9; 95% CI, 1.7-4.9], aspects of prior psychiatric inpatient and outpatient treatment (eg, number of antidepressant prescriptions filled in the past 12 months [OR, 1.3; 95% CI, 1.1-1.7]), and disorders diagnosed during the focal hospitalizations (eg, non-affective psychosis [OR, 2.9; 95% CI, 1.2-7.0]). A total of 52.9% of posthospitalization suicides occurred after the 5% of hospitalizations with highest predicted suicide risk (3824.1 suicides per 100 000 person-years). These highest-risk hospitalizations also accounted for significantly elevated proportions of several other adverse posthospitalization outcomes (unintentional injury deaths, suicide attempts, and subsequent hospitalizations).

Conclusions and Relevance: The high concentration of risk of suicide and other adverse outcomes might justify targeting expanded posthospitalization interventions to soldiers classified as having highest posthospitalization suicide risk, although final determination requires careful consideration of intervention costs, comparative effectiveness, and possible adverse effects.

Suicide acceptability as a mechanism of suicide clustering in a nationally representative sample of adolescents

Kleiman EM (USA)

Comprehensive Psychiatry 59, 17-20, 2015

Purpose: The goal of the present study was to examine suicide acceptability as a mechanism of suicide clustering in adolescents.

Methods: Data were drawn from The National Annenberg Survey of Youth, a sample of 3302 adolescents aged 14-22 collected between 2002 and 2004.

Results: Results indicated that beliefs of the acceptability of suicide partially mediated the effect of exposure to suicide (defined as knowing someone who attempted or completed suicide) on 1) serious suicidal ideation and 2) suicide planning behaviors.

Conclusions: The present study demonstrated that suicide acceptability is in small part a possible reason why suicides tend to cluster in adolescents. It contributes not only to the knowledge of how the phenomenon of suicide clustering might occur, but more broadly highlights the importance of examining mediators of suicide clustering.

Suicidal ideation and mental health disorders in young school children across Europe

Kovess-Masfety V, Pilowsky DJ, Goelitz D, Kuijpers R, Otten R, Moro MF, Bitfoi A, Koç C, Lesinskiene S, Mihova Z, Hanson G, Fermanian C, Pez O, Carta MG (Italy, Turkey, Romania, Bulgaria, Lithuania, Germany, The Netherlands)

Journal of Affective Disorders 177, 28-35, 2015

Introduction: The aim of this study is to measure the prevalence of suicidal ideation and thoughts of death in elementary school children in a European survey and to determine the associated socio-demographic and clinical factors.

Methods: Data refer to children aged 6-12 (N=7062) from Italy, Turkey, Romania, Bulgaria, Lithuania, Germany, and the Netherlands randomly selected in primary schools. Suicidal thoughts and death ideation were measured using a computerized pictorial diagnostic tool from the Dominic Interactive (DI) completed by the children. The Strengths and Difficulties Questionnaire (SDQ) was administered to teachers and parents along with a socio-demographic questionnaire.

Results: Suicidal ideation was present in 16.96% of the sample (from 9.9 in Italy to 26.84 in Germany), death thoughts by 21.93% (from 7.71% in Italy to 32.78 in Germany). SI and DT were more frequent in single-parent families and large families. Externalizing disorders were strongly correlated with SI and DT after controlling for other factors and this was true for internalizing disorders only when reported by the children.

Conclusion: Recognizing suicidal ideation in young children may be recommended as part of preventive strategies such as screening in the context of the presence of any mental health problems whether externalizing or internalizing.

Number of visits to the emergency department and risk of suicide: A population-based case-control study

Kvaran RB, Gunnarsdottir OS, Kristbjornsdottir A, Valdimarsdottir UA, Rafnsson V (Iceland)
BMC Public Health 15, 227, 2015

Background: The aim was to study whether number of visits to emergency department (ED) is associated with suicide, taking into consideration known risk factors.

Methods: This is a population-based case-control study nested in a cohort. Computerized database on attendees to ED (during 2002-2008) was record linked to nation-wide death registry to identify 152 cases, and randomly selected 1520 controls. The study was confined to patients attending the ED, who were subsequently discharged, and not admitted to hospital ward. Odds ratio (OR) and 95% confidence intervals (CI) of suicide risk according to number of visits (logistic regression) adjusted for age, gender, mental and behavioral disorders, non-causative diagnosis, and drug poisonings.

Results: Suicide cases had on average attended the ED four times, while controls attended twice. The OR for attendance due to mental and behavioral disorders was 3.08 (95% CI 1.61-5.88), 1.60 (95% CI 1.06-2.43) for non-causative diagnosis, and 5.08 (95% CI 1.69-15.25) for poisoning. The ORs increased gradually with increasing number of visits. Adjusted for age, gender, and the above mentioned diagnoses, the OR for three attendances was 2.17, for five attendances 2.60, for seven attendances 5.97, and for nine attendances 12.18 compared with those who had one visit.

Conclusions: Number of visits to the ED is an independent risk factor for suicide adjusted for other known and important risk factors. The prevalence of four or more visits was 40% among cases compared with 10% among controls. This new risk factor may open new venues for suicide prevention.

Dialectical behavior therapy for high suicide risk in individuals with borderline personality disorder: A randomized clinical trial and component analysis

Linehan MM, Korslund KE, Harned MS, Gallop RJ, Lungu A, Neacsiu AD, McDavid J, Comtois KA, Murray-Gregory AM (USA)

JAMA Psychiatry 72, 475-482, 2015

Importance: Dialectical behavior therapy (DBT) is an empirically supported treatment for suicidal individuals. However, DBT consists of multiple components, including individual therapy, skills training, telephone coaching, and a therapist consultation team, and little is known about which components are needed to achieve positive outcomes.

Objective: To evaluate the importance of the skills training component of DBT by comparing skills training plus case management (DBT-S), DBT individual therapy plus activities group (DBT-I), and standard DBT which includes skills training and individual therapy.

Design, Setting and Participants: We performed a single-blind randomized clinical trial from April 24, 2004, through January 26, 2010, involving 1 year of treatment and 1 year of follow-up. Participants included 99 women (mean age, 30.3 years; 69 [71%] white) with borderline personality disorder who had at least 2 suicide attempts and/or nonsuicidal self-injury (NSSI) acts in the last 5 years, an NSSI act or suicide attempt in the 8 weeks before screening, and a suicide attempt in the past year. We used an adaptive randomization procedure to assign participants to each condition. Treatment was delivered from June 3, 2004, through September 29, 2008, in a university-affiliated clinic and community settings by therapists or case managers. Outcomes were evaluated quarterly by blinded assessors. We hypothesized that standard DBT would outperform DBT-S and DBT-I.

Interventions: The study compared standard DBT, DBT-S, and DBT-I. Treatment dose was controlled across conditions, and all treatment providers used the DBT suicide risk assessment and management protocol.

Main Outcomes and Measures: Frequency and severity of suicide attempts and NSSI episodes.

Results: All treatment conditions resulted in similar improvements in the frequency and severity of suicide attempts, suicide ideation, use of crisis services due to suicidality, and reasons for living. Compared with the DBT-I group, interventions that included skills training resulted in greater improvements in the frequency of NSSI acts ($F_{1,85} = 59.1$ [P < .001] for standard DBT and $F_{1,85} = 56.3$ [P < .001] for DBT-S) and depression ($t_{399} = 1.8$ [P = .03] for standard DBT and $t_{399} = 2.9$ [P = .004] for DBT-S) during the treatment year. In addition, anxiety significantly improved during the treatment year in standard DBT ($t_{94} = -3.5$ [P < .001]) and DBT-S ($t_{94} = -2.6$ [P = .01]), but not in DBT-I. Compared with the DBT-I group, the standard DBT group had lower dropout rates from treatment (8 patients [24%] vs 16 patients [48%] [P = .04]), and patients were less likely to use crisis services in follow-up (ED visits, 1 [3%] vs 3 [13%] [P = .02]; psychiatric hospitalizations, 1 [3%] vs 3 [13%] [P = .03]).

Conclusions and Relevance: A variety of DBT interventions with therapists trained in the DBT suicide risk assessment and management protocol are effective for reducing suicide attempts and NSSI episodes. Interventions that include DBT skills training are more effective than DBT without skills training, and standard DBT may be superior in some areas.

Associations of racial/ethnic identities and religious affiliation with suicidal ideation among lesbian, gay, bisexual, and questioning individuals

Lytle MC, De Luca SM, Blosnich JR, Brownson C (USA)
Journal of Affective Disorders 178, 39-45, 2015

Background: Our aim was to examine the associations of racial/ethnic identity and religious affiliation with suicidal ideation among lesbian, gay, bisexual, and questioning (LGBQ) and heterosexual college students. An additional aim was to determine the prevalence of passive suicidal ideation (i.e., death ideation) and active suicidal ideation among culturally diverse LGBQ individuals.

Methods: Data from the National Research Consortium probability-based sample of college students from 70 postsecondary institutions (n=24,626) were used to examine active and passive suicidal ideation in the past 12-months and lifetime active suicidal ideation among students by sexual orientation, racial/ethnic identity, and religious affiliation.

Results: Across most racial/ethnic groups and religious affiliations, LGBQ students were more likely to report active suicidal ideation than non-LGBQ individuals. Among LGBQ students, Latino individuals had lower odds of reporting both past 12-month passive and active suicidal ideation than their non-Hispanic white LGBQ counterparts. Compared to Christian LGBQ students, Agnostic/Atheist LGBQ individuals had greater odds of reporting past 12-month passive suicidal ideation, and Jewish LGBQ students were less likely to endorse past 12-month passive and active suicidal ideation.

Limitations: Cross-sectional design and self-reported data.

Conclusions: Results corroborate previous research showing elevated prevalence of suicidal ideation among LGBQ individuals in comparison to their heterosexual counterparts. These findings are among the first to document prevalence differences within the LGBQ population based on intersectional identities (race/ethnicity and religious affiliation). Providers should recognize that LGBQ individuals might need support in negotiating the complex relationship between multiple identities, especially due to their elevated prevalence of suicidal ideation.

Clinical and social outcomes of adolescent self harm: Population based birth cohort study

Mars B, Heron J, Crane C, Hawton K, Lewis G, Macleod J, Tilling K, Gunnell D (UK)

BMJ 349, g5954, 2015

Objectives: To investigate the mental health, substance use, educational, and occupational outcomes of adolescents who self harm in a general population sample, and to examine whether these outcomes differ according to self reported suicidal intent.

Design: Population based birth cohort study.

Setting: Avon Longitudinal Study of Parents and Children (ALSPAC), a UK birth cohort of children born in 1991-92.

Participants: Data on lifetime history of self harm with and without suicidal intent were available for 4799 respondents who completed a detailed self harm questionnaire at age 16 years. Multiple imputation was used to account for missing data.

Main Outcome Measures: Mental health problems (depression and anxiety disorder), assessed using the clinical interview schedule-revised at age 18 years, self reported substance use (alcohol, cannabis, cigarette smoking, and illicit drugs) at age 18 years, educational attainment at age 16 and 19 years, occupational outcomes at age 19 years, and self harm at age 21 years.

Results: Participants who self harmed with and without suicidal intent at age 16 years were at increased risk of developing mental health problems, future self harm, and problem substance misuse, with stronger associations for suicidal self harm than for non-suicidal self harm. For example, in models adjusted for confounders the odds ratio for depression at age 18 years was 2.21 (95% confidence interval 1.55 to 3.15) in participants who had self harmed without suicidal intent at age 16 years and 3.94 (2.67 to 5.83) in those who had self harmed with suicidal intent. Suicidal self harm, but not self harm without suicidal intent, was also associated with poorer educational and employment outcomes.

Conclusions: Adolescents who self harm seem to be vulnerable to a range of adverse outcomes in early adulthood. Risks were generally stronger in those who had self harmed with suicidal intent, but outcomes were also poor among those who had self harmed without suicidal intent. These findings emphasise the need for early identification and treatment of adolescents who self harm.

Prevalence of suicidal ideation and other suicide warning signs in veterans attending an urgent care psychiatric clinic

McClure JR, Criqui MH, Macera CA, Ji M, Nievergelt CM, Zisook S (USA)

Comprehensive Psychiatry 60, 149-155, 2015

Background: Suicide prevention in the clinical setting is focused on evaluating risk in the coming hours to days, yet little is known about which factors increase acute risk.

Purpose: To determine the prevalence of factors that may serve as warnings of heightened acute risk.

Methods: Veterans attending an urgent care psychiatric clinic (n=473) completed a survey on suicidal ideation and other acute risk warning signs.

Results: More than half the sample (52%) reported suicidal ideation during the prior week. Of these, more than one-third (37%) had active ideation which included participants with a current suicide plan (27%) and those who had made preparations to carry out their plan (12%). Other warning signs were also highly prevalent, with the most common being: sleep disturbances (89%), intense anxiety (76%), intense agitation (75%), hopelessness (70%), and desperation (70%). Almost all participants (97%) endorsed at least one warning sign. Participants with depressive syndrome and/or who screened positive for post-traumatic stress disorder endorsed the largest number of warning signs. Those with both depressive syndrome and post-traumatic stress disorder were more likely to endorse intense affective states than those with either disorder alone. All p-values for group comparisons are <.008.

Conclusion: Our major findings are the strikingly high prevalence of past suicidal ideation, suicide attempts, current suicidal ideation and intense affective states in veterans attending an urgent care psychiatric clinic; and the strong associations between co-occurring post-traumatic stress disorder and depressive syndrome with intense affective states.

Patterns of stressful life events: Distinguishing suicide ideators from suicide attempters

McFeeters D, Boyda D, O'Neill S (UK)

Journal of Affective Disorders 175, 192-198, 2015

Background: Suicidal ideation is an important indicator for subsequent suicidal behaviour, yet only a proportion of ideators transit from thought to action. This has led to interest surrounding the factors that distinguish ideators who attempt from non-attempters. The study aimed to identify distinct classes of life event categories amongst a sample of ideators and assess the ability of the classes to predict the risk of a suicide attempt.

Methods: A subsample of ideators was extracted based on responses to the suicidality section of the Adult Psychiatric Morbidity Survey (N=7403). Fifteen stressful life events (SLEs) were grouped into six broad categories.

Results: Using Latent Class Analysis (LCA), three distinct classes emerged; class 1 had a high probability of encountering interpersonal conflict, class 2 reported a low probability of experiencing any of the SLE categories with the exception of minor life stressors, whereas class 3 had a high probability of endorsing multiple SLE categories. The Odds Ratio for attempted suicide were highest among members of Class 3.

Limitations: The use of broad event categories as opposed to discrete life events may have led to an underestimation of the true exposure to SLEs.

Conclusions: The findings suggest the experience of multiple types of SLEs may predict the risk of transitioning towards suicidal behaviour for those individuals who have contemplated suicide. In application, this re-emphasises the need for a routine appraisal of risk amongst this vulnerable group and an assessment of the variety of events which may signal the individuals who may be at immediate risk.

Suicidal ideation and suicide attempts in five groups with different severities of gambling: Findings from the National Epidemiologic Survey on Alcohol and Related Conditions

Moghaddam JF, Yoon G, Dickerson DL, Kim SW, Westermeyer J (USA)

American Journal on Addictions 24, 292-298, 2015

Background and Objectives: Problem and pathological gamblers show high rates of suicidal behavior. However, previous research of suicide among this population has been inconsistent. Discrepancies may stem from methodological issues, including variable use of suicide nomenclature and selection bias in study samples. Furthermore, earlier research has rarely examined gambling severity aside from problem or pathological categories. This study utilized subgroups derived from a nationally representative data set, examining different characteristics of suicidal behaviors and several gambling levels, including subclinical groups.

Methods: Participants included 13,578 individuals who participated in the National Epidemiologic Survey on Alcohol and Related Conditions (NESARC) and provided information on gambling behavior, lifetime suicidal ideation, and/or lifetime suicide attempts. Five gambling groups were derived using DSM-IV criteria for pathological gambling; non-gambling, low-risk gambling, at-risk gambling, problem gambling, and pathological gambling.

Results: Problem gambling was associated with suicidal ideation [adjusted odds ratio (AOR)=1.64, 95% confidence interval (CI)=1.19-2.26] and suicide attempts [(AOR)=2.42, 95% (CI)=1.60-3.67] after adjustment for sociodemographic variables. Pathological gambling was associated with suicidal ideation [(AOR)=2.86, 95% (CI)=1.98-4.11] and suicide attempts [(AOR)=2.77, 95% (CI)=1.72-4.47) after adjustment for sociodemographic variables.

Discussion, Conclusions, and Scientific Significance: Our results from this population sample reinforce increased rates of suicidal behavior amongst smaller, clinical samples of problem and pathological gamblers. Education for providers about gambling is recommended, including screening for gambling-related symptoms such as suicidal behavior.

Suicide-related internet use: A review

Mok K, Jorm AF, Pirkis J (Australia)

Australian and New Zealand Journal of Psychiatry. Published online: 19 February 2015. doi: 10.1177/0004867415569797

Objective: To systematically review research on how people use the Internet for suicide-related reasons and its influence on users. This review summarises the main findings and conclusions of existing work, the nature of studies that have been conducted, their strengths and limitations, and directions for future research.

Method: An online search was conducted through PsycINFO, PubMed, Ovid MEDLINE and CINAHL databases for papers published between 1991 and 2014. Papers were included if they examined how the Internet was used for suicide-related reasons, the influence of suicide-related Internet use, and if they presented primary data, including case studies of Internet-related suicide attempts and completions.

Results: Findings of significant relationships between suicide-related search trends and rates of suicide suggest that search trends may be useful in monitoring suicide risk in a population. Studies that examine online communications between people who are suicidal can further our understanding of individuals' suicidal experiences. While engaging in suicide-related Internet use was associated with higher levels of suicidal ideation, evidence of its influence on suicidal ideation over time was mixed. There is a lack of studies directly recruiting suicidal Internet users. Only case studies examined the influence of suicide-related Internet use on suicidal behaviours, while no studies assessed the influence of pro-suicide or suicide prevention websites. Online professional services can be useful to suicide prevention and intervention efforts, but require more work in order to demonstrate their efficacy.

Conclusions: Research has shown that individuals use the Internet to search for suicide-related information and to discuss suicide-related problems with one another. However, the causal link between suicide-related Internet use and suicidal thoughts and behaviours is still unclear. More research is needed, particularly involving direct contact with Internet users, in order to understand the impact of both informal and professionally moderated suicide-related Internet use.

Alcohol use and misuse, self-harm and subsequent mortality: An epidemiological and longitudinal study from the multicentre study of self-harm in England

Ness J, Hawton K, Bergen H, Cooper J, Steeg S, Kapur N, Clarke M, Waters K (UK)

Emergency Medicine Journal. Published online: 6 January 2015. doi:10.1136/emermed-2013-202753

Objectives: Alcohol use and misuse are strongly associated with self-harm and increased risk of future self-harm and suicide. The UK general population prevalence of alcohol use, misuse and alcohol-attributable harm has been rising. We have investigated the prevalence of and trends in alcohol use and misuse in self-harm patients and their associations with repeat self-harm and subsequent death.

Methods: We used patient data from the Multicentre Study of Self-Harm in England for 2000-2009 and UK mortality data for patients presenting from 2000 to 2007 who were followed up to the end of 2009.

Results: Alcohol involvement in acts of self-harm (58.4%) and alcohol misuse (36.1%) were somewhat higher than found previously in self-harm patients. Alcohol involvement and misuse were most frequent in men, those aged 35-54 years and those from white ethnicities. The frequency of alcohol misuse increased between 2000 and 2009, especially in women. Repetition of self-harm was associated with alcohol involvement in self-harm and particularly with alcohol misuse. Risk of suicide was increased significantly in women misusing alcohol.

Conclusions: Alcohol use and misuse in self-harm patients appears to have increased in recent years, particularly in women. The association of alcohol with greater risk of self-harm repetition and mortality highlights the need for clinicians to investigate alcohol use in self-harm patients. Ready availability of alcohol treatment staff in general hospitals could facilitate appropriate aftercare and the prevention of adverse outcomes.

The psychology of suicidal behaviour

O'Connor RC, Nock MK (UK)

Lancet Psychiatry 1, 73-85, 2014

The causes of suicidal behaviour are not fully understood; however, this behaviour clearly results from the complex interaction of many factors. Although many risk factors have been identified, they mostly do not account for why people try to end their lives. In this Review, we describe key recent developments in theoretical, clinical, and empirical psychological science about the emergence of suicidal thoughts and behaviours, and emphasise the central importance of psychological factors. Personality and individual differences, cognitive factors, social aspects, and negative life events are key contributors to suicidal behaviour. Most people struggling with suicidal thoughts and behaviours do not receive treatment. Some evidence suggests that different forms of cognitive and behavioural therapies can reduce the risk of suicide reattempt, but hardly any evidence about factors that protect against suicide is available. The development of innovative psychological and psychosocial treatments needs urgent attention.

The co-occurrence of aggression and self-harm: Systematic literature review

O'Donnell O, House A, Waterman M (UK)
Journal of Affective Disorders 175, 325-350, 2015

Background: Epidemiological research supports an association between aggression and self-harm through data on the frequency with which individuals exhibit both behaviours. Unbiased evidence, however, is needed to draw conclusions about the nature and extent of co-occurrence.

Method: Systematic review of published studies was undertaken to evaluate whether or not the frequency with which aggression and self-harm co-occur is beyond that which would be expected by chance. Outcome measures included: (a) between-group differences on a standardised aggression/self-harm measure - the groups defined by scores on a measure of the other behaviour; (b) correlations between the two behaviours; (c) co-occurrence rates in populations defined by the presence of either behaviour; (d) co-occurrence rates in populations not defined by either behaviour. Odds ratios were calculated for studies presenting complete frequency data.

Results: 123 studies, some yielding more than one type of result, met the inclusion criteria. Most case-control studies found elevated levels of aggression in self-harming populations (or self-harm in aggressive populations) compared to controls. The majority of correlational, co-occurrence rate, and odds ratio data found aggression and self-harm to be associated.

Limitations: Results were subject to descriptive synthesis only and thus, unable to report an overall effect size.

Conclusions: Evidence suggests that aggression and self-harm frequently co-occur. Such evidence necessitates more theoretical discussion and associated research on the source and nature of co-occurrence. Nonetheless, individuals who present with one behaviour may be considered an 'at-risk' group in terms of exhibiting the other. Such evidence holds implications for practice (e.g. risk assessment).

Frequency and functions of non-suicidal self-injury: Associations with suicidal thoughts and behaviors

Paul E, Tsypes A, Eidlitz L, Ernhout C, Whitlock J (USA)
Psychiatry Research 225, 276-282, 2015

Previous research has found associations between non-suicidal self-injury (NSSI) and suicidal thoughts and behaviors (STBs), yet the nature of this relationship remains equivocal. The goal of the present study was to examine how lifetime NSSI frequency and individual NSSI functions relate to a history of suicidal ideation, plan, and attempt. Data were collected via a large (N=13,396) web-based survey of university students between the ages of 18 and 29. After demographics and psychiatric conditions were controlled for, we found a positive curvilinear relationship between NSSI frequency and each of the suicide outcomes. When examined among those with STBs, bipolar disorder and problematic substance use remained positively associated with risk for suicide attempt, but not NSSI. Analyses of individual NSSI functions showed differential associations with STBs of varying severity. Specifically, nearly every NSSI function was significantly related to suicide attempt, with functions related to avoiding committing suicide, coping with self-hatred, and feeling generation (anti-dissociation) showing the strongest risks for suicide attempt. From both clinical and research perspectives, these findings suggest the importance of assessing multiple reasons for engaging in self-injury.

Is suicide under the influence of alcohol a deliberate self-harm syndrome? An autopsy study of lethality

Pennel L, Quesada JL, Begue L, Dematteis M (France)

Journal of Affective Disorders 177, 80-85, 2015

Background: Alcohol is a risk factor for suicide and is often involded in violent actions. The aim of the study was to assess the involvement of alcohol in suicides and its relationship with the lethality of suicide methods.

Methods: In a retrospective study on autopsy reports, we compared suicide and non-suicide victims, suicides with positive and negative blood alcohol concentration (BAC), and studied the lethality of suicide methods using a multivariate analysis.

Results: Suicide victims (n=88) were not different to non-suicide victims (n=270) for positive BAC and narcotics, but were more often positive for prescription medications (59.1 vs. 35.6%, p=0.003) and medications in blood (72.7 vs. 54.8%, p=0.004). Whereas non-suicidal victims died mainly of traumas (60%, p<0.001), two populations of suicides emerged with regard to BAC, self-poisoning predominating with positive BAC (38.9%, p=0.039) and asphyxiation with negative BAC (41.4%, p=0.025). Positive BAC appeared as the unique and strong independent predictive factor, increasing the risk of self-poisoning suicide by 4.36 [1.29-14.76], and decreasing the risk of suicidal asphyxiation by 84% (OR=0.16 [0.03-0.83]). Positive blood narcotics tended to behave in the similar way to alcohol.

Limitations: Recruitment bias (victims declared by the Forensic authorities) and incomplete autopsy reports are the two main limitations.

Conclusions: Characteristics of suicide victims with positive BAC are suggestive of Deliberate Self-Harm Syndrome (low lethality methods, substance misuse). These being at high risk of repeated suicide attempts, previous self-harm involving alcohol may represent a warning sign and access to medication should be limited to prevent recidivism.

Effects of suicide bereavement on mental health and suicide risk

Pitman A, Osborn D, King M, Erlangsen A (UK, Denmark)
Lancet Psychiatry 1, 86-94, 2014

Between 48 million and 500 million people are thought to experience suicide bereavement every year. Over the past decade, increased policy attention has been directed towards suicide bereavement, but with little evidence to describe the effect of exposure or to provide appropriate responses. We used a systematic approach to carry out a narrative review of studies of the effect of suicide bereavement on mortality, mental health, and social functioning, and compared them with effects from other bereavements. We found 57 studies that satisfied strict inclusion criteria. Results from these studies suggested that exposure to suicide of a close contact is associated with several negative health and social outcomes, depending on an individual's relationship to the deceased. These effects included an increased risk of suicide in partners bereaved by suicide, increased risk of required admission to psychiatric care for parents bereaved by the suicide of an offspring, increased risk of suicide in mothers bereaved by an adult child's suicide, and increased risk of depression in offspring bereaved by the suicide of a parent. Some evidence was shown for increased rejection and shame in people bereaved by suicide across a range of kinship groups when data were compared with reports of relatives bereaved by other violent deaths. Policy recommendations for support services after suicide bereavement heavily rely on the voluntary sector with little input from psychiatric services to address described risks. Policymakers should consider how to strengthen health and social care resources for people who have been bereaved by suicide to prevent avoidable mortality and distress.

Economic shocks, resilience, and male suicides in the great recession: Cross-national analysis of 20 EU countries

Reeves A, McKee M, Gunnell D, Chang S-S, Basu S, Barr B, Stuckler D (UK, China, USA)
European Journal of Public Health 25, 404-409, 2015

Background: During the 2007-11 recessions in Europe, suicide increases were concentrated in men. Substantial differences across countries and over time remain unexplained. We investigated whether increases in unaffordable housing, household indebtedness or job loss can account for these population differences, as well as potential mitigating effects of alternative forms of social protection.

Methods: Multivariate statistical models were used to evaluate changes in suicide rates in 20 EU countries from 1981-2011. Models adjusted for pre-existing time trends and country-fixed effects. Interaction terms were used to evaluate modifying effects.

Results: Changes in levels of unaffordable housing had no effect on suicide rates (P=0.32); in contrast, male suicide increases were significantly associated with each percentage point rise in male unemployment, by 0.94% (95% CI: 0.51-1.36%), and indebtedness, by 0.54% (95% CI: 0.02-1.06%). Spending on active labour market programmes (ALMP) (-0.26%, 95% CI: -0.08 to -0.45%) and high levels of social capital (-0.048%, 95% CI: -0.0096 to -0.087) moderated the unemployment-suicide association. There was no interaction of the volume of anti-depressant prescriptions (P=0.51), monetary benefits to unemployed persons (P=0.77) or total social protection spending per capita (P=0.37). Active labour market programmes and social capital were estimated to have prevented ~540 and ~210 male suicides, respectively, arising from unemployment in the countries studied.

Conclusion: Job losses were a critical determinant of variations in male suicide risks in Europe's recessions. Greater spending on ALMP and levels of social capital appeared to mitigate suicide risks.

Service use and unmet needs in youth suicide: A study of trajectories

Renaud J, Séguin M, Lesage AD, Marquette C, Choo B, Turecki G (Canada)
Canadian Journal of Psychiatry 59, 523-530, 2014

Objective: While 90% of suicide victims have suffered from mental health disorders, less than one-half are in contact with a mental health professional in the year preceding their death. Service use in the last year of life of young suicide victims and control subjects was studied in Quebec. We wanted to determine what kinds of health care services were needed and if they were actually received by suicide victims.

Method: We recruited 67 consecutive suicide victims and 56 matched living control subjects (aged 25 years and younger). We evaluated subjects' psychopathological profile and determined which services would have been indicated by conducting a needs assessment. We then compared this with what services were actually received.

Results: Suicide victims were more likely than living control subjects to have a psychiatric diagnosis. They were most in need of services to address substance use disorder, depression, interpersonal distress, and suicide-related problems. There were significant deficits in the domains of coordination and continuity of care, mental health promotion and training, and governance.

Conclusions: Our results show that we need to urgently take action to address these identified deficits to prevent further loss of life in our young people.

Social media and suicide prevention: A systematic review

Robinson J, Cox G, Bailey E, Hetrick S, Rodrigues M, Fisher S, Herrman H (Australia)
Early Intervention in Psychiatry. Published online: 19 February 2015. doi: 10.1111/eip.12229

Aim: Social media platforms are commonly used for the expression of suicidal thoughts and feelings, particularly by young people. Despite this, little is known about the ways in which social media can be used for suicide prevention. The aim of this study was to conduct a systematic review to identify current evidence pertaining to the ways in which social media are currently used as a tool for suicide prevention.

Methods: Medline, PsycInfo, Embase, CINHAL and the Cochrane Library were searched for articles published between 1991 and April 2014. English language articles with a focus on suicide-related behaviour and social media were included. No exclusion was placed on study design.

Results: Thirty studies were included; 4 described the development of social media sites designed for suicide prevention, 6 examined the potential of social media in terms of its ability to reach or identify people at risk of suicide, 15 examined the ways in which people used social media for suicide prevention-related purposes, and 5 examined the experiences of people who had used social media sites for suicide prevention purposes. No intervention studies were identified.

Conclusion: Social media platforms can reach large numbers of otherwise hard-to-engage individuals, may allow others to intervene following an expression of suicidal ideation online, and provide an anonymous, accessible and non-judgmental forum for sharing experiences. Challenges include difficulties controlling user behaviour and accurately assessing risk, issues relating to privacy and confidentiality and the possibility of contagion. Social media appears to hold significant potential for suicide prevention; however, additional research into its safety and efficacy is required.

Confronting death from drug self-intoxication (DDSI): Prevention through a better definition

Rockett IR, Smith GS, Caine ED, Kapusta ND, Hanzlick RL, Larkin GL, Naylor CP, Nolte KB, Miller TR, Putnam SL, De Leo D, Kleinig J, Stack S, Todd KH, Fraser DW (USA, Austria, New Zealand, Australia)

American Journal of Public Health 104, e49-e55, 2014

Suicide and other self-directed violence deaths are likely grossly underestimated, reflecting inappropriate classification of many drug intoxication deaths as accidents or unintentional and heterogeneous ascertainment and coding practices across states. As the tide of prescription and illicit drug-poisoning deaths is rising, public health and research needs would be better satisfied by considering most of these deaths a result of self-intoxication. Epidemiologists and prevention scientists could design better intervention strategies by focusing on premorbid behavior. We propose incorporating deaths from drug self-intoxication and investigations of all poisoning deaths into the National Violent Death Reporting System, which contains misclassified homicides and undetermined intent deaths, to facilitate efforts to comprehend and reverse the surging rate of drug intoxication fatalities.

Help-seeking behaviour and adolescent self-harm: A systematic review

Rowe SL, French RS, Henderson C, Ougrin D, Slade M, Moran P (UK)

Australian and New Zealand Journal of Psychiatry 48, 1083-1095, 2014

Objective: Self-harm is common in adolescence, but most young people who self-harm do not seek professional help. The aim of this literature review was to determine (a) the sources of support adolescents who self-harm access if they seek help, and (b) the barriers and facilitators to help-seeking for adolescents who self-harm.

Method: Using a pre-defined search strategy we searched databases for terms related to self-harm, adolescents and help-seeking. Studies were included in the review if participants were aged 11-19 years.

Results: Twenty articles met criteria for inclusion. Between a third and one half of adolescents who self-harm do not seek help for this behaviour. Of those who seek help, results showed adolescents primarily turned to friends and family for support. The Internet may be more commonly used as a tool for self-disclosure rather than asking for help. Barriers to help-seeking included fear of negative reactions from others including stigmatisation, fear of confidentiality being breached and fear of being seen as 'attention-seeking'. Few facilitators of help-seeking were identified.

Conclusions: Of the small proportion of adolescents who seek help for their self-harm, informal sources are the most likely support systems accessed. Interpersonal barriers and a lack of knowledge about where to go for help may impede help-seeking. Future research should address the lack of knowledge regarding the facilitators of help-seeking behaviour in order to improve the ability of services to engage with this vulnerable group of young people.

Brief cognitive-behavioral therapy effects on post-treatment suicide attempts in a military sample: Results of a randomized clinical trial with 2-year follow-up

Rudd MD, Bryan CJ, Wertenberger EG, Peterson AL, Young-McCaughan S, Mintz J, Williams SR, Arne KA, Breitbach J, Delano K, Wilkinson E, Bruce TO (USA)
The American Journal of Psychiatry 172, 441-449, 2015

Objective: The authors evaluated the effectiveness of brief cognitive-behavioral therapy (CBT) for the prevention of suicide attempts in military personnel.

Method: In a randomized controlled trial, active-duty Army soldiers at Fort Carson, Colo., who either attempted suicide or experienced suicidal ideation with intent, were randomly assigned to treatment as usual (N=76) or treatment as usual plus brief CBT (N=76). Assessment of incidence of suicide attempts during the follow-up period was conducted with the Suicide Attempt Self-Injury Interview. Inclusion criteria were the presence of suicidal ideation with intent to die during the past week and/or a suicide attempt within the past month. Soldiers were excluded if they had a medical or psychiatric condition that would prevent informed consent or participation in outpatient treatment, such as active psychosis or mania. To determine treatment efficacy with regard to incidence and time to suicide attempt, survival curve analyses were conducted. Differences in psychiatric symptoms were evaluated using longitudinal random-effects models.

Results: From baseline to the 24-month follow-up assessment, eight participants in brief CBT (13.8%) and 18 participants in treatment as usual (40.2%) made at least one suicide attempt (hazard ratio=0.38, 95% CI=0.16-0.87, number needed to treat=3.88), suggesting that soldiers in brief CBT were approximately 60% less likely to make a suicide attempt during follow-up than soldiers in treatment as usual. There were no between-group differences in severity of psychiatric symptoms.

Conclusions: Brief CBT was effective in preventing follow-up suicide attempts among active-duty military service members with current suicidal ideation and/or a recent suicide attempt.

Evaluating the implementation of "Managing the Risk of Suicide: A Suicide Prevention Strategy for the ACT 2009-2014": A whole-of-government/whole-of-community suicide prevention strategy

Sheehan J, Griffiths K, Rickwood D, Carron-Arthur B (Australia)

Crisis 36, 4-12, 2015

Background: Over the past two decades, governments have invested significantly in policies and strategies to prevent the tragic loss of life to suicide. However, there has been little focus on evaluating the implementation of such policies.

Aims: This paper reports on the evaluation of the implementation of "Managing the Risk of Suicide: A Suicide Prevention Strategy for the ACT 2009-2014," the Australian Capital Territory's (ACT) suicide prevention strategy. We sought to answer two questions: (1) Could agencies provide data reporting on their progress in implementing the activities for which they were responsible?; and (2) Could a judgment about implementation progress be made and, if so, to what extent was the activity implemented?

Method: Individually tailored electronic surveys were sent to 18 ACT agencies annually over 4 years to measure their progress in implementing activities for which they had responsibility.

Results: By year four, full data were provided for 64% of activities, maximal partial data for 9%, and minimal partial data for 27%. Forty-two per cent of activities were fully implemented, 20% were partially implemented, and 38% were not implemented or could not be measured.

Conclusion: It is possible to measure implementation of suicide prevention strategies, but appropriate processes and dedicated resources must be in place at the outset.

Suicide in children: A systematic review

Soole R, Kolves K, De Leo D (Australia)

Archives of Suicide Research. Published online: 17 December 2014. doi: 10.1080/13811118.2014.996694

Objectives: To provide a review of studies on suicide in children aged 14 years and younger.

Method: Articles were identified through a systematic search of Scopus, MEDLINE and PsychINFO. Key words were "children, suicide, psychological autopsy and case-study". Additional articles were identified through manual search of reference lists and discussion with colleagues.

Results: Fifteen published articles were identified, eight psychological autopsy studies (PA) and seven retrospective case-study series.

Conclusion: Suicide incidence and gender asymmetry increases with age. Hanging is the most frequent method. Lower rates of psychopathology are evident among child suicides compared to adolescents. Previous suicide attempts were an important risk factor. Children were less likely to consume alcohol prior to suicide. Parent-child conflicts were the most common precipitant.

Understanding the elevated suicide risk of female soldiers during deployments

Street AE, Gilman SE, Rosellini AJ, Stein MB, Bromet EJ, Cox KL, Colpe LJ, Fullerton CS, Gruber MJ, Heeringa SG, Lewandowski-Romps L, Little RJA, Naifeh JA, Nock MK, Sampson NA, Schoenbaum M, Ursano RJ, Zaslavsky AM, Kessler RC (USA)

Psychological Medicine 45, 717-726, 2015

Background: The Army Study to Assess Risk and Resilience in Servicemembers (Army STARRS) has found that the proportional elevation in the US Army enlisted soldier suicide rate during deployment (compared with the never-deployed or previously deployed) is significantly higher among women than men, raising the possibility of gender differences in the adverse psychological effects of deployment.

Method: Person-month survival models based on a consolidated administrative database for active duty enlisted Regular Army soldiers in 2004-2009 (n=975057) were used to characterize the gender*deployment interaction predicting suicide. Four explanatory hypotheses were explored involving the proportion of females in each soldier's occupation, the proportion of same-gender soldiers in each soldier's unit, whether the soldier reported sexual assault victimization in the previous 12 months, and the soldier's pre-deployment history of treated mental/behavioral disorders.

Results: The suicide rate of currently deployed women (14.0/100000 person-years) was 3.1-3.5 times the rates of other (i.e. never-deployed/previously deployed) women. The suicide rate of currently deployed men (22.6/100000 person-years) was 0.9-1.2 times the rates of other men. The adjusted (for time trends, sociodemographics, and Army career variables) female:male odds ratio comparing the suicide rates of currently deployed v. other women v. men was 2.8 (95% confidence interval 1.1-6.8), became 2.4 after excluding soldiers with Direct Combat Arms occupations, and remained elevated (in the range 1.9-2.8) after adjusting for the hypothesized explanatory variables.

Conclusions: These results are valuable in excluding otherwise plausible hypotheses for the elevated suicide rate of deployed women and point to the importance of expanding future research on the psychological challenges of deployment for women.

Are people at risk of psychosis also at risk of suicide and self-harm? A systematic review and meta-analysis

Taylor PJ, Hutton P, Wood L (UK)

Psychological Medicine 45, 911-926, 2015

Background: Suicide and self-harm are prevalent in individuals diagnosed with psychotic disorders. However, less is known about the level of self-injurious thinking and behaviour in those individuals deemed to be at ultra-high risk (UHR) of developing psychosis, despite growing clinical interest in this population. This review provides a synthesis of the extant literature concerning the prevalence of self-harm and suicidality in the UHR population, and the predictors and correlates associated with these events.

Method: A search of electronic databases was undertaken by two independent reviewers. A meta-analysis of prevalence was undertaken for self-harm, suicidal ideation and behaviour. A narrative review was also undertaken of analyses examining predictors and correlates of self-harm and suicidality.

Results: Twenty-one eligible studies were identified. The meta-analyses suggested a high prevalence of recent suicidal ideation (66%), lifetime self-harm (49%) and lifetime suicide attempts (18%). Co-morbid psychiatric problems, mood variability and a family history of psychiatric problems were among the factors associated with self-harm and suicide risk.

Conclusions: Results suggest that self-harm and suicidality are highly prevalent in the UHR population, with rates similar to those observed in samples with diagnosed psychotic disorders. Appropriate monitoring and managing of suicide risk will be important for services working with the UHR population. Further research in this area is urgently needed considering the high rates identified.

Age-specific suicide mortality following non-fatal self-harm: National cohort study in Sweden

Tidemalm D, Beckman K, Dahlin M, Vaez M, Lichtenstein P, Langstrom N, Runeson B (Sweden)

Psychological Medicine 45, 1699-1707, 2015

Background: Possible age-related differences in risk of completed suicide following non-fatal self-harm remain unexplored. We examined associations between self-harm and completed suicide across age groups of self-harming patients, and whether these associations varied by violent index method, presence of mental disorder, and repeated self-harm.

Method: The design was a cohort study with linked national registers in Sweden. The study population comprised individuals aged 10 years hospitalized during 1990-1999 due to non-fatal self-harm (n=53 843; 58% females) who were followed for 9-19 years. We computed hazard ratios (HRs) across age groups (age at index self-harm episode), with time to completed suicide as outcome.

Results: The 1-year HR for suicide among younger males (10-19 years) was 14.6

[95% confidence interval (CI) 4.1-51.9] for violent method and 8.4 (95% CI 1.8-40.0) for mental disorder. By contrast, none of the three potential risk factors increased the 1-year risks in the youngest females. Among patients aged 20 years, the 1-year HR for violent method was 4.6 (95% CI 3.8-5.4) for males and 10.4 (95% CI 8.3-13.0) for females. HRs for repeated self-harm during years 2-9 of follow-up were higher in 10- to 19-year-olds (males: HR 4.0, 95% CI 2.0-7.8; females: HR 3.7, 95% CI 2.1-6.5). The 20 years age groups had higher HRs than the youngest, particularly for females and especially within 1 year.

Conclusions: Violent method and mental disorder increase the 1-year suicide risk in young male self-harm patients. Further, violent method increases suicide risk within 1 year in all age and gender groups except the youngest females. Repeated self-harm may increase the long-term risk more in young patients. These aspects should be accounted for in clinical suicide risk assessment.

Suicide in U.S. workplaces, 2003-2010: A comparison with non-workplace suicides

Tiesman HM, Konda S, Hartley D, Menéndez CC, Ridenour M, Hendricks S (USA)
American Journal of Preventive Medicine 48, 674–682, 2015

Introduction: Suicide rates have risen considerably in recent years. National workplace suicide trends have not been well documented. The aim of this study is to describe suicides occurring in U.S. workplaces and compare them to suicides occurring outside of the workplace between 2003 and 2010.

Methods: Suicide data originated from the Census of Fatal Occupational Injury database and the Web-Based Injury Statistics Query and Reporting System. Suicide rates were calculated using denominators from the 2013 Current Population Survey and 2000 U.S. population census. Suicide rates were compared among demographic groups with rate ratios and 95% CIs. Suicide rates were calculated and compared among occupations. Linear regression, adjusting for serial correlation, was used to analyze temporal trends. Analyses were conducted in 2013-2014.

Results: Between 2003 and 2010, a total of 1,719 people died by suicide in the workplace. Workplace suicide rates generally decreased until 2007 and then sharply increased (p=0.035). This is in contrast with non-workplace suicides, which increased over the study period (p=0.025). Workplace suicide rates were highest for men (2.7 per 1,000,000); workers aged 65-74 years (2.4 per 1,000,000); those in protective service occupations (5.3 per 1,000,000); and those in farming, fishing, and forestry (5.1 per 1,000,000).

Conclusions: The upward trend of suicides in the workplace underscores the need for additional research to understand occupation-specific risk factors and develop evidence-based programs that can be implemented in the workplace.

The molecular bases of the suicidal brain

Turecki (Canada)

Nature Reviews Neuroscience 15, 802-816, 2014

Suicide ranks among the leading causes of death around the world and takes a heavy emotional and public health toll on most societies. Both distal and proximal factors contribute to suicidal behaviour. Distal factors - such as familial and genetic predisposition, as well as early-life adversity - increase the lifetime risk of suicide. They alter responses to stress and other processes through epigenetic modification of genes and associated changes in gene expression, and through the regulation of emotional and behavioural traits. Proximal factors are associated with the precipitation of a suicidal event and include alterations in key neurotransmitter systems, inflammatory changes and glial dysfunction in the brain. This review explores the key molecular changes that are associated with suicidality and discusses some promising avenues for future research.

The neurobiology of suicide

van Heeringen K, Mann JJ (Belgium, USA)

Psychiatry 1, 63-72, 2014

The stress-diathesis model posits that suicide is the result of an interaction between state-dependent (environmental) stressors and a trait-like diathesis or susceptibility to suicidal behaviour, independent of psychiatric disorders. Findings from post-mortem studies of the brain and from genomic and in-vivo neuroimaging studies indicate a biological basis for this diathesis, indicating the importance of neurobiological screening and interventions, in addition to cognitive and mood interventions, in the prevention of suicide. Early-life adversity and epigenetic mechanisms might explain some of the link between suicide risk and brain circuitry and neurochemistry abnormalities. Results from a range of studies using diverse designs and post-mortem and in-vivo techniques show impairments of the serotonin neurotransmitter system and the hypothalamic-pituitary-adrenal axis stress-response system in the diathesis for suicidal behaviour. These impairments manifest as impaired cognitive control of mood, pessimism, reactive aggressive traits, impaired problem solving, over-reactivity to negative social signs, excessive emotional pain, and suicidal ideation, leading to suicidal behaviour. Biomarkers related to the diathesis might help to inform risk-assessment procedures and treatment choice in the prevention of suicide.

Factors associated with suicide in the month following contact with different types of health services in Quebec

Vasiliadis HM, Ngamini-Ngui A, Lesage A (Canada)
Psychiatric Services 66, 121-126, 2015

Objective: The aim of the study was to identify factors associated with suicide death occurring in the month following an outpatient visit, emergency room contact, or hospitalization.

Methods: The results of this study are based on data for 8,851 individuals ages 11 years and older who died between January 1, 2000, and December 15, 2007, and whose death was confirmed as suicide by the coroner's office in Quebec, Canada. Health service use in the year prior to death was assessed by review of data from the province's public health insurance agency. Multivariate logistic regression models were used to assess the association of clinical and sociodemographic factors and the occurrence of suicide death in the month following versus more than one month after the last use of health services.

Results: A total of 81.6% of suicide decedents had consulted on an outpatient basis, 48.7% had visited an emergency department, and 28.5% were hospitalized in the year prior to death. Among individuals who had been discharged from an emergency department or a hospital closest to their death, 29.5% and 75.3%, respectively, died in the month following discharge. The most consistent modifiable factor associated with death in the month following last contact was number of outpatient consultations following discharge.

Conclusions: Ensuring follow-up care after an emergency department visit or hospitalization may be associated with a longer period between discharge and suicide, allowing for more time to intervene and, possibly, prevent suicide.

Meta-analysis of suicide rates among psychiatric in-patients

Walsh G, Sara G, Ryan CJ, Large M (Australia)
Acta Psychiatrica Scandinavica 131, 174-184, 2015

Objective: To examine factors associated with the number of psychiatric admissions per in-patient suicide and the suicide rate per 100 000 in-patient years in psychiatric hospitals.

Method: Random-effects meta-analysis was used to calculate pooled estimates, and meta-regression was used to examine between-sample heterogeneity.

Results: Forty-four studies published between 1945 and 2013 reported a total of 7552 in-patient suicides. The pooled estimate of the number of admissions per suicide calculated using 39 studies reporting 150 independent samples was 676 (95% CI: 604-755). Recent studies tended to report higher numbers of admissions per suicide than earlier studies. The pooled estimate of suicide rates per 100 000 in-patient years calculated using 27 studies reporting 95 independent samples was 147 (95% CI: 138-156). Rates of suicide per 100 000 in-patient years tended to be higher in more recent samples, in samples from regions with a higher whole of population suicide rate, in samples from settings with a shorter average length of hospital stay and in studies using coronial records to define suicide.

Conclusion: Rates of in-patient suicide in psychiatric hospitals vary remarkably and are disturbingly high. Further research might clarify the extent to which patient factors and the characteristics of in-patient facilities contribute to the unacceptable mortality in psychiatric hospitals.

Sick-leave measures, socio-demographic factors and health care as risk indicators for suicidal behavior in patients with depressive disorders — a nationwide prospective cohort study in Sweden

Wang M, Alexanderson K, Runeson B, Mittendorfer-Rutz E (Sweden)
Journal of Affective Disorders 173, 201-210, 2015

Background: Studies based on large data sets investigating a wide range of risk indicators on suicidal behavior in patients with depressive disorders are sparse. This study aimed to examine the association of sick-leave measured in different ways on one hand and socio-demographics, medication, and health care on the other hand with suicide attempt and suicide among patients with depressive disorders.

Methods: This is a population-based prospective cohort study using nationwide register data. All individuals who lived in Sweden 31.12.2004, then aged 16-64 years, and had psychiatric in- or out-patient care due to depressive disorders in 2005 were included (N=21,096). Univariate and multivariate hazard ratios (HR) and 95% Confidence Intervals (CI) with regard to suicide attempt and suicide during 2006-2010 were estimated by Cox regression.

Results: Those with new sick-leave spells, full-time spells, spells due to mental diagnoses and exceeding one year and those having ≥1 sick-leave spells had a higher risk of suicide attempt. Female sex, young age, lower education, living alone, prescription of antidepressants and anxiolytics, inpatient health care, and suicide attempts resulted in higher HRs of suicide attempt in the multivariate analyses (range of HRs 1.17-3.28). Male sex, combined antidepressant and anxiolytic prescription, mental inpatient health care, and suicide attempts predicted subsequent suicide (range of HRs 1.84-3.33).

Limitations: Focus on specialized health care limited generalization.

Conclusions: Sickness absence, social-demographics, and medical determinants were associated with suicidal behavior. These risk indicators should be considered when monitoring individuals with depressive disorders and assessing suicide risk.

The roles of culture and gender in the relationship between divorce and suicide risk: A meta-analysis

Yip PSF, Yousuf S, Chan CH, Yung T, Wu KCC (Hong Kong, Taiwan)
Social Science and Medicine 128, 87-94, 2015

With some exceptions, literature has consistently shown that divorced populations are at higher risk for suicide than married ones. Here we make use of coefficients of aggravation (COAs), suicide rate ratios of the divorcees over the married, to study patterns of COAs and test the contribution of international sociocultural factors and gender to the relationship between divorce and suicide. We conducted a systematic search of electronic databases to identify ecological studies reporting suicide rates and ratios of those rates within different marital statuses between Jan 1, 2000 and Dec 31, 2013. In total, ten studies consisting in suicide statistics of eleven countries/areas were selected. Using random-effect modeling, we noted that the pooled COA for men and women were 3.49 (95% CI 2.43-4.56) and 3.15 (95% CI 1.74-4.56), suggesting both divorced men and women exhibited a greater risk of suicide than their married counterparts. Subgroup analyses revealed that COAs in Asian countries are significantly higher than those in non-Asian ones. Among the sociocultural measures retrieved from the HOFSTEDE index and the World Values Surveys, we noted significant associations between COA and four measures, including the individualism-collectivism score, the long-term orientation scores, the survival/self-expression score, and the gender inequality indices. The magnitudes and the directions of the associations however differ by sex. The results confirm that overall divorced people have an aggregate higher suicide risk than married ones. The method used in our research could reveal what cultural indicators are exerting effect on the relationship between divorce and suicide risk, which might change with sociocultural transition. More investigation into the relationships and then the construction of culturally appropriate suicide prevention policy is recommended.

Citation List

FATAL SUICIDAL BEHAVIOR

Epidemiology

Ahmadi M, Ranjbaran H, Azadbakht M, Heidari Gorji M, Heidari Gorji A (2014). A survey of characteristics of self-immolation in the northern Iran. *Annals of Medical and Health Sciences Research* 4, S228-232.

Armitage CJ, Panagioti M, Abdul Rahim W, Rowe R, O'Connor RC (2015). Completed suicides and self-harm in Malaysia: A systematic review. *General Hospital Psychiatry* 37, 153-165.

Babanejad M, Delpisheh A, Asadollahi K, Khorshidi A, Sayehmiri K (2014). Attribution of mental disorders in suicide occurrence. *Omega* 69, 311-321.

Bahar N, Ismail WS, Hussain N, Haniff J, Bujang MA, Hamid AM, Yusuff Y, Nordin N, Ali NH (2014). Suicide among the youth in Malaysia: What do we know? *Asia-Pacific Psychiatry* 7, 223-229.

Bardale R. V., Dixit P. G. (2015). Suicide behind bars: A 10-year retrospective study. *Indian Journal of Psychiatry* 57, 81-84.

Baruah AM, Chaliha R (2014). Pattern of suicidal deaths brought for medico legal autopsy at Gauhati Medical College: A retrospective study. *Journal of Punjab Academy of Forensic Medicine and Toxicology* 14, 86-90.

Becker T, Rüsch N (2014). Balancing care for patients at risk of death by suicide. *The Lancet Psychiatry* 1, 98-99.

Behmanehsh Poor F, Tabatabaei SM, Bakhshani N-M (2014). Epidemiology of suicide and its associated socio-demographic factors in patients admitted to emergency department of Zahedan Khatam-Al-Anbia hospital. *International Journal of High Risk Behaviors and Addiction* 3, e22637.

Bhosle SH, Zanjad NP, Dake MD, Godbole HV (2014). Deaths due to hanging among adolescents — a 10-year retrospective study. *Journal of Forensic and Legal Medicine* 29, 30-33.

Bjerregaard P, Larsen CVL (2015). Time trend by region of suicides and suicidal thoughts among Greenland Inuit. *International Journal of Circumpolar Health* 74, 10.3402/ijch.v74.26053.

Branas CC, Kastanaki AE, Michalodimitrakis M, Tzougas J, Kranioti EF, Theodorakis PN, Carr BG, Wiebe DJ (2015). The impact of economic austerity and prosperity events on suicide in Greece: A 30-year interrupted time-series analysis. *BMJ Open* 5, e005619.

Cerel J, Moore M, Brown MM, van de Venne J, Brown SL (2014). Who leaves suicide notes? A six-year population-based study. *Suicide and Life-Threatening Behaviour.* Published online: 13 October 2014. doi: 10.1111/sltb.

Charrel C-L, Plancke L, Genin M, Defromont L, Ducrocq F, Vaiva G, Danel T (2015). Mortality of people suffering from mental illness: A study of a cohort of patients hospitalised in psychiatry in the north of France. *Social Psychiatry and Psychiatric Epidemiology* 50, 269-277.

Chibishev A, Glasnovic M, Miletic M, Smokovski I, Chitkushev L (2014). Influence of age on the survival and mortality rate in acute caustic poisonings. *Materia Socio-Medica* 26, 272-276.

Chinawa JM, Manyike PC, Obu HA, Odetunde OI, Aniwada EC, Ndu IK, Chinawa AT (2014). Behavioral disorder amongst adolescents attending secondary school in southeast Nigeria. *Behavioural Neurology* 2014, e705835.

Coffey MJ, Coffey CE, Ahmedani BK (2015). Suicide in a health maintenance organization population. *JAMA Psychiatry* 72, 294-296.

Corr WP (2014). Suicides and suicide attempts among active component members of the U.S. armed forces, 2010-2012; methods of self-harm vary by major geographic region of assignment. *Medical Surveillance Monthly Report* 21, 2-5.

Debata PK, Deswal S, Kumath M (2014). Causes of unnatural deaths among children and adolescents in northern India - a qualitative analysis of postmortem data. *Journal of Forensic and Legal Medicine* 26, 53-55.

Deckert A, Winkler V, Meisinger C, Heier M, Becher H (2015). Suicide and external mortality pattern in a cohort of migrants from the former Soviet Union to Germany. *Journal of Psychiatric Research* 63, 36-42.

Etzersdorfer E, Klein J, Baus N, Sonneck G, Kapusta ND (2015). Epidemiology of suicide in Austria during 2000–2010: Potential years of life lost: Time for the national suicide prevention program. *Wiener Klinische Wochenschrift*. Published online: 3 March 2015. doi: 10.1007/s00508-015-0729-3.

Fekadu A, Medhin G, Kebede D, Alem A, Cleare AJ, Prince M, Hanlon C, Shibre T (2015). Excess mortality in severe mental illness: 10-year population-based cohort study in rural Ethiopia. *British Journal of Psychiatry* 206, 289-296.

Fontanella CA, Hiance-Steelesmith DL, Phillips GS, Bridge JA, Lester N, Sweeney HA, Campo JV (2015). Widening rural-urban disparities in youth suicides, United States, 1996-2010. *JAMA Pediatrics*. Published online: 3 March 2015. doi: 10.1007/s00508-015-0729-3.

Fountoulakis KN, Savopoulos C, Apostolopoulou M, Dampali R, Zaggelidou E, Karlafti E, Fountoukidis I, Kountis P, Limenopoulos V, Plomaritis E, Theodorakis P, Hatzitolios AI (2015). Rate of suicide and suicide attempts and their relationship to unemployment in Thessaloniki Greece (2000-2012). *Journal of Affective Disorders* 174, 131-136.

Fuhr DC, Calvert C, Ronsmans C, Chandra PS, Sikander S, De Silva MJ, Patel V (2014). Contribution of suicide and injuries to pregnancy-related mortality in low-income and middle-income countries: A systematic review and meta-analysis. *Lancet Psychiatry* 1, 213-225.

Gauthier S, Reisch T, Bartsch C (2015). Swiss prison suicides between 2000 and 2010. *Crisis*. Published online: 23 February 2015. doi: 10.1027/0227-5910/a000302.

Graham L, Fischbacher CM, Stockton D, Fraser A, Fleming M, Greig K (2015). Understanding extreme mortality among prisoners: A national cohort study in Scotland using data linkage. *European Journal of Public Health*. Published online: 11 February 2015. doi: 10.1093/eurpub/cku252.

Granbichler CA, Oberaigner W, Kuchukhidze G, Bauer G, Ndayisaba J-P, Seppi K, Trinka E (2015). Cause-specific mortality in adult epilepsy patients from Tyrol, Austria: Hospital-based study. *Journal of Neurology* 262, 126-133.

Greenlee K, Hyde PS (2014). Suicide and depression in older adults: Greater awareness can prevent tragedy. *Generations* 38, 23-26.

Häkkinen M, Vuori E, Ojanperä I (2014). Prescription opioid abuse based on representative postmortem toxicology. *Forensic Science International* 245, 121-125.

Hall T, Chassler D, Blom B, Grahn R, Blom-Nilsson M, Sullivan L, Lundgren L (2015). Mortality among a national population sentenced to compulsory care for substance use disorders in Sweden: Descriptive study. *Evaluation and Program Planning* 49, 153-162.

Hassamal S, Keyser-Marcus L, Crouse Breden E, Hobron K, Bhattachan A, Pandurangi A (2015). A brief analysis of suicide methods and trends in Virginia from 2003 to 2012. *BioMed Research International* 2015, 104036.

Helaly AMN, Ali EF, Zidan EM (2015). The pattern of suicide in the western kingdom of Saudi Arabia: A retrospective study from 2008 to 2012. *American Journal of Forensic Medicine and Pathology* 36, 27-30.

Helema S, Holopainen J, Partonen T (2014). Suicide rates in Maltese islands (1955-2009) analysed in European context using WHO data. *Malta Medical Journal* 26, 8-10.

Hempstead KA, Phillips JA (2015). Rising suicide among adults aged 40-64 years: The role of job and financial circumstances. *American Journal of Preventive Medicine.* Published online: 26 February 2015. doi: 10.1016/j.amepre.2014.11.006.

Hong J, Knapp M (2014). Impact of macro-level socio-economic factors on rising suicide rates in South Korea: Panel-data analysis in east Asia. *Journal of Mental Health Policy and Economics* 17, 151-162

Ikeshita K, Shimoda S, Norimoto K, Arita K, Shimamoto T, Murata K, Makinodan M, Kishimoto T (2014). Profiling psychiatric inpatient suicide attempts in Japan. *International Journal of Emergency Mental Health* 16, 217-221.

Inoue K, Nishimura Y, Okazazi Y, Fukunaga T (2014). Discussion based on analysis of the suicide rate and the average disposable income per household in Japan. *West Indian Medical Journal* 63, 344-347.

Jia C-X, Wang X-T, Zhao Z-T (2014). Psychometric properties of the suicidal ideation questionnaire among Chinese high school students. *Omega* 70, 195-207.

Johnson NB, Hayes LD, Brown K, Hoo EC, Ethier KA (2014). CDC National Health Report: Leading causes of morbidity and mortality and associated behavioral risk and protective factors-United States, 2005-2013. *Morbidity and Mortality Weekly Report* 63, 3-27

Joshi R, Guggilla R, Praveen D, Maulik PK (2015). Suicide deaths in rural Andhra Pradesh—a cause for global health action. *Tropical Medicine and International Health* 20, 188-193.

Kang EH, Hyun MK, Choi SM, Kim JM, Kim GM, Woo JM (2014). Twelve-month prevalence and predictors of self-reported suicidal ideation and suicide attempt among Korean adolescents in a web-based nationwide survey. *Australian and New Zealand Journal of Psychiatry* 49, 47-53.

Klaassen Z, Jen RP, DiBianco JM, Reinstatler L, Li Q, Madi R, Lewis RW, Smith AM, Neal DE, Moses KA, Terris MK (2015). Factors associated with suicide in patients with genitourinary malignancies. *Cancer.* Published online: 17 February 2015. doi: 10.1002/cncr.29274.

Korhonen M, Puhakka M, Virén M (2014). Economic hardship and suicide mortality in Finland, 1875-2010. *European Journal of Health Economics.* Published online: 2 December 2014. doi: 10.1007/s10198-014-0658-5.

Kumar A, Sachan R, Verma A (2015). Medico-legal evaluation of firearm injuries-an original study from India with review of literature. *Journal of Forensic Sciences* 60 Suppl 1, S83-86.

Kumral B, Ozdes T, Avsar A, Buyuk Y (2014). Accidental deaths by hanging among children in Istanbul, Turkey: Retrospective analysis of medicolegal autopsies in 33 years. *The American Journal of Forensic Medicine and Pathology* 35, 271-274.

Lama BB, Duke JM, Sharma NP, Thapa B, Dahal P, Bariya ND, Marston W, Wallace HJ (2015). Intentional burns in Nepal: A comparative study. *Burns.* Published online: 21 February 2015. doi: 10.1016/j.burns.2015.01.006.

Lazar SG (2014). The mental health needs of military service members and veterans. *Psychodynamic Psychiatry* 42, 459-478.

Leenen I, Cervantes-Trejo A (2014). Temporal and geographic trends in homicide and suicide rates in Mexico, from 1998 through 2012. *Aggression and Violent Behavior* 19, 699–707.

Lim D, Ha M, Song I (2014). Trends in the leading causes of death in Korea, 1983-2012. *Journal of Korean Medical Science* 29, 1597-1603.

Liu T, Song X, Chen G, Paradis AD, Zheng X (2014). Prevalence of schizophrenia disability and associated mortality among Chinese men and women. *Psychiatry Research* 220, 181-187.

Logan JE, Skopp NA, Reger MA, Gladden M, Smolenski DJ, Floyd CF, Gahm GA (2015). Precipitating circumstances of suicide among active duty US army personnel versus US civilians, 2005-2010. *Suicide and Life-Threatening Behavior* 45, 65-77.

Maguen S, Skopp NA, Zhang Y, Smolenski DJ (2014). Gender differences in suicide and suicide attempts among US army soldiers. *Psychiatry Research* 225, 545-549.

Maniecka-Bryła I, Bryła M, Bryła P, Pikala M (2015). The burden of premature mortality in Poland analysed with the use of standard expected years of life lost. *BMC Public Health* 15, 101.

Matheson FI, Creatore MI, Gozdyra P, Park AL, Ray JG (2014). A population-based study of premature mortality in relation to neighbourhood density of alcohol sales and cheque cashing outlets in Toronto, Canada. *British Medical Journal Open* 4, e006032

McCarten JM, Hoffmire CA, Bossarte RM (2015). Changes in overall and firearm veteran suicide rates by gender, 2001-2010. *American Journal of Preventative Medicine.* Published online: 13 January 2015. doi: 10.1016/j.amepre.2014.10.013.

Mendes R, Santos S, Taveira F, Dinis-Oliveira RJ, Santos A, Magalhães T (2015). Child suicide in the north of Portugal. *Journal of Forensic Sciences* 60, 471-475.

Moebus S, Bödeker W (2015). Mortality of intentional and unintentional pesticide poisonings in Germany from 1980 to 2010. *Journal of Public Health Policy* 36, 170-180.

Muccino E, Crudele GD, Gentile G, Marchesi M, Rancati A, Zoja R (2014). Suicide drowning in the non-coastal territory of Milan. *International Journal of Legal Medicine.* Published online: 15 November 2014. doi: 10.1007/s00414-014-1115-9.

Ngui AN, Apparicio P, Moltchanova E, Vasiliadis H-M (2014). Spatial analysis of suicide mortality in Quebec: Spatial clustering and area factor correlates. *Psychiatry Research* 220, 20-30.

Norheim OF, Jha P, Admasu K, Godal T, Hum RJ, Kruk ME, Gomez-Dantes O, Mathers CD, Pan H, Sepulveda J, Suraweera W, Verguet S, Woldemariam AT, Yamey G, Jamison DT, Peto R (2015). Avoiding 40% of the premature deaths in each country, 2010-30: Review of national mortality trends to help quantify the UN sustainable development goal for health. *Lancet* 385, 239-252.

Orui M, Harada S, Hayashi M (2014). Changes in suicide rates in disaster-stricken areas following the Great East Japan Earthquake and their effect on economic factors: an ecological study. *Environmental Health and Preventive Medicin* 19, 459-466.

Papini S, Nakagawa LE (2014). Current status of rodenticide intoxication in Brazil: A preliminary survey from 2009 to 2011. *Brazilian Archives of Biology and Technology* 57, 685-688.

Park N, Peterson C (2014). Suicide in happy places revisited: The geographical unit of analysis matters. *Applied Psychology-Health and Well Being* 6, 318-323.

Park S (2015). Brief report: Sex differences in suicide rates and suicide methods among adolescents in South Korea, Japan, Finland, and the US. *Journal of Adolescence* 40, 74-77.

Pierce M, Bird SM, Hickman M, Millar T (2015). National record linkage study of mortality for a large cohort of opioid users ascertained by drug treatment or criminal justice sources in England, 2005-2009. *Drug and Alcohol Dependence* 146, 17-23.

Qasim AP, Tariq SA, Naeem M (2014). Profile of unnatural deaths; in Faisalabad. *Medical Forum Monthly* 25, 51-54.

Rachiotis G, Stuckler D, McKee M, Hadjichristodoulou C (2015). What has happened to suicides during the Greek economic crisis? Findings from an ecological study of suicides and their determinants (2003-2012). *British Medical Journal Open* 5, e007295.

Racz E, Konczol F, Meszaros H, Kozma Z, Mayer M, Porpaczy Z, Poor VS, Sipos K (2015). Drowning-related fatalities during a 5-year period (2008-2012) in south-west Hungary - a retrospective study. *Journal of Forensic and Legal Medicine* 31, 7-11.

Ramchandra Sane M, Mugadlimath AB, Zine KU, Farooqui JM, Phalke BJ (2015). Course of near-hanging victims succumbed to death: A seven year study. *Journal of Clinical and Diagnostic Research* 9, HC01-HC03.

Rancic N, Rankovic A, Savic D, Abramovic A, Rancic J, Jakovljevic M (2014). Intentional self-poisonings and unintentional poisonings of adolescents with nonfatal outcomes. *Journal of Child and Adolescent Substance Abuse* 24, 12-18.

Ranney ML, Locci N, Adams EJ, Betz M, Burmeister DB, Corbin T, Dalawari P, Jacoby JL, Linden J, Purtle J, North C, Houry DE (2014). Gender-specific research on mental illness in the emergency department: Current knowledge and future directions. *Academic Emergency Medicine* 21, 1395-1402.

Renard F, Tafforeau J, Deboosere P (2014). Premature mortality in Belgium in 1993-2009: Leading causes, regional disparities and 15 years change. *Archives of Public Health* 72, 34.

Roskar S, Zorko M, Podlesek A (2015). Suicide in Slovenia between 1997 and 2010. *Crisis*. Published online: 12 January 2015. doi: 10.1027/0227-5910/a000298.

Sabri B, Sanchez MV, Campbell JC (2014). Motives and characteristics of domestic violence homicides and suicides among women in India. *Health Care for Women International*. Published online: 22 Dec 2014. doi: 10.1080/07399332.2014.971954.

Sarma PG (2014). Suicide rate computation - methodological inexactitude. *Acta Medica International* 1, 82-84.

Sarma PG (2015). Time series analysis of Indian suicides: Correlation with human development index (HDI). *Acta Medica International* 2, 122-124.

Schwarcz SK, Vu A, Hsu LC, Hessol NA (2014). Changes in causes of death among persons with AIDS: San Francisco, California, 1996-2011. *AIDS Patient Care and STDs* 28, 517-523.

Sheu Y, Chen L-H, Hedegaard H (2014). Percentage of suicide deaths, by mechanism and age group - United States, 2011. *Morbidity and Mortality Weekly Report* 63, 845.

Shinsugi C, Stickley A, Konishi S, Ng CF, Watanabe C (2014). Seasonality of child and adolescent injury mortality in Japan, 2000-2010. *Environmental Health and Preventive Medicine* 20, 36-43.

Siegel M, Ross CS, King C (2014). Examining the relationship between the prevalence of guns and homicide rates in the USA using a new and improved state-level gun ownership proxy. *Injury Prevention* 20, 424-426.

Sinyor M, Schaffer A, Cheung AH (2014). An observational study of bullying as a contributing factor in youth suicide in Toronto. *Canadian Journal of Psychiatry* 59, 632-638.

Sinyor M, Schaffer A, Remington G (2015). Suicide in schizophrenia: An observational study of coroner records in Toronto. *Journal of Clinical Psychiatry* 76, e98-e103.

Sohn J, Cho J, Moon KT, Suh M, Ha KH, Kim C, Shin DC, Jung SH (2014). Medical care expenditure in suicides from non-illness-related causes. *Journal of Preventive Medicine and Public Health* 47, 327-335.

Sonderman JS, Munro HM, Blot WJ, Tarone RE, McLaughlin JK (2014). Suicides, homicides, accidents, and other external causes of death among blacks and whites in the southern community cohort study. *PLoS One* 9, e114852.

Straif-Bourgeois S, Ratard R (2014). Firearm-related mortality, Louisiana 1999-2010. *Journal of the Louisiana State Medical Society* 166, 168-174.

Sullivan EM, Annest JL, Simon TR, Luo F, Dahlberg LL (2015). Suicide trends among persons aged 10-24 years - United States, 1994-2012. *Morbidity and Mortality Weekly Report* 64, 201-205.

Sun L, Zhang J (2014). Characteristics of Chinese rural young suicides: Who did not have a strong intent to die. *Comprehensive Psychiatry* 57, 73-78.

Sun L, Zhang J (2015). Potential years of life lost due to suicide in China, 2006-2010. *Public Health*. Published online: 10 March 2015. doi: 10.1016/j.puhe.2015.02.012.

Szalontay A, Burtea V, Ifteni P (2014). Blood alcohol concentration in suicide: A 10 years study. *Revista De Cercetare Si Interventie Sociala* 46, 144-151.

Tejada-Vera B (2014). Age-adjusted suicide rates, by state - United States, 2012. *Morbidity and Mortality Weekly Report* 63, 1041.

Termorshuizen F, Braam AW, van Ameijden EJC (2014). Neighborhood ethnic density and suicide risk among different migrant groups in the four big cities in the Netherlands. *Social Psychiatry and Psychiatric Epidemiology*. Published online: 10 December 2014. doi: 10.1007/s00127-014-0993-y.

Vinita VE, Paul PM, Janani, Pradhan P, Kumar PS (2014). Pattern of neck tissue injuries in hanging - a prospective study. *Journal of Punjab Academy of Forensic Medicine and Toxicology* 14, 101-104.

Viswanathan KG, Gupta A, Santhosh CS, Siddesh RC, Prabal S (2014). Profile of fatal organophosphorus pesticide poisoning cases near Davangere. *Journal of Punjab Academy of Forensic Medicine and Toxicology* 14, 96-100.

Wilson AL, Sideras J (2015). Regional Infant and Child Mortality Review Committee 2013 final report. *South Dakota Journal of Medicine* 66, 415-9.

Wolodzko T, Kokoszka A (2014). Characteristics of groups after the suicide attempt. Cluster analysis of National Comorbidity Survey (NCS) 1990-1992. *Psychiatria Polska* 48, 1253-1267.

Xu J, Kochanek KD, Murphy SL, Arias E (2014). Mortality in the United States, 2012. *NCHS Data Brief* 168, 1-8.

Yoshioka E, Hanley SJ, Kawanishi Y, Saijo Y (2014). Time trends in method-specific suicide rates in Japan, 1990-2011. *Epidemiology and Psychiatric Sciences*. Published online: 6 November 2014. doi: 10.1017/S2045796014000675.

Yuen K, Harrigan SM, Mackinnon AJ, Harris MG, Yuen HP, Henry LP, Jackson HJ, Herrman H, McGorry PD (2014). Long-term follow-up of all-cause and unnatural death in young people with first-episode psychosis. *Schizophrenia Research* 159, 70-75.

Zhao S, Zhan J (2014). Suicide risks among adolescents and young adults in rural China. *International Journal of Environmental Research and Public Health* 12, 131-145.

Risk and protective factors

Åberg F, Gissler M, Karlsen TH, Ericzon BG, Foss A, Rasmussen A, Bennet W, Olausson M, Line PD, Nordin A, Bergquist A, Boberg KM, Castedal M, Pedersen CR, Isoniemi H (2015). Differences in long-term survival among liver transplant recipients and the general population: A population-based Nordic study. *Hepatology* 61, 668-677.

Ahmadi A, Mohammadi R, Almasi A, Amini-Saman J, Sadeghi-Bazargani H, Bazargan-Hejazi S, Svanström L (2014). A case-control study of psychosocial risk and protective factors of self-immolation in Iran. *Burns* 41, 386-393.

Ahn MH, Park S, Lee HB, Ramsey CM, Na R, Kim SO, Kim JE, Yoon S, Hong JP (2014). Suicide in cancer patients within the first year of diagnosis. *Psycho-Oncology* 24, 601-607.

Balbuena L, Tempier R (2015). Independent association of chronic smoking and abstinence with suicide. *Psychiatric Services* 66, 186-192.

Bender KA, Theodossiou I (2015). A reappraisal of the unemployment-mortality relationship: Transitory and permanent effects. *Journal of Public Health Policy* 36, 81-94.

Bixby H, Hodgson S, Fortunato L, Hansell A, Fecht D (2015). Associations between green space and health in English cities: An ecological, cross-sectional study. *PLoS One* 10, e0119495.

Bjorkenstam C, Alexanderson K, Bjorkenstam E, Lindholm C, Mittendorfer-Rutz E (2014). Diagnosis-specific disability pension and risk of all-cause and cause-specific mortality - a cohort study of 4.9 million inhabitants in Sweden. *BMC Public Health* 14, 1247.

Busse M, Busse S, Myint AM, Gos T, Dobrowolny H, Müller UJ, Bogerts B, Bernstein H-G, Steiner J (2014). Decreased quinolinic acid in the hippocampus of depressive patients: Evidence for local anti-inflammatory and neuroprotective responses? *European Archives of Psychiatry and Clinical Neuroscience.* Published online: 20 November 2014. doi: 10.1007/s00406-014-0562-0.

Chan SKW, So HC, Hui CLM, Chang WC, Lee EHM, Chung DWS, Tso S, Hung SF, Yip KC, Dunn E, Chen EYH (2014). 10-year outcome study of an early intervention program for psychosis compared with standard care service. *Psychological Medicine* 45, 1181-1193.

Chojnicka I, Fudalej S, Walczak A, Wasilewska K, Fudalej M, Stawinski P, Strawa K, Pawlak A, Wojnar M, Krajewski P, Ploski R (2014). Inverse association between obesity predisposing FTO genotype and completed suicide. *Plos One* 9, e108900.

Cobaugh DJ, Miller MJ, Pham TT, Krenzelok EP (2015). Risk of major morbidity and death in older adults with suicidal intent: A cross-sectional analysis from the National Poison Data System, 2000-2009. *Journal of the American Geriatrics Society* 63, 501-507.

Contis G, Foley TP (2015). Depression, suicide ideation, and thyroid tumors among Ukrainian adolescents exposed as children to Chernobyl radiation. *Journal of Clinical Medicine Research* 7, 332-338.

Costa LDS, Alencar ÁP, Neto PJN, Dos Santos MDSV, Da Silva CGL, Pinheiro SDFL, Teixeira Silveira R, Bianco BAV, Pinheiro Júnior RFF, De Lima MAP, Reis AOA, Neto MLR (2015). Risk factors for suicide in bipolar disorder: A systematic review. *Journal of Affective Disorders* 170, 237-254.

Crawford AA, Galobardes B, Jeffreys M, Davey Smith G, Gunnell D (2014). Risk of suicide for individuals reporting asthma and atopy in young adulthood: Findings from the Glasgow Alumni study. *Psychiatry Research* 225, 364-367.

D'Orio BM, Thompson MP, Lamis DA, Heron S, Kaslow NJ (2015). Social support, attachment, and drug misuse in suicidal African American women. *Addiction Research and Theory* 23, 170-176.

Darlington TM, Pimentel R, Smith K, Bakian AV, Jerominski L, Cardon J, Camp NJ, Callor WB, Grey T, Singleton M, Yandell M, Renshaw PF, Yurgelun-Todd DA, Gray D, Coon H (2014). Identifying rare variants for genetic risk through a combined pedigree and phenotype approach: Application to suicide and asthma. *Translational Psychiatry* 4, e471.

Davey Smith G, Munafó M (2015). Why is there a link between smoking and suicide? *Psychiatric Services* 66, 331.

Desmond E (2014). The legitimation of risk and Bt cotton: a case study of Bantala village in Warangal, Andhra Pradesh, India. *Journal of Risk Research*. Published online: 26 September 2014. doi: 10.1080/13669877.2014.961516.

Dixon PG, Sinyor M, Schaffer A, Levitt A, Haney CR, Ellis KN, Sheridan SC (2014). Association of weekly suicide rates with temperature anomalies in two different climate types. *International Journal of Environmental Research and Public Health* 11, 11627-11644.

Dobscha SK, Denneson LM, Kovas AE, Teo A, Forsberg CW, Kaplan MS, Bossarte R, McFarland BH (2014). Correlates of suicide among veterans treated in primary care: Case-control study of a nationally representative sample. *Journal of General Internal Medicine* 29, 853-860.

Espinoza M (2014). Land development and suicide rates in the United States. *Academic Excellence Showcase* 2014, e37.

Fan MD (2015). Disarming the dangerous: Preventing extraordinary and ordinary violence. *Indiana Law Journal* 90, 151-178.

Firebaugh G, Acciai F, Noah AJ, Prather C, Nau C (2014). Why lifespans are more variable among blacks than among whites in the United States. *Demography* 51, 2025-2045.

Gallaway MS, Lagana-Riordan C, Dabbs CR, Bell MR, Bender AA, Fink DS, Forys-Donahue K, Pecko JA, Schmissrauter SC, Perales R, Coombs MA, Rattigan MR, Millikan AM (2015). A mixed methods epidemiological investigation of preventable deaths among US army soldiers assigned to a rehabilitative warrior transition unit. *Work* 50, 21-36.

Gauthier S, Reisch T, Ajdacic-Gross V, Bartsch C (2015). Road traffic suicide in Switzerland. *Traffic Injury Prevention*. Published online: 20 March 2015. doi: 10.1080/15389588.2015.1021419.

Gissler M, Karalis E, Ulander V-M (2015). Decreased suicide rate after induced abortion, after the current care guidelines in Finland 1987-2012. *Scandinavian Journal of Public Health* 43, 99-101.

Goldberg S, Werbeloff N, Shelef L, Fruchter E, Weiser M (2015). Risk of suicide among female adolescents with eating disorders: A longitudinal population-based study. *Eating and Weight Disorders*. Published online: 18 January 2015. doi: 10.1007/s40519-015-0176-1.

Gunnarsdottir AS, Kristbjornsdottir A, Gudmundsdottir R, Gunnarsdottir OS, Rafnsson V (2014). Survival of patients with alcohol use disorders discharged from an emergency department: A population-based cohort study. *British Medical Journal Open* 4, e006327.

Hagens M, Pasman HRW, Onwuteaka-Philipsen BD (2014). Cross-sectional research into counselling for non-physician assisted suicide: Who asks for it and what happens? *BMC Health Services Research* 14, 455.

Haglund A, Tidemalm D, Jokinen J, Långström N, Lichtenstein P, Fazel S, Runeson B (2014). Suicide after release from prison: A population-based cohort study from Sweden. *Journal of Clinical Psychiatry* 75, 1047-1053.

Hankin BL, Barrocas AL, Young JE, Haberstick B, Smolen A (2015). 5-HTTLPR× interpersonal stress interaction and nonsuicidal self-injury in general community sample of youth. *Psychiatry Research* 225, 609-612.

Hoggatt KJ, Jamison AL, Lehavot K, Cucciare MA, Timko C, Simpson TL (2015). Alcohol and drug misuse, abuse, and dependence in women veterans. *Epidemiologic Reviews* 37, 23-37.

Hong SC, Lee J (2014). People on the verge of death: Evidence from impacts of celebrity suicides. *Applied Economics* 47, 710-724.

Hoti E, Levesque E, Sebagh M, Heneghan HM, Khalfallah M, Castaing D, Azoulay D (2014). Liver transplantation with grafts from donors who die from suicide by hanging: A matched cohort study. *Transplantation* 98, 1236-1243.

Huguet N, Lewis-Laietmark C (2015). Rates of homicide-followed-by-suicide among White, African American, and Hispanic men. *Public Health*. Published online: 24 February 2015. doi: 10.1016/j.puhe.2014.11.008.

Ishii N, Terao T, Araki Y, Kohno K, Mizokami Y, Shiotsuki I, Hatano K, Makino M, Kodama K, Iwata N (2015). Low risk of male suicide and lithium in drinking water. *Journal of Clinical Psychiatry* 76, 319-326.

Jalles JT, Andresen MA (2015). The social and economic determinants of suicide in Canadian provinces. *Health Economics Review* 5, 1.

Jia H, Zack MM, Thompson WW, Crosby AE, Gottesman II (2015). Impact of depression on quality-adjusted life expectancy (QALE) directly as well as indirectly through suicide. *Social Psychiatry and Psychiatric Epidemiology*. Published online: 7 February 2015. doi: 10.1007/s00127-015-1019-0.

Kawanishi C, Aruga T, Ishizuka N, Yonemoto N, Otsuka K, Kamijo Y, Okubo Y, Ikeshita K, Sakai A, Miyaoka H, Hitomi Y, Iwakuma A, Kinoshita T, Akiyoshi J, Horikawa N, Hirotsune H, Eto N, Iwata N, Kohno M, Iwanami A, Mimura M, Asada T, Hirayasu Y, Grp A-J (2014). Assertive case management versus enhanced usual care for people with mental health problems who had attempted suicide and were admitted to hospital emergency departments in Japan (ACTION-J): A multicentre, randomised controlled trial. *Lancet Psychiatry* 1, 193-201.

Kiamanesh P, Dyregrov K, Haavind H, Dieserud G (2014). Suicide and perfectionism: A psychological autopsy study of non-clinical suicides. *Omega* 69, 381-399.

Kim J, Choi N, Lee Y-J, An H, Kim N, Yoon H-K, Lee H-J (2014). High altitude remains associated with elevated suicide rates after adjusting for socioeconomic status: A study from South Korea. *Psychiatry Investigation* 11, 492-494.

Kimura G, Kadoyama K, Brown JB, Nakamura T, Miki I, Nisiguchi K, Sakaeda T, Okuno Y (2015). Antipsychotics-associated serious adverse events in children: An analysis of the FAERS database. *International Journal of Medical Sciences* 12, 135-140.

Kosidou K, Dalman C, Fredlund P, Magnusson C (2014). School performance and the risk of suicidal thoughts in young adults: Population-based study. *Plos One* 9, e109958.

Kumar S, Singh US, Verma AK, Ali W, Krishna A (2015). Intentional and non-intentional burn related deaths: A comparative study of socio-demographic profile. *Burns* 41, 265-270.

Lee BX, Wexler BE, Gilligan J (2014). Political correlates of violent death rates in the US, 1900-2010: Longitudinal and cross-sectional analyses. *Aggression and Violent Behavior* 19, 721-728.

Lin C, Yen T-H, Juang Y-Y, Lin J-L, Lee S-H (2014). Psychiatric comorbidity and its impact on mortality in patients who attempted suicide by paraquat poisoning during 2000-2010. *Plos One* 9, e112160-e112160.

Lo Vasco VR (2015). Impairment and reorganization of the phosphoinositide-specific phospholipase C enzymes in suicide brains. *Journal of Affective Disorders* 174, 324-328.

Mallon S, Rosato M, Galway K, Hughes L, Rondon-Sulbaran J, McConkey S, Leavey G (2014). Patterns of presentation for attempted suicide: Analysis of a cohort of individuals who subsequently died by suicide. *Suicide and Life-Threatening Behavior*. Published online: 24 October 2014. doi: 10.1111/sltb.12134.

Malpas PJ (2014). A time to die? Conversations with Jack. *Patient Education and Counseling* 97, 297-298.

McMahon EM, Keeley H, Cannon M, Arensman E, Perry IJ, Clarke M, Chambers D, Corcoran P (2014). The iceberg of suicide and self-harm in Irish adolescents: A population-based study. *Social Psychiatry and Psychiatric Epidemiology* 49, 1929-1935.

Myint S, Rerkamnuaychoke B, Peonim V, Riengrojpitak S, Worasuwannarak W (2014). Fatal firearm injuries in autopsy cases at central Bangkok, Thailand: A 10-year retrospective study. *Journal of Forensic and Legal Medicine* 28, 5-10.

Norström T, Grönqvist H (2014). The great recession, unemployment and suicide. *Journal of Epidemiology and Community Health*. Published online: 22 October 2014. doi: 10.1136/jech-2014-204602.

Oka M, Kubota T, Tsubaki H, Yamauchi K (2014). Analysis of the impact of geographical characteristics on the suicide rate and visualization of the result by GIS (Geographic Information System). *Psychiatry and Clinical Neurosciences*. Published online: 11 November 2014. doi: 10.1111/pcn.12254.

Oliffe JL, Han CSE, Drummond M, Sta Maria E, Bottorff JL, Creighton G (2014). Men, masculinities, and murder-suicide. *American Journal of Men's Health*. Published online: 7 October 2014. doi: 10.1177/1557988314551359.

Oquendo MA, Sullivan GM, Sudol K, Baca-Garcia E, Stanley BH, Sublette ME, Mann JJ (2014). Toward a biosignature for suicide. *American Journal of Psychiatry*. 171, 1259-1277.

Pan C-H, Jhong J-R, Tsai S-Y, Lin S-K, Chen C-C, Kuo C-J (2014). Excessive suicide mortality and risk factors for suicide among patients with heroin dependence. *Drug and Alcohol Dependence* 145, 224-230.

Picouto MD, Villar F, Braquehais MD (2014). The role of serotonin in adolescent suicide: Theoretical, methodological, and clinical concerns. *International Journal of Adolescent Medicine and Health* 27, 129-133.

Poorolajal J, Rostami M, Mahjub H, Esmailnasab N (2015). Completed suicide and associated risk factors: A six-year population based survey. *Archives of Iranian Medicine* 18, 39-43.

Pranji N, Males-Bili L (2014). Work ability index, absenteeism and depression among patients with burnout syndrome. *Materia Socio-Medica* 26, 249-252.

Rajarao P, Anjannamma TC (2013). A study of suicidal deaths in married women in province of Telangana area, Andhra Pradesh (India). *International Journal of Pharmaceutical and Biomedical Research* 4, 37-39.

Randall JR, Walld R, Finlayson G, Sareen J, Martens PJ, Bolton JM (2014). Acute risk of suicide and suicide attempts associated with recent diagnosis of mental disorders: A population-based, propensity score-matched analysis. *Canadian Journal of Psychiatry* 59, 531-538.

Remberk B, Bazynska AK, Bronowska Z, Potocki P, Krempa-Kowalewska A, Niwinski P, Rybakowski F (2014). Which aspects of long-term outcome are predicted by positive and negative symptoms in early-onset psychosis? An exploratory eight-year follow-up study. *Psychopathology* 48, 47-55.

Rich BA (2014). Pathologizing suffering and the pursuit of a peaceful death. *Cambridge Quarterly of Healthcare Ethics* 23, 403-416.

Rivera MP (2014). Priming the pump... Suicide and Latino teens. *The Hispanic Outlook In Higher Education* 25, 32.

Roswall N, Sandin S, Löf M, Skeie G, Olsen A, Adami HO, Weiderpass E (2015). Adherence to the healthy Nordic food index and total and cause-specific mortality among Swedish women. *European Journal of Epidemiology*. Published online: 18 March 2015. doi: 10.1007/s10654-015-0021-x.

Rubanzana W, Hedt-Gauthier BL, Ntaganira J, Freeman MD (2015). Exposure to genocide and risk of suicide in Rwanda: A population-based case-control study. *Journal of Epidemiology and Community Health* 69, 117-122.

Sandberg JV, Jakobsson J, Palsson E, Landen M, Mathe AA (2014). Low neuropeptide Y in cerebrospinal fluid in bipolar patients is associated with previous and prospective suicide attempts. *European Neuropsychopharmacology* 24, 1907-1915.

Schaffer A, Isometsa ET, Tondo L, D HM, Turecki G, Reis C, Cassidy F, Sinyor M, Azorin JM, Kessing LV, Ha K, Goldstein T, Weizman A, Beautrais A, Chou YH, Diazgranados N, Levitt AJ, Zarate CA, Jr., Rihmer Z, Yatham LN (2014). International Society for Bipolar Disorders Task Force on Suicide: meta-analyses and meta-regression of correlates of suicide attempts and suicide deaths in bipolar disorder. *Bipolar Disorders* 17, 1-16.

Shetty CK (2014). Suicide cases in Manipal, South India: An autopsy study. *International Journal of Forensic Science and Pathology* 2, e701.

Shigidi M, Mohammed O, Ibrahim M, Taha E (2014). Clinical presentation, treatment and outcome of paraphenylene-diamine induced acute kidney injury following hair dye poisoning: A cohort study. *Pan African Medical Journal.* Published online: 16 October 2014. doi:10.11604/pamj.2014.19.163.3740.

Smith C, Ryom L, Monforte AdA, Reiss P, Mocroft A, El-Sadr W, Weber R, Law M, Sabin C, Lundgren J (2014). Lack of association between use of efavirenz and death from suicide: Evidence from the D:A:D study. *Journal of the International AIDS Society* 17, 19512.

Smith NDL, Kawachi I (2014). State-level social capital and suicide mortality in the 50 U.S. States. *Social Science and Medicine* 120, 269-277.

Sousa S, Santos L, Dinis-Oliveira RJ, Magalhães T, Santos A (2014). Pedestrian fatalities resulting from train–person collisions. *Traffic Injury Prevention* 16, 208-212.

Strid JMC, Christiansen CF, Olsen M, Qin P (2014). Hospitalisation for chronic obstructive pulmonary disease and risk of suicide: A population-based case-control study. *British Medical Journal Open* 4, e006363.

Sun J, Guo X, Zhang J, Wang M, Jia C, Xu A (2015). Incidence and fatality of serious suicide attempts in a predominantly rural population in Shandong, China: A public health surveillance study. *British Medical Journal Open* 5, e006762.

Sun L, Li H, Zhang J, Wu Q (2015). Psychological strains and suicide intent: Results from a psychological autopsy study with Chinese rural young suicides. *International Journal of Social Psychiatry.* Published online: 12 March 2015. doi: 10.1177/0020764015573087.

Svensson T, Inoue M, Sawada N, Iwasaki M, Sasazuki S, Shimazu T, Yamaji T, Ikeda A, Kawamura N, Mimura M, Tsugane S (2014). The association between complete and partial nonresponse to psychosocial questions and suicide: The JPHC study. *European Journal of Public Health.* Published online: 13 December 2014. doi: 10.1093/eurpub/cku209.

Thomas KH, Martin RM, Potokar J, Pirmohamed M, Gunnell D (2014). Reporting of drug induced depression and fatal and non-fatal suicidal behaviour in the UK from 1998 to 2011. *BMC Pharmacology and Toxicology* 15, 54.

Tse S, Tang J, Wong P (2014). Fortune or foe: The fatal harm caused by a gambling disorder. *Addiction* 109, 2135.

Uggla C, Mace R (2015). Someone to live for: Effects of partner and dependent children on preventable death in a population wide sample from Northern Ireland. *Evolution and Human Behavior* 36, 1-7.

Vijayakumari N, Magendran J (2014). Relationship of menstruation with suicidal hanging: An autopsy study. *Indian Internet Journal of Forensic Medicine and Toxicology* 12, 11-13.

Webb RT, Kapur N (2015). Suicide, unemployment, and the effect of economic recession. *The Lancet Psychiatry* 2, 196-197.

Werbart Törnblom A, Werbart A, Rydelius P-A (2015). Shame and gender differences in paths to youth suicide: Parents' perspective. *Qualitative Health Research*. Published online: 25 March 2015. doi: 10.1177/1049732315578402.

Woo YS, Jun T-Y, Jeon Y-H, Song HR, Kim T-S, Kim J-B, Lee M-S, Kim J-M, Jo S-J (2014). Relationship of temperament and character in remitted depressed patients with suicidal ideation and suicide attempts—results from the CRESCEND study. *PLoS One* 9, e105860.

Yaylaci F (2015). Analysis of suicides related with educational failure. *Anthropologist* 19, 507-516.

Yur'yev A, Yur'yeva L, Värnik P, Lumiste K, Värnik A (2015). The complex impact of risk and protective factors on suicide mortality: A study of the Ukrainian general population. *Archives of Suicide Research*. Published online: 23 February 2015. doi: 10.1080/13811118.2015.1004471.

Zhang J, Sun L, Conwell Y, Qin P, Jia CX, Xiao S, Tu XM (2015). Suicides and medically serious attempters are of the same population in Chinese rural young adults. *Journal of Affective Disorders* 176, 176-182.

Zivin K, Yosef M, Miller EM, Valenstein M, Duffy S, Kales HC, Vijan S, Kim M (2015). Associations between depression and all-cause and cause-specific risk of death: A retrospective cohort study in the Veterans Health Administration. *Journal of Psychosomatic Research* 78, 324-331.

Prevention

Coleman D (2014). Traditional masculinity as a risk factor for suicidal ideation: Cross-sectional and prospective evidence from a study of young adults. *Archives of Suicide Research*. Published online: 10 November 2014. doi: 10.1080/13811118.2014.957453.

Draper J, Murphy G, Vega E, Covington DW, McKeon R (2014). Helping callers to the National Suicide Prevention Lifeline who are at imminent risk of suicide: The importance of active engagement, active rescue, and collaboration between crisis and emergency services. *Suicide and Life-Threatening Behavior*. Published online: 1 October 2014. doi: 10.1111/sltb.12128.

Hamilton E, Klimes-Dougan B (2015). Gender differences in suicide prevention responses: Implications for adolescents based on an illustrative review of the literature. *International Journal of Environmental Research and Public Health* 12, 2359-2372.

Kirsch DJ, Pinder-Amaker SL, Morse C, Ellison ML, Doerfler LA, Riba MB (2014). Population-based initiatives in college mental health: Students helping students to overcome obstacles. *Current Psychiatry Reports* 16, 525.

Kostunina NY (2014). Prevention of student youth suicidal behaviour. *Procedia - Social and Behavioral Sciences* 131, 57-60.

Luxton DD, O'Brien K, Pruitt LD, Johnson K, Kramer G (2014). Suicide risk management during clinical telepractice. *International Journal of Psychiatry in Medicine* 48, 19-31.

Madsen LB, Eddleston M, Hansen KS, Pearson M, Agampodi S, Jayamanne S, Konradsen F (2015). Cost-effectiveness analyses of self-harm strategies aimed at reducing the mortality of pesticide self-poisonings in Sri Lanka: A study protocol. *BMJ Open* 5, e007333.

Malakouti SK, Nojomi M, Poshtmashadi M, Hakim Shooshtari M, Mansouri Moghadam F, Rahimi-Movaghar A, Afghah S, Bolhari J, Bazargan-Hejazi S (2015). Integrating a suicide prevention program into the primary health care network: A field trial study in Iran. *BioMed Research International* 2015, 193729.

Robst J (2015). Suicide attempts after emergency room visits: The effect of patient safety goals. *Psychiatric Quarterly*. Published online: 29 January 2015. doi: 10.1007/s11126-015-9345-7.

Scott LN, Pilkonis PA, Hipwell AE, Keenan K, Stepp SD (2014). Non-suicidal self-injury and suicidal ideation as predictors of suicide attempts in adolescent girls: A multi-wave prospective study. *Comprehensive Psychiatry* 58, 1-10.

Scott M (2015). Teaching note - understanding of suicide prevention, intervention, and postvention: Curriculum for MSW students. *Journal of Social Work Education* 51, 177-185.

Shuchman M (2014). Suicide report indicates shift at WHO. *Canadian Medical Association Journal* 186, e532.

Tiatia-Seath J (2014). Pacific peoples, mental health service engagement and suicide prevention in Aotearoa New Zealand. *Ethnicity and Inequalities in Health and Social Care* 7, 111-121.

Varia SG, Ebin J, Stout ER (2014). Suicide prevention in rural communities: Perspectives from a community of practice. *Journal of Rural Mental Health* 38, 109-115.

Postvention and Bereavement

Bailey L, Bell J, Kennedy D (2014). Continuing social presence of the dead: Exploring suicide bereavement through online memorialisation. *New Review of Hypermedia and Multimedia.* Published online: 16 December 2014. doi: 10.1080/13614568.2014.983554.

Bardon C, Mishara BL (2015). Development of a comprehensive programme to prevent and reduce the negative impact of railway fatalities, injuries and close calls on railway employees. *Journal of Occupational Rehabilitation.* Published online: 13 January 2015. doi: 10.1007/s10926-014-9562-1.

Bentley B, O'Connor M (2015). Conducting research interviews with bereaved family carers: When do we ask? *Journal of Palliative Medicine* 18, 241-245 .

Boelen PA, de Keijser J, Smid G (2014). Cognitive-behavioral variables mediate the impact of violent loss on post-loss psychopathology. *Psychological Trauma: Theory, Research, Practice, and Policy.* Published online: 22 December 2014. doi: 10.1037/tra0000018.

Canning P, Gournay K (2014). The impact of patient suicide on community mental health teams. *British Journal of Mental Health Nursing* 3, 235-240.

Castelli Dransart DA, Gulfi A, Heeb J-L, Gutjahr E (2015). The impact of patient suicide on the professional practice of Swiss psychiatrists and psychologists. *Academic Psychiatry.* Published online: 9 January 2015. doi: 10.1007/s40596-014-0267-8.

Chapple A, Ziebland S, Hawton K (2015). Taboo and the different death? Perceptions of those bereaved by suicide or other traumatic death. *Sociology of Health and Illness.* Published online: 13 February 2015. doi: 10.1111/1467-9566.12224.

Greenberg D, Shefler G (2014). Patient suicide. *Israel Journal of Psychiatry and Related Sciences* 51, 193-198.

Hagström AS (2014). "The self-murderer from Orminge": A bereaved daughter's remonstrance to "rescue" her self through a performed memoir of revolt. *Narrative Inquiry* 24, 218-238.

Hunt QA, Hertlein KM (2015). Conceptualizing suicide bereavement from an attachment lens. *American Journal of Family Therapy* 43, 16-27

Jahn DR, Spencer-Thomas S (2014). Continuing bonds through after-death spiritual experiences in individuals bereaved by suicide. *Journal of Spirituality in Mental Health* 16, 311-324.

Jefee-Bahloul H, Hanna RC, Brenner AM (2014). Teaching psychiatry residents about suicide loss: Impact of an educational program. *Academic Psychiatry* 38, 768-770.

Mallon S, Stanley N (2015). Creation of a death by suicide. *Crisis.* Published online: 12 January 2015. doi: 10.1027/0227-5910/a000299.

Means JJ (2015). Personal reflections on a suicide. *Academic Psychiatry.* Published online: 13 January 2015. doi: 10.1007/s40596-014-0271-z.

Pettersen R, Omerov P, Steineck G, Dyregrov A, Titelman D, Dyregrov K, Nyberg U (2014). Suicide-bereaved siblings' perception of health services. *Death Studies.* Published online: 17 December 2014. doi: 10.1080/07481187.2014.946624.

Phillips T (2015). Wrestling with grief: Fan negotiation of professional/private personas in responses to the Chris Benoit double murder–suicide. *Celebrity Studies.* Published online: 19 January 2015. doi: 10.1080/19392397.2015.995470.

Santos S, Campos RC, Tavares S (2014). Suicidal ideation and distress in family members bereaved by suicide in Portugal. *Death Studies.* Published online: 31 December 2014. doi: 10.1080/07481187.2014.946626.

Santos S, Tavares S, Campos RC (2014). Distress in Portuguese family members bereaved by suicide: An exploratory study. *Journal of Loss and Trauma.* Published online: 24 October 2014. doi: 10.1080/15325024.2014.934618.

Sweeney L, Owens C, Malone K (2014). Communication and interpretation of emotional distress within the friendships of young Irish men prior to suicide: A qualitative study. *Health and Social Care in the Community* 23, 150-158.

Ward-Ciesielski EF, Wielgus MD, Jones CB (2014). Suicide-bereaved individuals' attitudes toward therapists. *Crisis.* Published online: 2 December 2014. doi: 10.1027/0227-5910/a000290.

Wilcox HC, Mittendorfer-Rutz E, Kjeldgard L, Alexanderson K, Runeso B (2015). Functional impairment due to bereavement after the death of adolescent or young adult offspring in a national population study of 1,051,515 parents. *Social Psychiatry and Psychiatric Epidemiology.* Published online: 1 January 2015. doi: 10.1007/s00127-014-0997-7.

NON FATAL SUICIDAL BEHAVIOR

Epidemiology

Adams K, Halacas C, Cincotta M, Pesich C (2014). Mental health and Victorian Aboriginal people: What can data mining tell us? *Australian Journal of Primary Health* 20, 350-355.

Aggarwal B, Rana SK, Chhavi N (2014). Pattern of poisoning in children, an experience from a teaching hospital in northern India. *JK Science* 16, 174-178.

Aichberger MC, Heredia Montesinos A, Bromand Z, Yesil R, Temur-Erman S, Rapp MA, Heinz A, Schouler-Ocak M (2015). Suicide attempt rates and intervention effects in women of Turkish origin in Berlin. *European Psychiatry*. Published online: 14 January 2015. doi: 10.1016/j.eurpsy.2014.12.003.

Al-Sayegh H, Lowry J, Polur RN, Hines RB, Liu F, Zhang J (2015). Suicide history and mortality: A follow-up of a national cohort in the United States. *Archives of Suicide Research* 19, 35-47.

Alves MAG, Cadete MMM (2015). Suicide attempts among children and adolescents: Partial or total injury? *Ciencia e Saude Coletiva* 20, 75-84.

Babakhanian M, Sadeghi M, Mohamadpur E, Rezazadeh H (2014). Deliberate self-harm among patients referring to the emergency room in Damghan, Iran. *Iranian Journal of Psychiatry and Behavioral Sciences* 8, 46–51.

Bayramoglu A, Saritemur M, Akgol Gur ST, Emet M (2015). Demographic and clinical differences of aggressive and non-aggressive suicide attempts in the emergency department in the eastern region of Turkey. *Iranian Red Crescent Medical Journal* 17, e24666.

Brière FN, Rohde P, Seeley JR, Klein D, Lewinsohn PM (2014). Adolescent suicide attempts and adult adjustment. *Depression and Anxiety* 32, 270-276.

Corcoran P, Griffin E, O'Carroll A, Cassidy L, Bonner B (2015). Hospital-treated deliberate self-harm in the western area of northern Ireland. *Crisis* 1-8 . Published online: 12 January 2015. doi: 10.1027/0227-5910/a000301.

Cotter P, Corcoran P, McCarthy J, O'Suilleabháin F, Carli V, Hoven C, Wasserman C, Sarchiapone M, Wasserman D, Keeley H (2014). Victimisation and psychosocial difficulties associated with sexual orientation concerns: A school-based study of adolescents. *Irish Medical Journal* 107, 310-313.

Eroglu M, Yildirim AO, Uzkeser M, Saritas A, Acemoglu H, Navruz M, Emet M (2014). Emergency room visits for suicide attempts: Rates, trends and sociodemographic characteristics of suicide attempts in Northeastern Anatolia. *Klinik Psikofarmakoloji Bulteni* 24, 350-359.

Falhammar H, Frisen L, Norrby C, Hirschberg AL, Almqvist C, Nordenskjold A, Nordenstrom A (2014). Increased mortality in patients with congenital adrenal hyperplasia due to 21-hydroxylase deficiency. *The Journal of Clinical Endocrinology & Metabolism* 99, e2715-2721.

Forrester MB, Bojes H (2015). Adolescent pesticide exposures reported to Texas poison centers. *International Journal of Adolescent Medicine and Health*. Published online: 7 March 2015. doi: 10.1515/ijamh-2014-0072.

Ghimire S, Devkota S, Budhathoki R, Thakur A, Sapkota N (2014). Psychiatric comorbidities in patients with deliberate self-harm in a tertiary care center. *Journal of the Nepal Medical Association* 52, 697-702.

Grover S., Sarkar S., Chakrabarti S., Malhotra S., Avasthi A. (2015). Intentional self-harm in children and adolescents: A study from psychiatry consultation liaison services of a tertiary care hospital. *Indian Journal of Psychological Medicine* 37, 12-16.

Guerreiro DF, Sampaio D, Figueira ML, Madge N (2015). Self-harm in adolescents: A self-report survey in schools from Lisbon, Portugal. *Archives of Suicide* Research. Published online: 12 March 2015. doi: 10.1080/13811118.2015.1004480.

Hart R, Doherty DA (2014). The potential implications of a PCOS diagnosis on a woman's long-term health using data linkage. *Journal of Clinical Endocrinology and Metabolism* 100, 911-919.

Hasegawa K, Espinola JA, Brown DFM, Camargo CA, Jr. (2014). Trends in U.S. Emergency department visits for opioid overdose, 1993-2010. *Pain Medicine* 15, 1765-1770.

Hawton K, Haw C, Casey D, Bale L, Brand F, Rutherford D (2014). Self-harm in Oxford, England: Epidemiological and clinical trends, 1996-2010. *Social Psychiatry and Psychiatric Epidemiology* 50, 695-704.

Henning J, Frangos S, Simon R, Pachter HL, Bholat OS (2015). Patterns of traumatic injury in New York City prisoners requiring hospital admission. *Journal of Correctional Health Care* 21, 53-58.

Herbert A, Gilbert R, Gonzalez-Izquierdo A, Li L (2015). Violence, self-harm and drug or alcohol misuse in adolescents admitted to hospitals in England for injury: A retrospective cohort study. *BMJ Open* 5, e006079.

Jonas JB, Nangia V, Rietschel M, Paul T, Behere P, Panda-Jonas S (2014). Prevalence of depression, suicidal ideation, alcohol intake and nicotine consumption in rural central India. The Central India Eye and Medical Study. *PLoS One* 9, e113550.

Kalantar Motamedi MH, Heydari M, Heydari M, Ebrahimi A (2015). Prevalence and pattern of facial burns: A 5-year assessment of 808 patients. *Journal of Oral and Maxillofacial Surgery* 73, 676-682.

Kamijo Y, Takai M, Fujita Y, Hirose Y, Iwasaki Y, Ishihara S, Yokoyama T, Yagi K, Sakamoto T (2014). A multicenter retrospective survey of poisoning after consumption of products containing synthetic chemicals in Japan. *Internal Medicine* 53, 2439-2445.

Kavalci G, Ethemoglu FB, Batuman A, Kumral D, Emre C, Surgit M, Akdikan A, Kavalci C (2014). Epidemiological and cost analysis of self-poisoning cases in Ankara, Turkey. *Iranian Red Crescent Medical Journal* 16, e10856.

Kaya E, Yilmaz A, Saritas A, Colakoglu S, Baltaci D, Kandis H, Kara IH (2015). Acute intoxication cases admitted to the emergency department of a university hospital. *World Journal of Emergency Medicine* 6, 54-59.

Kern JK, Geier DA, Bjørklund G, King PG, Homme KG, Haley BE, Sykes LK, Geier MR (2014). Evidence supporting a link between dental amalgams and chronic illness, fatigue, depression, anxiety, and suicide. *Neuro Endocrinology Letters* 35, 537-552.

Koc B, Tutal F, Urumdas M, Ozkurt Y, Erus T, Yavuz A, Kemik O (2014). The preliminary experience in the emergency department of a newly opened penitentiary institution hospital in Turkey. *North American Journal of Medical Sciences* 6, 460-465.

Ku CH, Hung HM, Leong WC, Chen HH, Lin JL, Huang WH, Yang HY, Weng CH, Lin CM, Lee SH, Wang IK, Liang CC, Chang CT, Lin WR, Yen TH (2015). Outcome of patients with carbon monoxide poisoning at a far-east poison center. *PLoS One* 10, e0118995.

Lahti M, Eriksson JG, Heinonen K, Kajantie E, Lahti J, Wahlbeck K, Tuovinen S, Pesonen AK, Mikkonen M, Osmond C, Raikkonen K (2014). Maternal grand multiparity and the risk of severe mental disorders in adult offspring. *PLoS One* 9, e114679.

Lipsicas CB, Mäkinen IH, Wasserman D, Apter A, Kerkhof A, Michel K, Renberg ES, Van Heeringen K, Värnik A, Schmidtke A (2014). Repetition of attempted suicide among immigrants in Europe. *Canadian Journal of Psychiatry* 59, 539-547.

McAndrew S, Warne T (2014). Hearing the voices of young people who self-harm: Implications for service providers. *International Journal of Mental Health Nursing* 23, 570-579.

Min A, Jang E-y, Park YC (2014). The predictor of suicidal ideation and attempt of middle school adolescents in an urban community. *Journal of Korean Neuropsychiatric Association* 53, 228-236.

Min K-B, Park S-G, Hwang SH, Min J-Y (2014). Precarious employment and the risk of suicidal ideation and suicide attempts. *Preventive Medicine* 71, 72-76.

Oktan V (2014). A characterization of self-injurious behavior among Turkish adolescents. *Psychological Reports* 115, 645-654.

Park S, Kim JW, Kim BN, Bae JH, Shin MS, Yoo HJ, Cho SC (2015). Clinical characteristics and precipitating factors of adolescent suicide attempters admitted for psychiatric inpatient care in South Korea. *Psychiatry Investigation* 12, 29-36.

Pavarin RM, Fioritti A, Fontana F, Marani S, Paparelli A, Boncompagni G (2014). Emergency department admission and mortality rate for suicidal behavior. *Crisis* 35, 406-414.

Rajabi MT, Maddah G, Bagheri R, Mehrabi M, Shabahang H, Lorestani F (2015). Corrosive injury of the upper gastrointestinal tract: Review of surgical management and outcome in 14 adult cases. *Iranian Journal of Otorhinolaryngology* 27, 15-21.

Ravi P, Karakiewicz PI, Roghmann F, Gandaglia G, Choueiri TK, Menon M, McKay RR, Nguyen PL, Sammon JD, Sukumar S, Varda B, Chang SL, Kibel AS, Sun M, Quoc-Dien T (2014). Mental health outcomes in elderly men with prostate cancer. *Urologic Oncology* 32, 1333-1340.

Saaiq M, Ashraf B (2014). Epidemiology and outcome of self-inflicted burns at Pakistan Institute of Medical Sciences, Islamabad. *World journal of plastic surgery* 3, 107-114.

Sari Dogan F, Ozaydin V, Varisli B, Incealtin O, Ozkok Z (2014). The analysis of poisoning cases presented to the emergency department within a one-year period. *Turkiye Acil Tip Dergisi* 14, 160-164.

Shen C-H, Peng C-K, Chou Y-C, Pan K-T, Chang S-C, Chang S-Y, Huang K-L (2015). Predicting duration of mechanical ventilation in patients with carbon monoxide poisoning: A retrospective study. *Journal of Critical Care* 30, 19-24.

Straub J, Keller F, Sproeber N, Koelch MG, Plener PL (2015). Prevalence and association with depressive and manic symptoms. *Zeitschrift Fur Kinder-Und Jugendpsychiatrie Und Psychotherapie* 43, 39-45.

Swain S, Mohanan P, Sanah N, Sharma V, Ghosh D (2014). Risk behaviors related to violence and injury among school-going adolescents in Karnataka, southern India. *International Journal of Adolescent Medicine and Health* 26, 551-558.

Taylor MR, Boden JM, Rucklidge JJ (2014). The relationship between ADHD symptomatology and self-harm, suicidal ideation, and suicidal behaviours in adults: A pilot study. *Attention Deficit and Hyperactivity Disorders* 6, 303-312.

Tossone K, Jefferis E, Bhatta MP, Bilge-Johnson S, Seifert P (2014). Risk factors for rehospitalization and inpatient care among pediatric psychiatric intake response center patients. *Child and Adolescent Psychiatry and Mental Health* 8, 27.

Verdolini N, Dean J, Elisei S, Quartesan R, Zaman R, Agius M (2014). Bipolar disorder: The importance of clinical assessment in identifying prognostic factors - an audit. Part 1: An analysis of potential prognostic factors. *Psychiatria Danubina* 26 Suppl 1, 289-300.

Wong YJ, Vaughan EL, Liu T, Chang TK (2014). Asian Americans' proportion of life in the United States and suicide ideation: The moderating effects of ethnic subgroups. *Asian American Journal of Psychology* 5, 237-242.

Yabanoglu H, Aytac HO, Turk E, Karagulle E, Belli S, Sakallioglu AE, Tarim MA, Moray G, Haberal M (2015). Evaluation of demographic and clinical characteristics of patients who attempted suicide by self-inflicted burn using catalyzer. *International Surgery* 100, 304-308 .

Yang LS, Zhang ZH, Sun L, Sun YH, Ye DQ (2015). Prevalence of suicide attempts among college students in China: A meta-analysis. *PLoS One* 10, e0116303.

Zelner I, Matlow J, Hutson JR, Wax P, Koren G, Brent J, Finkelstei Y (2015). Acute poisoning during pregnancy: Observations from the toxicology investigators consortium. *Journal of Medical Toxicology*. Published online: 18 March 2015. doi: 10.1007/s13181-015-0467-y.

Risk and protective factors

Abdollahi A, Abu Talib M (2015). Hardiness, spirituality, and suicidal ideation among individuals with substance abuse: The moderating role of gender and marital status. *Journal of Dual Diagnosis* 11, 12-21.

Abdollahi A, Abu Talib M, Yaacob SN, Ismail Z (2015). The role of hardiness in decreasing stress and suicidal ideation in a sample of undergraduate students. *Journal of Humanistic Psychology* 55, 202-222.

Ackerman JP, McBee-Strayer SM, Mendoza K, Stevens J, Sheftall AH, Campo JV, Bridge JA (2014). Risk-sensitive decision-making deficit in adolescent suicide attempters. *Journal of Child and Adolescent Psychopharmacology* 25, 109-113.

Adamowicz JL, Salwen JK, Hymowitz GF, Vivian D (2015). Predictors of suicidality in bariatric surgery candidates. *Journal of Health Psychology*. Published online: 18 February 2015. doi: 10.1177/1359105315569618.

Adler BA, Wink LK, Early M, Shaffer R, Minshawi N, McDougle CJ, Erickson CA (2015). Drug-refractory aggression, self-injurious behavior, and severe tantrums in autism spectrum disorders: A chart review study. *Autism* 19, 102-106.

Ahmadi A, Schwebel DC, Bazargan-Hejazi S, Taliee K, Karim H, Mohammadi R (2015). Self-immolation and its adverse life-events risk factors: Results from an Iranian population. *Journal of Injury and Violence Research* 7, 13-18.

Ai AL, Pappas C, Simonsen E (2015). Risk and protective factors for three major mental health problems among Latino American men nationwide. *American Journal of Men's Health* 9, 64-75.

Al-Asadi AM, Klein B (2014). Comorbidity structure of psychological disorders in the online e-pass data as predictors of psychosocial adjustment measures: Psychological distress, adequate social support, self-confidence, quality of life, and suicidal ideation. *Journal of Medical Internet Research* 16, e248.

Alexander CL, Reger MA, Smolenski DJ, Fullerton NR (2014). Comparing US army suicide cases to a control sample: Initial data and methodological lessons. *Military Medicine* 179, 1062-1066.

Alhusen JL, Frohman N, Purcell G (2015). Intimate partner violence and suicidal ideation in pregnant women. *Archives of Women's Mental Health*. Published online: 10 March 2015. doi: 10.1007/s00737-015-0515-2.

Allen J, Hopper K, Wexler L, Kral M, Rasmus S, Nystad K (2014). Mapping resilience pathways of indigenous youth in five circumpolar communities. *Transcultural Psychiatry* 51, 601-631.

Alpaslan AH, Soylu N, Avci K, Co kun KT, Kocak U, Ta HU (2015). Disordered eating attitudes, alexithymia and suicide probability among Turkish high school girls. *Psychiatry Research* 226, 224-229.

Alsaleh A (2014). The impact of community structural instability on Bedoon and suicidal behavior in Kuwait. *African and Asian Studies* 13, 272-290.

Altamura C, Fagiolini A, Galderisi S, Rocca P, Rossi A (2014). Schizophrenia today: Epidemiology, diagnosis, course and models of care. *Journal of Psychopathology* 20, 223-243.

Alter AL, Hershfield HE (2014). People search for meaning when they approach a new decade in chronological age. *Proceedings of the National Academy of Sciences of the United States of America* 111, 17066-17070.

Amer NRY, Hamdan-Mansour AM (2014). Psychosocial predictors of suicidal ideation in patients diagnosed with chronic illnesses in Jordan. *Issues in Mental Health Nursing* 35, 864-871.

Ammerman BA, Kleiman EM, Uyeji LL, Knorr AC, McCloskey MS (2015). Suicidal and violent behavior: The role of anger, emotion dysregulation, and impulsivity. *Personality and Individual Differences* 79, 57-62.

Anderson LM, Hayden BM, Tomasula JL (2014). Sexual assault, overweight, and suicide attempts in U.S. adolescents. *Suicide and Life-Threatening Behavior.* Published online: 19 December 2014. doi: 10.1111/sltb.12148.

Anderson R, Wilson T, Griffiths M (2014). Antidepressant use and suicide rate in England: The geographic divide. *Value in Health* 17, A464.

Anikeeva O, Bi P, Hiller JE, Ryan P, Roder D, Han GS (2015). Trends in migrant mortality rates in Australia 1981-2007: A focus on the national health priority areas other than cancer. *Ethnicity and Health* 20, 29-48.

Ansell EB, Wright AGC, Markowitz JC, Sanislow CA, Hopwood CJ, Zanarini MC, Yen S, Pinto A, McGlashan TH, Grilo CM (2015). Personality disorder risk factors for suicide attempts over 10 years of follow-up. *Personality Disorders* 6, 161-167.

Antai D, Oke A, Braithwaite P, Lopez GB (2014). The effect of economic, physical, and psychological abuse on mental health: A population-based study of women in the Philippines. *International Journal of Family Medicine* 2014, 852317.

Arnold EM, McCall VW, Anderson A, Bryant A, Bell R (2013). Sleep problems, suicidality and depression among American Indian youth. *Journal of Sleep Disorders* 2, 119.

Ashton LM, Hutchesson MJ, Rollo ME, Morgan PJ, Collins CE (2014). A scoping review of risk behaviour interventions in young men. *BMC Public Health* 14, 957.

Assari S (2014). Synergistic effects of lifetime psychiatric disorders on suicidal ideation among blacks in the USA. *Journal of Racial and Ethnic Health Disparities* 1, 275-282.

Athwal H (2015). 'I don't have a life to live': Deaths and UK detention. *Race and Class* 56, 50-68.

Avenevoli S, Swendsen J, He JP, Burstein M, Merikangas KR (2015). Major depression in the national comorbidity survey-adolescent supplement: Prevalence, correlates, and treatment. *Journal of the American Academy of Child & Adolescent Psychiatry* 54, 37-44.e2.

Baams L, Grossman AH, Russell ST (2015). Minority stress and mechanisms of risk for depression and suicidal ideation among lesbian, gay, and bisexual youth. *Developmental Psychology* 51, 688-696.

Baetens I, Claes L, Hasking P, Smits D, Grietens H, Onghena P, Martin G (2015). The relationship between parental expressed emotions and non-suicidal self-injury: The mediating roles of self-criticism and depression. *Journal of Child and Family Studies* 24, 491-498.

Bagalkot TR, Park J-I, Kim H-T, Kim H-M, Kim MS, Yoon M-S, Ko S-H, Cho H-C, Chung Y-C (2014). Lifetime prevalence of and risk factors for suicidal ideation and suicide attempts in a Korean community sample. *Psychiatry Interpersonal and Biological Processes* 77, 360-373.

Baiocco R, Ioverno S, Cerutti R, Santamaria F, Fontanesi L, Lingiardi V, Baumgartnert E, Laghi F (2014). Suicidal ideation in Spanish and Italian lesbian and gay young adults: The role of internalized sexual stigma. *Psicothema* 26, 490-496.

Baker CK, Helm S, Bifulco K, Chung-Do J (2014). The relationship between self-harm and teen dating violence among youth in Hawaii. *Qualitative Health Research* 25, 652-667.

Balbuena L, Tempier R (2015). Why is there a link between smoking and suicide? In reply. *Psychiatric Services* 66, 331-332.

Baldwin DS, Green M, Montgomery SA (2014). Lack of efficacy of moclobemide or imipramine in the treatment of recurrent brief depression: Results from an exploratory randomized, double-blind, placebo-controlled treatment study. *International Clinical Psychopharmacology* 29, 339-343.

Ballard ED, Lally N, Nugent AC, Furey ML, Luckenbaugh DA, Zarate CA, Jr. (2014). Neural correlates of suicidal ideation and its reduction in depression. *International Journal of Neuropsychopharmacology,* Published online: 31 October 2014. doi: 10.1093/ijnp/pyu069.

Ballard ED, Musci RJ, Tingey L, Goklish N, Larzelere-Hinton F, Barlow A, Cwik M (2015). Latent class analysis of substance use and aggressive behavior in American Indian youth who attempted suicide. *American Indian and Alaska Native Mental Health Research* 22, 77-94.

Ballard ED, Voort Jvd, Luckenbaugh DA, Richards EM, Ionescu DF, Niciu MJ, Brutsche NE, Ameli R, Zarate CA (2014). Suicidal ideation in the context of ketamine infusion: Relationship with depression and anxiety symptom clusters. *Comprehensive Psychiatry* 55, e45.

Barber C, Azrael D, Miller M (2014). Study findings on FDA antidepressant warnings and suicide attempts in young people: A false alarm? *British Medical Journal* 349, g5645.

Bartlett RO (2014). Proxy for suicide attempts was inappropriate in study of changes in antidepressant use after FDA warnings. *British Medical Journal* 349, g5644.

Batejan KL, Jarvi SM, Swenson LP (2015). Sexual orientation and non-suicidal self-injury: A meta-analytic review. *Archives of Suicide Research* 19, 131-150.

Batterham PJ, Calear AL, van Spijker BA (2014). The specificity of the interpersonal-psychological theory of suicidal behavior for identifying suicidal ideation in an online sample. *Suicide and Life-Threatening Behavior*. Published online: 12 November 2014. doi: 10.1111/sltb.12140.

Baumgartner JN, Parcesepe A, Mekuria YG, Abitew DB, Gebeyehu W, Okello F, Shattuck D (2014). Maternal mental health in Amhara region, Ethiopia: A cross-sectional survey. *Global Health, Science and Practice* 2, 482-486.

Berger E, Reupert A, Hasking P (2015). Pre-service and in-service teachers' knowledge, attitudes and confidence towards self-injury among pupils. *Journal of Education For Teaching* 41, 37-51.

Berman NC, Stark A, Cooperman A, Wilhelm S, Glenn Cohen I (2015). Effect of patient and therapist factors on suicide risk assessment. *Death Studies*. Published online: 12 February 2015. doi: 10.1080/07481187.2014.958630.

Bernert RA, Kim JS, Iwata NG, Perlis ML (2015). Sleep disturbances as an evidence-based suicide risk factor. *Current Psychiatry Reports* 17, 554-554.

Bernstein J, Bernstein E, Belanoff C, Cabral HJ, Babakhanlou-Chase H, Derrington TM, Diop H, Douriez C, Evans SR, Jacobs H, Kotelchuck M (2014). The association of injury with substance use disorder among women of reproductive age: An opportunity to address a major contributor to recurrent preventable emergency department visits? *Academic Emergency Medicine* 21, 1459-1468.

Bhalla D, Tchalla AE, Marin B, Ngoungou EB, Tan CT, Preux PM (2014). Epilepsy: Asia versus Africa. *Epilepsia* 55, 1317-1321.

Bhatta MP, Shakya S, Jefferis E (2014). Association of being bullied in school with suicide ideation and planning among rural middle school adolescents. *Journal of School Health* 84, 731-738.

Biétry D, Exadaktylos A, Müller T, Zbären P, Caversaccio M, Arnold A (2014). Sharp neck injuries in suicidal intention. *European Archives of Oto-Rhino-Laryngology*. Published online: 28 December 2014. doi: 10.1007/s00405-014-3471-y.

Binelli C, Muñiz A, Sanches S, Ortiz A, Navines R, Egmond E, Udina M, Batalla A, López-Sola C, Crippa JA, Subirà S, Martín-Santos R (2015). New evidence of heterogeneity in social anxiety disorder: Defining two qualitatively different personality profiles taking into account clinical, environmental and genetic factors. *European Psychiatry* 30, 160-165.

Birmaher B, Gill MK, Axelson DA, Goldstein BI, Goldstein TR, Yu H, Liao F, Iyengar S, Diler RS, Strober M, Hower H, Yen S, Hunt J, Merranko JA, Ryan ND, Keller MB (2014). Longitudinal trajectories and associated baseline predictors in youths with bipolar spectrum disorders. *American Journal of Psychiatry* 171, 990-999.

Bischof A, Meyer C, Bischof G, John U, Wurst FM, Thon N, Lucht M, Grabe HJ, Rumpf H-J (2015). Suicidal events among pathological gamblers: The role of comorbidity of axis I and axis II disorders. *Psychiatry Research* 225, 413-414.

Bishopp SA, Boots DP (2014). General strain theory, exposure to violence, and suicide ideation among police officers: A gendered approach. *Journal of Criminal Justice* 42, 538-548.

Biswas PS, Khess CRJ (2014). Gender difference and phenomenology of unipolar depression from Indian perspective. *International Journal of Culture and Mental Health* 7, 372-385.

Blank M, Zhang J, Lamers F, Taylor AD, Hickie IB, Merikangas KR (2015). Health correlates of insomnia symptoms and comorbid mental disorders in a nationally representative sample of US adolescents. *Sleep* 38, 197-2014.

Blasco-Fontecilla H, Artieda-Urrutia P, Berenguer-Elias N, Manuel Garcia-Vega J, Fernandez-Rodriguez M, Rodriguez-Lomas C, Gonzalez-Villalobos I, Iruela-Cuadrado L, de Leon J (2014). Are major repeater patients addicted to suicidal behavior? *Adicciones* 26, 321-333.

Blasco-Fontecilla H, Baca-Garcia E, Courtet P, García Nieto R, De Leon J (2015). Horror vacui: Emptiness might distinguish between major suicide repeaters and nonmajor suicide repeaters: A pilot study. *Psychotherapy and Psychosomatics* 84, 117-119.

Bodzy ME, Barreto S, Swenson LP, Liguori G, Costea G (2015). Self-reported psychopathology, trauma symptoms and emotion coping among child suicide attempters and ideators: An exploratory study of young children. *Archives of Suicide Research.* Published online: 9 March 2015. doi: 10.1080/13811118.2015.1004469.

Borges G, Orozco R, Breslau J, Miller M (2014). An observational study of the impact of service use on suicidality among adults with mental disorders. *Injury Epidemiology* 1, e29.

Borza T, Engedal K, Bergh S, Barca ML, Benth JŠ, Selbæk G (2015). The course of depressive symptoms as measured by the Cornell Scale for Depression in Dementia over 74 months in 1158 nursing home residents. *Journal of Affective Disorders* 175, 209-216.

Bourne T, Wynants L, Peters M, Van Audenhove C, Timmerman D, Van Calster B, Jalmbrant M (2015). The impact of complaints procedures on the welfare, health and clinical practise of 7926 doctors in the UK: A cross-sectional survey. *British Medical Journal Open* 5, e006687.

Braga C, Gonçalves S (2014). Non-suicidal self injury, psychopathology and attachment: A study with university students. *Spanish Journal of Psychology* 17, e66.

Brand-Gothelf A, Leor S, Apter A, Fennig S (2014). The impact of comorbid depressive and anxiety disorders on severity of anorexia nervosa in adolescent girls. *Journal of Nervous and Mental Disease* 202, 759-762.

Braquehais MD, Eiroa-Orosa FJ, Holmes KM, Lusilla P, Bravo M, Mozo X, Mezzatesta M, Casanovas M, Pujol T, Sher L (2014). Differences in physicians' and nurses' recent suicide attempts: An exploratory study. *Archives of Suicide Research.* Published online: 17 December 2015. doi: 10.1080/13811118.2014.996693.

Brausch AM, Boone SD (2015). Frequency of nonsuicidal self-injury in adolescents: Differences in suicide attempts, substance use, and disordered eating. *Suicide and Life-Threatening Behavior.* Published online: 13 February 2015. doi: 10.1111/sltb.12155.

Breen ME, Seifuddin F, Zandi PP, Potash JB, Willour VL (2015). Investigating the role of early childhood abuse and HPA axis genes in suicide attempters with bipolar disorder. *Psychiatric Genetics* 25, 106-111.

Breines JG, Ayduk O (2015). Rejection sensitivity and vulnerability to self-directed hostile cognitions following rejection. *Journal of Personality* 83, 1-13.

Bresin K, Schoenleber M (2015). Gender differences in the prevalence of nonsuicidal self-injury: A meta-analysis. *Clinical Psychology Review* 38, 55-64.

Bridge JA, Reynolds B, McBee-Strayer SM, Sheftall AH, Ackerman J, Stevens J, Mendoza K, Campo JV, Brent DA (2015). Impulsive aggression, delay discounting, and adolescent suicide attempts: Effects of current psychotropic medication use and family history of suicidal behavior. *Journal of Child and Adolescent Psychopharmacology* 25, 114-123.

Briere J, Godbout N, Dias C (2015). Cumulative trauma, hyperarousal, and suicidality in the general population: A path analysis. *Journal of Trauma and Dissociation* 16, 153-169.

Broadbent R, Papadopoulos T (2014). Improving mental health and wellbeing for young men in the building and construction industry. *Journal of Child and Adolescent Mental Health* 26, 217-227.

Brunoni AR, Nunes MA, Lotufo PA, Benseñor IM (2014). Acute suicidal ideation in middle-aged adults from Brazil. Results from the baseline data of the Brazilian longitudinal study of adult health (ELSA-Brasil). *Psychiatry Research* 225, 56-562.

Bryan CJ, Clemans TA, Leeson B, Rudd MD (2015). Acute vs. chronic stressors, multiple suicide attempts, and persistent suicide ideation in US soldiers. *Journal of Nervous and Mental Disease* 203, 48-53.

Bryan CJ, Hitschfeld MJ, Palmer BA, Schak KM, Roberge EM, Lineberry TW (2014). Gender differences in the association of agitation and suicide attempts among psychiatric inpatients. *General Hospital Psychiatry* 36, 726-731.

Bryan CJ, Rudd MD, Wertenberger E, Young-McCaughon S, Peterson A (2015). Nonsuicidal self-injury as a prospective predictor of suicide attempts in a clinical sample of military personnel. *Comprehensive Psychiatry* 59, 1-7.

Buckholdt KE, Parra GR, Anestis MD, Lavender JM, Jobe-Shields LE, Tull MT, Gratz KL (2015). Emotion regulation difficulties and maladaptive behaviors: Examination of deliberate self-harm, disordered eating, and substance misuse in two samples. *Cognitive Therapy and Research* 39, 140-152.

Burke TA, Stange JP, Hamilton JL, Cohen JN, O'Garro-Moore J, Daryanani I, Abramson LY, Alloy LB (2014). Cognitive and emotion-regulatory mediators of the relationship between behavioral approach system sensitivity and nonsuicidal self-injury frequency. *Suicide and Life-Threatening Behavior*. Published online: 2 December 2014. doi: 10.1111/sltb.12145.

Burns MN, Ryan DT, Garofalo R, Newcomb ME, Mustanski B (2015). Mental health disorders in young urban sexual minority men. *Journal of Adolescent Health* 56, 52-58.

Butwicka A, Frisén L, Almqvist C, Zethelius B, Lichtenstein P (2015). Risks of psychiatric disorders and suicide attempts in children and adolescents with type 1 diabetes: A population-based cohort study. *Diabetes Care* 38, 453-459.

Calkins ME, Moore TM, Merikangas KR, Burstein M, Satterthwaite TD, Bilker WB, Ruparel K, Chiavacci R, Wolf DH, Mentch F, Qiu H, Connolly JJ, Sleiman PA, Hakonarson H, Gur RC, Gur RE (2014). The psychosis spectrum in a young US community sample: Findings from the Philadelphia neurodevelopmental cohort. *World Psychiatry* 13, 296-305.

Campos RC, Holden RR (2014). Suicide risk in a Portuguese non-clinical sample of adults. *European Journal of Psychiatry* 28, 230-241.

Cannavale R, Itro A, Campisi G, Compilato D, Colella G (2015). Oral self-injuries: Clinical findings in a series of 19 patients. *Medicina Oral Patologia Oral y Cirugia Bucal* 20, e123-e129.

Cao J, Chen J-M, Kuang L, Ai M, Fang W-D, Gan Y, Wang W, Chen X-R, Xu X-M, Wang H-G, Lv Z (2015). Abnormal regional homogeneity in young adult suicide attempters with no diagnosable psychiatric disorder: A resting state functional magnetic imaging study. *Psychiatry Research* 23, 95-102.

Capron DW, Allan NP, Ialongo NS, Leen-Feldner E, Schmidt NB (2015). The depression distress amplification model in adolescents: A longitudinal examination of anxiety sensitivity cognitive concerns, depression and suicidal ideation. *Journal of Adolescence* 41, 17-24.

Carpenter GSJ, Carpenter TP, Kimbrel NA, Flynn EJ, Pennington ML, Cammarata C, Zimering RT, Kamholz BW, Gulliver SB (2015). Social support, stress, and suicidal ideation in professional firefighters. *American Journal of Health Behavior* 39, 191-196.

Carpenter RW, Trull TJ (2015). The pain paradox: Borderline personality disorder features, self-harm history, and the experience of pain. *Personality Disorders* 6, 141-151.

Carra G, Bartoli F, Crocamo C, Brady KT, Clerici M (2015). Cannabis use disorder as a correlate of suicide attempts among people with bipolar disorder. *Bipolar Disorders* 17, 113-114.

Case BG (2014). More data needed to interpret link between suicide and FDA warning on antidepressants. *British Medical Journal* 349, g5616.

Casey P, Jabbar F, O'Leary E, Doherty AM (2015). Suicidal behaviours in adjustment disorder and depressive episode. *Journal of Affective Disorders* 174, 441-446.

Castaneto MS, Gorelick DA, Desrosiers NA, Hartman RL, Pirard S, Huestis MA (2014). Synthetic cannabinoids: Epidemiology, pharmacodynamics, and clinical implications. *Drug and Alcohol Dependence* 144, 12-41.

Ceccon RF, Meneghel SN, Hirakata VN (2014). Women with HIV: Gender violence and suicidal ideation. *Revista de Saúde Pública* 48, 758-765.

Chan JW (2014). Eveningness and insomnia: Independent risk factors of nonremission in major depressive disorder. *Sleep* 37, 911-917.

Chang EC, Hirsch JK (2015). Social problem solving under assault: Understanding the impact of sexual assault on the relation between social problem solving and suicidal risk in female college students. *Cognitive Therapy and Research* 39, 403-414.

Chang EC, Lian X, Yu T, Qu J, Zhang B, Jia W, Hu Q, Li J, Wu J, Hirsch JK (2014). Loneliness under assault: Understanding the impact of sexual assault on the relation between loneliness and suicidal risk in college students. *Personality and Individual Differences* 72, 155-159.

Chaplo SD, Kerig PK, Bennett DC, Modrowski CA (2015). The roles of emotion dysregulation and dissociation in the association between sexual abuse and self-injury among juvenile justice-involved youth. *Journal of Trauma and Dissociation* 16, 272-285.

Cheatle MD (2014). Suicidal ideation in patients with chronic pain: The risk-benefit of pharmacotherapy. *Pain* 155, 2446-2447.

Chee KY, Tripathi A, Avasthi A, Chong MY, Xiang YT, Sim K, Si TM, Kanba S, He YL, Lee MS, Fung-Kum Chiu H, Yang SY, Kuga H, Udormatn P, Kallivayalil RA, Tanra AJ, Maramis M, Grover S, Chin LF, Dahlan R, Mohamad Isa MF, Ebenezer EGM, Nordin N, Shen WW, Shinfuku N, Tan CH, Sartorius N (2015). Country variations in depressive symptoms profile in Asian countries: Findings of the Research on Asia Psychotropic Prescription (REAP) studies. *Asia-Pacific Psychiatry.* Published online: 13 January 2015. doi: 10.1111/appy.

Chen H, Li Y, Wang L, Zhang B (2015). Causes of suicidal behaviors in men who have sex with men in China: A national questionnaire survey. *BMC Public Health*, 15: 91.

Cheng Y, Li X, Lou C, Sonenstein FL, Kalamar A, Jejeebhoy S, Delany-Moretlwe S, Brahmbhatt H, Olumide AO, Ojengbede O (2014). The association between social support and mental health among vulnerable adolescents in five cities: Findings from the study of the well-being of adolescents in vulnerable environments. *Journal of Adolescence Health* 55, S31-S38.

Chester DS, Merwin LM, Dewall CN (2014). Maladaptive perfectionism's link to aggression and self-harm: Emotion regulation as a mechanism. *Aggressive Behavior.* Published online: 12 December 2014. doi: 10.1002/AB.21578.

Cheung K, Aarts N, Noordam R, van Blijderveen JC, Sturkenboom MC, Ruiter R, Visser LE, Stricker BH (2014). Antidepressant use and the risk of suicide: A population-based cohort study. *Journal of Affective Disorders* 174C, 479-484.

Cho K-O (2014). Physical activity and suicide attempt of South Korean adolescents - evidence from the eighth Korea youth risk behaviors web-based survey. *Journal of Sports Science and Medicine* 13, 888-893.

Choi NG, DiNitto DM, Marti CN (2015). Middle-aged and older adults who had serious suicidal thoughts: Who made suicide plans and nonfatal suicide attempts? *International Psychogeriatrics* 27, 491-500.

Chong SJ, Johandi F, Kang GCW (2015). Self-inflicted burns in soldiers: The Singapore experience. *Annals of Plastic Surgery.* Published online: 17 March 2015. doi: 10.1097/SAP. 0000000000000495.

Choon MW, Abu Talib M, Yaacob SN, Awang H, Tan JP, Hassan S, Ismail Z (2015). Negative automatic thoughts as a mediator of the relationship between depression and suicidal behaviour in an at-risk sample of Malaysian adolescents. *Child and Adolescent Mental Health* 20, 89-93.

Christoffersen MN, Møhl B, DePanfilis D, Vammen KS (2014). Non-suicidal self-injury-does social support make a difference? An epidemiological investigation of a Danish national sample. *Child Abuse and Neglect.* Published online: 27 November 2014. doi: 10.1016/j.chiabu.2014.10.023.

Chu C-S, Tzeng N-S, Chang H-A, Chang C-C, Chen T-Y (2014). Killing two birds with one stone: The potential role of aripiprazole for patients with comorbid major depressive disorder and nicotine dependence via altering brain activity in the anterior cingulate cortex. *Medical Hypotheses* 83, 407-409.

Chung JH, Moon K, Kim DH, Min J-W, Kim TH, Hwang H-J (2014). Suicidal ideation and suicide attempts among diabetes mellitus: The Korea National Health and Nutrition Examination Survey (KNHANES IV, V) from 2007 to 2012. *Journal of Psychosomatic Research* 77, 457-461.

Cianfaglione R, Clarke A, Kerr M, Hastings RP, Oliver C, Moss J, Heald M, Felce D (2015). A national survey of Rett syndrome: Behavioural characteristics. *Journal of Neurodevelopmental Disorders* 7, 11.

Claes L, Bounnan WP, Witconnb G, Thurston M, Fernandez-Aranda F, Arcelus J (2015). Non-suicidal self-injury in trans people: Associations with psychological symptoms, victimization, interpersonal functioning, and perceived social support. *Journal of Sexual Medicine* 12, 168-179.

Claes L, Fagundo AB, Jimenez-Murcia S, Agueera Z, Giner-Bartolome C, Granero R, Sanchez I, Riesco N, Menchon JM, Tarrega S, Fernandez-Aranda F (2015). Is non-suicidal self-injury related to impulsivity in anorexia nervosa? Results from self-report and performance-based tasks. *European Eating Disorders Review* 23, 28-33.

Claes L, Luyckx K, Baetens I, Van De Ven M, Witteman C (2015). Bullying and victimization, depressive mood, and non-suicidal self-injury in adolescents: The moderating role of parental support. *Journal of Child and Family Studies.* Published online: 31 January 2015. doi: 10.1007/s10826-015-0138-2.

Claes L, Luyckx K, Bijttebier P, Turner B, Ghandi A, Smets J, Norre J, Van Assche L, Verheyen E, Goris Y, Hoksbergen I, Schoevaerts K (2015). Non-suicidal self-injury in patients with eating disorder: Associations with identity formation above and beyond anxiety and depression. *European Eating Disorders Review* 23, 119-125.

Clements C, Jones S, Morriss R, Peters S, Cooper J, While D, Kapur N (2015). Self-harm in bipolar disorders: Findings from a prospective clinical database. *Journal of Affective Disorders* 173, 113-119.

Colizzi M, Costa R, Todarello O (2015). Dissociative symptoms in individuals with gender dysphoria: Is the elevated prevalence real? *Psychiatry Research* 226, 173-180.

Colle R, Chupin M, Cury C, Vandendrie C, Gressier F, Hardy P, Falissard B, Colliot O, Ducreux D, Corruble E (2015). Depressed suicide attempters have smaller hippocampus than depressed patients without suicide attempts. *Journal of Psychiatric Research* 61, 13-18.

Colledge L, Hickson F, Reid D, Weatherburn P (2015). Poorer mental health in UK bisexual women than lesbians: Evidence from the UK 2007 Stonewall Women's Health Survey. *Journal of Public Health.* Published online: 13 January 2015. doi: 10.1093/pubmed/fdu105.

Congues JM (2014). Promoting collective well-being as a means of defying the odds: Drought in the Goulburn Valley, Australia. *Rural Society* 20, 229-242.

Conner KR, Wyman P, Goldston DB, Bossarte RM, Lu N, Kaukeinen K, Tu XM, Houston RJ, Lamis DA, Chan G, Bucholz KK, Hesselbrock VM (2014). Two studies of connectedness to parents and suicidal thoughts and behavior in children and adolescents. *Journal of Clinical Child and Adolescent Psychology.* Published online: 13 October 2014. doi: 10.1080/15374416.2014.952009.

Cook TB, Brenner LA, Cloninger CR, Langenberg P, Igbide A, Giegling I, Hartmann AM, Konte B, Friedl M, Brundin L, Groer MW, Can A, Rujescu D, Postolache TT (2015). "Latent" infection with toxoplasma gondii: Association with trait aggression and impulsivity in healthy adults. *Journal of Psychiatric Research* 60, 87-94.

Cornelius JR, Kirisci L, Reynolds M, Vanyukov M, Tarter R (2015). Does the Transmissible Liability Index (TLI) assessed in late childhood predict suicidal symptoms at young adulthood? *American Journal of Drug and Alcohol Abuse* 41, 264-268.

Correll CU (2014). Recognition of patients who would benefit from LAI antipsychotic treatment: How to assess adherence. *Journal of Clinical Psychiatry* 75, e29.

Coyle H, Clough P, Cooper P, Mohanraj R (2014). Clinical experience with perampanel: Focus on psychiatric adverse effects. *Epilepsy and Behavior* 41, 193-196.

Cramer RJ, Colbourn SL, Gemberling TM, Graham J, Stroud CH (2015). Substance-related coping, HIV-related factors, and mental health among an HIV-positive sexual minority community sample. *AIDS Care.* Published online: 23 March 2015. doi: 10.1080/09540121.2015.1024097.

Crane C, Heron J, Gunnell D, Lewis G, Evans J, Williams JMG (2015). Adolescent over-general memory, life events and mental health outcomes: Findings from a UK cohort study. *Memory.* Published online: 26 February 2014. doi: 10.1080/09658211.2015.1008014.

Crepeau-Hobson F, Leech NL (2015). Peer victimization and suicidal behaviors among high school youth. *Journal of School Violence.* Published online: 14 January 2015. doi: 10.1080/15388220.2014.996717.

Crombach A, Bambonye M, Elbert T (2014). A study on reintegration of street children in Burundi: Experienced violence and maltreatment are associated with mental health impairments and impeded educational progress. *Frontiers in Psychology* 5, 1441.

Crowe M (2014). From expression to symptom to disorder: The psychiatric evolution of self-harm in the DSM. *Journal of Psychiatric and Mental Health Nursing* 21, 857-858.

Cruz D, Narciso I, Pereira CR, Sampaio D (2014). Risk trajectories of self-destructiveness in adolescence: Family core influences. *Journal of Child and Family Studies* 23, 1172-1181.

Da Graça Cantarelli M, Nardin P, Buffon A, Eidt MC, Antônio Godoy L, Fernandes BS, Gonçalves CA (2015). Serum triglycerides, but not cholesterol or leptin, are decreased in suicide attempters with mood disorders. *Journal of Affective Disorders* 172, 403-409.

da Graça Cantarelli M, Tramontina AC, Leite MC, Gonçalves CA (2014). Potential neurochemical links between cholesterol and suicidal behavior. *Psychiatry Research* 30, 745-751.

Dai J, Zhong B-L, Xiang Y-T, Chiu HFK, Chan SSM, Yu X, Caine ED (2015). Internal migration, mental health, and suicidal behaviors in young rural Chinese. *Social Psychiatry and Psychiatric Epidemiology.* 50, 621-631.

Dalgard F, Gieler U, Tomas-Aragones L, Lien L, Poot F, Jemec GB, Misery L, Szabo C, Linder D, Sampogna F, Evers AW, Halvorsen JA, Balieva F, Szepietowski J, Romanov D, Marron SE, Altunay IK, Finlay AY, Salek SS, Kupfer J (2015). The psychological burden of skin diseases: A cross-sectional multicenter study among dermatological out-patients in 13 European countries. *Journal of Investigative Dermatology* 135, 984-991.

Dalglish SL, Melchior M, Younes N, Surkan PJ (2015). Work characteristics and suicidal ideation in young adults in France. *Social Psychiatry and Psychiatric Epidemiology* 50, 613-620.

Davis A (2014). Violence-related mild traumatic brain injury in women: Identifying a triad of post-injury disorders. *Journal of Trauma Nursing* 21, 300-308.

Davis B, Royne Stafford MB, Pullig C (2014). How gay-straight alliance groups mitigate the relationship between gay-bias victimization and adolescent suicide attempts. *Journal of the American Academy of Child & Adolescent Psychiatry* 53, 1271-1278.e1271.

Davison KM, Marshall-Fabien GL, Tecson A (2015). Association of moderate and severe food insecurity with suicidal ideation in adults: National survey data from three Canadian provinces. *Social Psychiatry and Psychiatric Epidemiology* 50, 963-972.

Daviss WB, Diler RS (2014). Suicidal behaviors in adolescents with ADHD: Associations with depressive and other comorbidity, parent-child conflict, trauma exposure, and impairment. *Journal of Attention Disorders* 18, 680-690.

Dazzi T, Gribble R, Wessely S, Fear NT (2015). Suicidal ideation and research ethics committees: A reply. *Psychological Medicine* 45, 217-218.

de Bolger AdP, Jones T, Dunstan D, Lykins A (2014). Australian trans men: Development, sexuality, and mental health. *Australian Psychologist* 49, 395-402.

De Jesus JR, De Campos BK, Galazzi RM, Martinez JLC, Arruda MAZ (2014). Bipolar disorder: Recent advances and future trends in bioanalytical developments for biomarker discovery. *Analytical and Bioanalytical Chemistry* 407, 661-667.

De Luca S, Schmeelk-Cone K, Wyman P (2015). Latino and Latina adolescents' help-seeking behaviors and attitudes regarding suicide compared to peers with recent suicidal ideation. *Suicide and Life-Threatening Behavior.* Published online: 12 January 2015. doi: 10.1111/sltb.12152.

Defife JA, Haggerty G, Smith SW, Betancourt L, Ahmed Z, Ditkowsky K (2015). Clinical validity of prototype personality disorder ratings in adolescents. *Journal of Personality Assessment* 97, 271-277.

Delgado-Casas C, Navarro JI, Garcia-Gonzalez-Gordon R, Marchena E (2014). Functional analysis of challenging behavior in people with severe intellectual disabilities. *Psychological Reports* 115, 655-669.

Dell Osso L, Massimetti G, Conversano C, Bertelloni C, Carta M, Ricca V, Carmassi C (2014). Alterations in circadian/seasonal rhythms and vegetative functions are related to suicidality in DSM-5 PTSD. *BMC Psychiatry* 14, 352-352.

Denneson LM, Teo AR, Ganzini L, Helmer DA, Bair MJ, Dobscha SK (2014). Military veterans' experiences with suicidal ideation: Implications for intervention and prevention. *Suicide and Life-Threatening Behavior.* Published online: 3 November 2014. doi: 10.1111/sltb.12136.

Denny S, Lucassen MFG, Stuart J, Fleming T, Bullen P, Peiris-John R, Rossen FV, Utter J (2014). The association between supportive high school environments and depressive symptoms and suicidality among sexual minority students. *Journal of Clinical Child and Adolescent Psychology.* Published online: 3 December 2014. doi: 10.1080/15374416.2014.958842.

DeShong HL, Tucker RP, O'Keefe VM, Mullins-Sweatt SN, Wingate LR (2015). Five factor model traits as a predictor of suicide ideation and interpersonal suicide risk in a college sample. *Psychiatry Research* 226, 217-223.

Di Thiene D, Alexanderson K, Tinghog P, Torre GL, Mittendorfer-Rutz E (2015). Suicide among first-generation and second-generation immigrants in Sweden: Association with labour market marginalisation and morbidity. *Journal of Epidemiology and Community Health* 69, 467-473.

Dickey LM, Reisner SL, Juntunen CL (2015). Non-suicidal self-injury in a large online sample of transgender adults. *Professional Psychology-Research and Practice* 46, 3-11.

Ding Y, Lawrence N, Olie E, Cyprien F, le Bars E, Bonafe A, Phillips ML, Courtet P, Jollant F (2015). Prefrontal cortex markers of suicidal vulnerability in mood disorders: A model-based structural neuroimaging study with a translational perspective. *Translational Psychiatry* 5, e516.

Dixon-Gordon KL, Chapman AL, Weiss NH, Rosenthal MZ (2014). A preliminary examination of the role of emotion differentiation in the relationship between borderline personality and urges for maladaptive behaviors. *Journal of Psychopathology and Behavioral Assessment* 36, 616-625.

Dorsey ER (2015). Safety, tolerability, and efficacy of PBT2 in Huntington's disease: A phase 2, randomised, double-blind, placebo-controlled trial. *Lancet Neurology* 14, 39-47.

Dou J, Tang J, Lu CH, Jiang ES, Wang PX (2015). A study of suicidal ideation in acute ischemic stroke patients. *Health and Quality of Life Outcomes* 13, 7.

Du J, Zhu M, Bao H, Li B, Dong Y, Xiao C, Zhang GY, Henter I, Rudorfer M, Vitiello B (2014). The role of nutrients in protecting mitochondrial function and neurotransmitter signaling: Implications for the treatment of depression, PTSD, and suicidal behaviors. *Critical Reviews in Food Science and Nutrition*. Published online: 3 November 2014. doi: 10.1080/10408398.2013.876960.

Duarte DW, Neumann CR, Weber ES (2015). Intentional injuries and patient survival of burns: A 10-year retrospective cohort in southern Brazil. *Burns* 41, 271-278.

Dubrey SW, Chehab O, Ghonim S (2015). Carbon monoxide poisoning: An ancient and frequent cause of accidental death. *British Journal of Hospital Medicine* 76, 159-162

Ducasse D, Olié E, Guillamme S, Artéro S, Courtet P (2015). A meta-analysis of cytokines in suicidal behavior. *Brain, Behavior, and Immunity* 46, 203-21.

Dudovitz RN, McCoy K, Chung PJ (2015). At-school substance use as a marker for serious health risks. *Academic Pediatrics* 15, 41-46.

Dufort M, Stenbacka M, Gumpert CH (2014). Physical domestic violence exposure is highly associated with suicidal attempts in both women and men. Results from the national public health survey in Sweden. *European Journal of Public Health*. Published online: 3 December 2014. doi: 10.1093/eurpub/cku198 413-418.

Dunlavy AC, Aquah EO, Wilson ML (2015). Suicidal ideation among school-attending adolescents in Dar es Salaam, Tanzania. *Tanzania Journal of Health Research*. Published online: January 2015. doi: 10.4314/thrb.v17i1.5.

Dunlop-Thomas CM, Bao G, Lim SS, Drenkard CM (2014). Social support and suicidal ideation in systemic lupus erythematosus: Georgians organized against lupus cohort. *Arthritis and Rheumatology* 66, S586.

Duppong Hurley K, Wheaton RL, Mason WA, Schnoes CJ, Epstein MH (2014). Exploring suicide risk history among youth in residential care. *Residential Treatment For Children and Youth* 31, 316-327.

Dworetzky BA, Weisholtz DS, Perez DL, Baslet G (2015). A clinically oriented perspective on psychogenic nonepileptic seizure-related emergencies. *Clinical EEG and Neuroscience* 46, 26-33.

Edinburgh L, Pape-Blabolil J, Harpin SB, Saewyc E (2014). Multiple perpetrator rape among girls evaluated at a hospital-based child advocacy center: Seven years of reviewed cases. *Child Abuse and Neglect* 38, 1540-1551.

Eggertson L (2014). Suicide rate lower among boys in Iqaluit. *Canadian Medical Association Journal* 186, E665-E666.

Ejaz R, Leibson T, Koren G (2014). Selective serotonin reuptake inhibitor discontinuation during pregnancy: At what risk? *Canadian Family Physician* 60, 1105-1106.

Elbogen EB, Johnson SC (2014). Violence, suicide, and all-cause mortality. *Lancet Psychiatry* 1, 6-8.

Elgar FJ, Napoletano A, Saul G, Dirks MA, Craig W, Poteat VP, Holt M, Koenig BW (2014). Cyberbullying victimization and mental health in adolescents and the moderating role of family dinners. *Journal of the American Medical Association Pediatricsics* 168, 1015-1022.

Elliott M, Naphan DE, Kohlenberg BL (2014). Suicidal behavior during economic hard times. *International Journal of Social Psychiatry*. Published online: 30 October 2014. doi: 10.1177/0020764014556391.

Ellis BH, Lankau EW, Ao T, Benson MA, Miller AB, Shetty S, Lopes Cardozo B, Geltman PL, Cochran J (2015). Understanding Bhutanese refugee suicide through the interpersonal-psychological theory of suicidal behavior. *American Journal of Orthopsychiatry* 85, 43-55.

Erskine HE, Moffitt TE, Copeland WE, Costello EJ, Ferrari AJ, Patton G, Degenhardt L, Vos T, Whiteford HA, Scott JG (2015). A heavy burden on young minds: The global burden of mental and substance use disorders in children and youth. *Psychological Medicine* 45, 1551-163.

Esan F, Chester V, Gunaratna IJ, Hoare S, Alexander RT (2015). The clinical, forensic and treatment outcome factors of patients with autism spectrum disorder treated in a forensic intellectual disability service. *Journal of Applied Research in Intellectual Disabilities* 28, 193-200.

Evren C, Bozkurt M, Dem rc AÇ, Evren B, Can Y, Umut G (2015). Gender differences according to psychological and behavioral variables among 10th grade students in Istanbul. *Anatolian Journal of Psychiatry* 16, 77-84.

Evren C, Dalbudak E, Evren B, Demirci AC (2014). High risk of internet addiction and its relationship with lifetime substance use, psychological and behavioral problems among 10th grade adolescents. *Psychiatria Danubina* 26, 330-339.

Evren C, Karabulut V, Can Y, Bozkurt M, Umut G, Evren B (2014). Predictors of outcome during a 6-month follow-up among heroin dependent patients receiving buprenorphine/naloxone maintenance treatment. *Bulletin of Clinical Psychopharmacology* 24, 311-322.

Fadum EA, Stanley B, Qin P, Diep LM, Mehlum L (2014). Self-poisoning with medications in adolescents: A national register study of hospital admissions and readmissions. *General Hospital Psychiatry* 36, 709-715.

Faedda GL, Marangoni C, Reginaldi D (2015). Depressive mixed states: A reappraisal of Koukopoulos'criteria. *Journal of Affective Disorders* 176, 18-23.

Falcone T, Janigro D, Lovell R, Simon B, Brown CA, Herrera M, Myint AM, Anand A (2015). S100B blood levels and childhood trauma in adolescent inpatients. *Journal of Psychiatric Research* 62, 14-22.

Fang L, Zhang VF, Poon HLM, Fung WLA, Katakia D (2014). Lifestyle practices, psychological well-being, and substance use among Chinese-Canadian youth. *Journal of Ethnic and Cultural Diversity in Social Work* 23, 207-222.

Faria YdO, Gandolfi L, Azevedo Moura LB (2014). Prevalence of risk behaviors in young university students. *Acta Paulista De Enfermagem* 27, 591-595.

Farrell CT, Bolland JM, Cockerham WC (2015). The role of social support and social context on the incidence of attempted suicide among adolescents living in extremely impoverished communities. *Journal of Adolescent Health* 56, 59-65.

Farrelly S, Jeffery D, Rusch N, Williams P, Thornicroft G, Clement S (2015). The link between mental health-related discrimination and suicidality: Service user perspectives. *Psychological Medicine* 45, 2013-2022.

Fazel S, Geddes JR, Kushel M (2014). The health of homeless people in high-income countries: Descriptive epidemiology, health consequences, and clinical and policy recommendations. *Lancet* 384, 1529-1540.

Fergusson DM, McLeod GFH, Horwood LJ (2014). Leaving school without qualifications and mental health problems to age 30. *Social Psychiatry and Psychiatric Epidemiology* 50, 469-478.

Filiptsova OV, Atramentova LA, Kobets Y (2014). Heritability of fear: Ukrainian experience. *Egyptian Journal of Medical Human Genetics* 15, 347-353.

Fink-Miller EL (2014). An examination of the interpersonal psychological theory of suicidal behavior in physicians. *Suicide and Life-Threatening Behavior*. Published online: 19 December 2014. doi: 10.1111/sltb.12147.

Fleehart S, Fan VS, Nguyen HQ, Lee J, Kohen R, Herting JR, Matute-Bello G, Adams SG, Pagalilauan G, Borson S (2014). Prevalence and correlates of suicide ideation in patients with COPD: A mixed methods study. *International Journal of Chronic Obstructive Pulmonary Disease* 9, 1321-1329.

Fletcher JB, Reback CJ (2015). Depression mediates and moderates effects of methamphetamine use on sexual risk taking among treatment-seeking gay and bisexual men. *Health Psychology.* Published online: 12 January 2015. doi: 10.1037/hea0000207.

Flett GL, Hewitt PL. A proposed framework for preventing perfectionism and promoting resilience and mental health among vulnerable children and adolescents. *Psychology in the Schools* 51, 899-912.

Flett GL, Hewitt PL, Heisel MJ (2014). The destructiveness of perfectionism revisited: Implications for the assessment of suicide risk and the prevention of suicide. *Review of General Psychology* 18, 156-172.

Ford JD, Gómez JM (2015). The relationship of psychological trauma, and dissociative and posttraumatic stress disorders to non-suicidal self-injury and suicidality: A review. *Journal of Trauma and Dissociation* 16, 232-271.

Forkmann T, Wichers M, Geschwind N, Peeters F, van Os J, Mainz V, Collip D (2014). Effects of mindfulness-based cognitive therapy on self-reported suicidal ideation: Results from a randomised controlled trial in patients with residual depressive symptoms. *Comprehensive Psychiatry* 55, 1883-1890.

Forrester A, Singh J, Slade K, Exworthy T, Sen P (2014). Mental health in-reach in an urban UK remand prison. *International Journal of Prisoner Health* 10, 155-163.

Forty L, Ulanova A, Jones L, Jones I, Gordon-Smith K, Fraser C, Farmer A, McGuffin P, Lewis CM, Hosang GM, Rivera M, Craddock N (2014). Comorbid medical illness in bipolar disorder. *British Journal of Psychiatry* 205, 465-472.

Fovet T, Geoffroy PA, Vaiva G, Adins C, Thomas P, Amad A (2015). Individuals with bipolar disorder and their relationship with the criminal justice system: A critical review. *Psychiatric Services* 66, 348-353.

Franzke I, Wabnitz P, Catani C (2015). Dissociation as a mediator of the relationship between childhood trauma and non-suicidal self-injury for females: A path analytic approach. *Journal of Trauma and Dissociation* 16, 286-302.

Fresán A, González-Castro TB, Peralta-Jiménez Y, Juarez-Rojop I, Pool-Garcia S, Velázquez-Sánchez MP, López-Narváez L, Tovilla-Zárate CA (2015). Gender differences in socio-demographic, clinical characteristics and psychiatric diagnosis in/of suicide attempters in a Mexican population. *Acta Neuropsychiatrica* 27, 182-188.

Friedman MJ (2015). Risk factors for suicides among army personnel. *JAMA* 313, 1154-1155.

Frost M, Casey L (2015). Who seeks help online for self-injury? *Archives of Suicide Research.* Published online: 23 February 2015. doi: 10.1080/13811118.2015.1004470.

Fry RA, Fry LE, Castanelli DJ (2015). A retrospective survey of substance abuse in anaesthetists in Australia and New Zealand from 2004 to 2013. *Anaesthesia and Intensive Care* 43, 111-117.

Fulginiti A, Brekke JS (2015). Escape from discrepancy: Self-esteem and quality of life as predictors of current suicidal ideation among individuals with schizophrenia. *Community Mental Health Journal.* Published online: 15 February 2015. doi: 10.1007/s10597-015-9846-8.

Gabrielli J, Hambrick EP, Tunno AM, Jackson Y, Spangler A, Kanine RM (2014). Longitudinal assessment of self-harm statements of youth in foster care: Rates, reporters, and related factors. *Child Psychiatry & Human Development.* Published online: 23 December 2014. doi: 10.1007/s10578-014-0529-4.

Gardner KJ, Dodsworth J, Selby EA (2014). Borderline personality traits, rumination, and self-injurious behavior: An empirical test of the emotional cascades model in adult male offenders. *Journal of Forensic Psychology Practice* 14, 398-417.

Germain M-L (2014). Work-related suicide: An analysis of US government reports and recommendations for human resources. *Employee Relations* 36, 148-164.

Gibbons RD, Perraillon MC, Hur K, Conti RM, Valuck RJ, Brent DA (2015). Antidepressant treatment and suicide attempts and self-inflicted injury in children and adolescents. *Pharmacoepidemiology and Drug Safety* 24, 208-214.

Gifuni AJ, Ding Y, Olie E, Lawrence N, Cyprien F, Le Bars E, Bonafe A, Phillips ML, Courtet P, Jollant F (2015). Subcortical nuclei volumes in suicidal behavior: Nucleus accumbens may modulate the lethality of acts. *Brain Imaging and Behavior.* Published online: 12 March 2015. doi: 10.1007/s11682-015-9369-5.

Gilchrist G, Davidson S, Middleton A, Herrman H, Hegarty K, Gunn J (2015). Factors associated with smoking and smoking cessation among primary care patients with depression: A naturalistic cohort study. *Advances in Dual Diagnosis* 8, 18-28.

Giletta M, Prinstein MJ, Abela JRZ, Gibb BE, Barrocas AL, Hankin BL (2015). Trajectories of suicide ideation and nonsuicidal self-injury among adolescents in mainland China: Peer predictors, joint development, and risk for suicide attempts. *Journal of Consulting and Clinical Psychology* 83, 265-279.

Gilreath TD, Wrabel SL, Sullivan KS, Capp GP, Roziner I, Benbenishty R, Astor RA (2015). Suicidality among military-connected adolescents in California schools. *European Child and Adolescent Psychiatry.* Published online: 20 March 2015. doi: 10.1007/s00787-015-0696-2.

Giotakos O, Tsouvelas G, Nisianakis P, Giakalou V, Lavdas A, Tsiamitas C, Panagiotis K, Kontaxakis V (2015). A negative association between lithium in drinking water and the incidences of homicides, in Greece. *Biological Trace Element Research* 164, 165-168.

Glasheen C, Pemberton MR, Lipari R, Copello EA, Mattson ME (2014). Binge drinking and the risk of suicidal thoughts, plans, and attempts. *Addictive Behaviors* 43, 42-49.

Glucksman ML (2014). Manifest dream content as a possible predictor of suicidality. *Psychodynamic Psychiatry* 42, 657-670.

Goldblatt MJ, Briggs S, Lindner R (2015). Destructive groups: The role of projective identification in suicidal groups of young people. *British Journal of Psychotherapy* 31, 38-53.

Goldman ML, Shah RN, Bernstein CA (2015). Depression and suicide among physician trainees: Recommendations for a national response. *JAMA Psychiatry* 72, 411-412.

Golmaryami FN, Frick PJ, Hemphill SA, Kahn RE, Crapanzano AM, Terranova AM (2015). The social, behavioral, and emotional correlates of bullying and victimization in a school-based sample. *Journal of Abnormal Child Psychology.* Published online: 22 March 2015. doi: 10.1007/s10802-015-9994-x.

Gómez JM, Becker-Blease K, Freyd JJ (2015). A brief report on predicting self-harm: Is it gender or abuse that matters? *Journal of Aggression, Maltreatment and Trauma* 24, 203-214.

Gonçalves A, Sequeira C, Duarte J, Freitas P (2014). Suicide ideation in higher education students: Influence of social support. *Atencion Primaria* 46 Suppl 5, 88-91.

Goutaudier N, Melioli T, Valls M, Bouvet R, Chabrol H (2014). Relations between cyclothymic temperament and borderline personality disorder traits in non-clinical adolescents. *European Review of Applied Psychology* 64, 345-351.

Gradus JL, Leatherman S, Raju S, Ferguson R, Miller M (2014). Posttraumatic stress disorder, depression, and non-fatal intentional self-harm in Massachusetts veterans. *Injury Epidemiology.* Published online: 27 August 2015. doi: 10.1186/s40621-014-0020-5.

Gradus JL, Smith BN, Vogt D (2015). Family support, family stress, and suicidal ideation in a combat-exposed sample of Operation Enduring Freedom/Operation Iraqi Freedom veterans. *Anxiety, Stress & Coping.* Published online: 16 February 2015. doi: 10.1080/10615806.2015.1006205.

Grah M, Mihanovic M, Ruljancic N, Restek-Petrovic B, Molnar S, Jelavic S (2014). Brain-derived neurotrophic factor as a suicide factor in mental disorders. *Acta Neuropsychiatrica* 26, 356-363.

Grandgenevre P, Warembourg F, Carrière N, Vaillant A, Defebvre L, Vaiva G (2015). Hypersexuality in Parkinson's disease. Advantage of the presence of the entourage for medical assessment. *Presse Medicale* 44, e51-e58.

Granö N, Salmijärvi L, Karjalainen M, Kallionpää S, Roine M, Taylor P (2015). Early signs of worry: Psychosis risk symptom visual distortions are independently associated with suicidal ideation. *Psychiatry Research* 225, 263-267.

Gratz KL, Bardeen JR, Levy R, Dixon-Gordon KL, Tull MT (2015). Mechanisms of change in an emotion regulation group therapy for deliberate self-harm among women with borderline personality disorder. *Behaviour Research and Therapy* 65, 29-35.

Gratz KL, Dixon-Gordon KL, Chapman AL, Tull MT (2015). Diagnosis and characterization of DSM-5 nonsuicidal self-injury disorder using the clinician-administered nonsuicidal self-injury disorder index. *Assessment.* Published online: 20 January 2015. doi: 10.1177/1073191114565878.

Graugaard C, Giraldi A, Frisch M, Falgaard Eplov L, Davidsen M (2015). Self-reported sexual and psychosocial health among non-heterosexual Danes. *Scandinavian Journal of Public Health* 43, 309-314.

Greist JH, Mundt JC, Gwaltney CJ, Jefferson JW, Posner K (2014). Predictive value of baseline electronic Columbia-Suicide Severity Rating Scale (eC-SSRS) assessments for identifying risk of prospective reports of suicidal behavior during research participation. *Innovations in Clinical Neuroscience* 11, 23-31.

Griffith J (2015). Homecoming of soldiers who are citizens: Re-employment and financial status of returning army national guard soldiers from Operations Iraqi Freedom (OIF) and Enduring Freedom (OEF). *Work* 50, 85-96.

Grisham JR, Williams AD (2014). Long-term outcomes of young people who attempted suicide. *JAMA* 312, 2277-2278.

Gualano MR, Bert F, Mannocci A, La Torre G, Zeppegno P, Siliquini R (2014). Consumption of antidepressants in Italy: Recent trends and their significance for public health. *Psychiatric Services* 65, 1226-1231.

Guan L, Hao B, Zhu T (2014). How did the suicide act and speak differently online? Behavioral and linguistic features of China's suicide microblog users. *Arxiv* 1407.0466.

Guclu O, Senormanci O, Aydin E, Erkiran M, Kokturk F (2015). Phenomenological subtypes of mania and their relationships with substance use disorders. *Journal of Affective Disorders* 174, 569-573.

Guendelman MD, Owens EB, Galán C, Gard A, Hinshaw SP (2015). Early-adult correlates of maltreatment in girls with attention-deficit/hyperactivity disorder: Increased risk for internalizing symptoms and suicidality. *Development and Psychopathology.* Published online: 27 February 2015. doi: 10.1017/S0954579414001485.

Guerreiro DF, Figueira ML, Cruz D, Sampaio D (2015). Coping strategies in adolescents who self-harm. *Crisis* 36, 31-37.

Guillén AI, Panadero S, Rivas E, Vázquez JJ (2015). Suicide attempts and stressful life events among female victims of intimate partner violence living in poverty in Nicaragua. *Scandinavian Journal of Psychology* 56, 349-356.

Gulbas LE, Zayas LH (2015). Examining the interplay among family, culture, and Latina teen suicidal behavior. *Qualitative Health Research* 25, 689-699.

Gunes G, Malkan UY, Aksu S, Haznedaroglu IC, Buyukasik Y, Sayinalp N, Ozcebe OI, Goker H, Demiroglu H (2014). Massive life-threatening hemorrhages due to toxic oral intake of 3750 mg dabigatran etexilate as a suicide attempt and the clinical management. *Blood* 124, 5091.

Gupta G, Avasthi A, Grover S, Singh SM (2014). Factors associated with suicidal ideations and suicidal attempts in patients with obsessive compulsive disorder. *Asian Journal of Psychiatry* 12, 140-146.

Gvion Y, Horesh N, Levi-Belz Y, Apter A (2015). A proposed model of the development of suicidal ideations. *Comprehensive Psychiatry* 56, 93-102.

Gyles C (2014). Mental health and veterinary suicides. *Canadian Veterinary Journal* 55, 1123-1126.

Hafizi S, Tabatabaei D, Koenig HG (2014). Borderline personality disorder and religion: A perspective from a Muslim country. *Iranian Journal of Psychiatry* 9, 137-141.

Haghighi H, Golmirzaee J, Mohammadi K, Moradabadi AS, Dadipoor S, Hesam AA (2015). Investigating the relationship between the demographic variables associated with suicide in different seasons, among suicidal people in the Shahid Mohammadi hospital, Bandar Abass, Iran. *Journal of Education and Health Promotion* 4, 3.

Hales H, Edmondson A, Davison S, Maughan B, Taylor PJ (2015). The impact of contact with suicide-related behavior in prison on young offenders. *Crisis* 36, 21-30.

Hammett JF, Ulloa EC (2014). The effect of gender and perpetrator-victim role on mental health outcomes and risk behaviors associated with intimate partner violence. *Journal of Interpersonal Violence.* Published online: 18 December 2014. doi: 10.1177/0886260514564163.

Han D-H (2014). The association between temporomandibular disorders and suicide ideation in a representative sample of the South Korean population. *Journal of Oral and Facial Pain and Headache* 28, 338-345.

Hansen BD, Wadsworth JP (2015). Effects of an antecedent intervention on repetitive behaviors of a child with autism. *Child and Family Behavior Therapy* 37, 51-62.

Hardt J, Bernert S, Matschinger H, Angermeier MC, Vilagut G, Bruffaerts R, De Girolamo G, De Graaf R, Haro JM, Kovess V, Alonso J (2015). Suicidality and its relationship with depression, alcohol disorders and childhood experiences of violence: Results from the ESEMeD study. *Journal of Affective Disorders* 175, 168-174.

Harland K, McCready S (2014). Rough justice: Considerations on the role of violence, masculinity, and the alienation of young men in communities and peacebuilding processes in Northern Ireland. *Youth Justice* 14, 269-283.

Hassanian-Moghaddam H, Zamani N, Sarjami S (2014). Violence and abuse against women who have attempted suicide by deliberate self-poisoning: A 2-year follow-up study in Iran. *Journal of Interpersonal Violence.* Published online: 29 December 2014. doi: 10.1177/0886260514564157.

Havermans RC, Vancleef L, Kalamatianos A, Nederkoorn C (2015). Eating and inflicting pain out of boredom. *Appetite* 85, 52-57.

Hayashi N, Igarashi M, Imai A, Yoshizawa Y, Asamura K, Ishikawa Y, Tokunaga T, Ishimoto K, Tatebayashi Y, Kumagai N, Ishii H, Okazaki Y (2015). The pathways from life-historical events and borderline personality disorder to symptomatic disorders among suicidal psychiatric patients: A study of structural equation modeling. *Psychiatry and the Clinical Neurosciences.* Published online: 27 January 2015. doi: 10.1111/pcn.12280.

He AS, Fulginiti A, Finno-Velasquez M (2015). Connectedness and suicidal ideation among adolescents involved with child welfare: A national survey. *Child Abuse and Neglect* 42, 54-62.

He imovi H, Popovi Z (2014). Risk factors for suicide in epilepsy patients. *Future Neurology* 9, 553-561.

Heintze K, Fuchs W (2015). Codeine ultra-rapid metabolizers: Age appears to be a key factor in adverse effects of codeine. *Drug Research.* Published online: 13 January 2015. doi: 10.1055/s-0034-1396885.

Hemmings S, Kalungi A, Seedat S, Joloba M, Kinyanda E (2014). Serotonin transporter gene variants are associated with increased risk of suicide in an HIV-positive Ugandan population. *South African Journal of Psychiatry* 20, 119.

Hendricks PS, Thorne CB, Clark CB, Coombs DW, Johnson MW (2015). Classic psychedelic use is associated with reduced psychological distress and suicidality in the United States adult population. *Journal of Psychopharmacology* 29, 280-288.

Henriksen CA, Stein MB, Afifi TO, Enns MW, Lix LM, Sareen J (2015). Identifying factors that predict longitudinal outcomes of untreated common mental disorders. *Psychiatric Services* 66, 163-170.

Herrell RK, Wilk JE, Hoge CW (2015). Symptoms of PTSD and depression in suicidal rumination, contemplation, and plans in US soldiers. *Comprehensive Psychiatry* 29, 280-288.

Heydari A, Teymoori A, Nasiri H (2015). The effect of parent and peer attachment on suicidality: The mediation effect of self-control and anomie. *Community Mental Health Journal* 51, 359-364.

Hides L, Limbong J, Vallmuur K, Barker R, Daglish M, Young RM (2015). Alcohol-related emergency department injury presentations in Queensland adolescents and young adults over a 13-year period. *Drug and Alcohol Review* 34, 177-184.

Hill A, Berner W, Briken P (2015). Risky sexual behavior. Forms of sexual self-harm. *Psychotherapeut* 60, 25-30.

Hirneth SJ, Hazell PL, Hanstock TL, Lewin TJ (2014). Bipolar disorder subtypes in children and adolescents: Demographic and clinical characteristics from an Australian sample. *Journal of Affective Disorders* 175, 98-107.

Hirsch JK, Nsamenang SA, Chang EC, Kaslow NJ (2014). Spiritual well-being and depressive symptoms in female African American suicide attempters: Mediating effects of optimism and pessimism. *Psychology of Religion and Spirituality* 6, 276-283.

Hoban C, Sareen J, Henriksen CA, Kuzyk L, Embil JM, Trepman E (2015). Mental health issues associated with foot complications of diabetes mellitus. *Foot and Ankle* 21, 49-55.

Hochard KD, Heym N, Townsend E (2015). The unidirectional relationship of nightmares on self-harmful thoughts and behaviors. *Dreaming* 25, 44-58.

Hodgson KJ, Shelton KH, van den Bree MB (2015). Psychopathology among young homeless people: Longitudinal mental health outcomes for different subgroups. *British Journal of Clinical Psychology*. Published online: 5 February 2015. doi: 10.1111/bjc.12075.

Hoertel N, Peyre H, Wall MM, Limosin F, Blanco C (2014). Examining sex differences in DSM-IV borderline personality disorder symptom expression Using Item Response Theory (IRT). *Journal of Psychiatric Research* 59, 213-219.

Holder SD, Wayhs A (2014). Schizophrenia. *American Family Physician* 90, 775-782.

Hollingshaus MS, Smith KR (2015). Life and death in the family: Early parental death, parental remarriage, and offspring suicide risk in adulthood. *Social Science and Medicine* 131, 181-189

Holloway IW, Padilla MB, Willner L, Guilamo-Ramos V (2014). Effects of minority stress processes on the mental health of Latino men who have sex with men and women: A qualitative study. *Archives of Sexual Behavior*. Published online: 4 November 2014. doi: 10.1007/s10508-014-0424-x.

Holm AL, Lyberg A, Berggren I, Aström S, Severinsson E (2014). Going around in a circle: A Norwegian study of suicidal experiences in old age. *Nursing Research and Practice* 2014, 734635.

Holt EW, DeMartini S, Davern TJ (2014). Acute liver failure due to acetaminophen poisoning in patients with prior weight loss surgery: A case series. *Journal of Clinical Gastroenterology*. Published online: 30 December 2014. doi: 10.1097/MCG.0000000000000278.

Holt MK, Vivolo-Kantor AM, Polanin JR, Holland KM, DeGue S, Matjasko JL, Wolfe M, Reid G (2015). Bullying and suicidal ideation and behaviors: A meta-analysis. *Pediatrics*. Published online: 5 January 2015. doi: 10.1542/peds.2014-1864.

Holt V, Skagerberg E, Dunsford M (2014). Young people with features of gender dysphoria: Demographics and associated difficulties. *Clinical Child Psychology and Psychiatry*. Published online: 26 November 2014. doi: 10.1177/1359104514558431.

Hooper LM, Tomek S, Bolland KA, Church Ii WT, Wilcox K, Bolland JM (2014). The impact of previous suicide ideations, traumatic stress, and gender on future suicide ideation trajectories among black American adolescents: A longitudinal investigation. *Journal of Loss and Trauma*. Published online: 13 October 2014. doi: 10.1080/15325024.2014.897573.

House A (2014). Self harm in young people. *BMJ* 349, g6204.

Hubbeling D (2015). Suicidal ideation and research ethics committees. *Psychological Medicine* 45, 217.

Hubers AAM, van der Mast RC, Pereira AM, Roos RAC, Veen LJ, Cobbaert CM, van Duijn E, Giltay EJ (2015). Hypothalamic-pituitary-adrenal axis functioning in Huntington's disease and its association with depressive symptoms and suicidality. *Journal of Neuroendocrinology* 27, 234-244.

Huey L, Hryniewicz D, Fthenos G (2014). 'I had a lot of anger and that's what kind of led me to cutting myself': Employing a social stress framework to explain why some homeless women self-injure. *Health Sociology Review* 23, 148-158.

Hulse EJ, Davies JOJ, Simpson AJ, Sciuto AM, Eddleston M (2014). Respiratory complications of organophosphorus nerve agent and insecticide poisoning: Implications for respiratory and critical care. *American Journal of Respiratory and Critical Care Medicine* 190, 1342-1354.

Husain Z, Janniger EJ, Krysicka JA, Micali G, Schwartz RA (2014). Body dysmorphic disorder: Beyond skin deep. *Giornale Italiano Di Dermatologia E Venereologia* 149, 447-452

Husky MM, Michel G, Richard JB, Guignard R, Beck F (2015). Gender differences in the associations of gambling activities and suicidal behaviors with problem gambling in a nationally representative French sample. *Addictive Behaviors* 45, 45-50.

Hussain A, Chandel RK, Ganie MA, Dar MA, Rather YH, Wani ZA, Shiekh JA, Shah MS (2015). Prevalence of psychiatric disorders in patients with a diagnosis of polycystic ovary syndrome in Kashmir. *Indian Journal of Psychological Medicine* 37, 66-70.

Innamorati M, Rihmer Z, Akiskal H, Gonda X, Erbuto D, Murri MB, Perugi G, Amore M, Girardi P, Pompili M (2015). Cyclothymic temperament rather than polarity is associated with hopelessness and suicidality in hospitalized patients with mood disorders. *Journal of Affective Disorders* 170, 161-165.

Inoue T, Inagaki Y, Kimura T, Shirakawa O (2015). Prevalence and predictors of bipolar disorder in patients with a major depressive episode: The Japanese epidemiological trial with latest measure of bipolar Disorder (JET-LMBP). *Journal of Affective Disorders* 174, 535-541.

Isung J, Aeinehband S, Mobarrez F, Nordstrom P, Runeson B, Asberg M, Piehl F, Jokinen J (2014). High interleukin-6 and impulsivity: Determining the role of endophenotypes in attempted suicide. *Translational Psychiatry* 4, e470.

Jabbar SA, Zaza HI (2014). Impact of conflict in Syria on Syrian children at the Zaatari refugee camp in Jordan. *Early Child Development and Care* 184, 1507-1530.

Jackowich RA, Vale R, Vale K, Wassersug RJ, Johnson TW (2014). Voluntary genital ablations: Contrasting the cutters and their clients. *Sexual Medicine* 2, 121-132.

Jacobson LH, Callander GE, Hoyer D (2014). Suvorexant for the treatment of insomnia. *Expert Review of Clinical Pharmacology* 7, 711-730.

Jahn DR, Poindexter EK, Cukrowicz KC (2015). Personality disorder traits, risk factors, and suicide ideation among older adults. *International Psychogeriatrics*. Published online: 23 February 2015. doi: 10.1017/S1041610215000174.

Jakši N, Aukst-Margetic B, Marcinko D, Brajkovi L, Loncar M, Jakovljevi M (2015). Temperament, character, and suicidality among Croatian war veterans with posttraumatic stress disorder. *Psychiatria Danubina* 27, 60-63.

Janiri D, Sani G, Danese E, Simonetti A, Ambrosi E, Angeletti G, Erbuto D, Caltagirone C, Girardi P, Spalletta G (2015). Childhood traumatic experiences of patients with bipolar disorder type I and type II. *Journal of Affective Disorders* 175, 92-97.

Jann MW (2014). Diagnosis and treatment of bipolar disorder in adults: A review of the evidence on pharmacologic treatments. *American Health and Drug Benefits* 7, 489-498.

Jenkins AL, McCloskey MS, Kulper D, Berman ME, Coccaro EF (2015). Self-harm behavior among individuals with intermittent explosive disorder and personality disorders. *Journal of Psychiatric Research* 60, 125-131.

Jeon HJ, Lee C, Fava M, Mischoulon D, Shim EJ, Heo JY, Choi H, Park JH (2014). Childhood trauma, parental death, and their co-occurrence in relation to current suicidality risk in adults. *Journal of Nervous and Mental Disease* 202, 870-876.

Jeon S, Eun H, Choi M, Kim B, Kim T (2014). The influence of parent and peer attachment in adolescent's suicidal ideation: Mediating effect of depression and anxiety. *Journal of Korean Neuropsychiatric Association* 53, 246-246.

Jewkes R, Gibbs A, Journal of the American Medical Association-Shai N, Willan S, Misselhorn A, Mushinga M, Washington L, Mbatha N, Skiweyiya Y (2014). Stepping Stones and Creating Futures intervention: Shortened interrupted time series evaluation of a behavioural and structural health promotion and violence prevention intervention for young people in informal settlements in Durban, South Africa. *BMC Public Health* 14, 1325.

Johansen P-Ø, Krebs TS (2015). Psychedelics not linked to mental health problems or suicidal behavior: A population study. *Journal of Psychopharmacology* 29, 270-272.

Jokinen J, Mattsson F, Lagergren K, Lagergren J, Ljung R (2015). Suicide attempt and future risk of cancer: A nationwide cohort study in Sweden. *Cancer Causes and Control* 26, 501-509.

Jones SE, Pezzi C, Rodriguez-Lainz A, Whittle L (2014). Health risk behaviors by length of time in the United States among high school students in five sites. *Journal of Immigrant and Minority Health*. Published online: 24 December 2014. doi: 10.1007/s10903-014-0151-3.

Jonsson U, Alexanderson K, Kjeldgard L, Mittendorfer-Rutz E (2014). Psychiatric diagnoses and risk of suicidal behaviour in young disability pensioners: Prospective cohort studies of all 19-23 year olds in Sweden in 1995, 2000, and 2005, respectively. *PLoS One* 9, e111618.

Jose J, Nandeesha H, Kattimani S, Meiyappan K, Sarkar S, S D (2015). Association between prolactin and thyroid hormones with severity of psychopathology and suicide risk in drug free male schizophrenia. *Clinica Chimica Acta* 15, 78-80.

Judd LL, Schettler PJ, Brown ES, Wolkowitz OM, Sternberg EM, Bender BG, Bulloch K, Cidlowski JA, de Kloet ER, Fardet L, Joels M, Leung DYM, McEwen BS, Roozendaal B, Van Rossum EFC, Ahn J, Brown DW, Plitt A, Singh G (2014). Adverse consequences of glucocorticoid medication: Psychological, cognitive, and behavioral effects. *American Journal of Psychiatry* 171, 1045.

Kaltiala-Heino R, Eronen M, Putkonen H (2014). Violent girls in adolescent forensic care are more often psychotic and traumatized than boys in the same level of care. *Journal of Forensic Psychiatry and Psychology* 25, 636-657.

Kanamuller J, Riala K, Nivala M, Hakko H, Rasanen P (2014). Correlates of sexual abuse in a sample of adolescent girls admitted to psychiatric inpatient care. *Journal of Child Sexual Abuse* 23, 804-823.

Kara K, Ozsoy S, Teke H, Congologlu MA, Turker T, Renklidag T, Karapirli M (2015). Non-suicidal self-injurious behavior in forensic child and adolescent populations. *Neurosciences* 20, 31-36.

Karpel MG, Jerram MW (2015). Levels of dissociation and non-suicidal self-injury: A quartile risk model. *Journal of Trauma and Dissociation*. Published online: 11 March 2015. doi: 10.1080/15299732.2015.989645.

Kattimani S, Sarkar S, Mukherjee A, Mathan K (2015). What do suicide attempters think about legal status of suicide in India? *Indian Journal of Psychiatry* 57, 103-104.

Katz J, Medoff D, Fang LJ, Dixon LB (2014). The relationship between the perceived risk of harm by a family member with mental illness and the family experience. *Community Mental Health Journal*. Published online: 23 December 2014. doi: 10.1007/s10597-014-9799-3.

Kavakci O, Semiz M, Kartal A, Dikici A, Kugu N (2014). Test anxiety prevalance and related variables in the students who are going to take the university entrance examination. *Dusunen Adam* 27, 301-307.

Kelly EV, Newton NC, Stapinski LA, Slade T, Barrett EL, Conrod PJ, Teesson M (2015). Suicidality, internalizing problems and externalizing problems among adolescent bullies, victims and bully-victims. *Preventive Medicine* 73, 100-105.

Kerns CM, Kendall PC, Zickgraf H, Franklin ME, Miller J, Herrington J (2015). Not to be overshadowed or overlooked: Functional impairments associated with comorbid anxiety disorders in youth with ASD. *Behavior Therapy* 46, 29-39.

Kettunen P, Koistinen E, Hintikka J (2014). Is postpartum depression a homogenous disorder: Time of onset, severity, symptoms and hopelessness in relation to the course of depression. *BMC Pregnancy Childbirth* 14, 402.

Keyser-Marcus LP, Alvanzo AMDMS, Rieckmann TP, Thacker LP, Sepulveda AP, Forcehimes AP, Islam LZP, Leisey MPMSW, Stitzer MP, Svikis DSP (2015). Trauma, gender, and mental health symptoms in individuals with substance use disorders. *Journal of Interpersonal Violence*. Published online: 8 May 2014. doi: 10.1177/0886260514532523.

Khazem LR, Law KC, Green BA, Anestis MD (2014). Examining the relationship between coping strategies and suicidal desire in a sample of United States military personnel. *Comprehensive Psychiatry* 57, 2-9.

Kiamanesh P, Dieserud G, Haavind H (2015). From a cracking facade to a total escape. Maladaptive perfectionism and suicide. *Death Studies* 39, 316-322.

Kidger J, Heron J, Leon DA, Tilling K, Lewis G, Gunnell D (2015a). Self-reported school experience as a predictor of self-harm during adolescence: A prospective cohort study in the south west of England (ALSPAC). *Journal of Affective Disorders* 173, 163-169.

Kim HJ, Kim GW, Oh SH, Park SH, Choi JH, Kim KH, Jeon WC, Lee HJ, Park KN, Korean Hypothermia Network I (2014). Therapeutic hypothermia after cardiac arrest caused by self-inflicted intoxication: A multicenter retrospective cohort study. *American Journal of Emergency Medicine* 32, 1378-1381.

Kim J, Shin J, Kim YA, Lee J (2015). Suicidal ideation in underweight adults who attempt to lose weight: Korea national health and nutrition examination survey, 2007-2012. *Korean Journal of Family Medicine* 36, 82-91.

Kim JS, Ha TH, Chang JS, Park YS, Huh I, Kim J, Hong KS, Park T, Ha K (2015). Seasonality and its distinct clinical correlates in bipolar II disorder. *Psychiatry Research* 225, 540-544.

Kim S, Kim H, Seo DC, Lee DH, Cho HI (2014). Suicidal ideation and its correlates among juvenile delinquents in South Korea. *Osong Public Health and Research Perspectives* 5, 258-265.

Kim SJ, Kang S-G, Cho IH, Lee Y-JG, Hong JP, Park J, Lee YJ (2015). The relationship between poor performance on attention tasks and increased suicidal ideation in adolescents. *European Child and Adolescent Psychiatry*. Published online: 8 February 2015. doi: 10.1007/s00787-015-0687-3.

Kim SM, Baek JH, Han DH, Lee YS, Yurgelun-Todd DA (2014). Psychosocial-environmental risk factors for suicide attempts in adolescents with suicidal ideation: Findings from a sample of 73,238 adolescents. *Suicide and Life-Threatening Behavior*. Published online: 2 December 2014. doi: 10.1111/sltb.12143.

King CA, Berona J, Czyz E, Horwitz AG, Gipson PY (2015). Identifying adolescents at highly elevated risk for suicidal behavior in the emergency department. *Journal of Child and Adolescent Psychopharmacology* 25, 100-108.

Kipping RR, Smith M, Heron J, Hickman M, Campbell R (2014). Multiple risk behaviour in adolescence and socio-economic status: Findings from a UK birth cohort. *European Journal of Public Health* 25, 44-49.

Kiss L, Pocock NS, Naisanguansri V, Suos S, Dickson B, Thuy D, Koehler J, Sirisup K, Pongrungsee N, Nguyen VA, Borland R, Dhavan P, Zimmerman C (2015). Health of men, women, and children in post-trafficking services in Cambodia, Thailand, and Vietnam: An observational cross-sectional study. *The Lancet Global Health* 3, e154-161.

Kitagawa Y, Shimodera S, Togo F, Okazaki Y, Nishida A (2014). Suicidal feelings interferes with help-seeking in bullied adolescents. *PLoS One* 9, e106031.

Kleiman EM, Ammerman BA, Kulper DA, Uyeji LL, Jenkins AL, McCloskey MS (2014). Forms of non-suicidal self-injury as a function of trait aggression. *Comprehensive Psychiatry* 59, 21-27.

Klingensmith K, Tsai J, Mota N, Southwick SM, Pietrzak RH (2014). Military sexual trauma in US veterans: Results from the national health and resilience in veterans study. *The Journal of Clinical Psychiatry* 75, e1133-1139.

Kmietowicz Z (2015). Doctors facing complaints have severe depression and suicidal thoughts, study finds. *BMJ* 350, h244.

Kolevzon A, Lim T, Schmeidler J, Martello T, Cook EH, Silverman JM (2014). Self-injury in autism spectrum disorder: An effect of serotonin transporter gene promoter variants. *Psychiatry Research* 220, 987-990.

Kong KA, Kim SI (2015). Mental health of single fathers living in an urban community in South Korea. *Comprehensive Psychiatry* 56, 188-197.

Konrad N, Opitz-Welke A (2014). The challenges of treating the mentally ill in a prison setting: The European perspective. *Clinical Practice* 11, 517-523.

Kopacz MS, McCarten JM, Pollitt MJ (2014). VHA chaplaincy contact with veterans at increased risk of suicide. *Southern Medical Journal* 107, 661-664.

Kopacz MS, McCarten JM, Vance CG, Connery AL (2015). A preliminary study for exploring different sources of guilt in a sample of veterans who sought chaplaincy services. *Military Psychology* 27, 1-8.

Koponen H, Kautiainen H, Leppanen E, Mantyselka P, Vanhala M (2014). Cardiometabolic risk factors in patients referred to depression nurse case managers. *Nordic Journal of Psychiatry* 69, 262-267.

Korb I, Plattner IE (2014). Suicide ideation and depression in university students in Botswana. *Journal of Psychology in Africa* 24, 420-426.

Kosaraju SKM, Vadlamani LN, Mohammed Bashir MS, Kalasapati LK, Rao GLVC, Rao GP (2015). Risk factors for suicidal attempts among lower socioeconomic rural population of Telangana region. *Indian Journal of Psychological Medicine* 37, 30-35.

Koyama A, Fujise N, Matsushita M, Ishikawa T, Hashimoto M, Ikeda M (2015). Suicidal ideation and related factors among dementia patients. *Journal of Affective Disorders* 178, 66-70.

Koyuncu A, Ertekin E, Ertekin BA, Binbay Z, Yuksel C, Deveci E, Tukel R (2015). Relationship between atypical depression and social anxiety disorder. *Psychiatry Research* 225, 79-84.

Krabbendam AA, Jansen LM, van de Ven PM, van der Molen E, Doreleijers TA, Vermeiren RR (2014). Persistence of aggression into adulthood in detained adolescent females. *Comprehensive Psychiatry* 55, 1572-1579.

Kraus GE, Yung E, Lebaron N, Zhang X, Iskric A, Lober J, Low NC (2014). The effect of childhood abuse and neglect on clinical severity in mood disorders. *Comprehensive Psychiatry* 55, e52-e53.

Krishna M, Rajendra R, Majgi SM, Heggere N, Parimoo S, Robinson C, Poole R (2014). Severity of suicidal intent, method and behaviour antecedent to an act of self-harm: A cross sectional study of survivors of self-harm referred to a tertiary hospital in Mysore, south India. *Asian Journal of Psychiatry* 12, 134-139.

Krni S, Pisk SV, Romac D, Tripkovi M (2014). Clinically significant depressive disorder in adolescence; cross-sectional study of two Croatian counties. *Psychiatria Danubina* 26, 428-434.

Kuyper L, Fernee H, Keuzenkamp S (2015). A comparative analysis of a community and general sample of lesbian, gay, and bisexual individuals. *Archives of Sexual Behavior*. Published online: 7 January 2015. doi: 10.1007/s10508-014-0457-1.

Lan WH, Bai YM, Hsu JW, Huang KL, Su TP, Li CT, Yang AC, Lin WC, Chang WH, Chen TJ, Tsai SJ, Chen MH (2015). Comorbidity of ADHD and suicide attempts among adolescents and young adults with bipolar disorder: A nationwide longitudinal study. *Journal of Affective Disorders* 176, 171-175.

Larson AM, Shinnick JE, Shaaya EA, Thiele EA, Thibert RL (2015). Angelman syndrome in adulthood. *American Journal of Medical Genetics* 167A, 331-344.

Latalova K, Prasko J, Kamaradova D, Ociskova M, Cinculova A, Grambal A, Kubinek R, Mainerova B, Smoldasova J, Tichackova A, Sigmundova Z (2014). Self-stigma and suicidality in patients with neurotic spectrum disorder - a cross sectional study. *Neuro Endocrinology Letters* 35, 474-480.

LeBaron N, Zhang X, Herrell R, Cho S, Iskric A, Low NC (2014). Anxious and suicidal behaviors among relatives are associated with suicide attempts and hospitalizations in mood disorder subjects. *Comprehensive Psychiatry* 55, e53.

Lee K-H, Pluck G, Lekka N, Horton A, Wilkinson ID, Woodruff PWR (2015). Self-harm in schizophrenia is associated with dorsolateral prefrontal and posterior cingulate activity. *Progress in Neuro-Psychopharmacology and Biological Psychiatry* 61, 18-23

Lee SH, Tsai YF, Chen CY, Huang LB (2014). Triggers of suicide ideation and protective factors of actually executing suicide among first onset cases in older psychiatric outpatients: A qualitative study. *BMC Psychiatry* 14, 269.

Legarreta M, Graham J, North L, Bueler CE, McGlade E, Yurgelun-Todd D (2015). DSM-5 posttraumatic stress disorder symptoms associated with suicide behaviors in veterans. *Psychological Trauma: Theory, Research, Practice, and Policy* 7, 277-85.

Leon SL, Cloutier P, BéLair M-A, Cappelli M (2014). Media coverage of youth suicides and its impact on paediatric mental health emergency department presentations. *Healthcare Policy* 10, 97-107.

Lester D (2015). Morningness-eveningness, current depression, and past suicidality. *Psychological Reports* 116, 331-336.

Levinger S, Somer E, Holden RR (2015). The importance of mental pain and physical dissociation in youth suicidality. *Journal of Trauma and Dissociation* 16, 322-339.

Levy BR, Pilver CE, Pietrzak RH (2014). Lower prevalence of psychiatric conditions when negative age stereotypes are resisted. *Social Science and Medicine* 119, 170-174.

Lewis KC, Meehan KB, Cain NM, Wong PS, Clemence AJ, Stevens J, Tillman JG (2015). Impairments in object relations and chronicity of suicidal behavior in individuals with borderline personality disorder. *Journal of Personality Disorders*. Published online: 24 February 2015. doi: 10.1521/pedi_2015_29_178.

Lian Q, Zuo X, Lou C, Gao E, Cheng Y (2015). Sexual orientation and risk factors for suicidal ideation and suicide attempts: A multi-centre cross-sectional study in three Asian cities. *Journal of Epidemiology* 25, 155-161.

Lim M, Lee SU, Park J-I (2014). Difference in suicide methods used between suicide attempters and suicide completers. *International Journal of Mental Health Systems* 8, 54.

Lin L, Zhang J (2015). Impulsivity, mental disorder, and suicide in rural China. *Archives of Suicide Research*. Published online: 12 March 2015. doi: 10.1080/13811118.2015.1004478.

Lindgren M, Manninen M, Kalska H, Mustonen U, Laajasalo T, Moilanen K, Huttunen MO, Cannon TD, Suvisaari J, Therman S (2015). Suicidality, self-harm and psychotic-like symptoms in a general adolescent psychiatric sample. *Early Intervention in Psychiatry*. Published online: 13 January 2015. doi: 10.1111/eip.12218.

Lukoo RN, Ngiyulu RM, Mananga GL, Gini-Ehungu JL, Ekulu PM, Tshibassu PM, Aloni MN (2014). Depression in children suffering from sickle cell anemia. *Journal of Pediatric Hematology-Oncology* 37, 20-24.

Luyckx K, Gandhi A, Bijttebier P, Claes L (2015). Non-suicidal self-injury in female adolescents and psychiatric patients: A replication and extension of the role of identity formation. *Personality and Individual Differences* 77, 91-96.

Mackelprang JL, Harpin SB, Grubenhoff JA, Rivara FP (2014). Adverse outcomes among homeless adolescents and young adults who report a history of traumatic brain injury. *American Journal of Public Health* 104, 1986-1992.

Madhok R (2014). Workforce. Look out for the 'second victim' of adverse events. *The Health Service Journal* 124, 25-27.

Madsen T, Karstoft K-I, Bertelsen M, Andersen SB (2014). Postdeployment suicidal ideations and trajectories of posttraumatic stress disorder in Danish soldiers: A 3-year follow-up of the usper study. *The Journal of Clinical Psychiatry* 75, 994-1000.

Malhi GS (2014). Thoughts on suicidal thinking in bipolar disorder. *Bipolar Disorders* 17, 19-21.

Mandelli L, Nearchou FA, Vaiopoulos C, Stefanis CN, Vitoratou S, Serretti A, Stefanis NC (2015). Neuroticism, social network, stressful life events: Association with mood disorders, depressive symptoms and suicidal ideation in a community sample of women. *Psychiatry Research* 226, 38-44.

Mandracchia JT, Smith PN (2014). The interpersonal theory of suicide applied to male prisoners. *Suicide and Life-Threatening Behavior* 45, 293-301.

Mann JJ, Oquendo MA, Watson KT, Boldrini M, Malone KM, Ellis SP, Sullivan G, Cooper TB, Xie S, Currier D (2014). Anxiety in major depression and cerebrospinal fluid free gamma-aminobutyric acid. *Depression and Anxiety* 31, 814-821.

Manning V, Koh PK, Yang Y, Ng A, Guo S, Kandasami G, Wong KE (2015). Suicidal ideation and lifetime attempts in substance and gambling disorders. *Psychiatry Research* 225, 706-709.

Mansbach-Kleinfeld I, Ifrah A, Apter A, Farbstein I (2014). Child sexual abuse as reported by Israeli adolescents: Social and health related correlates. *Child Abuse and Neglect* 40, 68-80.

Marion-Veyron R, Lambert M, Cotton SM, Schimmelmann BG, Gravier B, McGorry PD, Conus P (2015). History of offending behavior in first episode psychosis patients: A marker of specific clinical needs and a call for early detection strategies among young offenders. *Schizophrenia Research* 161, 163-168.

Marsic A, Berman ME, Barry TD, McCloskey MS (2015). The relationship between intentional self-injurious behavior and the loudness dependence of auditory evoked potential in research volunteers. *Journal of Clinical Psychology* 71, 250-257.

Marti CN, Choi NG, DiNitto DM, Choi BY (2015). Associations of lifetime abstention and past and current alcohol use with late-life mental health: A propensity score analysis. *Drug and Alcohol Dependence* 149, 245-251.

Martins CM, Von Werne Baes C, de Carvalho Tofoli SM, Juruena MF (2014). Emotional abuse in childhood is a differential factor for the development of depression in adults. *Journal of Nervous and Mental Disease* 202, 774-782.

Mavhandu-Mudzusi AH, Sandy PT (2015). Religion-related stigma and discrimination experienced by lesbian, gay, bisexual and transgender students at a South African rural-based university. *Culture, Health & Sexuality.* Published online: 3 March 2015. doi: 10.1080/13691058.2015.1015614.

Mayes SD, Baweja R, Calhoun SL, Syed E, Mahr F, Siddiqui F (2014). Suicide ideation and attempts and bullying in children and adolescents: Psychiatric and general population samples. *Crisis* 35, 301-309.

McCarthy-Jones S, McCarthy-Jones R (2014). Body mass index and anxiety/depression as mediators of the effects of child sexual and physical abuse on physical health disorders in women. *Child Abuse and Neglect* 38, 2007-2020.

McCullumsmith CB, Kalpazian C, Richards JS, Forchheimer M, Heinemann A, Richardson E, Wilson C, Barber J, Temkin N, Fann JR, Bombardier CH (2015). Novel risk factors associated with current suicidal ideation and lifetime suicide attempt in individuals with spinal cord injury. *Archives of Physical Medicine and Rehabilitation* 96, 799-808.

McCullumsmith CB, Williamson DJ, May RS, Bruer EH, Sheehan DV, Alphs LD (2014). Simple measures of hopelessness and impulsivity are associated with acute suicidal ideation and attempts in patients in psychiatric crisis. *Innovations in Clinical Neuroscience* 11, 47-53.

McMartin SE, Kingsbury M, Dykxhoorn J, Colman I (2014). Time trends in symptoms of mental illness in children and adolescents in Canada. *Canadian Medical Association Journal.* Published online: 3 November 2014. doi: 10.1503/cmaj.140064.

Miller AB, Adams LM, Esposito-Smythers C, Thompson R, Proctor LJ (2014). Parents and friendships: A longitudinal examination of interpersonal mediators of the relationship between Child Maltreatmentment and suicidal ideation. *Psychiatry Research* 220, 998-1006.

Miller AB, Esposito-Smythers C, Leichtweis RN (2015). Role of social support in adolescent suicidal ideation and suicide attempts. T*he Journal of Adolescent* 56, 286-292.

Miná VAL, Lacerda-Pinheiro SF, Maia LC, Pinheiro RFF, Meireles CB, De Souza SIR, Reis AOA, Bianco B, Rolim MLN (2014). The influence of inflammatory cytokines in physiopathology of suicidal behavior. *Journal of Affective Disorders* 172, 219-230.

Miravitlles M, Molina J, Quintano JA, Campuzano A, Pérez J, Roncero C (2014). Factors associated with depression and severe depression in patients with COPD. *Respiratory Medicine* 108, 1615-1625.

Misiak B, Kiejna A, Frydecka D (2015). Higher total cholesterol level is associated with suicidal ideation in first-episode schizophrenia females. *Psychiatry Research* 226, 383-388.

Mittal M, Harrison DL, Miller MJ, Brahm NC (2014). National antidepressant prescribing in children and adolescents with mental health disorders after an FDA boxed warning. *Research in Social and Administrative Pharmacy* 10, 781-790.

Modinos G, Allen P, Frascarelli M, Tognin S, Valmaggia L, Xenaki L, Keedwell P, Broome M, Valli I, Woolley J, Stone JM, Mechelli A, Phillips ML, McGuire P, Fusar-Poli P (2014). Are we really mapping psychosis risk? Neuroanatomical signature of affective disorders in subjects at ultra high risk. *Psychological Medicine* 44, 3491-3501.

Mohammadkhani P, Khanipour H, Azadmehr H, Mobramm A, Naseri E (2015). Trait mindfulness, reasons for living and general symptom severity as predictors of suicide probability in males with substance abuse or dependence. *Iranian Journal of Psychiatry* 10, 56-63.

Molina-Andreu O, González-Rodríguez A, Villanueva AP, Penadés R, Catalán R, Bernardo M (2014). Awareness of illness and suicidal behavior in delusional disorder patients. *Revista De Psiquiatria Clinica* 41, 156-158.

Moore TJ (2014). Antidepressants increase, rather than decrease, risk of suicidal behaviours in younger patients. *BMJ* 349, g5626.

Mousavi SG, Bateni S, Maracy MR, Mardanian F, Mousavi SH (2014). Recurrent suicide attempt and female hormones. *Advanced Biomedical Research* 3, 201.

Mueller AS, Abrutyn S (2015). Suicidal disclosures among friends: Using social network data to understand suicide contagion. *Journal of Health and Social Behavior* 56, 131-148.

Mueller AS, James W, Abrutyn S, Levin ML (2015). Suicide ideation and bullying among us adolescents: Examining the intersections of sexual orientation, gender, and race/ethnicity. *American Journal of Public Health* 105, 980-985.

Mula M, Sander JW (2015). Suicide and epilepsy: Do antiepileptic drugs increase the risk? *Expert Opinion on Drug Safety* 14, 553-558.

Mullins N, Hodgson K, Tansey KE, Perroud N, Maier W, Mors O, Rietschel M, Hauser J, Henigsberg N (2014). Investigation of blood MRNA biomarkers for suicidality in an independent sample. *Translational Psychiatry* 4, e474.

Muneer A (2014). Aripiprazole in the treatment of refractory mood disorders: A case series. *Clinical Psychopharmacology and Neuroscience* 12, 157-159.

Murray AL, McKenzie K, Murray KR, Richelieu M (2015). Do close supportive relationships moderate the effect of depressive symptoms on suicidal ideation? *British Journal of Guidance and Counselling.* Published online: 18 March 2015. doi: 10.1080/03069885.2015.1017804.

Nadorff MR, Salem T, Winer ES, Lamis DA, Nazem S, Berman ME (2014). Explaining alcohol use and suicide risk: A moderated mediation model involving insomnia symptoms and gender. *Journal of Clinical Sleep Medicine* 10, 1317-1323.

Nagata T, Nakagawa A, Matsumoto S, Shiina A, Iyo M, Hirabayashi N, Igarashi Y (2015). Characteristics of female mentally disordered offenders culpable under the new legislation in Japan: A gender comparison study. *Criminal Behavious and Mental Health.* Published online: 10 March 2015. doi: 10.1002/cbm.1949.

Nagesh O, Bastiampillai T, Fisher L, Mohan T (2015). Cyclical suicidal ideation following natalizumab infusion for multiple sclerosis. *Australian and New Zealand Journal of Psychiatry.* Published online: 16 February 2015. doi: 10.1177/0004867415572414.

Nahvi S, Ning Y, Segal KS, Richter KP, Arnsten JH (2014). Varenicline efficacy and safety among methadone maintained smokers: A randomized placebo-controlled trial. *Addiction* 109, 1554-1563.

Nascimento ER, Ornelas Maia AC, Soares-Filho G, Nardi AE, Cardoso A (2015). Predictors of suicidal ideation in coronary artery disease. *Comprehensive Psychiatry* 57, 16-20.

Näsi M, Räsänen P, Oksanen A, Hawdon J, Keipi T, Holkeri E (2014). Association between online harassment and exposure to harmful online content: A cross-national comparison between the United States and Finland. *Computers in Human Behavior* 41, 137-145.

Nishida A, Shimodera S, Sasaki T, Richards M, Hatch SL, Yamasaki S, Usami S, Ando S, Asukai N, Okazaki Y (2014). Risk for suicidal problems in poor-help-seeking adolescents with psychotic-like experiences: Findings from a cross-sectional survey of 16,131 adolescents. *Schizophrenia Research* 159, 257-262.

Noh H-M, Cho JJ, Park YS, Kim J-H (2015). The relationship between suicidal behaviors and atopic dermatitis in Korean adolescents. *Journal of Health Psychology*. Published online: 2 March 2015. doi: 10.1177/1359105315572453.

Nowotny KM, Peterson RL, Boardman JD (2015). Gendered contexts: Variation in suicidal ideation by female and male youth across U.S. States. *Journal of Health and Social Behavior* 56, 114-130.

O'Farrell IB, Corcoran P, Perry IJ (2015). Characteristics of small areas with high rates of hospital-treated self-harm: Deprived, fragmented and urban or just close to hospital? A national registry study. *Journal of Epidemiology and Community Health* 69, 162-167.

O'Keefe VM, Wingate LR, Cole AB, Hollingsworth DW, Tucker RP (2014). Seemingly harmless racial communications are not so harmless: Racial microaggressions lead to suicidal ideation by way of depression symptoms. *Suicide and Life-Threatening Behavior*. Published online: 30 December 2014. doi: 10.1111/sltb.12150.

Oglesby ME, Capron DW, Raines AM, Schmidt NB (2015). Anxiety sensitivity cognitive concerns predict suicide risk. *Psychiatry Research* 226, 252-256.

Oh SH, Lee KU, Kim SH, Park KN, Kim YM, Kim HJ (2014). Factors associated with choice of high lethality methods in suicide attempters: A cross-sectional study. *International Journal of Mental Health Systems* 8, 43.

Oktan V (2014). Investigation of self-injurious behavior in adolescents in terms of risk-taking behavior and self-esteem. *Egitim Ve Bilim* 39, 183-191.

Oktan V (2015). An investigation of problematic internet use among adolescents in terms of self-injurious and risk-taking behavior. *Children and Youth Services Review* 52, 63-67.

Olfson M, Schoenbaum M (2014). Link between FDA antidepressant warnings and increased suicide attempts in young people is questionable. *BMJ* 349, g5614.

Opperman K, Czyz EK, Gipson PY, King CA (2015). Connectedness and perceived burdensomeness among adolescents at elevated suicide risk: An examination of the interpersonal theory of suicidal behavior. *Archives of Suicide Research*. Published online: 9 March 2015. doi: 10.1080/13811118.2014.957451.

Orchard TJ, Nathan DM, Zinman B, Cleary P, Brillon D, Backlund JYC, Lachin JM (2015). Association between 7 years of intensive treatment of type 1 diabetes and long-term mortality. *JAMA* 313, 45-53.

Orui M, Sato Y, Tazaki K, Kawamura I, Harada S, Hayashi M (2015). Delayed increase in male suicide rates in tsunami disaster-stricken areas following the great east Japan earthquake: A three-year follow-up study in Miyagi Prefecture. *Tohoku Journal of Experimental Medicine* 235, 215-222.

Osafo J, Akotia CS, Andoh-Arthur J, Quarshie EN (2015). Attempted suicide in Ghana: Motivation, stigma and coping. *Death Studies*. Published online: 6 January 2015. doi: 10.1080/07481187.2014.991955.

Osama M, Islam MY, Hussain SA, Masroor SMZ, Burney MU, Masood MA, Menezes RG, Rehman R (2014). Suicidal ideation among medical students of Pakistan: A cross-sectional study. *Journal of Forensic and Legal Medicine* 27, 65-68.

Owen R., Gooding P., Dempsey R., Jones S. (2015). A qualitative investigation into the relationships between social factors and suicidal thoughts and acts experienced by people with a bipolar disorder diagnosis. *Journal of Affective Disorders* 176, 133-140.

Pan LA, Ramos L, Segreti A, Brent DA, Phillips ML (2014). Right superior temporal gyrus volume in adolescents with a history of suicide attempt. *British Journal of Psychiatry*. 206, 339-340.

Pani PP, Trogu E, Vigna-Taglianti F, Mathis F, Diecidue R, Kirchmayer U, Amato L, Davoli M, Ghibaudi J, Camposeragna A, Saponaro A, Faggiano F, Maremmani AGI, Maremmani I (2014). Psychopathological symptoms of patients with heroin addiction entering opioid agonist or therapeutic community treatment. *Annals of General Psychiatry* 13, 35.

Parikh N, Sharma P, Gandhi H, Banwari G (2014). A study on attempted suicide, its clinical and socio-demographic variables in a tertiary level hospital of Ahmedabad. *International Journal of Current Research and Review* 6, 57-63.

Park SC, Hahn SW, Hwang TY, Kim JM, Jun TY, Lee MS, Kim JB, Yim HW, Park YC (2014). Does age at onset of first major depressive episode indicate the subtype of major depressive disorder?: The clinical research center for depression study. *Yonsei Medical Journal* 55, 1712-1720.

Park SM (2014). Suicidal ideation and its determinants in Korean adults: The role of physical activity and functional limitations. *Psychology, Health and Medicine*. Published online: 1 December 2014. doi: 10.1080/13548506.2014.986144.

Patten SB (2014). Important messages for clinical care and health policy on suicide. *Canadian Journal of Psychiatry* 59, 509-510.

Patten SB, Williams JVA, Lavorato DH, Wang JL, McDonald K, Bulloch AGM (2015). Descriptive epidemiology of major depressive disorder in Canada in 2012. *Canadian Journal of Psychiatry* 60, 23-30.

Pease JL, Monteith LL, Hostetter TA, Forster JE, Bahraini NH (2015). Military service and suicidal thoughts and behaviors in a national sample of college students. *Crisis*. Published online: 12 January 2015. doi: 10.1027/0227-5910/a000300.

Peñas-Lledo E, Guillaume S, Delgado A, Naranjo MEG, Jaussent I, Llerena A, Courtet P (2014). ABCB1 gene polymorphisms and violent suicide attempt among survivors. *Journal of Psychiatric Research* 61, 52-56.

Pennington CR, Cramer RJ, Miller HA, Anastasi JS (2014). Psychopathy, depression, and anxiety as predictors of suicidal ideation in offenders. *Death Studies* 39, 288-295.

Perez S, Marco JH, Garcia-Alandete J (2014). Comparison of clinical and demographic characteristics among borderline personality disorder patients with and without suicidal attempts and non-suicidal self-injury behaviors. *Psychiatry Research* 220, 935-940.

Perlman G, Nelson B, Proudfit GH, Klein D, Kotov R (2014). Neural mechanisms of non-suicidal self-injury and suicidal behavior in adolescent girls. *Comprehensive Psychiatry* 55, e56.

Petersen I, Nazareth I (2015). Antidepressant dose and risk of deliberate self-harm: Is it the dose or the indication? *Journal of the American Medical Association Internal Medicine* 175, 463-464.

Podolak E (2014). Suicide risk assessment: Searching for true positive. *International Journal of Adolescent Medicine and Health* 27, 221-223.

Poindexter EK, Mitchell SM, Jahn DR, Smith PN, Hirsch JK, Cukrowicz KC (2015). PTSD symptoms and suicide ideation: Testing the conditional indirect effects of thwarted interpersonal needs and using substances to cope. *Personality and Individual Differences* 77, 167-172.

Polanco-Roman L, Jurska J, Quinones V, Miranda R (2014). Brooding, reflection, and distraction: Relation to non-suicidal self-injury versus suicide attempts. *Archives of Suicide Research*. Published online: 17 December 2014. doi: 10.1080/13811118.2014.981623.

Polanco-Roman L, Tsypes A, Soffer A, Miranda R (2014). Ethnic differences in prevalence and correlates of self-harm behaviors in a treatment-seeking sample of emerging adults. *Psychiatry Research* 220, 927-934.

Pompili M, Innamorati M, Gonda X, Serafini G, Erbuto D, Ricci F, Fountoulakis KN, Lester D, Vazquez G, Rihmer Z, Amore M, Girardi P (2014). Pharmacotherapy in bipolar disorders during hospitalization and at discharge predicts clinical and psychosocial functioning at follow-up. *Human Psychopharmacology* 29, 578-588.

Pompili M, Serafini G, Innamorati M, Montebovi F, Lamis DA, Milelli M, Giuliani M, Caporro M, Tisei P, Lester D, Amore M, Girardi P, Buttinelli C (2014). Factors associated with hopelessness in epileptic patients. *World Journal of Psychiatry* 4, 141-149.

Pratt SD, Jachna BR (2014). Care of the clinician after an adverse event. *International Journal of Obstetric Anesthesia* 24, 54-63.

Putnam K, Robertson-Blackmore E, Sharkey K, Payne J, Bergink V, Munk-Olsen T, Deligiannidis K, Altemus M, Newport J, Apter G, Devouche E, Vikorin A, Magnusson P, Lichtenstein P, Penninx B, Buist A, Bilszta J, O'Hara M, Stuart S, Brock R, Roza S, Tiemeier H, Guille C, Neill Epperson C, Kim D, Schmidt P, Martinez P, Wisner KL, Stowe Z, Jones I, Rubinow D, Sullivan P, Meltzer-Brody S (2015). Heterogeneity of postpartum depression: A latent class analysis. *The Lancet Psychiatry* 2, 59-67.

Quinones V, Jurska J, Fener E, Miranda R (2015). Active and passive problem solving: Moderating role in the relation between depressive symptoms and future suicidal ideation varies by suicide attempt history. *Journal of Clinical Psychology* 71, 402-412.

Rabinovitch SM, Kerr DCR, Leve LD, Chamberlain P (2014). Suicidal behavior outcomes of childhood sexual abuse: Longitudinal study of adjudicated girls. *Suicide and Life-Threatening Behavior*. Published online: 5 November 2014. doi: 10.1111/sltb.12141.

Rai NK, Goyal V, Kumar N, Shukla G, Srivastava AK, Singh S, Behari M (2015). Neuropsychiatric co-morbidities in non-demented Parkinson's disease. *Annals of Indian Academy of Neurology* 18, 33-38.

Rallis BA, Esposito-Smythers C, Mehlenbeck R (2015). Family environment as a moderator of the association between conduct disorder and suicidality. *Journal of Aggression, Maltreatment and Trauma* 24, 150-168.

Ramesh A, Kumar A, Aramandla MP, Nyanda AM (2014). Polycyclic aromatic hydrocarbon residues in serum samples of autopsied individuals from Tennessee. *International Journal of Environmental Research and Public Health* 12, 322-334.

Raposo S, El-Gabalawy R, Erickson J, Mackenzie CS, Sareen J (2014). Associations between anxiety disorders, suicide ideation, and age in nationally representative samples of Canadian and American adults. *Journal of Anxiety Disorders* 28, 823-829.

Rattaz C, Michelon C, Baghdadli A (2015). Symptom severity as a risk factor for self-injurious behaviours in adolescents with autism spectrum disorders. *Journal of Intellectual Disability Research*. Published online: 12 January 2015. doi: 10.1111/jir.12177.

Reading L, Bowen E (2014). A thematic analysis of how prisoners overcome suicidality. *International Journal of Prisoner Health* 10, 212-227.

Reas DL, Pedersen G, Karterud S, Ro O (2014). Self-harm and suicidal behavior in borderline personality disorder with and without bulimia nervosa. *Journal of Consulting and Clinical Psychology* 83, 643-648.

Rees S, Steel Z, Creamer M, Teesson M, Bryant R, McFarlane AC, Mills KL, Slade T, Carragher N, M OD, Forbes D, Silove D (2014). Onset of common mental disorders and suicidal behavior following women's first exposure to gender based violence: A retrospective, population-based study. *BMC Psychiatry* 14, 312.

Reeves R, Tamburello A (2014). Single cells, segregated housing, and suicide in the New Jersey department of corrections. *The Journal of the American Academy of Psychiatry and the Law* 42, 484-488.

Reisner SL, Vetters R, Leclerc M, Zaslow S, Wolfrum S, Shumer D, Mimiaga MJ (2015). Mental health of transgender youth in care at an adolescent urban community health center: A matched retrospective cohort study. *Journal of Adolescent Health* 56, 274-279.

Reynders A, Kerkhof AJFM, Molenberghs G, Van Audenhove C (2015). Help-seeking, stigma and attitudes of people with and without a suicidal past. A comparison between a low and a high suicide rate country. *Journal of Affective Disorders* 178, 5-11.

Rhodes AE, Boyle MH, Bridge JA, Sinyor M, Links PS, Tonmyr L, Skinner R, Bethell JM, Carlisle C, Goodday S, Hottes TS, Newton A, Bennett K, Sundar P, Cheung AH, Szatmari P (2014). Antecedents and sex/gender differences in youth suicidal behavior. *World Journal of Psychiatry* 4, 120-132.

Rhodes AE, Lu H, Skinner R (2014). Time trends in medically serious suicide-related behaviours in boys and girls. *Canadian Journal of Psychiatry* 59, 556-560.

Rice TR (2014). Violence among young men: The importance of a gender-specific developmental approach to adolescent male suicide and homicide. *International Journal of Adolescence Medicine and Health* 27, 177-181.

Rim TH, Lee CS, Lee SC, Chung B, Kim SS (2015). Influence of visual acuity on suicidal ideation, suicide attempts and depression in South Korea. *British Journal of Ophthalmology*. Published online: 2 March 2015. doi: 10.1136/bjophthalmol-2014-306518.

Rissanen I, Jaaskelainen E, Isohanni M, Koponen H, Joukamaa M, Alaraisanen A, Miettunen J (2014). Use of antidepressant medication and suicidal ideation - the Northern Finland Birth Cohort 1966. *Human Psychopharmacology* 29, 559-567.

Robert A, Suelves JM, Armayones M, Ashley S (2015). Internet use and suicidal behaviors: Internet as a threat or opportunity? *Telemedicine Journal and E-Health* 21, 306-311.

Robustelli BL, Trytko AC, Li A, Whisman MA (2015). Marital discord and suicidal outcomes in a national sample of married individuals. *Suicide and Life-Threatening Behavior*. Published online: 5 March 2015. doi: 10.1111/sltb.12157.

Rojas SM, Leen-Feldner EW, Blumenthal H, Lewis SF, Feldner MT (2014). Risk for suicide among treatment seeking adolescents: The role of positive and negative affect intensity. *Cognitive Therapy and Research* 39, 100-109.

Rolim-Neto ML, Alves Silva E, Teixeira Júnior AG, Sousa Cartaxo JD, Rolim Lima NN, Nascimento VB, Vieira Dos Santos MDS, Lima Da Silva CG, Romero De Sousa SI, Silva Costa LD, Nascimento Neto PJ (2014). Bipolar disorder incidence between children and adolescents: A brief communication. *Journal of Affective Disorders* 172, 171-174.

Rouse LM, Frey RA, López M, Wohlers H, Xiong I, Llewellyn K, Lucci SP, Wester SR (2015). Law enforcement suicide discerning etiology through psychological autopsy. *Police Quarterly* 18, 79-108.

Roux P, Lions C, Michel L, Mora M, Dauouède JP, Marcellin F, Spire B, Morel A, Carrieri PM, Morel A, Mora M, Aubertin JF, Robinet S, Desenclos JC, Cohen J, Herszkowicz A, Paul A, Porteret I, Sainte Marie T, Achard, Aubertin, Bijeau B, Bartolo, Bibette, Biderman, Bry, Cadart, Dewost, Daulouede, Gassmann, Guena, Guillet, Gutekunst, Herouin, Herran, Jacob, Kerlo h, Khouri, Lasalarié, Lavignasse, Magnin, Marre, Mauraycaplanne, Michel, Morel A, Nemayechi, Paillou, Partouche, Petit, Pouclet, Raulin, Regard, Roch, Rouille, Truffy, Vergez, Wajsbrot, Bachellier J, Beauverie P, Couteron JP, Marty-Double C, Vray M, Baker R, Catania H, Gossop M, Haemmig R, Torrens M, Wodak A, Carrieri MP, Mora M, Maradan G, Biemar J, Huguet S, Kurkdji P, Taieb C, Cohen J, Giovannini C, Kissikian MP, Desenclos JC, Job-Spira N, Dore V, Paul C, Porteret I, Vincent, Herszkowicz A, Prisse N, Richard N, Olivet F, Arditti J (2014). Factors associated with hcv risk practices in methadone-maintained patients: The importance of considering the couple in prevention interventions. *Substance Abuse: Treatment, Prevention, and Policy* 9, 37.

Rubin R (2014). Recent suicides highlight need to address depression in medical students and residents. *JAMA* 312, 1725-1727.

Rüsch N, Zlati A, Black G, Thornicroft G (2014). Does the stigma of mental illness contribute to suicidality? *British Journal of Psychiatry* 205, 257-259.

Safa M, Boroujerdi FG, Talischi F, Masjedi MR (2014). Relationship of coping styles with suicidal behavior in hospitalized asthma and chronic obstructive pulmonary disease patients: Substance abusers versus non- substance abusers. *Tanaffos* 13, 23-30.

Saffer BY, Glenn CR, David Klonsky E (2014). Clarifying the relationship of parental bonding to suicide ideation and attempts. *Suicide and Life-Threatening Behavior*. Published online: 22 December 2014. doi: 10.1111/sltb.12146.

Sajadi SF, Hajjari Z, Zargar Y, Mehrabizade Honarmand M, Arshadi N (2014). Predicting addiction potential on the basis of early traumatic events, dissociative experiences, and suicide ideation. *International Journal of High Risk Behaviors and Addiction* 3, e20995.

Sánchez-Teruel D, Robles-Bello MA (2014). Protective factors promoting resilience to suicide in young people and adolescents. *Papeles Del Psicologo* 35, 181-192.

Santaularia J, Johnson M, Hart L, Haskett L, Welsh E, Faseru B (2014). Relationships between sexual violence and chronic disease: A cross-sectional study. *BMC Public Health* 14, 1286.

Sara GE (2014). Mental disorder and suicide: A faulty connection, or a faulty argument? *Australian and New Zealand Journal of Psychiatry* 49, 84-86.

Sara GE, Burgess PM, Malhi GS, Whiteford HA, Hall WC (2014). Stimulant and other substance use disorders in schizophrenia: Prevalence, correlates and impacts in a population sample. *Australian and New Zealand Journal of Psychiatry* 48, 1036-1047.

Saraff PD, Trujillo N, Pepper CM (2015). Functions, consequences, and frequency of non-suicidal self-injury. *Psychiatric Quarterly*. Published online: 8 January 2015. doi: 10.1007/s11126-015-9338-6.

Scaruffi E, Gambineri A, Cattaneo S, Turra J, Vettor R, Mioni R (2014). Personality and psychiatric disorders in women affected by polycystic ovary syndrome. *Frontiers in Endocrinology* 5, 185.

Schäfer I, Gromus L, Atabaki A, Pawils S, Verthein U, Reimer J, Schulte B, Martens M (2014). Are experiences of sexual violence related to special needs in patients with substance use disorders? A study in opioid-dependent patients. *Addictive Behaviors* 39, 1691-1694.

Schäfer M, Quiring O (2014). The press coverage of celebrity suicide and the development of suicide frequencies in Germany. *Health Communication*. Published online: 3 November 2014. doi: 10.1080/10410236.2014.923273.

Scherer Zavaschi ML, Mardini V, Da Cunha GB, De Almeida Martins-Costa SH, Guarienti F, Pianca TG, Pechansky F, Paim Rohde LA, Kapczinski F, Cereser K, Szobot CM (2014). Socio-demographic and clinical characteristics of pregnant and puerperal crack-cocaine using women: Preliminary data. *Revista De Psiquiatria Clinica* 41, 121-123.

Schmidt NB, Capron DW, Raines AM, Allan NP (2014). Randomized clinical trial evaluating the efficacy of a brief intervention targeting anxiety sensitivity cognitive concerns. *Journal of Consulting and Clinical Psychology* 82, 1023-1033.

Segal DL, Gottschling J, Marty M, Meyer WJ, Coolidge FL (2015). Relationships among depressive, passive-aggressive, sadistic and self-defeating personality disorder features with suicidal ideation and reasons for living among older adults. *Aging and Mental Health*. Published online: 26 January 2015. doi: 10.1080/13607863.2014.1003280.

Seko Y, Kidd SA, Wiljer D, McKenzie KJ (2015). On the creative edge: Exploring motivations for creating non-suicidal self-injury content online. *Qualitative Health Research*. Published online: 6 February 2015. doi: 10.1177/1049732315570134.

Seo H-J, Song HR, Yim H-W, Kim J-B, Lee M-S, Kim J-M, Jun T-Y (2014). Age-related differences in suicidality between young people and older adults with depression: Data from a nationwide depression cohort study in Korea (the CRESCEND study). *Comprehensive Psychiatry* 56, 85-92.

Seo J-G, Lee J-J, Cho YW, Lee S-J, Kim J-E, Moon H-J, Park S-P (2015). Suicidality and its risk factors in Korean people with epilepsy: A MEPSY study. *Journal of Clinical Neurology* 11, 32-41.

Shah S, Mackinnon A, Galletly C, Carr V, McGrath JJ, Stain HJ, Castle D, Harvey C, Sweeney S, Morgan VA (2014). Prevalence and impact of childhood abuse in people with a psychotic illness. Data from the second Australian national survey of psychosis. *Schizophrenia Research* 159, 20-26.

Shahid M, Iqbal R, Khan MM, Khan MZ, Shamsi US, Nakeer R (2015). Risk factors for deliberate self-harm in patients presenting to the emergency departments of Karachi. *Journal of the College of Physicians and Surgeons* 25, 50-55.

Shaikh MA (2014). Prevalence, correlates, and changes in tobacco use between 2006 and 2010 among 13-15 year Moroccan school attending adolescents. *Journal of the Pakistan Medical Association* 64, 1306-1309.

Shakeri J, Farnia V, Valinia K, Hashemian AH, Bajoghli H, Holsboer-Trachsler E, Brand S (2014). The relationship between lifetime suicide attempts, serum lipid levels, and metabolic syndrome in patients with bipolar disorders. *International Journal of Psychiatry in Clinical Practice* 19, 124-131.

Shakya DR (2014). Psychiatric morbidities among mentally ill wives of Nepalese men working abroad. *Industrial Psychiatry Journal* 23, 52-57.

Shapiro J, Timmins ve, Swampillai B, Scavone A, Collinger K, Boulos C, Hatch J, Goldstein BI (2014). Correlates of psychiatric hospitalization in a clinical sample of Canadian adolescents with bipolar disorder. *Comprehensive Psychiatry* 55, 1855-1861.

Sharif F, Parsnia A, Mani A, Vosoghi M, Setoodeh G (2014). Comparison of personality traits, coping styles, and psychiatric disorders in adult suicidal and non-suicidal individuals. *International Journal of Community Based Nursing and Midwifery* 2, 148-156.

Sharma MK, Salim A (2014). Suicidal behavior among alcohol dependents: Relationship with anger and personality dimensions. *Industrial Psychiatry Journal* 23, 61-64.

Shelef L, Fruchter E, Spiegel DO, Shoval G, Mann JJ, Zalsman G (2014). Characteristics of soldiers with self harm in the Israeli defense forces. *Archives of Suicide Research* 18, 410-418.

Shim IH, Woo YS, Bahk WM (2014). Prevalence rates and clinical implications of bipolar disorder "with mixed features" as defined by DSM-5. *Journal of Affective Disorders* 173, 120-125.

Sigsbee B, Bernat JL (2014). Physician burnout: A neurologic crisis. *Neurology* 83, 2302-2306.

Silberschmidt A, Lee S, Zanarini M, Schulz SC (2015). Gender differences in borderline personality disorder: Results from a multinational, clinical trial sample. *Journal of Personality Disorders.* Published online: 6 January 2015. doi: 10.1521/pedi_2014_28_175.

Silva C, Ribeiro JD, Joiner TE (2015). Mental disorders and thwarted belongingness, perceived burdensomeness, and acquired capability for suicide. *Psychiatry Research* 226, 316-327.

Silva RJDS, Santos FALD, Soares NMM, Pardono E (2014). Suicidal ideation and associated factors among adolescents in northeastern Brazil. *Scientific World Journal* 2014, 450943.

Simon MA, Chen R, Chang ES, Dong X (2014). The association between filial piety and suicidal ideation: Findings from a community-dwelling Chinese aging population. *The Journals of Gerontology: Series A* 69, S90-S97.

Simonetti JA, Mackelprang JL, Rowhani-Rahbar A, Zatzick D, Rivara FP (2015). Psychiatric comorbidity, suicidality, and in-home firearm access among a nationally representative sample of adolescents. *JAMA Psychiatry* 72, 152-159.

Sisek-Šprem M, Križaj A, Juki V, Miloševi M, Petrovi Z, Herceg M (2014). Testosterone levels and clinical features of schizophrenia with emphasis on negative symptoms and aggression. *Nordic Journal of Psychiatry* 69, 102-109.

Slater T, Scourfield J, Greenland K (2015). Suicide attempts and social worker contact: Secondary analysis of a general population study. *British Journal of Social Work* 45, 378-394.

Smith AR, Yeager AE, Dodd DR (2014). The joint influence of acquired capability for suicide and stoicism on over-exercise among women. *Eating Behaviors* 17, 77-82.

Smith EG, Austin KL, Kim HM, Miller DR, Eisen SV, Christiansen CL, Kilbourne AM, Sauer BC, McCarthy JF, Valenstein M (2014). Suicide risk in Veterans Health Administration patients with mental health diagnoses initiating lithium or valproate: A historical prospective cohort study. *BMC Psychiatry* 14, 357.

Smith H, Power J (2014). Applying the dual-taxonomy of offending to self-injury: Do offenders exhibit life-course-persistent self-injurious behavior? *Victims and Offenders* 10, 179-213.

Soyka M, Zill P, Koller G, Samochowiec A, Grzywacz A, Preuss UW (2015). Val158Met COMT polymorphism and risk of aggression in alcohol dependence. *Addiction Biology* 20, 197-204.

Spitzer C, Masuhr O, Aalderink T, Rullkoetter N, Armbrust M (2015). Self-injury and childhood trauma in patients with borderline personality disorder. *Psychotherapeut* 60, 31-37.

Stange JP, Hamilton JL, Burke TA, Kleiman EM, O'Garro-Moore JK, Seligman ND, Abramson LY, Alloy LB (2015). Negative cognitive styles synergistically predict suicidal ideation in bipolar spectrum disorders: A 3-year prospective study. *Psychiatry Research* 226, 162-168.

Stansfeld S, Smuk M, Onwumere J, Clark C, Pike C, McManus S, Harris J, Bebbington P (2014). Stressors and common mental disorder in informal carers - an analysis of the English adult psychiatric morbidity survey 2007. *Social Science and Medicine* 120, 190-198.

Stoewen DL (2015). Suicide in veterinary medicine: Let's talk about it. *Canadian Veterinary Journal* 56, 89-92.

Stone DM, Luo F, Lippy C, McIntosh WL (2014). The role of social connectedness and sexual orientation in the prevention of youth suicide ideation and attempts among sexually active adolescents. *Suicide and Life-Threatening Behavior*. Published online: 12 November 2014. doi: 10.1111/sltb.12139.

Stone GD (2014). Farmer suicides. *Issues in Science and Technology* 30, 18.

Storch EA, Hanks CE, Mink JW, McGuire JF, Adams HR, Augustine EF, Vierhile A, Thatcher A, Bitsko R, Lewin AB, Murphy TK (2015). Suicidal thoughts and behaviors in children and adolescents with chronic tic disorders. *Depression and Anxiety*. Published online: 24 February 2015. doi: 10.1002/da.22357.

Straub J, Keller F, Sproeber N, Koelch MG, Plener PL (2015). Suicidal behavior in German adolescents. *Journal of Child and Adolescent Psychiatry and Psychotherapy* 43, 39-45.

Studd J (2014). Hormone therapy for reproductive depression in women. *Post Reproductive Health* 20, 132-137.

Subramaniam M, Abdin E, Seow EL, Picco L, Vaingankar JA, Chong SA (2014). Suicidal ideation, suicidal plan and suicidal attempts among those with major depressive disorder. *Annals of the Academy of Medicine, Singapore* 43, 412-421.

Sullivan GM, Oquendo MA, Milak M, Miller JM, Burke A, Ogden RT, Parsey RV, Mann JJ (2014). Positron emission tomography quantification of serotonin1A receptor binding in suicide attempters with major depressive disorder. *JAMA Psychiatry* 72, 169-178.

Sun L, Zhang J (2014). Coping skill as a moderator between negative life events and suicide among young people in rural China. *Journal of Clinical Psychology* 71, 258-266.

Sylvia LG, Thase ME, Reilly-Harrington NA, Salcedo S, Brody B, Kinrys G, Kemp D, Shelton RC, McElroy SL, Kocsis JH, Bobo WV, Kamali M, McInnis M, Friedman E, Tohen M, Bowden CL, Ketter TA, Singh V, Calabrese J, Nierenberg AA, Rabideau DJ, Elson CM, Deckersbach T (2015). Psychotherapy use in bipolar disorder: Association with functioning and illness severity. *Australian and New Zealand Journal of Psychiatry* 49, 453-461.

Takara K, Kondo T (2014). Autism spectrum disorder among first-visit depressed adult patients: Diagnostic clues from backgrounds and past history. *General Hospital Psychiatry* 36, 737-742.

Takara K, Kondo T (2014b). Comorbid atypical autistic traits as a potential risk factor for suicide attempts among adult depressed patients: A case-control study. *Annals of General Psychiatry* 13, 33-33.

Tandon VR, Singh P, Rani N, Roshi, Gupta R, Khajuria V (2014). Isoniazid induced psychosis (self harm behaviour) with neuropathy and vitamin B6 deficiency. *JK Science* 16, 34-36.

Tang F, Qin P (2015). Influence of personal social network and coping skills on risk for suicidal ideation in Chinese university students. *PLoS One* 10, e0121023.

Tang K-T, Hsieh C-W, Hsieh T-Y, Lan J-L, Chen Y-H, Chen D-Y (2014). Suicide attempts in patients with systemic lupus erythematosus: A single-center experience and literature review. *Psychosomatics* 56, 190-195.

Tanrıverdi D, Cuhadar D, Ciftci S (2014). Does the impairment of functional life increase the probability of suicide in cancer patients? *Asian Pacific Journal of Cancer Prevention* 15, 9549-9553.

Tapola V, Wahlstrom J, Kuittinen M, Lappalainen R (2015). The co-occurrence of nonsuicidal and suicidal self-injurious acts in adult women: A pilot study of similarities and differences. *Nordic Psychology* 67, 27-45.

Teofilo MM, Farias DR, Pinto Tde J, Vilela AA, Vaz Jdos S, Nardi AE, Kac G (2014). HDL-cholesterol concentrations are inversely associated with Edinburgh Postnatal Depression Scale scores during pregnancy: results from a Brazilian cohort study. *Journal of Psychiatric Research* 58, 181-188.

Tesfaye M, Hanlon C, Tessema F, Prince M, Alem A (2014). Common mental disorder symptoms among patients with malaria attending primary care in Ethiopia: A cross-sectional survey. *PLoS One* Published online: 30 September 2014. doi: 10.1371/journal.pone.0108923.

Thaipisuttikul P, Ittasakul P, Waleeprakhon P, Wisajun P, Jullagate S (2014). Psychiatric comorbidities in patients with major depressive disorder. *Neuropsychiatric Disease and Treatment* 10, 2097-2103.

Thomas JC (2014). Re-visioning medicine. *Journal of Medical Humanities* 35, 405-422.

Thompson SJ, Montgomery KL, Bender K (2014). Predictors of alcohol use among status-offending adolescents: Youth and parent perspectives. *Journal of Child and Adolescent Substance Abuse* 23, 389-397.

Thullen MJ, Taliaferro LA, Muehlenkamp JJ (2015). Suicide ideation and attempts among adolescents engaged in risk behaviors: A latent class analysis. *Journal of Research on Adolescence*. Published online: 6 March 2015. doi: : 10.1111/jora.12199.

Thurston WE, Tam DM, Dawson M, Jackson M, Kwok SM (2014). The intersection of gender and other social institutions in constructing gender-based violence in Guangzhou China. *Journal of Interpersonal Violence*. Published online: 18 November 2014. doi: 10.1177/0886260514556109.

Tong Y, Phillips MR, Duberstein P, Zhan W (2014). Suicidal behavior in relatives or associates moderates the strength of common risk factors for suicide. *Suicide and Life-Threatening Behavior*. Published online: 2 December 2014. doi: 10.1111/sltb.12144.

Tossone K, Jefferis ES, Grey SF, Bilge-Johnson S, Bhatta MP, Seifert P (2015). Poly-traumatization and harmful behaviors in a sample of emergency department psychiatric intake response center youth. *Child Abuse and Neglect* 40, 142-151.

Toussaint L, Wilson CM, Wilson LC, Williams DR (2015). Religiousness and suicide in a nationally representative sample of Trinidad and Tobago adolescents and young adults. *Social Psychiatry and Psychiatric Epidemiology*. Published online: 25 March 2015. doi: 10.1007/s00127-015-1045-y.

Tran KK, Wong YJ, Cokley KO, Brownson C, Drum D, Awad G, Wang MC (2015). Suicidal Asian American college students' perceptions of protective factors: A qualitative study. *Death Studies*. Published online: 13 February 2015. doi: 10.1080/07481187.2014.970299.

Tschiesner R, Basso D (2015). Consciousness, not only intentionality, yields self-harming behavior. *Frontiers in Human Neuroscience* 2015, 69.

Tseliou F, Johnson S, Major B, Rahaman N, Joyce J, Lawrence J, Mann F, Tapfumaneyi A, Chisholm B, Chamberlain-Kent N, Hinton MF, Fisher HL (2015). Gender differences in one-year outcomes of first-presentation psychosis patients in inner-city UK early intervention services. *Early Intervention in Psychiatry*. published online: 23 March 2015. doi: 10.1111/eip.12235.

Tucker CJ, Wiesen-Martin D (2015). Adolescent siblings' suicide ideation. *Journal of Family Issues* 36, 609-625.

Tundo A, Calabrese JR, Proietti L, de Filippis R (2015). Short-term antidepressant treatment of bipolar depression: Are ISBD recommendations useful in clinical practice? *Journal of Affective Disorders* 171, 155-160.

Tupler LA, Hong JY, Gibori R, Blitchington TF, Krishnan KRR (2015). Suicidal ideation and sex differences in relation to 18 major psychiatric disorders in college and university students: Anonymous web-based assessment. *Journal of Nervous and Mental Disease* 203, 269-278.

Turner BJ, Yiu A, Layden BK, Claes L, Zaitsoff S, Chapman AL (2015). Temporal associations between disordered eating and nonsuicidal self-injury: Examining symptom overlap over 1 year. *Behavior Therapy* 46, 125-138

Umubyeyi A, Mogren I, Ntaganira J, Krantz G (2014). Intimate partner violence and its contribution to mental disorders in men and women in the post genocide Rwanda: Findings from a population based study. *BMC Psychiatry* 14, 315

Urrila AS, Karlsson L, Kiviruusu O, Pankakoski M, Pelkonen M, Strandholm T, Marttunen M, The Adolescent Depression SG (2014). Sleep complaints in adolescent depression: One year naturalistic follow-up study. *BMC Psychiatry* 14, 283.

Ursano RJ, Heeringa SG, Stein MB, Jain S, Raman R, Sun X, Chiu WT, Colpe LJ, Fullerton CS, Gilman SE, Hwang I, Naifeh JA, Nock MK, Rosellini AJ, Sampson NA, Schoenbaum M, Zaslavsky AM, Kessler RC (2014). Prevalence and correlates of suicidal behavior among new soldiers in the U.S. army: Results from the Army Study to Assess Risk and Resilience in Servicemembers (Army STARRS). *Depression and Anxiety* 71, 514-522.

Valois RF, Zullig KJ, Hunter AA (2015). Association between adolescent suicide ideation, suicide attempts and emotional self-efficacy. *Journal of Child and Family Studies* 24, 237-248.

van der Molen E, Blokland AAJ, Hipwell AE, Vermeiren RRJM, Doreleijers TAH, Loeber R (2014). Girls' childhood trajectories of disruptive behavior predict adjustment problems in early adolescence. *Journal of Child Psychology and Psychiatry*. Published online: 10 October 2014. doi: 10.1111/jcpp.12339.

van Heeringen K, Bijttebier S, Desmyter S, Vervaet M, Baeken C (2014). Is there a neuroanatomical basis of the vulnerability to suicidal behavior? A coordinate-based meta-analysis of structural and functional MRI studies. *Frontiers in Human Neuroscience* 8, e824.

Van Niel C, Pachter LM, Wade R, Jr., Felitti VJ, Stein MT (2014). Adverse events in children: Predictors of adult physical and mental conditions. *Journal of Developmental & Behavioral Pediatrics* 35, 549-551.

Vanderploeg RD, Nazem S, Brenner LA, Belanger HG, Donnell AJ, Scott SG (2014). Suicidal ideation among Florida National Guard members: Combat deployment and non-deployment risk and protective factors. *Archives of Suicide Research*. Published online: 17 December 2014. doi: 10.1080/13811118.2014.957454.

Vanyukov PM, Szanto K, Siegle GJ, Hallquist MN, Reynolds CF, Aizenstein HJ, Dombrovski AY (2014). Impulsive traits and unplanned suicide attempts predict exaggerated prefrontal response to angry faces in the elderly. *American Journal of Geriatric Psychiatry*. Published online: 18 October 2014. doi: 10.1016/j.jagp.2014.10.004.

Vatne M, Nåden D (2014). Crucial resources to strengthen the desire to live: Experiences of suicidal patients. *Nursing Ethics*. Published online: 24 December 2014. doi: 10.1177/0969733014562990.

Vaughn MG, Salas-Wright CP, DeLisi M, Larson M (2015). Deliberate self-harm and the nexus of violence, victimization, and mental health problems in the United States. *Psychiatry Research* 225, 588-595

Venables NC, Sellbom M, Sourander A, Kendler KS, Joiner TE, Drislane LE, Sillanmaki L, Elonheimo H, Parkkola K, Multimaki P, Patrick CJ (2015). Separate and interactive contributions of weak inhibitory control and threat sensitivity to prediction of suicide risk. *Psychiatry Research* 226, 461-466.

Vilibi M, Juki V, Pandži-Sakoman M, Bili P, Miloševi M (2014). Association between total serum cholesterol and depression, aggression, and suicidal ideations in war veterans with posttraumatic stress disorder: A crosssectional study. *Croatian Medical Journal* 55, 520-529.

Visher CA, Bakken NW (2014). Reentry challenges facing women with mental health problems. *Women and Health* 54, 768-780.

Wachtel S, Siegmann P, Ocklenburg C, Hebermehl L, Willutzki U, Teismann T (2014). Acquired capability for suicide, pain tolerance, and fearlessness of pain - validation of the pain tolerance scale of the German Capability for Suicide Questionnaire. *Suicide and Life-Threatening Behavior*. Published online: 23 December 2014. doi: 10.1111/sltb.12149.

Wall M, Schenck-Gustafsson K, Minucci D, Sendén MG, Løvseth LT, Fridner A (2014). Suicidal ideation among surgeons in Italy and Sweden - a cross-sectional study. *BMC Psychology* 2, 53.

Walsh K, Copello A (2014). Severe and enduring mental health problems within an established substance misuse treatment partnership. *The Psychiatric Bulletin* 38, 216-219.

Wang Y, Sareen J, Afifi TO, Bolton S, Johnson EA, Bolton JM (2015). A population-based longitudinal study of recent stressful life events as risk factors for suicidal behavior in major depressive disorder. *Archives of Suicide Research* 19, 202-217.

Weinstein SM, Van Meter A, Katz AC, Peters AT, West AE (2015). Cognitive and family correlates of current suicidal ideation in children with bipolar disorder. *Journal of Affective Disorders* 173, 15-21.

Weinstock J, Scott TL, Burton S, Rash CJ, Moran S, Biller W, Kruedelbach N (2014). Current suicidal ideation in gamblers calling a helpline. *Addiction Research and Theory* 22, 398-406.

Weis D, Rothenberg L, Moshe L, Brent DA, Hamdan S (2014). The effect of sleep problems on suicidal risk among young adults in the presence of depressive symptoms and cognitive processes. *Archives of Suicide Research*. Published online: 17 December 2014. doi: 10.1080/13811118.2014.986697.

Weiss NH, Dixon-Gordon KL, Duke AA, Sullivan TP (2014). The underlying role of posttraumatic stress disorder symptoms in the association between intimate partner violence and deliberate self-harm among African American women. *Comprehensive Psychiatry* 59, 8-16.

West NA, Severtson SG, Green JL, Dart RC (2015). Trends in abuse and misuse of prescription opioids among older adults. *Drug and Alcohol Dependence* 149, 117-121.

Widger T (2015). Suicide and the 'poison complex': Toxic relationalities, child development, and the Sri Lankan self-harm epidemic. *Medical Anthropology Quarterly*. Published online: 4 February 2015. doi: 10.1080/01459740.2015.1012616.

Wilchek-Aviad Y, Malka M (2014). Religiosity, meaning in life and suicidal tendency among Jews. *Journal of Religion and Health*. Published online: 31 December 2014. doi: 10.1007/s10943-014-9996-y.

Williams GE, Daros AR, Graves B, McMain SF, Links PS, Ruocco AC (2015). Executive functions and social cognition in highly lethal self-injuring patients with borderline personality disorder. *Personality Disorders* 6, 107-116.

Williams MT, Wetterneck C, Tellawi G, Duque G (2014). Domains of distress among people with sexual orientation obsessions. *Archives of Sexual Behavior* 44, 783-789.

Wilson EC, Chen Y-H, Arayasirikul S, Wenzel C, Raymond HF (2015). Connecting the dots: Examining transgender women's utilization of transition-related medical care and associations with mental health, substance use, and HIV. *Journal of Urban Health* 92, 182-192.

Wisco BE, Marx BP, Wolf EJ, Miller MW, Southwick SM, Pietrzak RH (2014). Posttraumatic stress disorder in the US veteran population: Results from the national health and resilience in veterans study. *Journal of Clinical Psychiatry* 75, 1338-1346.

Wolford-Clevenger C, Febres J, Zapor H, Elmquist J, Bliton C, Stuart GL (2014). Interpersonal violence, alcohol use, and acquired capability for suicide. *Death Studies* 39, 234-241.

Woosley JA, Lichstein KL, Taylor DJ, Riedel BW, Bush AJ (2014). Hopelessness mediates the relation between insomnia and suicidal ideation. *Journal of Clinical Sleep Medicine* 10, 1223-1230.

Woznica AA, Carney CE, Kuo JR, Moss TG (2014). The insomnia and suicide link: Toward an enhanced understanding of this relationship. *Sleep Medicine Reviews*. Published online: 16 October 2014. doi: 10.1016/j.smrv.2014.10.004

Wu J, He Y, Lu C, Deng X, Gao X, Guo L, Wu H, Chan F, Zhou Y (2015). Bullying behaviors among Chinese school-aged youth: A prevalence and correlates study in Guangdong Province. *Psychiatry Research* 225, 716-722.

Yadegarfard M, Meinhold-Bergmann ME, Ho R (2014). Family rejection, social isolation, and loneliness as predictors of negative health outcomes (depression, suicidal ideation, and sexual risk behavior) among Thai male-to-female transgender adolescents. *Journal of LGBT Youth* 11, 347-363.

Ybarra ML, Mitchell KJ, Kosciw JG, Korchmaros JD (2014). Understanding linkages between bullying and suicidal ideation in a national sample of LGB and heterosexual youth in the United States. *Prevention Science* 16, 451-462.

Yeh Y-W, Ho P-S, Chen C-Y, Kuo S-C, Liang C-S, Ma K-H, Shiue C-Y, Huang W-S, Cheng C-Y, Wang T-Y, Lu R-B, Huang S-Y (2014). Incongruent reduction of serotonin transporter associated with suicide attempts in patients with major depressive disorder: a positron emission tomography study with 4-[18F]-ADAM. *International Journal of Neuropsychopharmacology*. Published online: 31 October 2014. doi: 10.1093/ijnp/pyu065.

Yen CF, Chou WJ, Liu TL, Ko CH, Yang P, Hu HF (2014). Cyberbullying among male adolescents with attention-deficit/hyperactivity disorder: Prevalence, correlates, and association with poor mental health status. *Research in Developmental Disabilities* 35, 3543-3553.

Yen S, Kuehn K, Tezanos K, Weinstock LM, Solomon J, Spirito A (2014). Perceived family and peer invalidation as predictors of adolescent suicidal behaviors and self-mutilation. *Journal of Child and Adolescent Psychopharmacology* 25, 124-130.

Yiu A, Turner BJ, Layden BK, Chapman AL, Zaitsoff SL (2014). Prevalence and correlates of eating disorder symptoms in a community sample with non-suicidal self-injury. *Journal of Psychopathology and Behavioral Assessment*. Published online: 21 October 2014. doi: 10.1007/s10862-014-9470-x.

Yoon DH, Kim SJ, Lee JH, Kim PM, Park DH, Ryu SH, Yu J, Ha JH (2015). The relationship between type D personality and suicidality in low-income, middle-aged adults. *Psychiatry Investigation* 12, 16-22.

You J, Lin M-P (2015). Predicting suicide attempts by time-varying frequency of nonsuicidal self-injury among Chinese community adolescents. *Journal of Consulting and Clinical Psychology* 83, 524-533.

Youssef NA, Bradford DW, Kilts JD, Szabo ST, Naylor JC, Allen TB, Strauss JL, Hamer RM, Brunca M, Shampine LJ, Marx CE (2014). Exploratory investigation of biomarker candidates for suicide in schizophrenia and bipolar disorder. *Crisis* 36, 46-54.

Zai CC, Manchia M, Sonderby IE, Yilmaz Z, De Luca V, Tiwari AK, Squassina A, Zai GC, Shaikh SA, Strauss J, King N, Le Foll B, Kaplan AS, Finseth PI, Vaaler AE, Djurovic S, Andreassen OA, Vincent JB, Kennedy JL (2014). Investigation of the genetic interaction between BDNF and DRD3 genes in suicidical behaviour in psychiatric disorders. *World Journal of Biological Psychiatry* 16, 171-179.

Zaninotto L, Souery D, Calati R, Scudellari P, Janiri L, Montgomery S, Kasper S, Zohar J, Mendlewicz J, Serretti A (2014). Mixed, melancholic, and anxious features in depression: A cross-sectional study of sociodemographic and clinical correlates. *Annals of Clinical Psychiatry* 26, 243-253.

Zeng R, Cohen LJ, Tanis T, Qizilbash A, Lopatyuk Y, Yaseen ZS, Galynker I (2015). Assessing the contribution of borderline personality disorder and features to suicide risk in psychiatric inpatients with bipolar disorder, major depression and schizoaffective disorder. *Psychiatry Research* 226, 361-367.

Zeppegno P, Gramaglia C, Castello L, Bert F, Gualano M, Ressico F, Coppola I, Avanzi G, Siliquini R, Torre E (2015). Suicide attempts and emergency room psychiatric consultation. *BMC Psychiatry* 15, 13.

Zetumer S, Young I, Shear MK, Skritskaya N, Lebowitz B, Simon N, Reynolds C, Mauro C, Zisook S (2015). The impact of losing a child on the clinical presentation of complicated grief. *Journal of Affective Disorders* 170, 15-21.

Zhai H, Bai B, Chen L, Han D, Wang L, Qiao Z, Qiu X, Yang X, Yang Y (2015). Correlation between family environment and suicidal ideation in university students in China. *International Journal of Environmental Research and Public Health* 12, 1412-1424.

Zhang J, Jia C-X, Wang L-L (2015). Testosterone differs between suicide attempters and community controls in men and women of China. *Physiology and Behavior* 141, 40-45.

Zhang J, Lin L (2014). The moderating effect of social support on the relationship between impulsivity and suicide in rural China. *Community Mental Health Journal.* Published online: 25 December 2014. doi: 10.1007/s10597-014-9811-y.

Zhang W, Finy MS, Bresin K, Verona E (2015). Specific patterns of family aggression and adolescents' self- and other-directed harm: The moderating role of personality. *Journal of Family Violence* 30, 161-170.

Zhang WC, Jia CX, Zhang JY, Wang LL, Liu XC (2015). Negative life events and attempted suicide in rural China. *PLoS One* 10, e0116634.

Zhang XQ, Wang ZM, Pan YL, Chiu HF, Ng CH, Ungvari GS, Lai KY, Cao XL, Li Y, Zhong BL, Xiang YT (2014). Use of electroconvulsive therapy in older Chinese psychiatric patients. *International Journal of Geriatric Psychiatry.* Published online: 3 November 2014. doi: 10.1002/gps.4227.

Zhao H, Guo W, Niu W, Zhong A, Zhou X (2015). Brain area-related neurological soft signs in depressive patients with different types of childhood maltreatment. *Asia Pacific Psychiatry.* Published online: 14 January 2015. doi: 10.1111/appy.12172.

Zheng A, Wang Z (2014). Social and psychological factors of the suicidal tendencies of Chinese medical students. *Biopsychosocial Medicine* 8, 23.

Zhong QY, Gelaye B, Rondon MB, Sanchez SE, Simon GE, Henderson DC, Barrios YV, Sanchez PM, Williams MA (2014). Using the Patient Health Questionnaire (PHQ-9) and the Edinburgh Postnatal Depression Scale (EPDS) to assess suicidal ideation among pregnant women in Lima, Peru. *Archives of Women's Mental Health*. Published online: 5 November 2015. doi: 10.1007/s00737-014-0481-0.

Zhu Q, Lou C, Gao E, Cheng Y, Zabin LS, Emerson MR (2015). Drunkenness and its association with health risk behaviors among adolescents and young adults in three Asian cities: Hanoi, Shanghai, Taipei. *Drug and Alcohol Dependence* 147, 251-256.

Zimmerman EM, Konopka LM (2014). Preliminary findings of single- and multifocused epileptiform discharges in nonepileptic psychiatric patients. *Clinical EEG and Neuroscience* 45, 285-292.

Zoghbi AW, Al Jurdi RK, Deshmukh PR, Chen da C, Xiu MH, Tan YL, Yang FD, Zhang XY (2014). Cognitive function and suicide risk in Han Chinese inpatients with schizophrenia. *Psychiatry Research* 220, 188-192.

Zöhre E, Ayrık C, Bozkurt S, Kose A, Narcı H, Çevik , Toker , Demir F, Ovla D (2015). Retrospective analysis of poisoning cases admitted to the emergency medicine. *Archives of Iranian Medicine* 18, 117-122.

Zschoche M, Schlarb AA (2015). Is there an association between insomnia symptoms, aggressive behavior, and suicidality in adolescents? *Adolescent Health, Medicine and Therapeutics* 6, 29-36.

Zunner B, Dworkin SL, Neylan TC, Bukusi EA, Oyaro P, Cohen CR, Abwok M, Meffert SM (2015). HIV, violence and women: Unmet mental health care needs. *Journal of Affective Disorders* 174, 619-626.

Zuromski KL, Witt K (2014). Fasting and acquired capability for suicide: A test of the interpersonal-psychological theory of suicide in an undergraduate sample. *Psychiatry Research* 226, 61-67.

Prevention

Arbore P (2014). A San Francisco-based center reaches out with supportive services for mid-life and older adults at risk for depression and suicide. *Generations* 38, 27-29.

Bartlett A, Walker T, Harty MA, Abel KM (2014). Health and social care services for women offenders: Current provision and a future model of care. *Journal of Forensic Psychiatry and Psychology* 25, 625-635.

Brent DA, Brown CH (2015). Effectiveness of school-based suicide prevention programmes. *The Lancet* 385, 1489–1491.

Brown JSL, Evans-Lacko S, Aschan L, Henderson MJ, Hatch SL, Hotopf M (2014). Seeking informal and formal help for mental health problems in the community: A secondary analysis from a psychiatric morbidity survey in South London. *BMC Psychiatry* 14, 275.

Decker KP, Peglow SL, Samples CR (2014). Participation in a novel treatment component during residential substance use treatment is associated with improved outcome: A pilot study. *Addiction Science and Clinical Practice* 9, 7.

Finney EJ, Buser SJ, Schwartz J, Archibald L, Swanson R (2015). Suicide prevention in fire service: The Houston Fire Department (HFD) model. *Aggression and Violent Behavior* 21, 1-4.

Hall CA, Reynolds-Iii CF (2014). Late-life depression in the primary care setting: Challenges, collaborative care, and prevention. *Maturitas* 79, 147-152.

Hassanian-Moghaddam H, Sarjami S, Kolahi AA, Lewin T, Carter G (2015). Postcards in Persia: A 12-24 month follow-up of a randomised controlled trial for hospital treated deliberate self-poisoning. *Archives of Suicide Research*. Published online: 16 March 2015. doi: 10.1080/13811118.2015.1004473.

Hibbeln JR, Gow RV (2014). The potential for military diets to reduce depression, suicide, and impulsive aggression: A review of current evidence for omega-3 and omega-6 fatty acids. *Military Medicine* 179, 117-128.

Hogan MF, Clymer JM (2014). Suicide in the health care neighborhood: More can be done, now. *American Journal of Lifestyle Medicine* 8, 438-440.

Joshi SV, Hartley SN, Kessler M, Barstead M (2015). School-based suicide prevention: Content, process, and the role of trusted adults and peers. *Child and Adolescent Psychiatric Clinics of North America* 24, 353-370

Kim BN, Masud MA, Kim Y (2014). Optimal implementation of intervention to control the self-harm epidemic. *Osong Public Health and Research Perspectives* 5, 315-323

King CA, Eisenberg D, Zheng K, Czyz E, Kramer A, Horwitz A, Chermack S (2015). Online suicide risk screening and intervention with college students: A pilot randomized controlled trial. *Journal of Consulting and Clinical Psychology*. 83, 630-636.

Lawson-Te Aho K (2014). The healing is in the pain: Revisiting and re-narrating trauma histories as a starting point for healing. *Psychology and Developing Societies* 26, 181-212.

Le TN, Gobert JM (2015). Translating and implementing a mindfulness-based youth suicide prevention intervention in a native American community. *Journal of Child and Family Studies* 24, 12-23.

Levi-Belz Y (2014). Stress-related growth among suicide survivors: The role of interpersonal and cognitive factors. *Archives of Suicide Research*. Published online: 15 December 2014. doi: 10.1080/13811118.2014.957452.

Mann JJ, Kuehn BM (2014). Rate of suicide increases in middle age: Primary care key to suicide prevention. *JAMA* 312, 1727-1728

Moutier C (2014). Tactics of the war on suicide. *Depression and Anxiety* 31, 961-963

Petrova M, Wyman PA, Schmeelk-Cone K, Pisani AR (2015). Positive-themed suicide prevention messages delivered by adolescent peer leaders: Proximal impact on classmates' coping attitudes and perceptions of adult support. *Suicide and Life-Threatening Behavior* Published online: 18 February 2015. doi: 10.1111/sltb.12156.

Pitman A, Stevenson F (2014). Suicide reporting within British newspapers' arts coverage. *Crisis* 36, 13-20.

Pridmore S, Auchincloss S (2015). Preventing suicide: A global imperative. *Australasian Psychiatry* 23, 81-82

Stone DM, Crosby AE (2014). Suicide prevention: State of the art review. *American Journal of Lifestyle Medicine* 8, 404-420.

Susanne Condron D, Garraza LG, Walrath CM, McKeon R, Goldston DB, Heilbron NS (2014). Identifying and referring youths at risk for suicide following participation in school-based gatekeeper training. *Suicide and Life-Threatening Behavior*. Published online: 2 December 2014. doi: 10.1111/sltb.12142.

van Spijker BAJ, Calear AL, Batterham PJ, Mackinnon AJ, Gosling JA, Kerkhof AJFM, Solomon D, Christensen H (2015). Reducing suicidal thoughts in the Australian general population through web-based self-help: Study protocol for a randomized controlled trial. *Trials* 16, 62.

Walrath C, Godoy Garraza L, Reid H, Goldston DB, McKeon R (2015). Impact of the Garrett Lee Smith youth suicide prevention program on suicide mortality. *American Journal of Public Health* 105, 986-993.

Wexler L, Chandler M, Gone JP, Cwik M, Kirmayer LJ, Lafromboise T, Brockie T, O'Keefe V, Walkup J, Alle J (2015). Advancing suicide prevention research with rural American Indian and Alaska native populations. *American Journal of Public Health* 105, 891-899.

Care and support

Achal KS, Shute J, Gill DS, Collins JM (2014). The role of the general dental practitioner in managing patients who self-harm. *British Dental Journal* 217, 503-506.

Adams J, Carroll A (2015). Mixed emotions: A response to - Large MM and Ryan CJ. Suicide risk categorisation of psychiatric inpatients: What it might mean and why it is of no use. Australasian Psychiatry 2014; 22(4):390-2. *Australasian Psychiatry* 23, 85-86.

Alghamdy MS, Randhawa MA, Al-Wahhas MH, Al-Jumaan MA (2015). Admissions for drug-related problems at the emergency department of a university hospital in the kingdom of Saudi Arabia. *Journal of Family and Community Medicine* 22, 44-48.

Almanzar S, Shah N, Vithalani S, Shah S, Squires J, Appasani R, Katz CL (2014). Knowledge of and attitudes toward clinical depression among health providers in Gujarat, India. *Annals of Global Health* 80, 89-95.

Anderson HD, Pace WD, Brandt E, Nielsen RD, Allen RR, Libby AM, West DR, Valuck RJ (2015). Monitoring suicidal patients in primary care using electronic health records. *Journal of the American Board of Family Medicine* 28, 65-71.

Andrew E, Williams J, Waters C (2014). Dialectical behaviour therapy and attachment: Vehicles for the development of resilience in young people leaving the care system. *Clinical Child Psychology and Psychiatry* 19, 503-515.

Barrett EA, Mork E, Færden A, Nesvåg R, Agartz I, Andreassen OA, Melle I (2015). The development of insight and its relationship with suicidality over one year follow-up in patients with first episode psychosis. *Schizophrenia Research* 162, 97-10.

Bedics JD, Atkins DC, Harned MS, Linehan MM (2015). The therapeutic alliance as a predictor of outcome in dialectical behavior therapy versus nonbehavioral psychotherapy by experts for borderline personality disorder. *Psychotherapy* 52, 67-77

Berk MS, Asarnow JR (2014). Assessment of suicidal youth in the emergency department. *Suicide and Life-Threatening Behavior*. Published online: 20 October 2014. doi: 10.1111/sltb.12133.

Berrouiguet S, Alavi Z, Vaiva G, Courtet P, Baca-Garcia E, Vidailhet P, Gravey M, Guillodo E, Brandt S, Walter M (2014). SIAM (suicide intervention assisted by messages): The development of a post-acute crisis text messaging outreach for suicide prevention. *BMC Psychiatry* 14, 294.

Bhat S, Kenchetty KP (2015). N-acetyl cysteine in the management of rodenticide consumption - life saving? *Journal of Clinical and Diagnostic Research* 9, OC10–OC13.

Boccio DE (2015). A school-based suicide risk assessment protocol. *Journal of Applied School Psychology* 31, 31-62.

Bolton JM (2015). Suicide risk assessment in the emergency department: Out of the darkness. *Depression and Anxiety* 32, 73-75.

Britton PC, Bryan CJ, Valenstein M (2014). Motivational interviewing for means restriction counseling with patients at risk for suicide. *Cognitive and Behavioral Practice*. Published online: 6 October 2014. doi: 10.1016/j.cbpra.2014.09.004.

Burgess AW, Sekula LK, Carretta CM (2015). Homicide-suicide and duty to warn. *Psychodynamic Psychiatry* 43, 67-90.

Call NA, Simmons CA, Mevers JE, Alvarez JP (2015). Clinical outcomes of behavioral treatments for pica in children with developmental disabilities. *Journal of Autism and Developmental Disorders*. Published online: 31 January 2015. doi: 10.1007/s10803-015-2375-z.

Card AJ, Simsekler MCE, Clark M, Ward JR, Clarkson PJ (2014). Use of the Generating Options for Active Risk Control (GO-ARC) technique can lead to more robust risk control options. *International Journal of Risk and Safety in Medicine* 26, 199-211.

Carlsson C, Nilsson Ranta D, Traeen B (2015). Mentalizing and emotional labor facilitate equine-assisted social work with self-harming adolescents. *Child and Adolescent Social Work Journal.* Published online: 20 January 2015. doi: 10.1007/s10560-015-0376-6.

Chong SJ, Johandi F, Kang GCW (2015). Self-inflicted burns in soldiers: The Singapore experience. *Annals of Plastic Surgery.* Published online: 24 April 2015. doi: 10.1097/SAP.0000000000000495.

Clarke MC, Coughlan H, Harley M, Connor D, Power E, Lynch F, Fitzpatrick C, Cannon M (2014). The impact of adolescent cannabis use, mood disorder and lack of education on attempted suicide in young adulthood. *World Psychiatry* 13, 322-323.

Coffey MJ (2015). Perfect depression care spread: The traction of zero suicides. *Journal of Clinical Outcomes Management* 22, 123-129.

Collimore KC, Rector NA (2014). Treatment of anxiety disorders with comorbid depression: A survey of expert CBT clinicians. *Cognitive and Behavioral Practice* 21, 485-493.

Comtois KA, Kerbrat AH, Atkins DC, Roy-Byrne P, Katon W (2015). Self-reported usual care for self-directed violence during the 6 months before emergency department admission. *Medical Care* 53, 45-53.

Coulter ID (2014). The response of an expert panel to nutritional armor for the warfighter: Can omega-3 fatty acids enhance stress resilience, wellness, and military performance? *Military Medicine* 179, 192-198.

Curry JF, Hersh J (2014). Development and evolution of cognitive behavior therapy for depressed adolescents. *Journal of Rational-Emotive and Cognitive-Behavior Therapy* 32, 15-30.

Diderich HM, Pannebakker FD, Dechesne M, Buitendijk SE, Oudesluys-Murphy AM (2014). Support and monitoring of families after child abuse detection based on parental characteristics at the emergency department. *Child* 41, 194-202.

Dosani S, Harding C, Wilson S (2014). Online groups and patient forums. *Current Psychiatry Reports* 16, 507.

Ebrahimi H, Kazemi AH, Fallahi Khoshknab M, Modabber R (2014). The effect of spiritual and religious group psychotherapy on suicidal ideation in depressed patients: A randomized clinical trial. *Journal of Caring Sciences* 3, 131-140.

Elger BS, Handtke V, Wangmo T (2015). Paternalistic breaches of confidentiality in prison: Mental health professionals' attitudes and justifications. *Journal of Medical Ethics.* Published online: 13 January 2015. doi: 10.1136/medethics-2013-101981.

Evans R (2014). Samaritans radar app. *Nursing Standard* 29, 33.

Ewing ESK, Diamond G, Levy S (2015). Attachment-based family therapy for depressed and suicidal adolescents: Theory, clinical model and empirical support. *Attachment and Human Development* 17, 136-156.

Fennig S, Brunstein Klomek A, Shahar B, Sarel-Michnik Z, Hadas A (2015). Inpatient treatment has no impact on the core thoughts and perceptions in adolescents with anorexia nervosa. *Early Intervention in Psychiatry.* Published online: 24 March 2015. doi: 10.1111/eip.12234.

Girlanda F, Cipriani A, Agrimi E, Appino MG, Barichello A, Beneduce R, Bighelli I, Bisoffi G, Bisogno A, Bortolaso P, Boso M, Calandra C, Cascone L, Castellazzi M, Corbascio C, Parise VF, Gardellin F, Gennaro D, Hanife B, Lintas C, Lorusso M, Luca A, Luca M, Luchetta C, Lucii C, Maio F, Marsilio A, Mattei C, Moretti D, Nose M, Occhionero G, Papanti D, Pecile D, Percudani M, Prestia D, Purgato M, Restaino F, Romeo S, Sciarma T, Strizzolo S, Tamborini S, Todarello O, Tozzi F, Ziero S, Zotos S, Barbui C (2014). Effectiveness of lithium in subjects with treatment-resistant depression and suicide risk: Results and lessons of an underpowered randomised clinical trial. *BMC Research Notes* 7, 731.

Goldblatt MJ, Briggs S, Lindner R, Schechter M, Ronningstam E (2015). Psychodynamic psychotherapy with suicidal adolescents. *Psychoanalytic Psychotherapy* 29, 20-37.

Goldstein TR, Fersch-Podrat RK, Rivera M, Axelson DA, Merranko J, Yu H, Brent DA, Birmaher B (2015). Dialectical behavior therapy for adolescents with bipolar disorders: Results from a pilot randomized trial. *Journal of Child and Adolescent Psychopharmacology* 25, 140-149.

Gorlyn M, Keilp J, Burke A, Oquendo M, Mann JJ, Grunebaum M (2015). Treatment-related improvement in neuropsychological functioning in suicidal depressed patients: Paroxetine vs. Bupropion. *Psychiatry Research* 225, 407-412.

Grudnikoff E, Soto EC, Frederickson A, Birnbaum ML, Saito E, Dicker R, Kane JM, Correll CU (2014). Suicidality and hospitalization as cause and outcome of pediatric psychiatric emergency room visits. *European Child and Adolescent Psychiatry*. Published online: 21 October 2014. doi: 10.1007/s00787-014-0624-x.

Guilfoyle SM, Monahan S, Wesolowski C, Modi AC (2015). Depression screening in pediatric epilepsy: Evidence for the benefit of a behavioral medicine service in early detection. *Epilepsy and Behavior* 44, 5-10.

Hall TD, Shah S, Ng B, Feberwee HM, Dotchin L, Vandermost M, King MA (2014). Changes in mood, depression and suicidal ideation after commencing pregabalin for neuropathic pain. *Australian Family Physician* 43, 705-708.

Hendin H (2014). An innovative approach to treating combat veterans with PTSD at risk for suicide. *Suicide and Life-Threatening Behavior* 44, 582-590.

Hepworth I, McGowan L (2015). Understanding the management of people seeking voluntary psychiatric hospitalization who do not meet the criteria for inpatient admission: A qualitative study of mental health liaison nurses working in accident and emergency departments in the north of England. *Archives of Psychiatric Nursing* 29, 26-32.

Herbeck Belnap B, Schulberg HC, He F, Mazumdar S, Reynolds CF, Rollman BL (2014). Electronic protocol for suicide risk management in research participants. *Journal of Psychosomatic Research* 78, 340-345.

Idenfors H, Kullgren G, Renberg ES (2015). Professional care after deliberate self-harm: A qualitative study of young people's experiences. *Patient Preference and Adherence* 9, 199-207.

Jeong YS, Kim HW, Park DS, Park JH (2014). Efficient clustering simulator for hierarchical management of high-risk with wellness. *Journal of Internet Technology* 15, 1151-1159.

Kahng S, Hausman NL, Fisher AB, Donaldson JM, Cox JR, Lugo M, Wiskow KM (2014). The safety of functional analyses of self-injurious behavior. *Journal of Applied Behavior Analysis*. 48, 107-114.

Kasckow J, Gao S, Hanusa B, Rotondi A, Chinman M, Zickmund S, Gurklis J, Fox L, Cornelius J, Richmond I, Haas GL (2015). Telehealth monitoring of patients with schizophrenia and suicidal ideation. *Suicide and Life-Threatening Behavior*. Published online: 17 February 2015. doi: 10.1111/sltb.

King CA, Gipson PY, Horwitz AG, Opperman KJ (2014). Teen options for change: An intervention for young emergency patients who screen positive for suicide risk. *Psychiatric Services* 66, 97-100.

Levi-Belz Y, Gamliel E (2015). The effect of perceived burdensomeness and thwarted belongingness on therapists' assessment of patients' suicide risk. *Psychotherapy Research* Published online: 9 March 2015. doi: 10.1080/10503307.2015.1013161.

Lindgren B-M, Aminoff C, Graneheim UH (2015). Features of everyday life in psychiatric inpatient care for self-harming: An observational study of six women. *Issues in Mental Health Nursing* 36, 82-88.

Lindgren BM, Hallgren Graneheim U (2015). Meanings of caring for people who self-harm as disclosed in narratives of dialectical behaviour therapy professionals. *Journal of Psychiatric and Mental Health Nursing*. Published online: 6 February 2015. doi: 10.1111/jpm.12196.

Long M, Manktelow R, Tracey A (2014). The healing journey: Help seeking for self-injury among a community population. *Qualitative Health Research*. Published online: 7 October 2014. doi: 10.1177/1049732314554092.

Looi GM, Engstrom A, Savenstedt S (2015). A self-destructive care: Self-reports of people who experienced coercive measures and their suggestions for alternatives. *Issues in Mental Health Nursing* 36, 96-103.

Malla A (2015). Opportunities for suicide risk reduction. *Psychiatric Services* 66, 109-109.

Matuskey D, Sondik T (2014). Memory reconsolidation for treatment-resistant aggression and self-injurious behaviors. *Journal of Clinical Psychopharmacology* 35, 104-105.

McCall WV, Benca RM, Rosenquist PB, Riley MA, Hodges C, Gubosh B, McCloud L, Newman JC, Case D, Rumble M, Mayo M, White KH, Phillips M, Krystal AD (2015). A multi-site randomized clinical trial to reduce suicidal ideation in suicidal adult outpatients with major depressive disorder: Development of a methodology to enhance safety. *Clinical Trials*. Published online: 1 March 2015. doi: 10.1177/1740774515573958.

McDermott E (2014). Asking for help online: Lesbian, gay, bisexual and trans youth, self-harm and articulating the 'failed' self. *Health*. Published online: 19 November 2014. doi: 10.1177/1363459314557967.

Meyers LLP, Landes SJP, Thuras PP (2014). Veterans' service utilization and associated costs following participation in dialectical behavior therapy: A preliminary investigation. *Military Medicine* 179, 1368-1373.

Miller I (2014). Teen suicide risk: A practitioner guide to screening, assessment, and management. *Journal of Youth and Adolescence* 43, 2077-2079.

Milner AJ, Carter G, Pirkis J, Robinson J, Spittal MJ (2015). Letters, green cards, telephone calls and postcards: Systematic and meta-analytic review of brief contact interventions for reducing self-harm, suicide attempts and suicide. *British Journal of Psychiatry* 206, 184-190.

Mormont E, Jamart J, Jacques D (2014). Symptoms of depression and anxiety after the disclosure of the diagnosis of Alzheimer disease. *Journal of Geriatric Psychiatry and Neurology* 27, 231-236l.

Mousavi SG, Zohreh R, Maracy MR, Ebrahimi A, Sharbafchi MR (2014). The efficacy of telephonic follow up in prevention of suicidal reattempt in patients with suicide attempt history. *Advanced Biomedical Research* 3, 198-198.

Niola P, Gross JA, Lopez JP, Chillotti C, Deiana V, Manchia M, Georgitsi M, Patrinos GP, Alda M, Turecki G, Del Zompo M, Squassina A (2014). Lithium-induced differential expression of SAT1 in suicide completers and controls is not correlated with polymorphisms in the promoter region of the gene. *Psychiatry Research* 220, 1167-1168.

Nolta K (2014). A school-based suicide risk assessment strategy. *National Association of School Nurses* 29, 295-298.

Omer H, Dolberger DI (2015). Helping parents cope with suicide threats: An approach based on nonviolent resistance. *Family Process*. Published online: 16 January 2015. doi: 10.1111/famp.12129.

Oruch R, Elderbi MA, Khattab HA, Pryme IF, Lund A (2014). Lithium: A review of pharmacology, clinical uses, and toxicity. *European Journal of Pharmacology* 740, 464-473.

Panksepp J, Yovell Y (2014). Preclinical modeling of primal emotional affects (seeking, panic and play): Gateways to the development of new treatments for depression. *Psychopathology* 47, 383-393.

Phillips G, Gerdtz MF, Elsom SJ, Weiland TJ, Castle D (2014). Mental health nurses' dispositional decision-making for people presenting to the emergency department with deliberate self-harm: An exploratory study. *Perspectives in Psychiatric Care* 51, 148-153.

Pinta ER (2015). Realities after suicide can be a deterrent. *American Journal of Psychiatry* 172, 96.

Puri M, Hall EG, Erisman M, Vwich Y (2014). Acting strange after trying to 'get numb'. *Current Psychiatry* 13, 50-54.

Rahman T, Cole EF, Parmar DD (2014). Depressed, suicidal, and brittle in her bones. *Current Psychiatry* 13, 55-60.

Rant B, Bregar B (2014). Understanding the attitudes of paramedics towards suicidal patients. *Obzornik Zdravstvene Nege* 48, 177-194.

Reinstatler L, Youssef NA (2015). Ketamine as a potential treatment for suicidal ideation: A systematic review of the literature. *Drugs In R and D* 15, 37-43.

Restifo E, Kashyap S, Hooke GR, Page AC (2015). Daily monitoring of temporal trajectories of suicidal ideation predict self-injury: A novel application of patient progress monitoring. *Psychotherapy Research*. Published online: 3 March 2015. doi: 10.1080/10503307.2015.1006707.

Ribeiro RB, Tully J, Fotiadou M (2015). Clinical characteristics and outcomes on discharge of women admitted to a medium secure unit over a 4-year period. *International Journal of Law and Psychiatry* 39, 83-89.

Rice TR (2014). Emotion regulation and adolescent suicide: A proposal for physician education. *International Journal of Adolescent Medicine and Health* 27, 189-194.

Saini P, Chantler K, Kapur N (2015). General practitioners' perspectives on primary care consultations for suicidal patients. *Health and Social Care in the Community*. Published online: 9 February 2015. doi: 10.1111/hsc.12198.

Saleh SN, Buckingham CD (2014). Handling varying amounts of missing data when classifying mental-health risk levels. *Studies in Health Technology and Informatics* 207, 92-101.

Santos JC, Pereira Simoes RM, Queiroz de Azevedo Erse MP, Neto Facanha JD, Fernandes Alves Marques LA (2014). Impact of " plus contigo" training on the knowledge and attitudes of health care professionals about suicide. *Revista Latino-Americana De Enfermagem* 22, 679-684.

Serpa JG, Taylor SL, Tillisch K (2014). Mindfulness-based stress reduction (MBSR) reduces anxiety, depression, and suicidal ideation in veterans. *Medical Care* 52 Suppl 5, S19-24.

Shea SC, Barney C (2015). Teaching clinical interviewing skills using role-playing: Conveying empathy to performing a suicide assessment: A primer for individual role-playing and scripted group role-playing. *Psychiatric Clinics of North America* 38, 147-183.

Shtivelband A, Aloise-Young PA, Chen PY (2015). Sustaining the effects of gatekeeper suicide prevention training. *Crisis*. Published online: 23 February 2015. doi: 10.1027/0227-5910/a000304.

Sinclair H, Pretorius A, Stein DJ (2014). A counselling line for problem and pathological gambling in South Africa: Preliminary data analysis. *Journal of Behavioral Addictions* 3, 199-202.

Taha F, Zhang H, Snead K, Jones AD, Blackmon B, Bryant RJ, Siegelman AE, Kaslow NJ (2014). Effects of a culturally informed intervention on abused, suicidal African American women. *Cultural Diversity and Ethnic Minority Psychology*. Published online: 17 November 2014. doi: 10.1037/cdp0000018.

Tang MH, Pinsky EG (2015). Mood and affect disorders. *Pediatrics in Review* 36, 52-61.

Targum SD, Friedman F, Pacheco MN (2014). Assessment of suicidal behavior in the emergency department. *Innovations in Clinical Neuroscience* 11, 194-200.

Tofthagen R, Talseth A-G, Fagerström L (2014). Mental health nurses' experiences of caring for patients suffering from self-harm. *Nursing Research and Practice* 2014, e905741-e905741.

Torio CM, Encinosa W, Berdahl T, McCormick MC, Simpson LA (2015). Annual report on health care for children and youth in the United States: National estimates of cost, utilization and expenditures for children with mental health conditions. *Academic Pediatrics* 15, 19-35.

Tørmoen AJ, Grøholt B, Haga E, Brager-Larsen A, Miller A, Walby F, Stanley B, Mehlum L (2014). Feasibility of dialectical behavior therapy with suicidal and self-harming adolescents with multi-problems: Training, adherence, and retention. *Archives of Suicide Research* 18, 432-444.

Trockel M, Karlin BE, Taylor CB, Brown GK, Manber R (2015). Effects of cognitive behavioral therapy for insomnia on suicidal ideation in veterans. *Sleep* 38, 259-265.

Turner BJMA, Austin SBBA, Chapman ALP (2014). Treating nonsuicidal self-injury: A systematic review of psychological and pharmacological interventions. *Canadian Journal of Psychiatry* 59, 576-585

Venkat A, Drori J (2014). When to say when: Responding to a suicide attempt in the acute care setting. *Narrative Inquiry in Bioethics* 4, 263-270.

Walker T, Shaw J, Ranote S, Doyle M, Poursanidou K, Meacock R, Abel K (2014). Medical skin camouflage: A recovery intervention for female prisoners who self-harm? *Criminal Behavious and Mental Health* 24, 317-320.

Waseem M, Diaz-Guerrero RJ, Cosme R, Ain Y, Leber M, Gerber LM (2014). Do all children with suicidal ideation receive a significant psychiatric intervention? *Pediatrics International*. Published online: 20 October 2014. doi: 10.1111/ped.12527.

While AE, Clark LL (2014). Development of a competency tool for adult trained nurses caring for people with intellectual disabilities. *Journal of Nursing Management* 22, 803-810.

Whisenhunt JL, Chang CY, Flowers LR, Brack GL, O'Hara C, Raines TC (2014). Working with clients who self-injure: A grounded theory approach. *Journal of Counseling and Development* 92, 387-397.

Williams B, Boyle M, Fielder C (2015). Empathetic attitudes of undergraduate paramedic and nursing students towards four medical conditions: A three-year longitudinal study. *Nurse Education Today* 35, e14-e18.

Wolk CB, Kendall PC, Beidas RS (2015). Cognitive-behavioral therapy for child anxiety confers long-term protection from suicidality. *Journal of the American Academy of Child and Adolescent Psychiatry* 54, 175-179.

Xu Z, Chen B, Li G, DW (2014). The interference in the suicide ideation of patients with malignant tumors by mental clinical nursing pathway. *Patient Preference and Adherence* 8, 1665-166.

CASE REPORTS

Abedini M, Fatehi F, Tabrizi N (2014). Ischemic stroke as a rare manifestation of aluminum phosphide poisoning: A case report. *Acta Medica Iranica* 52, 947-949.

Adit, Sachan A, Chaturvedi TP, Agrawal R, Parihar AV (2014). Dermatillomania: In patient undergoing orthodontic treatment. *Indian Journal of Dental Research* 25, 544-545.

Agrawal VK, Bansal A, Kumar R, Kumawat BL, Mahajan P (2014). Potassium permanganate toxicity: A rare case with difficult airway management and hepatic damage. *Indian Journal of Critical Care Medicine* 18, 819-821.

Ahmadi J, Ahmadi N, Soltani F, Bayat F (2014). Gender differences in depression scores of Iranian and German medical students. *Iranian Journal of Psychiatry and Behavioral Sciences* 8, 70-73.

Akinci E, Koylu R, Yortanli M, Gumus H, Koylu O, Altintepe L, Cander B (2015). Acute bismuth intoxication: Acute renal failure, tonsillar ulceration and posterior reversible encephalopathy syndrome. *Hong Kong Journal of Emergency Medicine* 22, 121-125.

Alby E, Bhat R (2014). Electroconvulsive therapy after division and repair of strap muscle and anterior jugular vein. *Journal of ECT* 30, e32-e33.

Aldemir E, Akyel B, Altintoprak AE, Aydin R, Co kunol H (2015). LPG dependence after a suicide attempt. *Case Reports in Psychiatry* 2015, e643253.

Alunni V, Grevin G, Buchet L, Gaillard Y, Quatrehomme G (2014). An amazing case of fatal self-immolation. *Forensic Science International* 244, e30-e33.

Amiri S, Arfaei A, Farhang S (2015). Self-inflicted needle injuries to the eye: A curing pain. *Case Reports in Psychiatry* 2015, 960579.

Aquila I, Pepe F, Di Nunzio C, Ausania F, Serra A, Ricci P (2014). Suicide case due to phosphoric acid ingestion: Case report and review of literature. *Journal of Forensic Sciences*. Published online: 20 October 2014. doi: 10.1111/1556-4029.12538.

Arifin MZ, Yudoyono F, Setiawan C, Sidabutar R, Sutiono AB, Faried A (2014). Comprehensive management of frontal and cerebellar tumor patients with personality changes and suicidal tendencies. *Surgical Neurology International* 5, 174.

Ashwini S, Amit DR, Ivan NS, Alka PV (2015). Pregabalin dependence with pregabalin induced intentional self-harm behavior: A case report. *Indian Journal of Psychiatry* 57, 110-111.

Atreya A, Kanchan T, Nepal S, Niroula R (2015). EEG and psychological assessment in attempted hangings: A case of near-hanging from Nepal. *Journal of South India Medicolegal Association* 7, 40-44.

Badhiwala JH, Blackham JR, Bhardwaj RD (2014). Neuropsychiatric changes following penetrating head injury in children. *Surgical Neurology International* 5, 154.

Bagayogo IP, Schneider JA, Tobia A, Schineller TM, Kaufman KR (2014). Hypersexuality after self-inflicted nail gun penetrating traumatic brain injury and neurosurgery: Case analysis with literature review. *Annals of Clinical Psychiatry* 27, 65-68.

Bakovic M, Petrovecki V, Strinovic D, Mayer D (2014). Shot through the heart - firepower and potential lethality of air weapons. *Journal of Forensic Sciences* 59, 1658-1661.

Barbera N, Indorato F, Spitaleri A, Bosco A, Carpinteri M, Busardo FP, Romano G (2014). A singular case of survival after acute methanol poisoning: Toxicological and neuroimaging findings. *The American Journal of Forensic Medicine and Pathology* 35, 253-255.

Bartschat S, Mercer-Chalmers-Bender K, Beike J, Rothschild MA, Jübner M (2014). Not only smoking is deadly: Fatal ingestion of e-juice—a case report. *International Journal of Legal Medicine* 129, 481-486.

Bayat A, Christensen M, Wibrand F, Duno M, Lund A (2015). Mild Lesch-Nyhan disease in a boy with a null mutation in HPRT1: An exception to the known genotype-phenotype correlation. *JIMD Reports* 18, 135-137.

Behera C, Mridha AR, Kumar R, Millo T (2015). Characteristic autopsy findings in hair dye poisoning. *BMJ Cas Reports* 2015, e2014-206692.

Behera C, Swain R, Mridha AR, Pooniya S (2015). Suicide by injecting lispro insulin with an intravenous cannula. *Medico-Legal Journal,* Published online: 6 March 2015. doi: 10.1177/0025817215573171.

Boonstra JJ, Kan AA, de Vries I, Deneer VHM, Meinders AJ (2015). A potentially fatal intoxication with colchicine. *Nederlands Tijdschrift voor Geneeskunde* 159, A8144.

Brodrick J, Mitchell BG (2015). Hallucinogen persisting perception disorder and risk of suicide. *Journal of Pharmacy Practice.* Published online: 27 January 2015. doi: 10.1177/0897190014566314.

Carlier J, Romeuf L, Guitton J, Priez-Barallon C, Bevalot F, Fanton L, Gaillard Y (2014). A validated method for quantifying atractyloside and carboxyatractyloside in blood by HPLC-HRMS/MS, a non-fatal case of intoxication with Atractylis gummifera L. *Journal of Analytical Toxicology* 38, 619-627.

Chandra G, Jayanth SH, Saralaya PK, Udaya Shankar BS, Praveen S (2014). Accidental cut throat injury: A case report. *Journal of South India Medicolegal Association* 6, 88-92.

Chavez P, Casso Dominguez A, Herzog E (2014). Evolving electrocardiographic changes in lamotrigine overdose: A case report and literature review. *Cardiovascular Toxicology.* Published online: 2 December 2014. doi: 10.1007/s12012-014-9300-0.

Chowdhury FR, Bari MS, Alam MMJ, Rahman MM, Bhattacharjee B, Qayyum JA, Mridha MS (2014). Organophosphate poisoning presenting with muscular weakness and abdominal pain - a case report. *BMC Research Notes* 7, 140.

Confer JR, White M, Groat MM, Madan A, Allen JG, Fowler JC, Kahn DA (2015). Integrating real-time feedback of outcome assessment for individual patients in an inpatient psychiatric setting: A case study of personalized psychiatric medicine. *Journal of Psychiatric Practice* 21, 72-78.

Dalhaug A, Pawinski A, Norum J, Nieder C (2014). Presentation and course of brain metastases from breast cancer in a paranoid-schizophrenic patient: A case report. *Cases Journal* 1, 195.

Danzer G (2014). Multidimensional family therapy in theory and in practice. *Child and Youth Services* 35, 16-34.

Debnath CR, Debnath MR, Alam MM, Moshwan MM (2014). A case of acute insulin poisoning with attempt to suicide. *Mymensingh Medical Journal* 23, 800-802.

Dettling A, Stadler K, Eisenbach C, Skopp G, Haffner HT (2015). Systemic inflammatory response due to chloroform intoxication - an uncommon complication. *International Journal of Legal Medicine.* Published online: 13 February 2015. doi: 10.1007/s00414-015-1156-8.

Eroglu MZ, Gunes T, Nebioglu M (2014). Suicide attempt by subcutaneous injection of cyanide: A case report. *Dusunen Adam* 27, 257-260.

Eryilmaz G, Gul IG, Yorbik O, Isiten N (2014). Long-acting methylphenidate toxicity: A case report. *Klinik Psikofarmakoloji Bulteni* 24, 384-386.

Fletcher R (2014). Contesting the cruel treatment of abortion-seeking women. *Reproductive Health Matters* 22, 10-21.

Fox DMBM (2014). It really was that bad, but I came back. *Canadian Medical Association Journal* 186, 1112.

Gauffin H, Landtblom A-M (2014). Epilepsy and violence: Case series concerning physical trauma in children of persons with epilepsy. *Neuropsychiatric Disease and Treatment* 10, 2183-2189.

Giddens JM, Sheehan DV (2014). The complexity of assessing overall severity of suicidality: A case study. *Innovations in Clinical Neuroscience* 11, 164-171

Giddens JM, Sheehan DV (2014). Do the five combinations of suicidal ideation in the FDA 2012 draft guidance document and the C-SSRS adequately cover all suicidal ideation combinations in practice? A case study. *Innovations in Clinical Neuroscience* 11, 172-178.

Giddens JM, Sheehan DV (2014). How the timing of a patient's self-ratings of suicidality and the relationship to the recipient affect patient responses: A case study. *Innovations in Clinical Neuroscience* 11, 191-193

Giddens JM, Sheehan DV (2014). Is a count of suicidal ideation and behavior events useful in assessing global severity of suicidality? A case study. *Innovations in Clinical Neuroscience* 11, 179-181.

Giddens JM, Sheehan DV (2014). Is there value in asking the question "Do you think you would be better off dead?" in assessing suicidality? A case study. *Innovations in Clinical Neuroscience* 11, 182-190.

Gokten ES, Kilicoglu AG (2015). Case report: An extreme homicide-suicide by a 12-year-old girl. *Aggression and Violent Behavior* 21, 110-112.

Graham N (2014). Polyamory: A call for increased mental health professional awareness. *Archives of Sexual Behavior* 43, 1031-1034.

Gulec H, Babayigit M, Kurtay A, Sahap M, Ulus F, Tutal Z, Horasanli E (2014). Seizure due to multiple drugs intoxication: A case report. *Revista Brasileira de Anestesiologia*. Published online: 3 June 2014. doi: 10.1016/j.bjane.2014.02.013.

Gupta MK, Kant K, Vishnoi A, Kumar A (2014). "Jodhpur bezoar": Giant polyurethane bezoar. *Indian Journal of Surgery*. 7 November 2014. doi: 10.1007/s12262-014-1192-5.

Harnish C, Gross B, Rittenhouse K, Bupp K, Vellucci A, Anderson J, Riley D, Rogers FB (2014). An alarming presentation of Creutzfeldt-Jakob disease following a self-inflicted gunshot wound to the head. *Injury* 46, 926-928.

Hassan S, Flett GL, Ganguli R, Hewitt PL (2014). Perfectionistic self-presentation and suicide in a young woman with major depression and psychotic features. *Case Reports in Psychiatry* 2014, 901981.

Hiraiwa T, Okada H, Sawada N, Nakayama K, Senda N, Kawanishi M (2014). Complex regional pain syndrome in a patient with acute drug poisoning: A case report. *Japanese Journal of Toxicology* 27, 323-326.

Iragavarapu C, Gupta T, Chugh SS, Aronow WS, Frishman WH (2014). Type B lactic acidosis associated with venlafaxine overdose. *American Journal of Therapeutics*. Published online: 17 November 2014. doi: 10.1097/MJT.0000000000000114.

Ishigaki S, Fukasawa H, Kinoshita-Katahashi N, Yasuda H, Kumagai H, Furuya R (2014). Caffeine intoxication successfully treated by hemoperfusion and hemodialysis. *Internal Medicine* 53, 2745-2747.

Jeckell AS, Durand D (2014). Premorbid antisocial personality and substance use disorder in traumatic brain injury: A case report and review of literature. *Addictive Disorders and their Treatment*. Published online: 9 December 2014. doi: 10.1097/ADT.0000000000000064.

Kakkar A, Kumar S (2014). Alprazolam poisoning. *Journal of Indian Academy of Forensic Medicine* 36, 432-433.

Kasckow J, Zickmund S, Rotondi A, Welch A, Gurklis J, Chinman M, Fox L, Haas GL (2014). Optimizing scripted dialogues for an e-health intervention for suicidal veterans with major depression. *Community Mental Health Journal*. Published online: 24 October 2014. 10.1007/s10597-014-9775-y.

Ketola RA, Viinamäki J, Rasanen I, Pelander A, Goebeler S (2015). Fatal kavalactone intoxication by suicidal intravenous injection. *Forensic Science International* 249, e7-e11 .

Kharbach Y, Tenkorang S, Ahsaini M, Mellas S, El Ammari J, Tazi MF, Khallouk A, El Fassi MJ,Farih MH (2014). Suicide attempt by self-stabbing of the bladder: A case report. *Journal of Medical Case Reports* 8, 391.

Khashaba S, Abuhassan K, Al-Reefy H, Tierney E (2014). Management of a self-inflicted laryngeal injury. *Bahrain Medical Bulletin* 36, 258-260.

Kim R, Jun J, Nam H (2015). Residency training: Bilateral facial nerve palsies after a suicide attempt by hanging. *Neurology* 84, e46-47.

Kiraly DD, Sher L (2014). Low testosterone in a young combat veteran with dual diagnosis and suicidal behavior: A case study. *International Journal of Adolescent Medicine and Health*. Published online: 22 December 2014. doi: 10.1515/ijamh-2015-5018.

Kiraly DD, Sher L (2014). Suicidal behavior in a medical professional with comorbid depression and substance use disorder: An educational case report. *International Journal of Adolescent Medicine and Health*. Published online: 20 November 2014. doi: 10.1515/ijamh-2015-5017.

Kopacz P, Kula K (2014). Lethal poisoning with theophylline in the form of rectally administered tablets. *Archiwum Medycyny Sadowej i Kryminologii* 64, 158-164.

Koschny R, Lutz M, Seckinger J, Schwenger V, Stremmel W, Eisenbach C (2014). Extracorporeal life support and plasmapheresis in a case of severe polyintoxication. *Journal of Emergency Medicine* 47, 527-531.

Kupeli A, Demirer M, Kalayci I, Gonen O, Gurpinar SS (2014). Is the victim daughter or the granddaughter of the perpetrator? (incest case report). *Procedia - Social and Behavioral Sciences* 131, 373-376.

Kuruc R, Sidlo J, Baloghová A, Zdarilek M, Zummerová A, Sikuta J (2014). The motivation behind extended suicide. *Archiwum Medycyny Sadowej i Kryminologii* 64, 127-133 .

Kustermann A, Möbius C, Oberstein T, Müller HH, Kornhuber J (2014). Depression and attempted suicide under pregabalin therapy. *Annals of General Psychiatry* 13, 37.

Kyong YY (2014). Serial monitoring of sedation scores in benzodiazepine overdose. *The American Journal of Emergency Medicine* 32, 1438.e5–1438.e6

Lee A, Sikka N, O'Connell F, Dyer A, Boniface K, Betz J (2015). Telepsychiatric assessment of a mariner expressing suicidal ideation. *International Maritime Health* 66, 49-51.

Lee E, Won Kim S, Enright RD (2014). Case study of a survivor of suicide who lost all family members through parent-child collective suicide. *Crisis* 36, 71-75.

Libbon R, Hamalian G, Yager J (2015). Self-cannibalism (autosarcophagy) in psychosis: A case report. *Journal of Nervous and Mental Disease* 203, 152-153.

Loredo J, Manalai P (2014). Suicide in men is systematically underreported in Afghanistan. *Journal of Medicine in the Tropics* 16, 109-110.

Malbranque S, Jousset N, Nedelcu C, Rougé-Maillart C (2014). Bone-patch type secondary projectiles: A report on two shots fired at point-blank range using hollow point bullets. *Forensic Science International* 245, e6-e10.

Matthews SS, Ringeisen AL, Wedro B (2014). Intentional overdose of warfarin in an adult: Anticoagulant reversal in the ED. *American Journal of Emergency Medicine* 32, 1150.e1-2.

McIntyre IM, Trochta A, Stolberg S, Campman SC (2015). Mitragynine 'Kratom' related fatality: A case report with postmortem concentrations. *Journal of Analytical Toxicology* 39, 152-155.

Meshi A, Belkin A, Koval T, Kornhouser T, Assia EI, Rotenstreich Y (2014). An experimental treatment of ocular quinine toxicity with high-dose 9-cis beta-carotene. *Retinal Cases and Brief Reports* 9, 157-161.

Miyauchi M, Hayashida M, Yokota H (2014). Benzalkonium chloride intoxication caused by intravenous self-injection. *Japanese Journal of Toxicology* 27, 327-332.

Moehle F, Madea B, Fronhoffs K, Doberentz E (2015). Questionable self-injury by a young girl with acid. *Rechtsmedizin* 25, 62-66.

Mohan A, Lee T, Sachdev P (2014). Surviving acute cyanide poisoning: A longitudinal neuropsychological investigation with interval mri. *BMJ Case Reports*. Published online: 19 March 2014. doi: 10.1136/bcr-2013-203025.

Montelescaut E, Vermeersch V, Commandeur D, Huynh S, Danguy Des Deserts M, Sapin J, Ould-Ahmed M, Drouillard I (2014). Acute arsenic poisoning. *Annales de Biologie Clinique* 72, 735-738.

Morrison J, Schwartz TL (2014). Adolescent angst or true intent? Suicidal behavior, risk, and neurobiological mechanisms in depressed children and teenagers taking antidepressants. *International Journal of Emergency Mental Health* 16, 247-250.

Motlhatlhedi K, Firth JA, Setlhare V, Kaguamba JK, Mmolaatshepe M (2014). A novel and fatal method of copper sulphate poisoning. *African Journal of Emergency Medicine* 4, e23–e25.

Nagashima G, Kamimura M, Kato A, Fukuda Y, Noda M, Morishima H, Tanaka T, Umano Y (2014). A case of self-harm by alcohol intoxication resulted in unintended in-hospital death. *Clinical Case Reports* 2, 45-47.

Nakano H, Iseki K, Ozawa A, Tominaga A, Sadahiro R, Otani K (2014). Conservative treatment improved corrosive esophagitis and pneumomediastinum in a patient who ingested bleaching agent containing sodium hypochlorite and sodium hydroxide. *Japanese Journal of Toxicology* 27, 39-44.

Nikoli S, Živkovi V (2015). Suicidal krönlein shot with a home manufactured firearm. *Forensic Science, Medicine, and Pathology*. Published online: 3 March 2015. doi: 10.1007/s12024-015-9666-8.

Perlis RH (2014). Use of large data sets and the future of personalized treatment. *Depression and anxiety* 31, 916-919.

Petrea S, Brezean I (2014). Self-ingested intraduodenal foreign bodies - expectancy or surgical sanction? *Journal of Medicine and Life* 7, 421-427.

Petrova V (2014). A case of an infiltrative astrocytoma in a suicidal woman. *Journal of Neuroimmunology* 275, 37.

Piedimonte F, Andreani JC, Piedimonte L, Micheli F, Graff P, Bacaro V (2015). Remarkable clinical improvement with bilateral globus pallidus internus deep brain stimulation in a case of Lesch-Nyhan disease: Five-year follow-up. *Neuromodulation* 18, 118-122.

Piskac O, Stribrny J, Rakovcová H, Maly M (2014). Cardiotoxicity of yew. *Cor et Vasa*. Published online: 23 December 2014. doi: 10.1016/j.crvasa.2014.11.003.

Pradeep Kumar MP, Havanur BL (2015). Hanging by hand kerchief: A rare case report. *Journal of South India Medicolegal Association* 7, 45-47.

Pradipkumar Singh K, Keisham S, Rishilu K, Meera Devi T (2014). Suicidal death due to stabbing: A case of rare occurrence. *Journal of Indian Academy of Forensic Medicine* 36, 434-436.

Radhakrishnan H, Gopi M, Arumugam A (2014). Ammonium dichromate poisoning: A rare cause of acute kidney injury. *Indian Journal of Nephrology* 24, 380-381.

Raslan M, Donaldson J, Royle J (2015). Penile self-harm: A case report and concise clinical review. *Scandinavian Journal of Urology and Nephrology*. Published online: 3 February 2015. doi: 10.3109/21681805.2015.1006248.

Ratnayake MKN, Pathiraja C, Ranathunga AN (2015). Ischaemic changes in electrocardiography (ECG) after attempted suicide by hanging (transient left ventricular apical ballooning). *Sri Lankan Journal of Anaesthesiology* 23, 39-42.

Rautji R, Kumar A (2014). A case of suicide or accidental death due to self stabbing. *Journal of Indian Academy of Forensic Medicine* 36, 437-438.

Re L, Birkhoff JM, Sozzi M, Andrello L, Osculati AMM (2015). The choking game: A deadly game. Analysis of two cases of "self-strangulation" in young boys and review of the literature. *Journal of Forensic and Legal Medicine* 30, 29-33.

Rossouw TI (2015). The use of mentalization-based treatment for adolescents (MBT-A) with a young woman with mixed personality disorder and tendencies to self-harm. *Journal of Clinical Psychology* 71, 178-187.

Ruder JB, Ward JG, Taylor S, Giles K, Higgins T, Haan JM (2015). Hydrogen sulfide suicide: A new trend and threat to healthcare providers. *Journal of Burn Care and Research* 36, e23-25.

Sabermoghaddam M, Abad M, Golmakani E, Mozaffari N (2015). Survival after judicial hanging. *American Journal of Forensic Medicine and Pathology*. Published online: 15 March 2015. doi: 10.1097/PAF.0000000000000140.

Sarkar S, Srinivas B, Grover S (2014). Quadruple pact suicide attempt involving a man and three adolescents. *Indian Journal of Psychological Medicine* 36, 422-424.

Sawamoto K, Hase M, Uemura S, Kasai T, Narimatsu E (2015). Takotsubo cardiomyopathy induced by suicidal neck hanging. *Journal of Emergency Medicine* 48, e35-e38.

Shah AH, Gordon CE, Bregy A, Shah N, Komotar RJ (2014). Considering iatrogenic psychosis after malignant glioma resection. *BMJ Case Reports*. Published online: 23 April 2014. doi: 10.1136/bcr-2013-201318.

Shang A-D, Lu Y-Q (2015). A case report of severe paraquat poisoning in an HIV-positive patient: An unexpected outcome and inspiration. *Medicine* 94, e587.

Sharma P, Manning S, Baronia R, Mushtaq S (2014). Pyrethroid as a substance of abuse. *Case Reports in Psychiatry* 2014, 169294.

Shirota T, Ikegami T, Sugiyama S, Kubota K, Shimizu A, Ohno Y, Mita A, Urata K, Nakazawa Y, Kobayashi A, Iwaya M, Miyagawa S (2015). Successful living donor liver transplantation for acute liver failure after acetylsalicylic acid overdose. *Clinical Journal of Gastroenterology* 8, 97-102.

Simoncini M, Miniati M, Vanelli F, Callari A, Vannucchi G, Mauri M, Dell'Osso L (2014). Lifetime autism spectrum features in a patient with a psychotic mixed episode who attempted suicide. *Case Reports in Psychiatry* 2014, 459524.

Straight B, Pike I, Hilton C, Oesterle M (2014). Suicide in three East African pastoralist communities and the role of researcher outsiders for positive transformation: A case study. *Culture, Medicine and Psychiatry*. Published online: 9 Nov 2014. doi: 10.1007/s11013-014-9417-4.

Suresh V, Vinay HN (2015). Suicidal suffocation using plastic bag - a case report. *Journal of South India Medicolegal Association* 7, 48-50.

Suzuki J, Poklis JL, Poklis A (2014). "My friend said it was good LSD": A suicide attempt following analytically confirmed 25I-NBOMe ingestion. *Journal of Psychoactive Drugs* 46, 379-382.

Tanrikulu Y, Sen Tanrikulu C, Karaman S, Sahin H (2015). Ingestion of multiple magnets for suicide. *Hong Kong Journal of Emergency Medicine* 22, 50-52.

Thangaraj K, Suresh ASS, Gambhir Singh O (2014). Suicidal hanging masquerading as a homicidal hanging. *Journal of Indian Academy of Forensic Medicine* 36, 322-324.

Tikka T, Al Abduwani J, Costello D (2015). Deliberate self-harming application of superglue in the nose: Case report and literature review. *The Journal of Laryngology and Otology* 129, 98-100.

Ueki C, Shintani T, Akimoto T, Sakaguchi G (2014). Successful endovascular treatment of traumatic thoracic aortic injury complicated by severe pelvic hemorrhage. *Annals of Vascular Diseases* 7, 410-412.

W growska-Danilewicz M, Danilewicz M, Zbrog Z (2014). Mercury-induced nephrotic syndrome: A case report and review of the literature. *Polish Journal of Pathology* 65, 322-326.

Weerdenburg K, Finkelstein Y (2015). Is suicide really painless?: A 12-year-old girl with seizures. *Pediatric Emergency Care* 31, 217-219.

Welman T, Wong JM, Le Vay R, Kader P (2014). Librium for bed 1, a bottle of scotch for bed 2. *BMJ Case Reports.* Published online: 11 March 2014. doi:10.1136/bcr-2013-202809.

Wiergowski M, Gos T, Sumi ska-Ziemann B, Kaliszan M, Jankowski Z (2014). Helium detection in the lungs in case of suicide by helium inhalation-case report and literature review. *Romanian Journal of Legal Medicine* 22, 153-156.

Wijeratne T, Ratnatunga C, Dharrmapala A, Samarasinghe T (2015). Corrosive acid injury of the stomach. *Ceylon Medical Journal* 60, 25-27.

Wilkinson S (2015). X. Refusing to live with advanced dementia: Contemporaneous and prospective decision-making. *Feminism and Psychology* 25, 148-154.

You MJ, Shin GW, Lee CS (2015). Clostridium tertium bacteremia in a patient with glyphosate ingestion. *American Journal of Case Reports* 16, 4-7.

Zátopková L, Hejna P, Janík M (2014). Hemolytic staining of the endocardium of the left heart chambers: A new sign for autopsy diagnosis of freshwater drowning. *Forensic Science, Medicine, and Pathology* 11, 65-68.

Zhu X, Wen J, Xu M, Chen P, Wan C (2015). A rare self-injurious case of multiple penetrating brain injury by nails in a young patient with depressive disorder. *Acta Neurologica Belgica* ePub, Published online: 5 March 2015. doi:. 10.1007/s13760-015-0439-7.

MISCELLANEOUS

Anonymous (2014). Suicide in India: From criminalisation to compassion. *The Lancet* 384, 2174.

Abrutyn S, Mueller AS (2014). The socioemotional foundations of suicide: A microsociological view of Durkheim's suicide. *Sociological Theory* 32, 327-351.

Adis Medical Writers (2014). Consider using lithium to augment antidepressant therapy or as a preventative maintenance therapy in patients with major depressive disorder. *Drugs and Therapy Perspectives* 30, 386-389.

Agrawal VK, Bansal A, Singh RK, Kumawat BL, Mahajan P (2015). Aluminum phosphide poisoning: Possible role of supportive measures in the absence of specific antidote. *Indian Journal Of Critical Care Medicine* 19, 109-112.

Ahn JH, Kim WH, Choi HJ, Jeon JY, Song IG, Bae JN (2015). Stigma of mental illnesses as perceived by North Korean defectors living in South Korea. *Psychiatry Investigation* 12, 9-15.

Ak S (2014). The association between times of war and suicide attempts: Hakkari experience. *Turkish Journal of Psychiatry* 25, 221-222.

Al-Sharifi A, Krynicki CR, Upthegrove R (2015). Self-harm and ethnicity: A systematic review. *International Journal of Social Psychiatry*. Published online: 17 March 2015. doi: 10.1177/0020764015573085.

Albuhairan F, Almutairi A, Al Eissa M, Naeem M, Almuneef M (2015). Non-suicidal self-strangulation among adolescents in Saudi Arabia: Case series of the choking game. *Journal of Forensic and Legal Medicine* 30, 43-45.

Alderson M, Parent-Rocheleau X, Mishara B (2015). Critical review on suicide among nurses. *Crisis*. Published online: 23 February 2015. doi: 10.1027/0227-5910/a000305.

Alexander BK (2014). Bodies yearning on the borders of becoming: A performative reflection on three embodied axes of social difference. *Qualitative Inquiry* 20, 1169-1178.

Allen TE (2014). Life of Pi and the moral wound. *Journal of the American Psychoanalytic Association* 62, 965-982.

Aloba O, Akinsulore A, Mapayi B, Oloniniyi I, Mosaku K, Alimi T, Esan O (2015). The Yoruba version of the Beck hopelessness scale: Psychometric characteristics and correlates of hopelessness in a sample of Nigerian psychiatric outpatients. *Comprehensive Psychiatry* 56, 258-271.

Altamura AC, Serati M, Buoli M (2015). Is duration of illness really influencing outcome in major psychoses? *Nordic Journal of Psychiatry*. Published online: 13 March 2015. doi: 10.3109/08039488.2014.990919.

Amado DM, Beamon DA, Sheehan DV (2014). Linguistic validation of the pediatric versions of the Sheehan Suicidality Tracking Scale (S-STS). *Innovations in Clinical Neuroscience* 11, 141-163.

Ambrus L, Sunnqvist C, Ekman A, Suchankova P, Träskman-Bendz L, Westrin Å (2014). Associations between avoidant focused coping strategies and polymorphisms in genes coding for brain-derived neurotrophic factor and vascular endothelial growth factor in suicide attempters: A preliminary study. *Psychiatry Research* 220, 732-733.

Anderson DM, Rees DI, Sabia JJ (2015). Anderson et al. respond to critics: Marijuana and suicide. *American Journal of Public Health* 105, e8-e9.

Andover MS, Morris BW (2014). Expanding and clarifying the role of emotion regulation in non-suicidal self-injury. *Canadian Journal of Psychiatry* 59, 569-575.

Andrews J (2015). II. Keeping older women safe from harm. *Feminism and Psychology* 25, 105-108.

Andriessen K (2014). Suicide bereavement and postvention in major suicidology journals: Lessons learned for the future of postvention. *Crisis* 35, 338-348.

Anestis MD, Selby EA (2015). Grit and perseverance in suicidal behavior and non-suicidal self-injury. *Death Studies*, 39, 211-218.

Anestis MD, Soberay KA, Gutierrez PM, Hernandez TD, Joiner TE (2014). Reconsidering the link between impulsivity and suicidal behavior. *Personality and Social Psychology Review* 18, 366-386.

Angelotta C (2015). Defining and refining self-harm: A historical perspective on nonsuicidal self-injury. *Journal of Nervous and Mental Disease* 203, 75-80.

Antonius D, Mathew N, Picano J, Hinds A, Cogswell A, Olympia J, Brooks T, Di Giacomo M, Baker J, Willer B, Leddy J (2014). Behavioral health symptoms associated with chronic traumatic encephalopathy: A critical review of the literature and recommendations for treatment and research. *Journal of Neuropsychiatry and Clinical Neurosciences* 26, 313-322.

Arbise BS, Amerson NL (2014). Tracking youth self-inflicted injury hospitalizations to target high-risk communities, leverage resources, and unify stakeholder efforts: Illinois Department of Public Health. *Preventing Chronic Disease* 11, E197-E197.

Armey MF, Schatten HT, Haradhvala N, Miller IW (2015). Ecological momentary assessment (EMA) of depression-related phenomena. *Current Opinion in Psychology* 4, 21-25.

Auxemery Y (2015). The mass murderer history: Modern classifications, sociodemographic and psychopathological characteristics, suicidal dimensions, and media contagion of mass murders. *Comprehensive psychiatry* 56, 149-154.

Aycock RD (2014). Commentary on "VHA chaplaincy contact with veterans at increased risk of suicide". *Southern Medical Journal* 107, 665.

Badami S (2014). Suicide as a counter-narrative in Wayanad, Southern India: The invisible death. *South Asia Research* 34, 91-112.

Baethge C (2015). A bold meta-analysis on suicidality in bipolar disorder. *Bipolar Disorders* 17, 17-18.

Bakian AV, Huber RS, Coon H, Gray D, Wilson P, McMahon WM, Renshaw PF (2015). Bakian et al. Respond to "assessing air pollution and suicide risk". *American Journal of Epidemiology* 181, 309-310.

Balon R (2014). Clinical factor 2013. *Psychotherapy and Psychosomatics* 83, 330-340.

Batterham PJ, Ftanou M, Pirkis J, Brewer JL, Mackinnon AJ, Beautrais A, Fairweather-Schmidt AK, Christensen H (2014). A systematic review and evaluation of measures for suicidal ideation and behaviors in population-based research. *Psychological Assessment.* Published online: 15 December 2014. doi: 10.1037/pas0000053.

Bejerot S, Edman G, Anckarsater H, Berglund G, Gillberg C, Hofvander B, Humble MB, Mortberg E, Rastam M, Stahlberg O, Frisen L (2014). The Brief Obsessive-Compulsive Scale (BOCS): A self-report scale for OCD and obsessive-compulsive related disorders. *Nordic Journal of Psychiatry* 68, 549-559.

Bennett DT, Reece TB, Smith PD, Grandhi MS, Yu Rove JA, Justison GA, Mitchell JD, Fullerton DA, Zamora MR, Weyant MJ (2014). Ex vivo lung perfusion allows successful transplantation of donor lungs from hanging victims. *Annals of Thoracic Surgery* 98, 1051-1056.

Bentley KH, Cassiello-Robbins CF, Vittorio L, Sauer-Zavala S, Barlow DH (2015). The association between nonsuicidal self-injury and the emotional disorders: A meta-analytic review. *Clinical Psychology Review* 37, 72-88.

Bernert RA, Nadorff MR (2014). Sleep disturbances and suicide risk. *Sleep Medicine Clinics* 10, 35-39.

Biel S, Plakun EM (2015). Psychodynamic systems of residential treatment: Another view from Riggs. *Psychodynamic Psychiatry* 43, 91-116.

BinDhim NF, Shaman AM, Trevena L, Basyouni MH, Pont LG, Alhawassi TM (2015). Depression screening via a smartphone app: Cross-country user characteristics and feasibility. *Journal of the American Medical Informatics Association* 22, 29-34.

Black C, Miller BJ (2014). Meta-analysis of cytokines and chemokines in suicidality: Distinguishing suicidal versus nonsuicidal patients. *Biological Psychiatry.* Published online: 30 October 2014. doi: 10.1016/j.biopsych.2014.10.014.

Black EB, Mildred H (2014). A cross-sectional examination of non-suicidal self-injury, disordered eating, impulsivity, and compulsivity in a sample of adult women. *Eating Behaviors* 15, 578-581.

Boden ZV, Gibson S, Owen GJ, Benson O (2015). Feelings and intersubjectivity in qualitative suicide research. *Qualitative Health Research.* Published online: 20 March 2015. doi:10.1177/1049732315576709.

Boege I, Corpus N, Schepker R, Fegert JM (2014). Pilot study: Feasibility of using the Suicidal Ideation Questionnaire (SIQ) during acute suicidal crisis. *Child and Adolescent Psychiatry And Mental Health* 8, 28.

Bondü R, Beier S (2015). Two of a kind? Differences and similarities of attacks in schools and in institutes of higher education. *Journal of Interpersonal Violence* 30, 253-271.

Borum V (2014). African Americans' perceived sociocultural determinants of suicide: Afrocentric implications for public health inequalities. *Social Work in Public Health* 29, 656-670.

Brady MT (2014). Cutting the silence: Initial, impulsive self-cutting in adolescence. *Journal of Child Psychotherapy* 40, 287-301.

Brent DA, Koplewicz HS, Steingard R (2015). New approaches to the assessment and treatment of suicidal adolescents. *Journal of Child and Adolescent Psychopharmacology* 25, 99.

Brossard B (2014). Fighting with oneself to maintain the interaction order: A sociological approach to self-injury daily process. *Symbolic Interaction* 37, 558-575.

Browne JL, Nefs G, Pouwer F, Speight J (2015). Suicidal ideation or non-suicidal self-harm? A mismatch between the DSM-IV criterion and PHQ-9 item nine. *Diabetes Research and Clinical Practice* 108, e5-e6.

Bruffaerts R, Posada-Villa J, Al-Hamzawi AO, Gureje O, Huang Y, Hu C, Bromet EJ, Viana MC, Hinkov HR, Karam EG, Borges G, Florescu SE, Williams DR, Demyttenaere K, Kovess-Masfety V, Matschinger H, Levinson D, De Girolamo G, Ono Y, de Graaf R, Oakley Browne M, Bunting B, Xavier M, Haro JM, Kessler RC (2014). Proportion of patients without mental disorders being treated in mental health services worldwide. *British Journal of Psychiatry* 206, 101-109.

Brunet A, Monson E (2014). Suicide risk among active and retired Canadian soldiers: The role of posttraumatic stress disorder. *Canadian Journal of Psychiatry* 59, 457-459.

Brunner J, Russel M, Herr K, Benjamin E, Myers L, Boyko O, Jaffray P, Reddy S (2015). Nonsuicidal self-injury-related foreign bodies in the emergency department. *Seminars in Ultrasound, CT, and MR* 36, 80-87.

Buser TJ, Pitchko A, Buser JK (2014). Naturalistic recovery from nonsuicidal self-injury: A phenomenological inquiry. *Journal of Counseling and Development* 92, 438-446.

Casali MB, Battistini A, Blandino A, Cattaneo C (2015). Corrigendum to "the injury pattern in fatal suicidal falls from a height: An examination of 307 cases" [forensic sci int 244 (2014) 57-62]. *Forensic Science International* 249, 52.

Caulkins CG (2015). Bridge over troubled discourse: The influence of the Golden Gate bridge on community discourse and suicide. *Journal of Aggression, Conflict and Peace Research* 7, 47-56.

Chandramouleeswaran S, Edwin NC, Victor PJ, Tharyan P (2014). The emergency physician's assessment of suicide risk in intentional self-poisoning using the modified sad persons scale versus standard psychiatric evaluation in a general hospital in South India: A cross-sectional study. *Tropical Doctor* 45, 21-26.

Chapman CL, Large MM (2014). Should clozapine be available to people with early schizophrenia and suicidal ideation? *Australian and New Zealand Journal of Psychiatry*. Published online: 19 December 2014. doi: 10.1177/0004867414563193.

Chappell PB, Mahableshwarkar AR, Alphs LD, Bangs ME, Butler A, DuBrava SJ, Greist JH, Lenderking WR, Mundt JC, Stewart M (2014). Prospective assessment of suicidal ideation and behavior: An internet survey of pharmaceutical sponsor practices. *Innovations in Clinical Neuroscience* 11, 14-22.

Chaurasia A, Harel O (2015). Partial f-tests with multiply imputed data in the linear regression framework via coefficient of determination. *Statistics in Medicine* 34, 432-443.

Chevalier L, Goldfarb E, Miller J, Hoeppner B, Gorrindo T, Birnbaum RJ (2015). Gaps in preparedness of clergy and healthcare providers to address mental health needs of returning service members. *Journal of Religion and Health* 54, 327-338.

Choong MY, Tee SF, Tang PY (2014). Meta-analysis of polymorphisms in TPH2 gene and suicidal behavior. *Psychiatry Research* 220, 1163-1166.

Church EJ (2015). Examining suicide: Imaging's contributions. *Radiologic Technology* 86, 275-295.

Clapp J. D., Patton S. C., Beck J. G. (2015). Expressive inhibition in response to stress: Implications for emotional processing following trauma. *Journal of Anxiety Disorders* 29, 109-118.

Clarke MC, Coughlan H, Harley M, Connor D, Power E, Lynch F, Fitzpatrick C, Cannon M (2014). The impact of adolescent cannabis use, mood disorder and lack of education on attempted suicide in young adulthood. *World Psychiatry* 13, 322-323.

Clarner A, Graessel E, Scholz J, Niedermeier A, Uter W, Drexler H (2015). Work-related post-traumatic stress disorder (PTSD) and other emotional diseases as consequence of traumatic events in public transportation: A systematic review. *International Archives of Occupational and Environmental Health* 88, 549-564.

Colak S, Erdogan MO, Baydin A, Afacan MA, Kati C, Duran L (2014). Epidemiology of organophosphate intoxication and predictors of intermediate syndrome. *Turkish Journal of Medical Sciences* 44, 279-282.

Conard PL, Armstrong ML, Young C, Hogan LM (2015). Nursing advocacy for women veterans and suicide. *Journal of Psychosocial Nursing and Mental Health Services* 53, 24-30.

Conner KR, Simons K (2015). State of innovation in suicide intervention research with military populations. *Suicide and Life-Threatening Behavior* 45, 281-292.

Cousins L, Goodyer IM (2015). Antidepressants and the adolescent brain. *Journal of Psychopharmacology* 29, 545-555.

Curnow K (2014). A right to choose how to live: The Australian common law position on refusals of care. *Journal of Law and Medicine* 22, 398-414.

Currier GW, Brown G, Walsh PG, Jager-Hyman S, Chaudhury S, Stanley B (2015). Screening for sexual orientation in psychiatric emergency departments. *Western Journal of Emergency Medicine* 16, 80-84.

Czyz EK, Berona J, King CA (2015). A prospective examination of the interpersonal-psychological theory of suicidal behavior among psychiatric adolescent inpatients. *Suicide and Life-Threatening Behavior* 45, 243-259.

Dahlstrom O, Zetterqvist M, Lundh L, Svedin CG (2015). Functions of nonsuicidal self-injury: Exploratory and confirmatory factor analyses in a large community sample of adolescents. *Psychological Assessment* 27, 302-313.

Daniels K, Loganathan M, Wilson R, Kasckow J (2014). Appointment attendance in patients with schizophrenia. *Clinical Practice* 11, 467-482.

Daray FM, Teti GL, Rojas SM, Fantini AP, Cárdenas-Delgado C, Armesto A, Derito MNC, Rebok F (2015). Time left for intervention in the suicidal process in borderline personality disorder. *Archives of Suicide Research.* Published online: 20 February 2015, doi: 10.1080/13811118.2014.1002875.

Dargan P, Reid G, Hodge S (2015). Exploring the role of mental imagery in the experience of self-injury: An interpretative phenomenological analysis. *Behavioural and cognitive psychotherapy* ePub, ePub-ePub ,

Daruwalla N, Belur J, Kumar M, Tiwari V, Sarabahiji S, Tilley N, Osrin D (2014). A qualitative study of the background and in-hospital medicolegal response to female burn injuries in India. *BMC Womens Health* 14, 142.

De Berardis D, Serroni N, Campanella D, Rapini G, Olivieri L, Feliziani B, Carano A, Valchera A, Iasevoli F, Tomasetti C, Mazza M, Fornaro M, Perna G, Di Nicola M, Martinotti G, Di Giannantonio M (2014). Alexithymia, responsibility attitudes and suicide ideation among outpatients with obsessive-compulsive disorder: An exploratory study. *Comprehensive Psychiatry* 58, 82-87.

De Leo D (2015). Can we rely on suicide mortality data? *Crisis* 36, 1-3.

De Souza MLP, Ferreira LO (2014). Jurupari committed suicide?: Notes for suicide investigation in indigenous context. *Saude e Sociedade* 23, 131-142.

De Vogli R, Owusu JT (2015). The causes and health effects of the great recession: From neoliberalism to 'healthy de-growth'. *Critical Public Health* 25, 15-31.

Debowska A, Boduszek D, Dhingra K (2015). Victim, perpetrator, and offense characteristics in filicide and filicide-suicide. *Aggression and Violent Behavior* 21, 113-124.

Delack JB (2015). "Mental health and veterinary suicides" - a comment. *Canadian Veterinary Journal* 56, 113-113.

DeVylder JE, Thompson E, Reeves G, Schiffman J (2015). Psychotic experiences as indicators of suicidal ideation in a non-clinical college sample. *Psychiatry Research* 226, 489-493.

Dickstein DP, Puzia ME, Cushman GK, Weissman AB, Wegbreit E, Kim KL, Nock MK, Spirito A (2015). Self-injurious implicit attitudes among adolescent suicide attempters versus those engaged in nonsuicidal self-injury. *Journal of Child Psychology and Psychiatry.* Published online: 11 February 2015. doi: 10.1111/jcpp.12385.

Dignam PT (2015). Suicide prevention: Let's start at the very beginning. *Australian and New Zealand Journal of Psychiatry* 49, 16-17.

Donovan DM, Hatch-Maillette MA, Phares MM, McGarry E, Michelle Peavy K, Taborsky J (2015). Lessons learned for follow-up phone booster counseling calls with substance abusing emergency department patients. *Journal of Substance Abuse Treatment* 50, 67-75.

Dubrey SW, Chehab O, Ghonim S (2015). Carbon monoxide poisoning: An ancient and frequent cause of accidental death. *British Journal of Hospital Medicine* 76, 159-162.

Ducasse D, Rene E, Beziat S, Guillaume S, Courtet P, Olie E (2014). Acceptance and commitment therapy for management of suicidal patients: A pilot study. *Psychotherapy and Psychosomatics* 83, 374-376.

Easson A, Agarwal A, Duda S, Bennett K (2014). Portrayal of youth suicide in Canadian News. *Journal of the Canadian Academy of Child and Adolescent Psychiatry* 23, 167-173.

Egnoto MJ, Griffin DJ, Svetieva E, Winslow L (2014). Information sharing during the University of Texas at Austin active shooter/suicide event. *Journal of School Violence.* Published online: 25 September 2014. doi: 10.1080/15388220.2014.949376.

Ellis TE, Rufino KA (2014). A psychometric study of the Suicide Cognitions Scale with psychiatric inpatients. *Psychological Assessment* 27, 82-89.

Engel CC, Bray RM, Jaycox LH, Freed MC, Zatzick D, Lane ME, Brambilla D, Rae Olmsted K, Vandermaas-Peeler R, Litz B, Tanielian T, Belsher BE, Evatt DP, Novak LA, Unützer J, Katon WJ (2014). Implementing collaborative primary care for depression and posttraumatic stress disorder: Design and sample for a randomized trial in the U.S. military health system. *Contemporary Clinical Trials* 39, 310-319.

Fang X, Fry DA, Ji K, Finkelhor D, Chen J, Lannen P, Dunne MP (2015). The burden of child maltreatment in China: A systematic review. *Bulletin of the World Health Organization* 93, 176-185.

Farabaugh A, Nyer M, Holt D, Baer L, Petrie S, DiPierro M, Nierenberg A, Pedrelli P, Cusin C, Fava M, Mischoulon D (2015). Screening for suicide risk in the college population. *Journal of Rational - Emotive and Cognitive - Behavior Therapy* 33, 78-94.

Feng J, Li S, Chen H (2015). Impacts of stress, self-efficacy, and optimism on suicide ideation among rehabilitation patients with acute pesticide poisoning. *PLoS One* 10, e0118011.

Feng P, Hu Y, Vurbic D, Akladious A, Strohl KP (2014). Chromosome 1 replacement increases brain orexins and antidepressive measures without increasing locomotor activity. *Journal of Psychiatric Research* 59, 140-147.

Fernandez J, Lang M (2015). Suicide and organ donors: Spillover effects of mental health insurance mandates. *Health Economics* 24, 491-497.

Ferrarese S (2014). Whose life? Whose body? Sovereignty and the early modern subject in Radicati's Philosophical Dissertation upon Death. *Italian Studies* 69, 328-339.

Finlay IG (2015). What is it to do good medical ethics? From the perspective of a practising doctor who is in parliament. *Journal of Medical Ethics* 41, 83-86.

Fitzgerald P, Kulkarni J (2014). Suicide rates and mental health disorder prevention. *Australian and New Zealand Journal of Psychiatry* 49, 91-92.

Fleischmann A, De Leo D (2014). The World Health Organization's report on suicide. *Crisis* 35, 289-291.

Fonseca-Machado MdO, Alves LC, Freitas PS, Monteiro JCdS, Gomes-Sponholz F (2014). Mental health of women who suffer intimate partner violence during pregnancy. *Investigación y Educación en Enfermería* 32, e19968-e19968.

Ford JD, Gómez JM (2015). Self injury & suicidality: The impact of trauma and dissociation. *Journal of Trauma and Dissociation* 16, 225-231.

Fornaro M, De Berardis D, De Pasquale C, Indelicato L, Pollice R, Valchera A, Perna G, Iasevoli F, Tomasetti C, Martinotti Gn, Koshy AS, Fasmer OB, Oedegaard KJ (2015). Prevalence and clinical features associated to bipolar disorder-migraine comorbidity: A systematic review. *Comprehensive Psychiatry* 56, 1-16.

Fountoulakis KN, Gonda X, Baghai TC, Baldwin DS, Bauer M, Blier P, Gattaz W, Hasler G, Moller H, Tandon R, Vieta E, Kasper S (2014). Report of the WPA section of pharmacopsychiatry on the relationship of antiepileptic drugs with suicidality in epilepsy. *International Journal of Psychiatry in Clinical Practice*. Published online: 23 April 2015. doi: 10.3109/13651501.2014.1000930.

Friedman RA (2014). Antidepressants' black-box warning - 10 years later. *New England Journal of Medicine* 371, 1666-1668.

Galynker I, Yaseen Z, Briggs J (2014). Assessing risk for imminent suicide. *Psychiatric Annals* 44, 431-436.

García-Nieto R, Blasco-Fontecilla H, de León-Martinez V, Baca-García E (2014). Clinical features associated with suicide attempts versus suicide gestures in an inpatient sample. *Archives of Suicide Research* 18, 419-431.

Giddens JM, Sheehan KH, Sheehan DV (2014). The Columbia-Suicide Severity Rating Scale (C-SSRS): Has the "gold standard" become a liability? *Innovations in Clinical Neuroscience* 11, 66-80.

Gilbert F (2014). Self-estrangement & deep brain stimulation: Ethical issues related to forced explantation. *Neuroethics*. Published online: 25 October 2014. doi: 10.1007/s12152-014-9224-1.

Gipson PY, Agarwala P, Opperman KJ, Horwitz A, King CA (2015). Columbia-Suicide Severity Rating Scale: Predictive validity with adolescent psychiatric emergency patients. *Pediatric Emergency Care* 31, 88-94.

Gispert R, Gallo B, Barbería E, Puigdefàbregas A, Ribas G, Medallo J (2014). Comments about the differences in the number of suicide deaths in Spain. *Revista de Psiquiatría y Salud Mental* 7, 208-209 .

Gøtzsche PC (2014). Study of study of changes in antidepressant use after FDA warnings is not reliable. *BMJ* 349, g5623.

Goes FS (2015). The importance of anxiety states in bipolar disorder. *Current Psychiatry Reports*. Published online: 24 January 2015. doi: 10.1007/s11920-014-0540-2.

Graham Martin OAM (2014). On child suicide. *Advances in Mental Health* 12, 88-92.

Gray JS, McCullagh JA (2014). Suicide in Indian country: The continuing epidemic in rural Native American communities. *Journal of Rural Mental Health* 38, 79-86.

Greenberg PE, Fournier A-A, Sisitsky T, Pike CT, Kessler RC (2015). The economic burden of adults with major depressive disorder in the United States (2005 and 2010). *The Journal of Clinical Psychiatry* 76, 155-162.

Grobler C, Smith N (2014). Suicide attempts among bipolar patients in Limpopo province, South Africa. *South African Journal of Psychiatry* 20, 118-119.

Grunberg PH, Lewis SP (2015). Self-injury and readiness to recover: Preliminary examination of components of the stages of change model. *Counselling Psychology Quarterly*. Published online: 23 January 2015. doi: 10.1080/09515070.2014.998627.

Guo Y, Barnett AG (2015). Invited commentary: Assessment of air pollution and suicide risk. *American Journal of Epidemiology*. Published online: 10 February 2015. doi: 10.1093/aje/kwu342.

Güven FMK, Türkdogan KA, Duman A, Akpinar O, Kapcı M, Sonmez E, Co kun A, Akpınar H, Sogut O, Korkmaz I (2014). Cost analysis of different venues for treating suicide cases presented to the emergency department. *Biomedical Research* 25, 431-436.

Haghighi F, Xin Y, Chanrion B, O'Donnell AH, Ge Y, Dwork AJ, Arango V, Mann JJ (2014). Increased DNA methylation in the suicide brain. *Dialogues in Clinical Neuroscience* 16, 430-438.

Hamza CA, Willoughby T, Heffer T (2015). Impulsivity and nonsuicidal self-injury: A review and meta-analysis. *Clinical Psychology Review* 38, 13-24.

Haouzi P, Sonobe T, Torsell-Tubbs N, Prokopczyk B, Chenuel B, Klingerman CM (2014). In vivo interactions between cobalt or ferric compounds and the pools of sulphide in the blood during and after H2S poisoning. *Toxicological Sciences* 141, 493-504.

Harrod CS, Goss CW, Stallones L, DiGuiseppi C (2014). Interventions for primary prevention of suicide in university and other post-secondary educational settings. *Cochrane Database of Systematic Reviews* 10, CD009439.

Hashimoto K, Sugawara N, Tanaka O, Nakamura K, Yasui-Furukori N (2014). Parental bonding and attitudes toward suicide among medical college students in Japan. *Neuropsychiatric Disease and Treatment* 10, 2015-2020.

Hawton K (2014). Suicide prevention: A complex global challenge. *Lancet Psychiatry* 1, 2-3.

Hawton K (2015). Suicide in doctors while under fitness to practise investigation. *BMJ* 350, h813.

Hayes JF, Miles J, Walters K, King M, Osborn DP (2015). A systematic review and meta-analysis of premature mortality in bipolar affective disorder. *Acta Psychiatrica Scandinavica*. Published online: 3 March 2015. doi: 10.1111/acps.12408.

Hermens ML, Oud M, Sinnema H, Nauta MH, Stikkelbroek Y, van Duin D, Wensing M (2015). The multidisciplinary depression guideline for children and adolescents: An implementation study. *European Child & Adolescent Psychiatry.* Published online: 15 January 2015. doi: 10.1007/s00787-014-0670-4.

Hill BJ, Barnett JT (2014). Mental health and the army. *JAMA Psychiatry* 71, 967.

Hill RM, Rey Y, Marin CE, Sharp C, Green KL, Pettit JW (2014). Evaluating the interpersonal needs questionnaire: Comparison of the reliability, factor structure, and predictive validity across five versions. *Suicide and Life-Threatening Behavior* 45, 302-314.

Hlásny V, Jung BJ (2014). Wellington Chung: Child of the Korean independence movement crushed by cold war regimes. *Korea Journal* 54, 106-146.

Hoge CW, Warner CH, Castro CA (2014). Mental health and the army. *JAMA Psychiatry* 71, 965-966.

Holliday C, Vandermause R (2015). Teen experiences following a suicide attempt. *Archives of Psychiatric Nursing* 29, 168-173.

Horton M, Wright N, Dyer W, Wright-Hughes A, Farrin A, Mohammed Z, Smith J, Heyes T, Gilbody S, Tennant A (2014). Assessing the risk of self-harm in an adult offender population: An incidence cohort study. *Health Technology Assessment.* Published online: October 2014. doi: 10.3310/hta18640.

Hughes LS (2015). You can't hide the bridges. *Annals of Family Medicine* 13, 181-183.

Ickowicz A, Schachar R (2015). Suicide prevention strategies: Adventures in the grey zone. *Journal of the Canadian Academy of Child and Adolescent Psychiatry* 24, 4.

Iliceto P, Fino E (2015). Beck Hopelessness Scale (BHS): A second-order confirmatory factor analysis. *European Journal of Psychological Assessment* 31, 31-37.

Ingelman-Sundberg M, Persson A, Jukic MM (2014). Polymorphic expression of CYP2C19 and CYP2D6 in the developing and adult human brain causing variability in cognition, risk for depression and suicide: The search for the endogenous substrates. *Pharmacogenomics* 15, 1841-1844.

Ioannou M, Debowska A (2014). Genuine and simulated suicide notes: An analysis of content. *Forensic Science International* 245, 151-160.

Iyer R, Iken B, Leon A (2015). Developments in alternative treatments for organophosphate poisoning. *Toxicology Letters* 2, 200-206.

Jasiewicz A, Samochowiec A, Samochowiec J, Malecka I, Suchanecka A, Grzywacz A (2014). Suicidal behavior and haplotypes of the dopamine receptor gene (DRD2) and ANKK1 gene polymorphisms in patients with alcohol dependence - preliminary report. *PLoS One* 9, e111798.

Jena AB, Prasad V (2014). Primary care physicians' role in counseling about gun safety. *American Family Physician* 90, 619-620.

Ji N-J, Hong Y-P, Stack SJ, Lee W-Y (2014). Influence of media on suicide: Proper coverage of media on suicide report response. *Journal of Korean Medical Science* 29, 1584-1585.

Jimenez-Trevino L, Alejandra Saiz P, Corcoran P, Buron P, Paz Garcia-Portilla M, Ramon Chinea E, Navio M, Fernandez V, Angel Jimenez-Arriero M, Gracia R, Bobes J (2015). Factors associated with hospitalization after suicide spectrum behaviors: Results from a multicenter study in Spain. *Archives of Suicide Research* 19, 17-34.

Jin U, Park J-S, Min Y-G, Yang H-M, Lim H-S, Choi B-J, Choi S-Y, Yoon M-H, Hwang G-S, Tahk S-J, Shin J-H (2015). Hanging-associated left ventricular systolic dysfunction. *Resuscitation* 88, 1-5.

Jordans M, Kaufman A, Brenman NF, Adhikari RP, Luitel N, Tol WA, Komproe I (2014). Suicide in South Asia: A scoping review. *BMC Psychiatry* 14, 12.

Kar N, Arun M, Mohanty MK, Bastia BK (2014). Scale for assessment of lethality of suicide attempt. *Indian Journal of Psychiatry* 56, 337-343.

Karanovi J, Švikovi S, Pantovi M, Durica S, Brajuškovi G, Damjanovi A, Jovanovi V, Ivkovi M, Romac S, Savi Pavi evi D (2015). Joint effect of ADARB1 gene, HTR2C gene and stressful life events on suicide attempt risk in patients with major psychiatric disorders. *World Journal of Biological Psychiatry* 16, 261-271.

Karman P, Kool N, Poslawsky IE, Van Meijel B (2015). Nurses' attitudes towards self-harm: A literature review. *Journal of Psychiatric and Mental Health Nursing* 22, 65-75.

Katada R, Nishitani Y, Okazaki S, Matsumoto H (2014). Decapitation by force to the body: A case report and a review of the literature. *Journal of Forensic Research* 5, e232.

Kattimani S, Bharadwaj B, Sarkar S, Mukherjee A (2015). Interrater reliability of the Silverman et al. nomenclature for suicide-related ideations, behaviors, and communications. *Crisis* 36, 61-64.

Kelleher E, Kelleher MF, Grad O (2014). Effects of patient suicide on the multidisciplinary care team. *Lancet Psychiatry* 1, 174-175.

Kern JK, Geier DA, Bjørklund G, King PG, Homme KG, Haley BE, Sykes LK, Geier MR (2014). Evidence supporting a link between dental amalgams and chronic illness, fatigue, depression, anxiety, and suicide. *Neuroendocrinology Letters* 35, 537-552 ,

Keshaviah A, Edkins K, Hastings ER, Krishna M, Franko DL, Herzog DB, Thomas JJ, Murray HB, Eddy KT (2014). Re-examining premature mortality in anorexia nervosa: A meta-analysis redux. *Comprehensive Psychiatry* 55, 1773-1784.

Kessler RC, Nock MK, Schoenbaum M (2014). Mental health and the army reply. *JAMA Psychiatry* 71, 967-968.

Khokhlov VD (2015). Trauma to the hyoid bone and laryngeal cartilages in hanging: Review of forensic research series since 1856. *Legal Medicine* 17, 17-23.

Kiffel J, Sher L (2015). Prevention and management of depression and suicidal behavior in men with prostate cancer. *Frontiers in Public Health* 3, 28.

Kim J-W, Szigethy EM, Melhem NM, Saghafi EM, Brent DA (2014). Inflammatory markers and the pathogenesis of pediatric depression and suicide: A systematic review of the literature. *The Journal of Clinical Psychiatry* 75, 1242-1253.

Kitamura T, Kiyohara K, Sakai T, Iwami T, Nishiyama C, Kajino K, Nishiuchi T, Hayashi Y, Katayama Y, Yoshiya K, Shimazu T (2014). Epidemiology and outcome of adult out-of-hospital cardiac arrest of non-cardiac origin in Osaka: A population-based study. *BMJ Open* 4, e006462.

Kivivuori J, Suonpaa K, Lehti M (2014). Patterns and theories of European homicide research. *European Journal of Criminology* 11, 530-551.

Klonsky ED, Victor SE, Saffer BY (2014). Nonsuicidal self-injury: What we know, and what we need to know. *Canadian Journal of Psychiatry-Revue Canadienne De Psychiatrie* 59, 565-568 ,

Kongerslev M, Simonsen S, Bo S (2015). The quest for tailored treatments: A meta-discussion of six social cognitive therapies. *Journal of Clinical Psychology* 71, 188-198.

Kopacz MS, Hoffmire CA, Morley SW, Vance CG (2014). Using a spiritual distress scale to assess suicide risk in veterans: An exploratory study. *Pastoral Psychology* 64, 381-390.

Kopacz MS, Pollitt MJ (2015). Delivering chaplaincy services to veterans at increased risk of suicide. *Journal of Health Care Chaplaincy* 21, 1-13.

Kostro K, Lerman JB, Attia E (2014). The current status of suicide and self-injury in eating disorders: A narrative review. *Journal of Eating Disorders* 2, 19.

Kroll H (2015). Mental health first aid: Addressing mental health as a public health priority. *Perspectives in Public Health* 135, 12-14.

Kumar A, Mahto T, Kumar S, Kishore K (2013). Different methods of suicide: A review. *Journal of Evolution of Medical and Dental Sciences* 2, 256-264.

Kuppens T, Pollet TV (2014). Mind the level: Problems with two recent nation-level analyses in psychology. *Frontiers in Psychology*. Published online: 30 September 2014. doi: 10.3389/fpsyg.2014.01110.

Laanani M, Ghosn W, Jougla E, Rey G (2015). Impact of unemployment variations on suicide mortality in western European countries (2000-2010): Authors' reply. *Journal of Epidemiology and Community Health*. Published online: 13 January 2015. doi: 10.1136/jech-2014-205382.

Law KC, Khazem LR, Anestis MD (2015). The role of emotion dysregulation in suicide as considered through the ideation to action framework. *Current Opinion in Psychology* 3, 30-35.

Lee HJ (2014). Fearless love, death for dignity: Female suicide and gendered subjectivity in rural north China. *China Journal* 71, 25-42.

Lee HY, Hong JP, Hwang JA, Lee HJ, Yoon HK, Lee BH, Kim YK (2015). Possible association between serotonin transporter gene polymorphism and suicide behavior in major depressive disorder. *Psychiatry Investigation* 12, 136-141.

Lee YJ, Bernstein K, Lee M, Nokes KM (2014). Bullying in the nursing workplace: Applying evidence using a conceptual framework. *Nursing Economics* 32, 255-267.

Lees C (2014). The GMC and doctors' suicides. *BMJ* 349, g7740.

Lesen E, Wiktorsson S, Carlsten A, Waern M, Hedenrud T (2015). Beliefs about antidepressants among persons aged 70 years and older in treatment after a suicide attempt. *International Psychogeriatrics*. Published online: 2 March 2015. doi: 10.1017/S1041610215000216.

Lester D, Hathaway D (2014). Organ donation by suicides: Sex and ethnicity. *Psychological Reports* 115, 948-950.

Lewis MJ (2014). "Am I not really dead?" Pseudocide, individuation, and the fictional awakening. *Literary Imagination* 16, 344-365.

Li W, Li W, Wan Y, Ren J, Li T, Li C (2014). Appraisal of the methodological quality and summary of the findings of systematic reviews on the relationship between SSRIs and suicidality. *Shanghai Archives of Psychiatry* 26, 248-258.

Liotta M, Mento C, Settineri S (2015). Seriousness and lethality of attempted suicide: A systematic review. *Aggression and Violent Behavior* 21, 97-109.

Lopez-Castroman J, Baca-Garcia E, World Research Consortium For Suicide W, Courtet P, Oquendo MA (2014). A cross-national tool for assessing and studying suicidal behaviors. *Archives of Suicide Research*. Published online: 20 December 2014. doi: 10.1080/13811118.2014.981624.

Lopez-Castroman J, Courtet P, Baca-Garcia E, Oquendo MA (2015). Identification of suicide risk in bipolar disorder. *Bipolar Disorders* 17, 22-23.

Lu D-Y, Lu T-R, Che J-Y, Zhu P-P (2014). Genetic and bioinformatic studies of antidepressant drug therapeutic efficacy and toxicity: A current overview. *Recent Patents on CNS Drug Discovery* 9, 193-199.

Luley S (2015). 'Suicide tourism': Creating misleading 'scientific' news. *Journal of Medical Ethics*. Published online: 26 February 2015. doi: 10.1136/medethics-2014-102467.

Lunawat VK, Karale M (2014). Repeat users of crisis resolution and home treatment team. *Psychiatria Danubina* 26 Suppl 1, 10-14.

Lusk J, Brenner LA, Betthauser LM, Terrio H, Scher AI, Schwab K, Poczwardowski A (2015). A qualitative study of potential suicide risk factors among Operation Iraqi Freedom/Operation Enduring Freedom soldiers returning to the Continental United States (CONUS). *Journal of Clinical Psychology*. Published online: 10 March 2015. doi: 10.1002/jclp.22164.

Maiese A, Gitto L, dell'Aquila M, Bolino G (2014). When the hidden features become evident: The usefulness of PMCT in a strangulation-related death. *Legal Medicine* 16, 364-366.

Mailloux S (2014). Fatal families: Why children are killed in familicide occurrences. *Journal of Family Violence* 29, 921-926.

Manning CL, Peters D, Lewith G (2015). Doctors' suicides: Economic considerations and beyond. *BMJ* 350, h1412.

Manning J (2014). The social structure of homicide-suicide. *Homicide Studies*. Published online: 21 August 2014. doi: 10.1177/1088767914547819.

Manoloudakis N, Labiris G, Karakitsou N, Kim JB, Sheena Y, Niakas D (2015). Characteristics of women who have had cosmetic breast implants that could be associated with increased suicide risk: A systematic review, proposing a suicide prevention model. *Archives of Plastic Surgery* 42, 131-142.

Mansoor S, Afshar M, Barrett M, Smith GS, Barr EA, Lissauer ME, McCurdy MT, Murthi SB, Netzer G (2015). Acute respiratory distress syndrome and outcomes after near hanging. *American Journal of Emergency Medicine* 33, 359-362.

Massaro L (2015). Unusual suicide in Italy: Criminological and medico-legal observations-a proposed definition of "atypical suicide" suitable for international application. *Journal of Forensic Sciences* 60, 790-800.

Matthieu MMP, Gardiner G, Ziegemeier E, Buxton M, Han L, Cross W (2014). Personal and professional knowledge of and experience with suicide and suicide prevention among stakeholders in clinical and community practice. *Social Work in Mental Health* 12, 443-456.

McCarthy M (2015). Youth suicide rate in rural US is nearly double that of urban areas, study finds. *BMJ* 350, h1376.

McEwen BS (2015). Biomarkers for assessing population and individual health and disease related to stress and adaptation. *Metabolism* 64 Suppl 1, S2-S10.

McLaren S, Gomez R, Gill P, Chesler J (2014). Marital status and suicidal ideation among Australian older adults: The mediating role of sense of belonging - corrigendum. *International Psychogeriatrics* 27, 155.

McLoughlin AB, Gould MS, Malone KM (2015). Global trends in teenage suicide: 2003-2014. *QJM*. Published online: 31 January 2015. doi: http://dx.doi.org/10.1093/qjmed/hcv026.

McNamara RF (2014). The sorrow of soreness: Infirmity and suicide in medieval England. *Parergon* 31, 11-34.

Meissner B, Bantjes J, Kagee A (2015). I would rather just go through with it than be called a wussy: An exploration of how a group of young South African men think and talk about suicide. *American Journal of Men's Health*. Published online: 27 January 2015. doi: 0.1177/1557988314568183.

Menon V (2014). Silverman revisited: A relook at some of the pitfalls and challenges in suicide nomenclature and few suggestions. *Industrial Psychiatry Journal* 23, 73-74.

Michelsen N (2015). The political subject of self-immolation. *Globalizations* 12, 83-100.

Mille D, Bernal AT (2014). Utilizing the integrated problem-centered metaframeworks perspective to help families cope with chronic physical pain: A case illustration. *Journal of Family Psychotherapy* 25, 316-329.

Miller M, Swanson S, Stürmer T (2015). In reply: Antidepressant dose and risk of deliberate self-harm: Is it the dose or the indication? *JAMA Internal Medicine* 175, 464.

Miller S, Dell'Osso B, Ketter TA (2014). The prevalence and burden of bipolar depression. *Journal of Affective Disorders* 169, S3-S11.

Minshawi NF, Hurwitz S, Morriss D, McDougle CJ (2015). Multidisciplinary assessment and treatment of self-injurious behavior in autism spectrum disorder and intellectual disability: Integration of psychological and biological theory and approach. *Journal of Autism and Developmental Disorders* 45, 1541-1568.

Miron J (2014). Suicide, coroner's inquests, and the parameters of compassion in Ontario, 1830-1900. *Social History* 47, 577-599.

Misnec ML (2014). Get back in line: How minor revisions to AR 600-8-4 would rejuvenate suicide line of duty investigations. *Military Law Review* 221, 183-214.

Mizen CS (2014). Towards a relational affective theory of personality disorder. *Psychoanalytic Psychotherapy* 28, 357-378.

Mohammadi S, Khazaie H, Rahimi Z, Vaisi-Raygani A, Zargooshi N, Rahimi Z (2015). The serotonin transporter (5-HTTLPR) but not serotonin receptor (5-HT2C CYS23SER) variant is associated with bipolar I disorder in Kurdish population from western Iran. *Neuroscience Letters* 590, 91-95.

Mohite PN, Patil NP, Sabashnikov A, Zych B, Garcia Saez D, Popov AF, De Robertis F, Bahrami T, Amrani M, Reed A, Carby M, Simon AR (2015). "Hanging donors": Are we still skeptical about the lungs? *Transplantation Proceedings* 47, 261-266.

Monteiro RA, Bahia CA, Paiva EA, Sá NNBd, Minayo MCdS (2015). Hospitalizations due to self-inflicted injuries - Brazil, 2002 to 2013. *Ciencia e Saude Coletiva* 20, 689-699.

Moore J (2014). Coroners' recommendations about healthcare-related deaths as a potential tool for improving patient safety and quality of care. *The New Zealand Medical Journal* 127, 35-53.

Moran P (2015). Adolescents who self-harm are at increased risk of health and social problems as young adults. *Evidence-Based Mental Health* 18, 52.

Moscarelli M, Manning W (2014). The impact of socio-economic factors on suicide rates in South Korea. *Journal of Mental Health Policy and Economics* 17, 149-150.

Mosholder AD, Taylor LG, Crentsil V (2014). Reservations about study on antidepressant use by young people and suicidal behaviour after FDA warnings. *BMJ* 349, g6503.

Moulton CD, Hopkins CWP, Bevan-Jones WR (2014). Systematic review of pharmacological treatments for depressive symptoms in Huntington's disease. *Movement Disorders* 29, 1556-1561.

Murray JL (2015). Suicidal–homicidal ideation in mass killers and transcendence. *Deviant Behavior* 36, 581-588.

Mutumba M, Resnicow K, Bauermeister JA, Harper GW, Musiime V, Snow RC, Lepkowski JM (2015). Development of a psychosocial distress measure for Ugandan adolescents living with HIV. *AIDS and Behavior* 19, 380-392.

Nadar S, Iqbal M, Raja KS, Rana PA, Khokhar JI (2014). Position of the knot in hanging and strangulation in asphyxiai deaths in medico-legal autopsies in Lahore. *Medical Forum Monthly* 25, 32-35.

Nazem S, Spitzer EG, Brenner LA, Bahraini NH (2014). Beyond categorical classifications: The importance of identifying posttrauma symptom trajectories and associated negative outcomes. *Journal of Clinical Psychiatry* 75, E947-E949

Nett RJ, Witte TK, Holzbauer SM, Elchos BL, Campagnolo ER, Musgrave KJ, Carter KK, Kurkjian KM, Vanicek C, O'Leary DR, Pride KR, Funk RH (2015). Prevalence of risk factors for suicide among veterinarians - United States, 2014. *Morbidity and Mortality Weekly Report* 64, 131-132.

Niezen R (2015). The Durkheim-Tarde debate and the social study of Aboriginal youth suicide. *Transcultural Psychiatry* 52, 96-114.

Nikolaev NI, Shvetsova TV (2015). Suicide motives in Russian and European literary tradition. *Asian Social Science* 11, 344-350.

Noguchi M, Iwase T, Suzuki E, Kishimoto Y, Takao S (2015). Erratum to: Social support and suicidal ideation in Japan: Are home visits by commissioned welfare volunteers associated with a lower risk of suicidal ideation among elderly people in the community? *Social Psychiatry and Psychiatric Epidemiology* 50, 505-506.

Novak MA, El-Mallah SN, Menard MT (2014). Use of the cross-translational model to study self-injurious behavior in human and nonhuman primates. *ILAR Journal* 55, 274-283.

Nrugham L, Holen A, Sund AM (2015). Prognosis and psychosocial outcomes of attempted suicide by early adolescence: A 6-year follow-up of school students into early adulthood. *Journal of Nervous and Mental Disease* 203, 294-301.

Nutt R, Kidd B, Matthews K (2014). Assessing the adherence to guidelines of media reporting of suicide using a novel instrument - the "risk of imitative suicide scale" (RISC). *Suicide and Life-Threatening Behavior* 45, 360-375.

O'Connor M, Groom J, Watson M, Harris P (2014). Developing organizational guidelines for the prevention and management of suicide in clients and carers receiving palliative care in Australia. *American Journal of Hospice and Palliative Care*. Published online: 29 December 2014. doi: 10.1177/1049909114565659.

O'Shea LE, Picchioni MM, Dickens GL (2015). The predictive validity of the short-term assessment of risk and treatability (START) for multiple adverse outcomes in a secure psychiatric inpatient setting. *Assessment*. Published online: 27 February 2015. doi: 10.1177/1073191115573301.

Olfson M, Gerhard T (2014). Re-examining antidepressant risk of self-injury in children and adolescents. *Pharmacoepidemiology and Drug Safety* 24, 215-217.

Oppong Asante K, Meyer-Weitz A, Petersen I (2015). Correlates of psychological functioning of homeless youth in Accra, Ghana: A cross-sectional study. *International Journal of Mental Health Systems* 9, 1.

Osborne K (2015). Inquiry finds link between patient suicide and inexperienced staff. *Nursing Standard (1987)* 29, 11.

Ougrin D, Tranah T, Stahl D, Moran P, Asarnow JR (2015). Therapeutic interventions for suicide attempts and self-harm in adolescents: Systematic review and meta-analysis. *Journal of the American Academy of Child and Adolescent Psychiatry* 54, 97-107.

Özerdem A (2014). Suicide: The shark of psychiatry. *Noropsikiyatri Arsivi* 51, 187-188

Pae C-U (2014). Influence of media on suicide: Proper coverage of media on suicide report. *Journal of Korean Medical Science* 29, 1583-1585.

Panagioti M, Gooding PA, Triantafyllou K, Tarrier N (2014). Suicidality and posttraumatic stress disorder (PTSD) in adolescents: A systematic review and meta-analysis. *Social Psychiatry and Psychiatric Epidemiology* 50, 525-537.

Park S, Lee SK, Oh HS, Jun T, Lee M, Kim J, Kim J, Yim H, Park YC (2015). Hazardous drinking-related characteristics of depressive disorders in Korea: The CRESCEND study. *Journal of Korean Medical Science* 30, 74-81.

Parkhurst KA, Conwell Y, Van Orden KA (2015). The interpersonal needs questionnaire with a shortened response scale for oral administration with older adults. *Aging and Mental Health*. Published online: 30 January 2015. doi: 10.1080/13607863.2014.1003288.

Parpa E, Tsilika E, Gennimata V, Mystakidou K (2014). Elderly cancer patients' psychopathology: A systematic review: Aging and mental health. *Archives of Gerontology and Geriatrics* 60, 9-15.

Pawlak J, Dmitrzak-Weglarz M, Maciukiewicz M, Wilkosc M, Leszczy ska-Rodziewicz A, Zaremba D, Kapelski P, Hauser J (2015). Suicidal behavior in the context of disrupted rhythmicity in bipolar disorder - data from an association study of suicide attempts with clock genes. *Psychiatry Research* 226, 517-520.

Perrin AJ (2014). Intentional misuse of veterinary medications in human suicide. *Journal of Veterinary Pharmacology and Therapeutics* 38, 209-213.

Phillips MR (2014). Pregnancy and suicide: Towards a coherent narrative. *Lancet Psychiatry* 1, 168-170.

Pierre JM (2014). Suicide, swords, and cultural sanctioning. *American Journal of Forensic Medicine and Pathology* 35, 284.

Pietrzak RH, Tsai J, Armour C, Mota N, Harpaz-Rotem I, Southwick SM (2015). Functional significance of a novel 7-factor model of DSM-5 PTSD symptoms: Results from the National Health And Resilience In Veterans Study. *Journal of Affective Disorders* 174, 522-526.

Piette A, Muchirahondo F, Mangezi W, Iversen A, Cowan F, Dube M, Grant-Peterkin H, Araya R, Abas M (2015). Simulation-based learning in psychiatry for undergraduates at the University of Zimbabwe medical school. *BMC Medical Education* 15, 23.

Pike I, McDonald RJ, Piedt S, Macpherson AK (2014). Developing injury indicators for First Nations and Inuit children and youth in Canada: A modified Delphi approach. *Chronic Diseases and Injuries in Canada* 34, 203-209.

Pirkis J, Robinson J (2014). Improving our understanding of youth suicide clusters. *The Lancet Psychiatry* 1, 5-6.

Pompili M, Venturini P, Lamis DA, Giordano G, Serafini G, Belvederi Murri M, Amore M, Girardi P (2014). Suicide in stroke survivors: Epidemiology and prevention. *Drugs and Aging* 32, 21-29.

Santos JC, Simoes RMP, Erse MPQdA, Facanha JDN, Marques LAFA (2014). Impact of "+Contigo" training on the knowledge and attitudes of health care professionals about suicide. *Revista Latino-Americana de Enfermagem* 22, 679-684.

Saunders KE, Hawton K (2014). Suicidal behaviour in bipolar disorder: Understanding the role of affective states. *Bipolar Disorders* 17, 24-26.

Saxena S, Fleischmann A (2014). WHO launches the first world suicide report. *The Lancet Psychiatry* 1, 255-256.

Seeman MV (2015). The impact of suicide on co-patients. *Psychiatric Quarterly*. Published online: 25 January 2015. doi: 10.1007/s11126-015-9346-6.

Sen P, Exworthy T, Forrester A (2014). Mental health care for foreign national prisoners in England and Wales. *Journal of Mental Health* 23, 333-339.

Sheehan DV, Alphs LD, Mao L, Li Q, May RS, Bruer EH, McCullumsmith CB, Gray CR, Li X, Williamson DJ (2014). Comparative validation of the S-STS, the ISST-plus, and the C-SSRS for assessing the suicidal thinking and behavior FDA 2012 suicidality categories. *Innovations in Clinical Neuroscience* 11, 32-46.

Sheehan DV, Giddens JM, Sheehan IS (2014). Status update on the Sheehan-Suicidality Tracking Scale (S-STS) 2014. *Innovations in Clinical Neuroscience* 11, 93-140.

Sheehan DV, Giddens JM, Sheehan KH (2014). Current assessment and classification of suicidal phenomena using the FDA 2012 draft guidance document on suicide assessment: A critical review. *Innovations in Clinical Neuroscience* 11, 54-65.

Sher L (2015). Suicide medical malpractice: An educational overview. *International Journal of Adolescent Medicine and Health* 27, 203-206.

Shetty CK (2015). Laws in relation to suicide in India and pleas for humanization and decriminalization of attempt to suicide- an overview. *Journal of South India Medicolegal Association* 7, 26-30.

Shilubane HN, Bos AE, Ruiter RA, van den Borne B, Reddy PS (2015). High school suicide in South Africa: Teachers' knowledge, views and training needs. *BMC Public Health* 15, 1599-1599.

Shilubane HN, Ruiter RA, Bos AE, Reddy PS, van den Borne B (2014). High school students' knowledge and experience with a peer who committed or attempted suicide: A focus group study. *BMC Public Health* 14, 1081.

Siamouli M, Samara M, Fountoulakis KN (2014). Is antiepileptic-induced suicidality a data-based class effect or an exaggeration? A comment on the literature. *Harvard Review of Psychiatry* 22, 379-381.

Simon RI (2014). How do you score on this self-assessment of suicide risk management? *Current Psychiatry* 13, 26-32.

Simon RI (2014). Suicide assessment and management self-test: How do you score? *Current Psychiatry* 13, 21-32.

Sinyor M, Cheung AH (2015). Antidepressants and risk of suicide. *BMJ* 350, h783-h783.

Sinyor M, Schaffer A, Hull I, Peisah C, Shulman K (2014). Last wills and testaments in a large sample of suicide notes: Implications for testamentary capacity. *Br J Psychiatry* ,

Siskind D, Harris M, Diminic S, Carstensen G, Robinson G, Whiteford H (2014). Predictors of mental health-related acute service utilisation and treatment costs in the 12 months following an acute psychiatric admission. *Australian and New Zealand Journal of Psychiatry* 48, 1048-1058.

Slavin-Mulford J, Perkey H, Blais M, Stein M, Sinclair SJ (2015). External validity of the Symptom Assessment-45 questionnaire (SA-45) in a clinical sample. *Comprehensive Psychiatry* 58, 205-212.

Slomski A (2014). Suicide runs in families with ADHD. *JAMA* 312, 1184-1184.

Sodhi-Berry N, Knuiman M, Alan J, Morgan VA, Preen DB (2015). Pre- and post-sentence mental health service use by a population cohort of older offenders (≥45 years) in Western Australia. *Social Psychiatry and Psychiatric Epidemiology* , Published online: 22 January 2015. doi: 10.1007/s00127-015-1008-3.

Sørensen JB, Rheinländer T, Sørensen BR, Pearson M, Agampodi T, Siribaddana S, Konradsen F (2014). An investigation into the role of alcohol in self-harm in rural Sri Lanka: A protocol for a multimethod, qualitative study. *BMJ Open* 4, e005860-e005860.

Staniloiu A, Markowitsch HJ (2014). Dissociative amnesia. *The Lancet Psychiatry* 1, 226-241.

Starcevic V, Aboujaoude E (2015). Cyberchondria, cyberbullying, cybersuicide, cybersex: "New" psychopathologies for the 21st century? *World Psychiatry* 14, 97-100.

Stone MB (2014). The FDA warning on antidepressants and suicidality - why the controversy? *New England Journal of Medicine* 371, 1668-1671.

Strawn JR, Welge JA, Wehry AM, Keeshin B, Rynn MA (2015). Efficacy and tolerability of antidepressants in pediatric anxiety disorders: A systematic review and meta-analysis. *Depression and Anxiety* 32, 149-157.

Suarez L, Beach SR, Moore SV, Mastromauro CA, Januzzi JL, Celano CM, Chang TE, Huffman JC (2015). Use of the Patient Health Questionnaire-9 and a detailed suicide evaluation in determining imminent suicidality in distressed patients with cardiac disease. *Psychosomatics* 56, 181-189.

Sulaj Z, Drishti A, Ceko I, Gashi A, Vyshka G (2015). Fatal aluminum phosphide poisonings in Tirana (Albania), 2009 - 2013. *Daru* 23, 8.

Sutherland O, Dawczyk A, De Leon K, Cripps J, Lewis SP (2014). Self-compassion in online accounts of nonsuicidal self-injury: An interpretive phenomenological analysis. *Counselling Psychology Quarterly* 27, 409-433.

Sykes MJ, Brabban A, Reilly J (2015). Balancing harms in support of recovery. *Journal of Mental Health* 24, 140-144.

Takeshima T, Yamauchi T, Inagaki M, Kodaka M, Matsumoto T, Kawano K, Katsumata Y, Fujimori M, Hisanaga A, Takahashi Y (2015). Suicide prevention strategies in Japan: A 15-year review (1998-2013). *Journal of Public Health Policy* 36, 52-66.

Talisse RB (2015). On Sidney Hook's "The ethics of suicide". *Ethics* 125, 549-551.

Tartaro C (2015). What is obvious? Federal courts' interpretation of the knowledge requirement in post-Farmer v. Brennan custodial suicide cases. *Prison Journal* 95, 23-42.

Teismann T, Forkmann T, Wachtel S, Edel MA, Nyhuis P, Glaesmer H (2015). The German version of the Painful and Provocative Events Scale: A psychometric investigation. *Psychiatry Research* 226, 264-272.

Terao T, Ishii N, Shiotsuki I (2014). Lithium in drinking water for dementia and suicide. *Austin Journal of Psychiatry and Behavioral Sciences* 1, 1022.

Teti GL, Rebok F, Rojas SM, Grendas L, Daray FM (2014). Systematic review of risk factors for suicide and suicide attempt among psychiatric patients in Latin America and Caribbean. *Revista Panamericana de Salud Publica* 36, 124-133.

Thelma Beatriz G-C, Isela J-R, Alma G, Maria Lilia L-N, Carlos Alfonso T-Z (2014). Association between HTR2C gene variants and suicidal behaviour: A protocol for the systematic review and meta-analysis of genetic studies. *BMJ Open* 4, e005423.

Thomas KH, Martin RM, Knipe DW, Higgins JP, Gunnell D (2015). Risk of neuropsychiatric adverse events associated with varenicline: Systematic review and meta-analysis. *BMJ* 350, h1109.

Tominaga M, Michiue T, Inamori-Kawamoto O, Hishmat AM, Oritani S, Takama M, Ishikawa T, Maeda H (2015). Efficacy of drug screening in forensic autopsy: Retrospective investigation of routine toxicological findings. *Legal Medicine* 17, 172-176.

Torisky EV, Jr. (2015). Minimally intentional suicide and "the falling man". *Journal of Value Inquiry* 49, 69-79.

Torjesen I (2015). Children whose parents attempted suicide are at raised risk of similar behaviour, study finds. *BMJ* 350, g7862-g7862.

Umamaheswari V, Avasthi A, Grover S (2014). Risk factors for suicidal ideations in patients with bipolar disorder. *Bipolar Disorders* 16, 642-651.

Vallance AK, Hemani A, Fernandez V, Livingstone D, McCusker K, Toro-Troconis M (2014). Using virtual worlds for role play simulation in child and adolescent psychiatry: An evaluation study. *The Psychiatric Bulletin* 38, 204-210.

van Hal G (2015). The true cost of the economic crisis on psychological well-being: A review. *Psychology Research and Behavior Management* 8, 17-25.

Vriniotis M, Barber C, Frank E, Demicco R (2015). A suicide prevention campaign for firearm dealers in New Hampshire. *Suicide and Life-Threatening Behavior* 45, 157-163.

Waghmare PB, Chikhalkar BG, Nanandkar SD (2014). Analysis of asphyxial deaths due to hanging. *Journal of Indian Academy of Forensic Medicine* 36, 343-345.

Wahlbeck K (2015). Public mental health: The time is ripe for translation of evidence into practice. *World Psychiatry* 14, 36-42.

Washburn JJ, Potthoff LM, Juzwin KR, Styer DM (2015). Assessing DSM-5 nonsuicidal self-injury disorder in a clinical sample. *Psychological Assessment* 27, 31-41.

Wei Y, Kutcher S, LeBlanc JC (2015). Hot idea or hot air: A systematic review of evidence for two widely marketed youth suicide prevention programs and recommendations for implementation. *Journal of the Canadian Academy of Child and Adolescent Psychiatry* 24, 5-16.

West JC, Rae DS, Mojtabai R, Duffy FF, Kuramoto J, Moscicki E, Narrow WE (2015). Planning patient-centered health homes for Medicaid psychiatric patients at greatest risk for intensive service use. *Community Mental Health Journal*. Published online: 10 February 2015. doi: 10.1007/s10597-015-9834-z.

White B, Willmott L, Savulescu J (2014). Voluntary palliated starvation: A lawful and ethical way to die? *Journal of Law And Medicine* 22, 376-386.

Wille R (2014). The shame of existing: An extreme form of shame. *International Journal of Psychoanalysis* 95, 695-717.

Willmot P, McMurran M (2015). Development of a self-report measure of social functioning for forensic inpatients. *International journal of Law and Psychiatry* 39, 72-76.

Wilson MP, Brennan JJ, Modesti L, Deen J, Anderson L, Vilke GM, Castillo EM (2015). Lengths of stay for involuntarily held psychiatric patients in the ED are affected by both patient characteristics and medication use. *American Journal of Emergency Medicine* 33, 527-530.

Wintemute GJ (2015). The epidemiology of firearm violence in the twenty-first century United States. *Annual Review of Public Health* 36, 5-19.

Winzer R, Lindblad F, Sorjonen K, Lindberg L (2014). Positive versus negative mental health in emerging adulthood: A national cross-sectional survey. *BMC Public Health* 14, 1238.

Wong PWC (2014). Active engagement for people bereaved by suicide. *The Lancet Psychiatry* 1, 109.

Woo YS, Jun TY, Jeon YH, Song HR, Kim TS, Kim JB, Lee MS, Kim JM, Jo SJ (2014). Relationship of temperament and character in remitted depressed patients with suicidal ideation and suicide attempts-results from the CRESCEND study. *PLoS One* 9, e105860.

Woodbury-Farina MA (2014). The importance of glia in dealing with stress. *Psychiatric Clinics of North America* 37, 679-705.

Yang K-C, Wang S-J, Hsieh W-C, Lirng J-F, Yang C-C, Deng J-F, Lin C-L, Chou Y-H (2015). Longitudinal changes in the dopamine transporter and cognition in suicide attempters with charcoal burning. *Psychiatry Research* 231, 160-167.

Yap MBH, Reavley NJ, Jorm AF (2015). Is the use of accurate psychiatric labels associated with intentions and beliefs about responses to mental illness in a friend? Findings from two national surveys of Australian youth. *Epidemiology and Psychiatric Sciences* 24, 54-68.

Yehia F, Nahas Z, Saleh S (2014). Perspectives a roadmap to parity in mental health financing: The case of Lebanon. *Journal of Mental Health Policy and Economics* 17, 131-141.

Ylijoki-Sørensen S, Boldsen JL, Lalu K, Sajantila A, Baandrup U, Boel LWT, Ehlers LH, Bøggild H (2014). Cost-consequence analysis of cause of death investigation in Finland and in Denmark. *Forensic Science International* 245, 133-142.

Yuodelis-Flores C, Ries RK (2015). Addiction and suicide: A review. *American Journal on Addictions* 24, 98-104.

Zhang J, Zhao Y, Bai Y, Lv G, Wu J, Chen Y (2015). The significance of serum uric acid level in humans with acute paraquat poisoning. *Scientific Reports* 5, 9168.

Zhang L, Huang X, Liu T, Chen Z, Zhu T (2014). Using linguistic features to estimate suicide probability of Chinese microblog users. *arXiv* 1411.0861.

Zonda T, Kmetty Z, Lester D, Tóth MD (2015). Effects of parliamentary elections on suicide rates in Hungary. *Crisis*. Published online: 24 February 2015. doi: 10.1027/0227-5910/a000303.

Zunner B, Dworkin SL, Neylan TC, Bukusi EA, Oyaro P, Cohen CR, Abwok M, Meffert SM (2015). HIV, violence and women: Unmet mental health care needs. *Journal of Affective Disorders* 174, 619-626.